T0211021

Lecture Notes in Computer Science　　　　**14052**

Founding Editors

Gerhard Goos
Juris Hartmanis

The series Lecture Notes in Computer Science (LNCS), including its subseries Lecture Notes in Artificial Intelligence (LNAI) and Lecture Notes in Bioinformatics (LNBI), has established itself as a medium for the publication of new developments in computer science and information technology research, teaching, and education.

LNCS enjoys close cooperation with the computer science R & D community, the series counts many renowned academics among its volume editors and paper authors, and collaborates with prestigious societies. Its mission is to serve this international community by providing an invaluable service, mainly focused on the publication of conference and workshop proceedings and postproceedings. LNCS commenced publication in 1973.

Gavriel Salvendy · June Wei
Editors

Design, Operation and Evaluation of Mobile Communications

4th International Conference, MOBILE 2023
Held as Part of the 25th HCI International Conference, HCII 2023
Copenhagen, Denmark, July 23–28, 2023
Proceedings

 Springer

Editors
Gavriel Salvendy
University of Central Florida
Orlando, FL, USA

June Wei
University of West Florida
Pensacola, FL, USA

ISSN 0302-9743   ISSN 1611-3349 (electronic)
Lecture Notes in Computer Science
ISBN 978-3-031-35920-0   ISBN 978-3-031-35921-7 (eBook)
https://doi.org/10.1007/978-3-031-35921-7

This Springer imprint is published by the registered company Springer Nature Switzerland AG
The registered company address is: Gewerbestrasse 11, 6330 Cham, Switzerland

Foreword

Human-computer interaction (HCI) is acquiring an ever-increasing scientific and industrial importance, as well as having more impact on people's everyday lives, as an ever-growing number of human activities are progressively moving from the physical to the digital world. This process, which has been ongoing for some time now, was further accelerated during the acute period of the COVID-19 pandemic. The HCI International (HCII) conference series, held annually, aims to respond to the compelling need to advance the exchange of knowledge and research and development efforts on the human aspects of design and use of computing systems.

The 25th International Conference on Human-Computer Interaction, HCI International 2023 (HCII 2023), was held in the emerging post-pandemic era as a 'hybrid' event at the AC Bella Sky Hotel and Bella Center, Copenhagen, Denmark, during July 23–28, 2023. It incorporated the 21 thematic areas and affiliated conferences listed below.

A total of 7472 individuals from academia, research institutes, industry, and government agencies from 85 countries submitted contributions, and 1578 papers and 396 posters were included in the volumes of the proceedings that were published just before the start of the conference, these are listed below. The contributions thoroughly cover the entire field of human-computer interaction, addressing major advances in knowledge and effective use of computers in a variety of application areas. These papers provide academics, researchers, engineers, scientists, practitioners and students with state-of-the-art information on the most recent advances in HCI.

The HCI International (HCII) conference also offers the option of presenting 'Late Breaking Work', and this applies both for papers and posters, with corresponding volumes of proceedings that will be published after the conference. Full papers will be included in the 'HCII 2023 - Late Breaking Work - Papers' volumes of the proceedings to be published in the Springer LNCS series, while 'Poster Extended Abstracts' will be included as short research papers in the 'HCII 2023 - Late Breaking Work - Posters' volumes to be published in the Springer CCIS series.

I would like to thank the Program Board Chairs and the members of the Program Boards of all thematic areas and affiliated conferences for their contribution towards the high scientific quality and overall success of the HCI International 2023 conference. Their manifold support in terms of paper reviewing (single-blind review process, with a minimum of two reviews per submission), session organization and their willingness to act as goodwill ambassadors for the conference is most highly appreciated.

This conference would not have been possible without the continuous and unwavering support and advice of Gavriel Salvendy, founder, General Chair Emeritus, and Scientific Advisor. For his outstanding efforts, I would like to express my sincere appreciation to Abbas Moallem, Communications Chair and Editor of HCI International News.

July 2023

Constantine Stephanidis

HCI International 2023 Thematic Areas and Affiliated Conferences

Thematic Areas

- HCI: Human-Computer Interaction
- HIMI: Human Interface and the Management of Information

Affiliated Conferences

- EPCE: 20th International Conference on Engineering Psychology and Cognitive Ergonomics
- AC: 17th International Conference on Augmented Cognition
- UAHCI: 17th International Conference on Universal Access in Human-Computer Interaction
- CCD: 15th International Conference on Cross-Cultural Design
- SCSM: 15th International Conference on Social Computing and Social Media
- VAMR: 15th International Conference on Virtual, Augmented and Mixed Reality
- DHM: 14th International Conference on Digital Human Modeling and Applications in Health, Safety, Ergonomics and Risk Management
- DUXU: 12th International Conference on Design, User Experience and Usability
- C&C: 11th International Conference on Culture and Computing
- DAPI: 11th International Conference on Distributed, Ambient and Pervasive Interactions
- HCIBGO: 10th International Conference on HCI in Business, Government and Organizations
- LCT: 10th International Conference on Learning and Collaboration Technologies
- ITAP: 9th International Conference on Human Aspects of IT for the Aged Population
- AIS: 5th International Conference on Adaptive Instructional Systems
- HCI-CPT: 5th International Conference on HCI for Cybersecurity, Privacy and Trust
- HCI-Games: 5th International Conference on HCI in Games
- MobiTAS: 5th International Conference on HCI in Mobility, Transport and Automotive Systems
- AI-HCI: 4th International Conference on Artificial Intelligence in HCI
- MOBILE: 4th International Conference on Design, Operation and Evaluation of Mobile Communications

List of Conference Proceedings Volumes Appearing Before the Conference

47. CCIS 1836, HCI International 2023 Posters - Part V, edited by Constantine Stephanidis, Margherita Antona, Stavroula Ntoa and Gavriel Salvendy

https://2023.hci.international/proceedings

Preface

With the rapid technological advances of mobile communications, mobile applications are not only changing people's living style but also changing organizations', industries', and governments' operation, management, and innovation in a new way, which further impacts the economy, society, and culture all over the world. Human-computer interaction plays an important role in this transition.

The 4th International Conference on Design, Operation and Evaluation of Mobile Communications (MOBILE 2023), an affiliated conference of the HCI International conference, addresses the design, operation, evaluation, and adoption of mobile technologies and applications for consumers, industries, organizations, and governments. The purpose of this conference is to provide a platform for researchers and practitioners from academia, industry, and government to discuss challenging ideas, novel research contributions, and the current theory and practice of related mobile communications research topics and applications.

The papers accepted for publication this year offer a comprehensive overview of the prevalent themes and subjects in the field of mobile communications. In particular, in the domain of mobile UX and interaction design the accepted papers discuss topics including users' behavior, mobile design, mobile communication, and user personalization. A considerable number of papers address the topic of voice assistants and conversational Artificial Intelligence (AI), focusing on design and evaluation aspects, as well as on decision-making in conversational AI, opinion building of argumentative dialogue systems, and anonymity in voice assistants. Finally, articles in this volume showcase examples of mobile applications, detailing their design and overall user experience. Emphasis is placed on application domains where mobile apps have gained significant traction, including but not limited to education, healthcare, and eCommerce.

One volume of the HCII 2023 proceedings is dedicated to this year's edition of the MOBILE conference and focuses on topics related to mobile user experience and interaction design, design and evaluation of Voice User Interfaces and conversational AI, as well as mobile Information Systems in education, healthcare, eCommerce, and beyond.

The papers of this volume were included for publication after a minimum of two single-blind reviews from the members of the MOBILE Program Board or, in some cases, from members of the Program Boards of other affiliated conferences. We would like to thank all of them for their invaluable contribution, support, and efforts.

July 2023

Gavriel Salvendy
June Wei

4th International Conference on Design, Operation and Evaluation of Mobile Communications (MOBILE 2023)

Program Board Chairs: **Gavriel Salvendy,** *University of Central Florida, USA* and **June Wei,** *University of West Florida, USA*

Program Board:

The full list with the Program Board Chairs and the members of the Program Boards of all thematic areas and affiliated conferences of HCII2023 is available online at:

http://www.hci.international/board-members-2023.php

HCI International 2024 Conference

The 26th International Conference on Human-Computer Interaction, HCI International 2024, will be held jointly with the affiliated conferences at the Washington Hilton Hotel, Washington, DC, USA, June 29 – July 4, 2024. It will cover a broad spectrum of themes related to Human-Computer Interaction, including theoretical issues, methods, tools, processes, and case studies in HCI design, as well as novel interaction techniques, interfaces, and applications. The proceedings will be published by Springer. More information will be made available on the conference website: http://2024.hci.international/.

General Chair
Prof. Constantine Stephanidis
University of Crete and ICS-FORTH
Heraklion, Crete, Greece
Email: general_chair@hcii2024.org

https://2024.hci.international/

Contents

Mobile Information Systems in Education, Healthcare, eCommerce and Beyond

Mobile User Experience and Interaction Design

Users' Sophisticated Information Search Behaviour

Adel Alhejaili[1,2](✉) and James Blustein[1]

[1] Dalhousie University, Halifax, NS, Canada
adel.alhejaili@dal.ca, jamie@ACM.org
[2] Taibah University, Medina, Saudi Arabia

Abstract. Smartphone use has become a part of many people's everyday life. Over the past years, the number of smartphone users has increased significantly. Understanding how and why users select apps to install is essential for app developers, designers and store owners.

Using a multi-method design, we combined an observational lab study with qualitative and think-aloud protocol to explore the users' scrolling behaviour when choosing which apps to install.

This work argues, showcases and explains that users' behaviour is dynamic and constantly changing throughout the app search process. Our findings indicate that users adjust and adapt to accommodate the implications of the acquired knowledge gained from the environment.

Keywords: HCI Theories and Methods · Apps · Decision-making · Information Search · Laboratory experiment · Search adaptation · Learning from search

1 Introduction

Before downloading any app, users type the search keyword for the desired app in the app store's search bar. Based on the entered keyword, screen size, and app store, a list of 2 to 7 apps is displayed to users [13], which is the starting point of the decision-making process [10]. Then, in the "information-gathering stage" [10, p. 129], if users are interested and think this app seems relevant to their needs, they can open the app description page to view more details about the app or consider other information cues. The last step is when users decide whether to install the app [13].

People undertake different strategies when making choices based "on the size and complexity of the available options" [30, p. 94]. "People can adjust their rate of information processing (i.e., acceleration), may choose to filter incoming information (filtration), or may queue information for later processing" [7, p. 95]. To some extent, the nature of the information is considered to be "elusive and hard" to explain since it is used differently by different people in different contexts. [2, p. 147].

© The Author(s), under exclusive license to Springer Nature Switzerland AG 2023
G. Salvendy and J. Wei (Eds.): HCII 2023, LNCS 14052, pp. 3–17, 2023.
https://doi.org/10.1007/978-3-031-35921-7_1

Our preliminary analysis [1] created a model of how users choose apps, discussed the heuristic decision-making processes and applied data mining approaches for pattern discovery to investigate the relationships between the information cues. As part of a bigger research project in the app domain, we provide additional analysis.

This research aims to showcase the users' scrolling behaviour when choosing which apps to install, addressing and providing an overview of the following aspects: information search and processing, choices and decision-making, problem recognition, evaluation of alternatives, search adaptation, and learning from search [5, 7, 12, 14, 22, 23, 28, 30, 31].

This work contributes to the growing area of understanding users' search behaviour in the following ways: First, we found that when users' searched for apps, they were not restricted by the default information (e.g., no scrolling) available on the app search results screen of the app store. In fact, in 39% of the app search instances, participants have scrolled past the default screen. Second, based on our observations, we found a significant difference between participants who employed different scrolling behaviour when searching for apps. Third, we used multiple theories that guided us throughout this work, creating a new perspective of users' scrolling behaviour in the app domain. Fourth, we found that when users look for apps, they adjust and adapt to accommodate the implications of the acquired knowledge gained from the environment. Fifth, our research suggests that developers must design their apps and content carefully because the salience of certain information cues may lead users to select specific apps over others.

2   Background and Related Work

We provide an overview of prior research regarding the theories and models of the following domains: information search and processing, choices and decision-making, problem recognition, evaluation of alternatives, search adaptation, and learning from search [5, 7, 12, 14, 22, 23, 28, 30, 31].

2.1   Information Search and Decision-Making Process

The most common method for discovering apps is through app stores operated and maintained by smartphone platform providers [9, 19]. The app selection platforms present a list of apps to the users based on the used search terms. However, the "information about the complex algorithms used to determine what apps appear higher in a search than others is not publicly known" [21, p. 2].

Usually, when users search for apps in the app stores, they have specific targets in their minds, such as the app name or keywords [20]. Apple reported that 70% of their app store visitors have used the search bar to find apps and that 65% of the downloaded apps occur after searching [3, 20]. The remaining 35% of the app store downloads are for users who might be scrolling and looking through the app lists to judge the information presented by the app publishers [20, 24].

In most information-seeking contexts, people can inspect several results. Users can only sometimes find the information they require with a single search. If they select an app that is not useful, they can quickly return to the results list and look for another option [4]. Users change their used keyword terms to create subsequent searches after viewing the results from the last used terms [29], called reformulation.

There are many models describing the consumer decision-making process. One model created by Solomon et al. [28] consists of several steps:

(1) problem recognition, where there is a need of a product or an app in our context,
(2) information search, where consumers are searching for options,
(3) evaluation of alternatives, where consumers evaluating and comparing options to make the best choice,
(4) product choice, where the consumer select the desired option and,
(5) the outcomes of the chosen choice.

Solomon et al. [28] stated that since the importance of decisions varies, people's effort in each stage differs. The decision-making process does not require going through all the above steps since it involves some degree of information search and deliberations based on the degree of people engaged in these decisions [24, 28]. Solomon et al. [28, p. 354] reported that it is common sense that people "do not undergo" the "elaborate sequence" whenever buying something. If people do that, they would "spend their entire lives making these decisions" [28].

2.2 Information Processing and Decision Theory

One essential "assumption about the nature of information processing" is that "people rarely process" it under "perfect conditions" [31, p. 196]. Some constraints are related either to the environment (external, e.g., the complexity of the information) or people's cognitive abilities (internal, e.g., prior knowledge) [27, 33].

When making complex decisions in the web environment, in addition, to coping with the amount of information available, people tend to prefer simplified decision strategies that only incorporate some of the available information into their decision available at hand [33]. This type uses, to some extent, the "least effort principle," which assumes that "people prefer less effort to more effort, not because they are lazy, but because they are economy-minded processors who spend their cognitive resources only when they are truly needed" [6, p. 38].

When encountering a "small number of well-understood alternatives," people generally tend to "examine all the attributes of all the alternatives and then make trade-offs when necessary." However, "when the choice set gets large, we must use alternative strategies, and these can get us into trouble" [30, p. 94].

For example, when faced with two choices, a reasonable strategy would be looking at all the alternatives and how they differ in terms of their attributes and then making some decisions based on the importance of such attributes as app reviews, size and screenshots. This type of strategy is called in the choice literature as a "compensatory," in which, for example, the (app reviews) attribute has a higher value that compensates for the (app size) attribute that has a low-value [30]. Noticeably, the same strategy cannot be used in a different context, where the set of options are larger, and it is harder to evaluate each option. Instead, one might simplify this task using the "elimination by aspects" strategy. First, a decision needs to be made regarding choosing which attribute is important, setting up a cutoff level, and eliminating all the options that do not satisfy the standard of the desired attributes [30]. In this process, attribute by attribute is evaluated until a choice is reached or the set of finalists' features is narrowed down enough to move on to compensatory evaluation [30]. Similarly, the anchoring strategy [32] is "the tendency to relay heavily, or anchor, on one piece of information in order to arrive at a decision" [26, p. 915].

People do not choose randomly between the equated alternatives. In contrast, they choose the superior option on the more important dimension, which appears to provide a compelling reason to choose [16]. "Reason-based conception of choice" focuses on the reasons that seem closer to how people think and talk about when making choices. When facing a difficult choice, people try to come up with reasons for and against each option at hand because most would only sometimes attempt to estimate the overall values of those options [16, p. 1112].

2.3   Adaptation in Search

Adaptation in the decision-making process is greatly affected by the time pressure, which affects how the information is examined. "Several types of adaptations" have been found, such as "acceleration, selective filtration, and the use of less information" [7, p. 96].

"People can adjust their rate of information processing (i.e., acceleration), may choose to filter incoming information (filtration), or may queue information for later processing." Acceleration can take the form of a participant working faster to complete the task, spending less time on each stage of the decision-making process, processing more information at the same time, or reducing the amount of time spent on each piece of information" [7, p. 95]. Participants may filter or select according to what they already know, seek more general information, or focus on the most reliable or salient attribute [7].

Overall, it has also been found that people seeking information are selective in the information they use to decide, either filtering information to focus on a subset of the available information or choosing different information sources [7]. They also may "shift their search strategy by more shallowly inspecting search results, more superficially processing found information, or by satisficing" [7, p. 95].

2.4 Learning from Search

Learning occurs throughout the search process as users plan, formulate and modify their search, and select and interact with all the information sources, while "gaining new or modifying and reinforcing existing knowledge" [22, p. 202]. In behavior science, it refers to "any change in behaviour which comes about as a result of experience [12, p. 39]. "Consumer behaviour is a process of learning; it is modified according to the customer's past experience and the objectives he or she has set" [12, p. 41]. Sometimes, they tend to supplement their knowledge with external searches, in which they might obtain information from different resources such as advertisements and friends' recommendations [28].

3 Research Objective

Our earlier work examined the heuristic decision-making processes while participants navigated through the app store by observing the information cues they considered when searching for apps [1]. The concepts of heuristics, information search and processing, decision-making and choices theories are intertwined.

Prior work conducted by Dogruel et al. [10] reported that half of their participants did not scroll past the default list of 5 apps in the app search results and that participants were mainly restricted by what is available on the default information on the app search screen.

This research aims to provide insights into the users' scrolling behaviour and how far they will go when searching for apps. The theories and models introduced earlier inform and guide our research discovery, especially the interpretations of the collected data.

Based on earlier work, our research seeks to address the following questions:

- Do users scroll beyond the default app screen looking for apps?
- How far will the users go?
- Does the total number of apps seen on the app selection page influence or affect users' scrolling search behaviour?
- Do the information cues presented by app developers in the app stores impact or affect users' scrolling search behaviour?
- Does prior knowledge affect users' scrolling search behaviour?
- Do users always choose the highest-rated apps?

4 Method

4.1 Participants

In this study, twenty-six students were recruited through the university e-mail lists as a convenience sample from a Canadian university with ages ranging from 18 to 40 years. Participants had to be 18 years old and own an Android smartphone to participate. The participants received $10 compensation for participating.

4.2 Procedure

Using a multi-method design [8], we combined an observational lab study with qualitative and think-aloud protocol followed by semi-structured interviews to explore the users' scrolling behaviour when choosing which apps to install [11, 17,18]. Also, we collected demographic information via a short questionnaire. Participants completed the study in about 30 min.

For the app selection tasks, participants were asked to help out a hypothetical friend who asked for advice to find two specific apps for given scenarios. The researcher gave two scenarios out of five for the following categories: Nutrition and health, Music, Twitter, Flight tracking, Scanning receipts, and Word games. When participants verbalized their advice of the app name for the selection task, they were given an Android smartphone to complete the tasks, and they were told to imagine it was their friend's smartphone. The complete study guide is reported in [1].

4.3 Measures

To guide our research discovery, we adapted some coding rules from the work of Dogruel et al. [10] while analyzing users' scrolling search behaviour when choosing apps. The complete guide of those rules can be found in [1]. For this work, we have recorded the following variables during each app search:

(1) The total number of apps seen by participants on the app search results in the app store with and without scrolling (e.g., five apps by default at the time of the study).
(2) The total time of the app search task from seeing the first app till the conclusion of the app search process.
(3) The time spent before selecting the first app for viewing.
(4) The lowest and the highest average ratings[1] of the list of apps displayed on the app search results in the app store.
(5) The rating of the selected app.
(6) Participants' scrolling behaviours were recorded using built-in software.
(7) The participants given advice was used to determine prior knowledge.
(8) Other variables were gathered, but reported as a part of another study [1].

In addition to the collected variables, it is important to note that the total number of app search instances was 84. For the statistical test analysis, we used Chi-square to report any significant differences. Also, we used the letter N to represent the total number of occurrences. Zeros used in Figs. 1 and 2, indicate that some participants did not see the app search results page and went directly to the app description page itself after initiating the search task by writing a keyword for an app. Furthermore, the ID represents the participant number. Lastly, the discussed theories guided us throughout the research discovery.

---

[1] When refer to the average rating on a five-point scale as the *rating* from here on.

5   Results

First, we describe users' search behaviour in terms of scrolling, how far they will go, influence or affected by the number of apps seen in the search results and the impact or effect of the information cues when searching for apps. Second, we shed some light on users' scrolling search behaviour concerning their given advice and prior knowledge of the given scenario. Third, we report our observations regarding the ratings of the lowest and highest apps in addition to the ratings of the selected apps. Lastly, we detail and reflect on the impact of adopting multiple theories and models regarding users' scrolling search behaviour.

5.1   Users' Scrolling Search Behaviour

When investigating users' search behaviour to find an app, it is crucial to consider their scrolling behaviour. This behaviour involves the total number of apps seen on the app selection page and the impact and effect of the information cues (e.g., app reviews). Figure 1 shows that the range of the number of apps seen by participants on the app search results varied from seeing nothing (e.g., opening the app page directly based on the user search keyword) to seeing up to 54 apps before making up their minds to select an app to view.

Interestingly, we found that participants have scrolled past the default screen in almost 39% ($N = 33$ out of 84) of the app instances. This shows that some participants, within a few seconds, had decided to view their first app to evaluate, while others spent up to one minute and 45 s scrolling through the apps list to view an app.

For example, the search behaviour of ID22 differed from other participants. Before even starting the search process of inputting a search keyword to look for an app, this participant went to Categories, then Top Free, and then scrolled down until he found an app that matched the given scenario. That participant stated that they would reach 54 apps in the app list, and if they could not find what they were seeking, they would start the search process using the Google Play Store search bar.

Based on the previous observations, the chi-square test revealed a difference ($p = 0.007 < 0.05$) between the participants and the total number of apps seen on the app search results, which confirms that participants employed different scrolling behaviours while searching for apps.

Information Cues Effect on Users' Scrolling Search Behaviour. One of the aspects that might extend or shorten users' scrolling behaviour is the quality of the information cues presented in the app stores.

For example, the participant with ID19 took 1 min and 45 s before choosing an app to view and saw 15 apps in total in the app search results. Then, he checked the short description of an app called Smart Receipts. They read *"track expenses, scan receipts, create PDF reports all from your phone,"* and then said *"I think this one is appropriate."* It was interesting that, from one cue and within only 19 s, he decided to install the app because this short description was well-written by the app developer/company, which summed up all the aspects that this participant needed in the app.

For the participant with the ID8, the first cue they considered in both app search tasks was the app logo. For the first app they chose, it only took them 23 s. For the second task, while scrolling through the app search results, he said that he *"has broad assumptions of their logos; they look all right."* It took that participant 48 s, perhaps a bit longer than his first task[2], and the number of apps they saw on the search results was 16. Interestingly, when he was asked why he considered the app logo in both tasks, he said, *"it looks professional, especially if it has the look of that it was designed by a graphical designer, something like that; they have been more committed on their app."*

Overall, the information cues in the app store environment have a considerable impact on their users [15], and it can trigger a change in users' behaviour while scrolling or judging the app content.

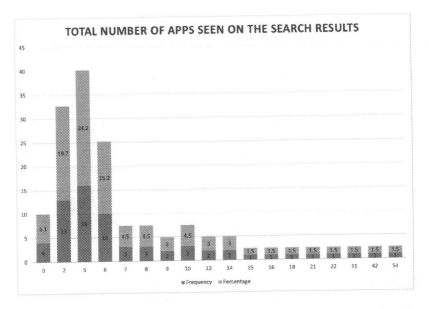

Fig. 1. The overall distribution of the frequency and percentage of the number of apps seen on the app search results page.

5.2 Prior Knowledge

We describe whether the participants followed the suggestion they were given of the category to consider when they were asked if they have specific app names

---

[2] We have not yet tested for a statistically significant difference between these times.

in mind before the app selection tasks based on the given scenarios. We wanted to see if prior knowledge would affect users' scrolling behaviour when searching for apps.

We found that fourteen participants did not have any app names in mind for the given scenarios. Some participants suggested some app names but searched for other apps. What was interesting is that a few participants suggested to search for a possible function that the app has to have based on the given scenario such as cam scanner.

Recall that our earlier work reported seven instances of the factor knew the apps where participants installed familiar apps [1]. In five instances, participants installed familiar apps in one of the search tasks, and in two instances, one participant installed apps that he already knew in both tasks.

The time spent to install an app ranged from 22 s to two minutes and a half. In five cases, the time spent was measured in seconds as the following: 22, 32, 49, 61, and 72. On the other hand, the participant with the ID9 spent two minutes and a half because he initially suggested an app but searched for another and then decided to install what he suggested. The participant with ID15 spent over two minutes. At first, he suggested a word game app, then while he was searching, navigating the app categories, he saw 42 apps in total on the app selection results. He stated that he recognized an app from the search results that he heard in the newspaper and installed it.

Overall, due to the low number of occurrences, we could not further investigate the effect of prior knowledge on the users' behaviour when searching for apps even though there are some indications that the installation process is, to some extent, quicker.

5.3   App Ratings

One of our research questions was observing participants if they would always choose the highest-rating apps. We first report the overall frequencies for the following variables: lowest rating displayed, highest rating displayed and the rating of the selected app.

The rating variable was divided into three parts: the rating of the selected apps and the lowest and highest ratings displayed on the app search results. We have observed participants in these three domains. We wanted to see if the app rating displayed on the app search results would influence their app selections.

The lowest displayed rating was 2.9, as Fig. 2a shows, and the highest displayed rating was 4.8, as Fig. 2b displays. It's important to note that, as we have mentioned earlier that some of our participants have gone directly to the app page description without displaying the app search results and because of that, the zero percent is shown in Fig. 2a and Fig. 2b.

Figure 2a displayed that the highest percentage of our participants have seen the app rating 3.9 with 17% ($N - 12$) of the cases followed by the app rating 3.6 with 16% ($N = 11$) of the cases. Apps rated 4 and 4.3 had the same percentage of 10% ($N = 7$) each. On the other hand, Fig. 2b showed that 28% ($N = 20$) of the cases were for apps with a rating of 4.5. Twenty percent ($N = 14$) of the

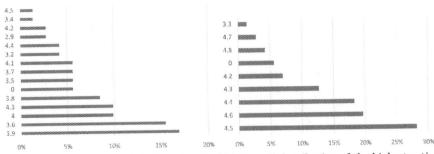

(a) Overall distribution of the lowest rating (b) Overall distribution of the highest rating

Fig. 2. Distribution of the lowest and highest ratings displayed on the search results.

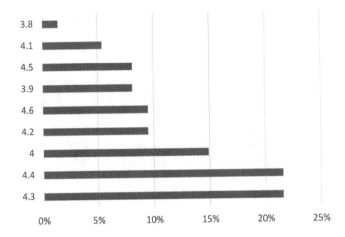

Fig. 3. The overall distribution of the rating of the selected app.

cases have seen apps with a 4.6 rating, followed by 18% ($N = 13$) for apps with a rating of 4.4.

For the rating of the selected app as seen in Fig. 3, 22% ($N = 16$) have chosen an app with a rating of 4.3, and similarly, apps with a rating of 4.4. Interestingly, 4% ($N = 3$) of our participants have seen an app on the search results with a rating of 4.8, the highest app rating in our sample. That does not necessarily mean that it would influence participants only to choose the highest ratings available since none of them has selected an app with a rating of 4.8. Indeed, with 1.5% ($N = 1$), one participant had chosen an app with a rating of 3.8.

More importantly, we thought we might find significant differences between participants concerning the three above variables. Regarding the rating of the selected app, the Chi-Square test found no difference between participants ($p = 0.467 > 0.05$). However, Chi-Square tests found significant differences between participants regarding the lowest and highest displayed ratings on the app search results (both $p = 0.001 < 0.05$).

5.4   Applicability of the Discussed Theories

In this section, we reflect on why we included multiple theories. We provide an overview of the aspects we learned from the "Return to the First" heuristic [1], information search and processing, choices and decision-making, problem recognition, evaluation of alternatives, search adaptation, and learning from search.

Concerning the consumer decision-process model created by Solomon et al. [28] as mentioned in Sects. 2.1 (p. 2) and 2.2 (p. 3), our earlier work found [1] that a few participants stated that they first must have a problem that creates the need to download an app that would solve the issue (problem recognition). For example, the participant with the ID5 stated *"I will see what problem this app would solve for me before installing anything."* Also, our earlier work reported that some participants evaluated multiple alternatives (apps) before deciding to install one and in 8% (N=7) out of the 84 instances of viewing apps, some participants returned to the first app they had initially considered [1].

Regarding the information search and processing, decision theories, and the constraints in the environment regarding the complexity of the information presented mentioned in Sect. 2.2 (p. 3), some participants would use the "least effort principle" when evaluating the app information cues. As we mentioned, from observing one information cue (e.g., app description), the participant with ID19 concluded his search task by installing the app. He did not need to look for other apps because what he found matched his needs. On the other hand, other participants were engaged in thorough comparative analysis when searching for apps till they found what they needed.

In terms of choices and the adaptation in search (selectivity or filtration), as reported in Sects. 2.2 (p. 3) and 2.3 (p. 4), we found that while participants were searching for apps in the app selection platform, they sometimes changed the information cues that they initially considered by adding or disregarding some of them since they had already used them previously [1]. Similarly, it is somewhat related to the "elimination by aspects" strategy, anchoring strategy, and the reason-based conception of choice concerning the importance of one attribute (information cue). All of them can be combined and employed in the same context in which the number of features is reduced when they evaluate other choices by focusing only on a single dominant feature [25]. For example, one participant indicated that he would discard choosing an app if it does not have a specific functionality (e.g., a QR code reader).

With respect to the aspect of learning from search is reported in Sect. 2.4 (p. 5), we found that users gather information along the search process that may aid them in narrowing their search of the apps they are comparing or are interested in downloading.

In summary, these theories have changed our perspective regarding users' decision-making strategies and their scrolling behaviours while selecting which apps to install.

6   Discussion

In this section, we discuss some of our interpretations of the reported results.

Everything in the environment (app stores in our context) does not have the same impact because it influences users' scrolling search behaviour when looking for apps. We showcased that the length in the browsing sequences that precede downloads indicates that some users deliberately browse options and consider multiple information cues for comparison before selecting an app to download [1,14]. On the other hand, based on the quality of the information cues, some participants found that focusing on only one cue was enough to determine the app's quality. It shows that when needed, participants use different strategies to cope with the amount of information presented in the app store by evaluating multiple alternatives or filtering and selecting specific salient cues to reach a decision.

More importantly, we found that the app ratings do not matter because it is based on the app quality in terms of the information cues and the efforts the app developer/publisher or company put in when designing their apps. It can be seen that, although participants have seen some apps with high ratings, still, it did not affect them in choosing those apps because none of the participants chose the highest-rated app with a rating of 4.8.

Overall, this analysis indicates that users adjust and adapt to accommodate the implications of the acquired knowledge gained from the environment. Their search behaviours can be unexpected.

7   Limitations

The studies of information-seeking behaviour and decision-making theories did not agree on the types of search activities that users tend to engage in while seeking information [2]. This could be related to the unpredictable behaviour of users when searching for apps because anything in the environment can trigger a change in their scrolling search behaviours.

Also, one of the limitations is that we could not find a single theory that can be applied or applicable to fit users' search scrolling behaviour. Because of that, we cannot determine the type of decision-making or strategy followed. To some extent, we are just trying to present our perspectives and interpretations of how users search for apps.

8   Future Work

In this work, we attempted to understand users' search scrolling behaviours when choosing apps. Still, further research is needed to include "users' characteristics (e.g., expertise, background, and topic knowledge)" since it may affect their search behaviours [4, p. 27].

Lastly, we aim to investigate further the importance and salience of some information cues because some users apparently prefer and value specific cues over others based on what they learned during their search. The importance of information cues shows the app's quality, and it can determine its success or failure.

9   Conclusion

Everything in the app store environment can impact and influences users' behaviours. Using a multi-method design, we combined an observational lab study with qualitative and think-aloud protocol to explore the users' scrolling behaviours when choosing which apps to install. We used and combined multiple theories that guided us throughout this work, creating a new perspective in the app domain.

Interestingly, users might not choose apps with high ratings since they focus on the app's quality represented by the information cues. Therefore, app developers and publishers need to pay attention when designing their apps because one single information cue could be why users install their apps.

In conclusion, our work showed that users' behaviour is dynamic and constantly changing throughout the app search process. They can adjust and adapt to accommodate the implications of the acquired knowledge gained from the environment.

Acknowledgments. The first author gratefully acknowledges a scholarship from Taibah University, Saudi Arabia.

References

1. Alhejaili, A., Blustein, J.: A study on how users choose apps. In: Kurosu, M. (ed.) HCII 2022. LNCS, vol. 13304, pp. 3–22. Springer, Cham (2022). https://doi.org/10.1007/978-3-031-05412-9_1
2. Allam, H., Bliemel, M., Nassiri, N., Toze, S., Peet, L.M., Banerjee, R.: A review of models of information seeking behavior. In: 2019 Sixth HCT Information Technology Trends (ITT), pp. 147–153 (2019). https://doi.org/10.1109/ITT48889.2019.9075095
3. Apple: Be Discoverd (2022). https://searchads.apple.com
4. Azzopardi, L.: Cognitive biases in search: a review and reflection of cognitive biases in information retrieval. In: Proceedings of the 2021 Conference on Human Information Interaction and Retrieval, CHIIR 2021, pp. 27–37. Association for Computing Machinery, New York (2021). https://doi.org/10.1145/3406522.3446023
5. Beresford, B., Sloper, P.: Understanding the dynamics of decision-making and choice: a scoping study of key psychological theories to inform the design and analysis of the panel study. Social Policy Research Unit, University of York, York (2008)
6. Bohner, G., Moskowitz, G.B., Chaiken, S.: The interplay of heuristic and systematic processing of social information. Eur. Rev. Soc. Psychol. **6**(1), 33–68 (1995). https://doi.org/10.1080/14792779443000003

7. Crescenzi, A., Capra, R., Choi, B., Li, Y.: Adaptation in information search and decision-making under time constraints. In: Proceedings of the 2021 Conference on Human Information Interaction and Retrieval, CHIIR 2021, pp. 95–105. Association for Computing Machinery, New York (2021). https://doi.org/10.1145/3406522.3446030

8. Creswell, J.W., Creswell, J.D.: Research Design: Qualitative, Quantitative & Mixed Methods Approaches, 5th edn. SAGE, Los Angeles (2018)

9. Dieter, M., Gerlitz, C., Helmond, A., Tkacz, N., van der Vlist, F.N., Esther Weltevrede, A.: Multi-situated app studies: methods and propositions. Soc. Media + Soc. 5(2) (2019). https://doi.org/10.1177/2056305119846486

10. Dogruel, L., Joeckel, S., Bowman, N.D.: Choosing the right app: an exploratory perspective on heuristic decision processes for smartphone app selection. Mob. Media Commun. 3, 125–144 (2015). https://doi.org/10.1177/2050157914557509

11. Felt, A.P., Ha, E., Egelman, S., Haney, A., Chin, E., Wagner, D.: Android permissions: user attention, comprehension, and behavior. In: Proceedings of the Eighth Symposium on Usable Privacy and Security, SOUPS 2012. ACM (2012). https://doi.org/10.1145/2335356.2335360

12. Foxoll, G.R.: Consumer Behaviour: A Practical Guide. Cengage Learning Emea (2016)

13. Google: Google play store (2022). https://play.google.com/store. Accessed 29 Dec 2022

14. He, J., Fang, X., Liu, H., Li, X.: Mobile app recommendation: an involvement-enhanced approach. MIS Q. 43(3), 827–850 (2019). https://doi.org/10.25300/MISQ/2019/15049

15. Helf, C., Hlavacs, H.: Apps for life change: critical review and solution directions. Entertainment Comput. 14, 17–22 (2016). https://www.sciencedirect.com/science/article/pii/S1875952115000075

16. Kahneman, D., Tversky, A.: Choices, Values, and Frames. Russell Sage Foundation. Cambridge University Press, New York (2000)

17. Kelley, P.G., Consolvo, S., Cranor, L.F., Jung, J., Sadeh, N., Wetherall, D.: A conundrum of permissions: installing applications on an android smartphone. In: Blyth, J., Dietrich, S., Camp, L.J. (eds.) FC 2012. LNCS, vol. 7398, pp. 68–79. Springer, Heidelberg (2012). https://doi.org/10.1007/978-3-642-34638-5_6

18. Kelley, P.G., Cranor, L.F., Sadeh, N.: Privacy as part of the app decision-making process. In: Proceedings of the SIGCHI Conference on Human Factors in Computing Systems, CHI 2013, pp. 3393–3402. Association for Computing Machinery, New York (2013). https://doi.org/10.1145/2470654.2466466

19. Larsen, M.E., Huckvale, K., Nicholas, J., Torous, J., Birrell, L., Li, E., Reda, B.: Using science to sell apps: evaluation of mental health app store quality claims. NPJ Digit. Med. 2(1), 18 (2019). https://doi.org/10.1038/s41746-019-0093-1

20. Lin, C.H., Chen, M.: The icon matters: how design instability affects download intention of mobile apps under prevention and promotion motivations. Electron. Commer. Res. 19(1), 211–229 (2019). https://doi.org/10.1007/s10660-018-9297-8

21. Marshall, J.M., Dunstan, D.A., Bartik, W.: The digital psychiatrist: in search of evidence-based apps for anxiety and depression. Front. Psychiatry 10, 831 (2019). https://doi.org/10.3389/fpsyt.2019.00831

22. O'Brien, H., Cole, A., Kampen, A., Brennan, K.: The effects of domain and search expertise on learning outcomes in digital library use. In: ACM SIGIR Conference on Human Information Interaction and Retrieval, CHIIR 2022, pp. 202–210. Association for Computing Machinery, New York (2022). https://doi.org/10.1145/3498366.3505761

23. Payne, J.W.: Heuristic search processes in decision making. Adv. Consum. Res. **3**(1), 321–327 (1976). https://scholars.duke.edu/display/pub1057867

24. Pol, M.: App icon preferences: The Influence of App Icon Design and Involvement on Quality and Intention to Download (2015). http://essay.utwente.nl/67044/

25. Proctor, R.W., Zandt, T.V.: Human Factors in Simple and Complex Systems. CRC Press (2018)

26. Saini, R., Monga, A.: How I decide depends on what I spend: use of heuristics is greater for time than for money. J. Consum. Res. **34**(6), 914–922 (2008)

27. Simon, H.A.: A behavioral model of rational choice. Q. J. Econ. **69**(1), 99–118 (1955). http://www.jstor.org/stable/1884852

28. Solomon, M.R., Bamossy, G.J., Askegaard, S., Hogg, M.K.: Consumer Behaviour: A European Perspective. Pearson Education (2016)

29. Suvanaphen, E., Roberts, J.C.: Visualizing evolving searches with EvoBerry. In: Proceedings of the 11th International Conference Information Visualization, IV 2007, pp. 238–244. IEEE Computer Society (2007). https://doi.org/10.1109/IV.2007.135

30. Thaler, R.H., Sunstein, C.R.: Nudge. Yale University Press, New Haven, CT and London (2008)

31. Todorov, A., Chaiken, S., Henderson, M.D.: The Heuristic-Systematic Model of Social Information Processing, pp. 195–212. SAGE Publications Inc., Thousand Oaks (2002). https://doi.org/10.4135/9781412976046. https://sk.sagepub.com/reference/hdbk_persuasion

32. Tversky, A., Kahneman, D.: Judgment under uncertainty: heuristics and biases. Science **185**(4157), 1124–1131 (1974). https://www.science.org/doi/abs/10.1126/science.185.4157.1124

33. Wirth, W., Böcking, T., Karnowski, V., Von Pape, T.: Heuristic and systematic use of search engines. J. Comput.-Mediated Commun. **12**(3), 778–800 (2007). https://doi.org/10.1111/j.1083-6101.2007.00350.x

A Model-Based Approach for Expansion of Androids Status-Bar-Notification

Emiliandro Carlos De Moraes Firmino and Aasim Khurshid$^{(\boxtimes)}$

Sidia Institute of Science and Technology, Manaus, AM, Brazil
emiliandro.firmino@sidia.com, Aasim.khurshid@sidia.com

Abstract. Workarounds are required to assist in interpreting the received message information in developing android applications that use notifications. The applications require making decisions on how to utilize the received notification.

Arguably, notifications are the most dynamic objects that may appear at any time, and it is vital to decide which notifications are expandable. This work proposes a formal model for expanding notifications for Android applications.

The model utilizes two algorithms that cooperate in evaluating errors in the status-Bar-Notifications (SBN) and decides on the expansion of the notification. This model-based decision-making increases the efficiency of discriminating the expandable notifications from the non-expandable ones using the linear classification based on the frequency distribution of dynamic values inside a Status-Bar-Notification.

Keywords: Android notifications · status-bar notifications · Model-based decision making · expandable notifications

1 Introduction

Notification is described as a vocabulary broken down into small bits of information. A large number of applications use this feature to present a variety of information in the text format [8].

Formally, notifications are presented since the first iteration of the operating system's Application Programmable Interface (API) and are developed to appear in different formats. However, notifications have suffered many updates since the first android interface [8].

Developing applications that use notification inside Android can be divided into two categories: create and receive. The act of creating a notification is well documented over many articles in sites, books, and forums, but to intercept a notification to read its contents is more demanding due to its specificity [7].

To access information on other applications, understanding the legal issues is necessary. Due to privacy and security reasons, android has the proxy to filter

This work is partially supported by Sidia institute of science and technology, and Samsung Eletrônica da Amazônia Ltda, under the auspice of the Brazilian informatics law no 8.387/91.

the information that can be utilized for third-party development. This exported information it's the formal model-based parcel known as Status-Bar-Notification (SBN).

SBN is a combination of static and dynamic mechanisms, and a service to filter the intercepted/received notification [1]. Due to the enforcement of these mechanisms, the interpretation of these bits of information ended up being unnecessarily complex. The creation of notification is not the focus of this article, but it is necessary to understand the input data while creating so that it is partly accessible inside an SBN's value [8]. Considering that, to objectify the use of those dynamic accessible data received by the application a study of the values presented inside SBN and the additional semantic data using data science techniques were used to develop a formal model.

Fig. 1. Status Bar region is also known as the notification drawer

The status bar is the region of the phone screen where information is presented in the application framework level of the android system process, the drawer commonly accessed by a swipe-down gesture started at the top corner of the screen area is visible in the Fig. 1. Information about time, battery, cell signal, and other specifics are present in the region. Everything presented in there is accessible for the developer to use until dismissed by the app or the user. This data is delivered via SBN in small bits of dynamic and static information.

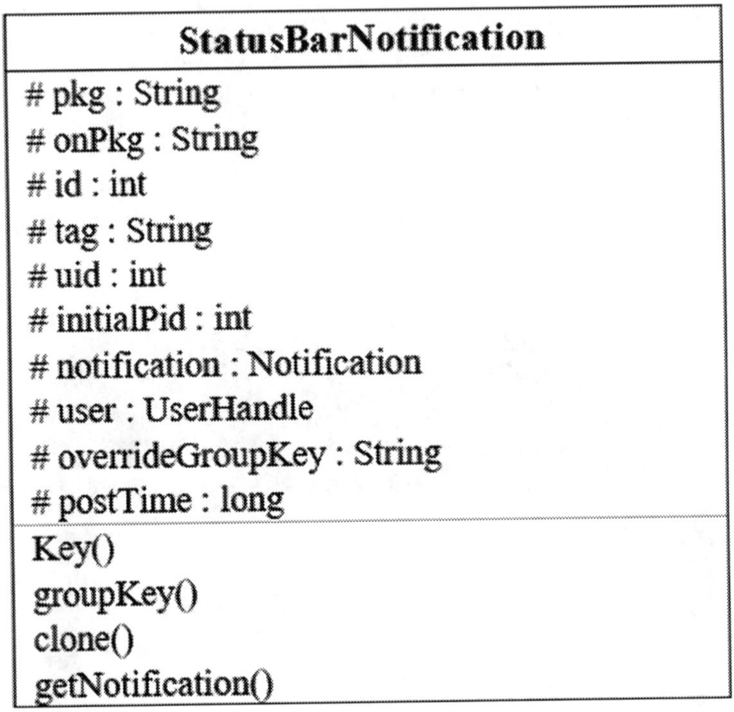

StatusBarNotification
# pkg : String
# onPkg : String
# id : int
# tag : String
# uid : int
# initialPid : int
# notification : Notification
# user : UserHandle
# overrideGroupKey : String
# postTime : long
Key()
groupKey()
clone()
getNotification()

Fig. 2. Status Bar Notification Model

Figure 2 presents the Status-Bar-Notification formal model and its static and dynamic information. The static portion represents data from the source that posted the notification inside the drawer, while the dynamic portion represents displayed content.

Table 1 provide information about the data available in the status-bar-notifications. The data is composed of static and dynamic data, as explained below:

Static data:

1. "Pkg" and "onPkg" values represent the application that initializes the notification.
2. "Uid" is the fixed id of the installation of the application on the phone.
3. "User" is a formal model representing the currently logged user on the phone. The "experimental analysis" section is explaining how was handle the information present in the bundle.

Table 1. Static and dynamic data inside Status-Bar-Notification.

Method	Values	Definition
Static	Pkg, onPkg, Uid, user	Every data that remains fixed with an information that point to the user logged on the cell phone and the notified application
Dynamic	Tag, notification, postTime, id, overrideGroupKey	Dynamic data is everything that is to be displayed inside the notification drawer and everything that changes from message to message

Dynamic data:

1. "post-time" value is the millisecond of when the notification was posted.
2. "Groupkey" value is a concatenation of many texts (pkg, id, tag, uid, and many more) that allows the location of the displayed information, it is a more detailed and specific version of the id parameter. As it is a more detailed id, it is ideal for tracking issues.
3. "Notification" value is every metadata to be displayed is inside a builder named extras. The builder contains information regarding what the app inputted for the notification being displayed. Information regarding text values, images values, and action values.

The rest of the paper is organized as follows. The legal obligations about notification data collection is detailed in the Sect. 2. Next, The proposed approach is explained in Sect. 3, followed by the experimental results in Sect. 4. Finally, Sect. 5 provides the conclusions and future work in this direction.

2   Legal Obligations

The research of a notification involves collecting data of hundreds of third-party apps. To understand its messages might get in conflict with copyright law and/or competition law [6]. This articles studies do not involve interpretation of explicit values in text or images encrypted or not. Thus, images and its related values collected will not be covered. The proposed study only involves patterns in which the information is received in the dynamic portion of an easily accessible bundle inside the Status-Bar-Notification.

3   Proposed Approach

Developing the applications that contain notification can be divided into two categories: create and receive [3]. The notification creation is well documented [7], however, to intercept a notification and its contents requires specificity: filtering the relevance and legal obligations in Sect. 2.

This work develops a formal model-based usage of accessible and non-accessible content followed by the expansion of the notification. A large amount of data is collected for the model development that classifies these notifications, and the relevant data is filtered using an empirical approach. We developed a formal model-based algorithm to reconstruct the notification in a controlled environment. Next, a linear classification model for the expandable and non-expandable notifications.

The model-based approach uses two algorithms to decide the expansion of the notification, and they coordinate with each other for decision-making. Firstly, the listener service intercepts the notification, which is sent to get evaluated for status bar notification errors and is processed as in Fig. 3(a). Then, the approach follows the process as in Fig. 3(b) to expand the dynamic notification.

Firstly, we present the working of the error evaluation of the proposed method in Fig. 3(a) and explained next.

(a) Block diagram of the error evaluation;(b) Block diagram of the Expansion of the dynamic notification.

Fig. 3. The block diagram of the working of the proposed method.

1. The listener intercepts the notification;
2. SBN reference is sent for the notification usage;
3. Next, all the static values are saved, which are classified using the binary classifier;

4. Next, the notification is checked for the string value;
5. If the notification checked is not in a string format, the value is converted to String.
6. Next, the value in a string format is saved.
7. Next, the notification is checked for the visibility of a Boolean value;
8. If the visibility value is not found, the value inside notification usage is set to default as false;
9. If the visibility value is found. The value inside notification usage is set as the same found;
10. Next, the notification saves the most common dynamic values such as "text" and "title";
11. Next, the notification is checked for the string value;
12. If the notification checked is not in a string format, the value is converted to String.
13. Then, "Text" and "Title" are saved in a string format.
14. Next, the notification is check for the "template" and "bigText" values.
15. If none of the values are present, the value inside notification usage is set as false;
16. If one of the values are present, the value inside notification usage is set as true;
17. If one of the values are present, all other dynamic values are saved inside a bundle;

Next, the working of the proposed method is explained as shown in Fig. 3(b), which intecepts the notification, and sends for error evaluation to the Notification usage application, and if there is no error, it follows to the classification of expandable and non-expandable notification.

1. The listener intercepts the notification;
2. The notification is sent to a Activity inside an Intent;
3. The Main Activity checks the intent for errors as shown in Fig. 3(a), and is already explained above;
4. If an error is found, the process ends here;
5. If an error is not found, the activity's list view generates a new item;
6. Next, the list view checks check for the "template" and "bigText" values;
7. Then, if the value is true, a new item for the list view is generated with a badge in its bottom right corner is created;
8. If the value is false, a new item with no badge is created;
9. The most common values inside the notification are used to fill the TextViews.

4   Experimental Evaluation

The devices used in our experiments were the Galaxy S20 5G and the Galaxy M62. For training and evaluation of the both the algorithms, a Samsung Book 4 GB RAM Intel® Celeron® is used. The application is created using android studio[1], and Kotlin is used as a programming language for efficiency[2].

---

[1] https://developer.android.com/studio.
[2] https://kotlinlang.org/.

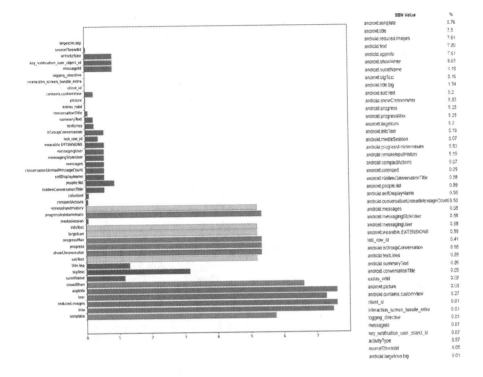

Fig. 4. Data collected for analysis in percentage

4.1 Data Collection

A total of 7412 Status-Bar-Notification were used to record their dynamics values. Figure 4 shows the percentage of frequency of those 44 unique values recorded 97372 times. Each unique value is highlighted in a color-coded pattern.

The blue color shows the most common values that were received, of those 4, "Text" and "Title" are explicitly stated as the main parameters to compose a notification [3, 4].

In an orange tint, the "template" and "showWhen" are represented, which specifies values stating if a notification should be displayed for the user and how to be displayed, furthermore in a red tint that is a parameter correlated to the "template" one that complement those in a blue tint when the user expands a notification inside the drawer [3–5].

Those in a green tint correspond to situational cases. In a light green are values that correspond to chat-based features and in a dark green that are the ones that correspond to upload and download feedback for the user [2, 4].

Finally, in a gray tint in Fig. 4 are the uncommon values and are discarded.

This filtered data is used to train the linear classifier, where data from 5929 status-bar-notifications is used for training and data from the other 1483 status-bar-notifications is used for evaluation.

```
+-----+-------------------------------------------+------------------+
|     | KEY NAMES                                 |    PERCENTAGE    |
+-----+-------------------------------------------+------------------+
|  0  | android.template                          |       10.46      |
|  1  | android.title                             |       13.77      |
|  2  | android.text                              |       13.06      |
|  3  | android.showWhen                          |       10.72      |
|  4  | android.substName                         |        4.09      |
|  5  | android.bigText                           |        7.33      |
|  6  | android.title.big                         |        4.33      |
|  7  | android.subText                           |        5.84      |
|  8  | android.showChronometer                   |        6.32      |
|  9  | android.infoText                          |        5.84      |
| 10  | android.mediaSession                      |        0.14      |
| 11  | android.remoteInputHistory                |        5.84      |
| 12  | android.compactActions                    |        0.14      |
| 13  | android.colorized                         |        0.31      |
| 14  | android.hiddenConversationTitle           |        1.11      |
| 15  | android.people.list                       |        1.55      |
| 16  | android.selfDisplayName                   |        1.11      |
| 17  | android.conversationUnreadMessageCount    |        1.11      |
| 18  | android.messages                          |        1.11      |
| 19  | android.messagingStyleUser                |        1.11      |
| 20  | android.messagingUser                     |        1.11      |
| 21  | android.wearable.EXTENSIONS               |        1.11      |
| 22  | android.isGroupConversation               |        1.11      |
| 23  | android.textLines                         |        0.6       |
| 24  | android.summaryText                       |        0.54      |
| 25  | android.conversationTitle                 |        0.2       |
| 26  | android.contains.customView               |        0.04      |
+-----+-------------------------------------------+------------------+
```

Fig. 5. Table representation of data collected using tabulate library

The relevant challenges towards a formal model-based usage of a Status-Bar-Notification are twofold: 1) patterns of additional semantic data; 2) Evaluation.

4.2 Patterns of Additional Semantic Data

Relevant information analysis of the status-bar-notification, needs a study of pattern present inside the additional semantic data. Using union-find techniques on collected sample, a data frame was created for binary search.

Moreover, it is recommended to utilize binary classification based on the collected data for the classification of the expandable and non-expandable notifications.

To summarize, chat rooms, search engines, system messages, multimedia recording, and multimedia viewing have dynamic data keys manipulated and counted to determine the ones with the highest frequency in percentage. Based on the frequency of those 27 valid values in Fig. 5, they were grouped in three and were correlated to direct the research. Each group serves as a feature for expandable and non-expandable notification classifier. These three groups include 1)common; 2)uncommon; and specific as shown in Fig. 6.

	KEY NAMES	PERCENTAGE
0	android.template	10.46
1	android.title	13.77
2	android.text	13.06
3	android.showWhen	10.72

	KEY NAMES	PERCENTAGE
0	android.subtName	4.09
1	android.bigText	7.33
2	android.title.big	4.33
3	android.subText	5.84
4	android.showChronometer	6.32
5	android.infoText	5.84
6	android.remoteInputHistory	5.84

	KEY NAMES	PERCENTAGE
0	android.mediaSession	0.14
1	android.compactActions	0.14
2	android.colorized	0.33
3	android.hiddenConversationTitle	1.11
4	android.people.list	1.55
5	android.selfDisplayName	1.11
6	android.conversationUnreadMessageCount	1.11
7	android.messages	1.11
8	android.messagingStyleUser	1.33
9	android.messagingUser	1.33
10	android.wearable.EXTENSIONS	1.11
11	android.isGroupConversation	1.11
12	android.textLines	0.6
13	android.summaryText	0.34
14	android.conversationTitle	0.2
15	android.contains.customView	0.04

Fig. 6. Three-group subdivision.

The correlation in Fig. 7, uses the grouped data presented in Fig. 6. Figure 7 shows the correlation of the notification data, and it shows a discriminate behavior of expandable and non-expandable notifications. Hence, the grouped data is used to train a classifier for expandable and non-expandable notifications.

4.3   Evaluation

For the evaluation of the proposed approach, we use two measures: 1) R^2, which measures the correlation of the grouped values with the ground-truth data, and 2) Root Mean Square Error (RMSE) of the grouped values with the ground-truth data.

The classifier is evaluated using R^2 and RMSE method. The linear classifier for expandable and non-expandable notifications has R^2 score of 0.792 on the training set and 0.829 on the test set, whereas, RMSE of 0.221 on the training set and 0.203 on the test set.

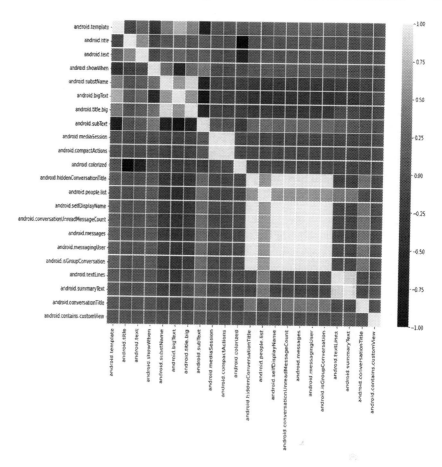

Fig. 7. Correlation heat map between values.

5   Conclusions

This paper proposed a formal model-based usage of accessible notification contents, that discriminates the expandable and non-expandable notifications. It uses empirical approach for the selection of features used by the classifier. Following this, a formal model-based algorithm was developed that reconstruct notifications in a controlled ambient. A linear classifier is trained on the filtered feature data. For the test, the features are extracted using the same process and passed to the classifier make an inference.

The results from the direct usage of the information given by Android's Proxy, known as Status-Bar-Notification, proves that a series of checks is necessary to find the relevant content and to prevent a number of exceptions. The developed algorithm succeed in decreasing the number of exceptions, however, improvements are required for a better performance and for error reduction.

References

1. Arden, O., George, M.D., Liu, J., Vikram, K., Askarov, A., Myers, A.C.: Sharing mobile code securely with information flow control. In: 2012 IEEE Symposium on Security and Privacy, pp. 191–205. IEEE (2012)
2. Android Developers: 10 remote input. https://developer.android.com/reference/android/app/RemoteInput. Accessed 31 Oct 2021
3. Android Developers: Notification. https://developer.android.com/reference/android/app/Notification. Accessed 31 Oct 2021
4. Android Developers: Notification builder. https://developer.android.com/reference/android/app/Notification.Builder#setSubText(java.lang.CharSequence). Accessed 31 Oct 2021
5. Android Developers: Notification builder. https://developer.android.com/reference/android/app/Notification.BigTextStyle?hl=en. Accessed 31 Oct 2021
6. Maass, M., Pridöhl, H., Herrmann, D., Hollick, M.: Best practices for notification studies for security and privacy issues on the internet. arXiv preprint arXiv:2106.08029 (2021)
7. Riadh, M.H.: Notification system to students using an Android application. Int. J. Comput. Appl. **140**(1), 22–27 (2016)
8. Schneegass, C., Sigethy, S., Eiband, M., Buschek, D.: Comparing concepts for embedding second-language vocabulary acquisition into everyday smartphone interactions. In: Mensch und Computer 2021 (2021). https://doi.org/10.1145/3473856.3473863

Research on Usability Design of Leisure Agriculture APP Interface Based on Kano-QFD

Huiqian He[1], Wei Sun[2(✉)], Yuan He[1], and Biru He[1]

[1] Guangdong Technology College, Zhaoqing 526100, Guangdong, China
939192573@qq.com, 263308130@qq.com
[2] South China University of Technology, Guangzhou 510006, Guangdong, China
1123832530@qq.com

Abstract. By mining the needs of land renting and land transfer groups, analyzing the correlation between user needs and functional requirements, obtaining the absolute weight of functional requirements, designing a leisure agriculture app that meets user needs and has a good user experience, and improves rural land use. Utilization rate and operational efficiency help rural revitalization and development. Based on the Kano model, through questionnaires and user interviews, determine the demand elements of the land transaction crowd, draw a user experience journey map, and establish a demand framework to prioritize functions. Through the quality function deployment theory (QFD), the mapping relationship between user needs and functional characteristics is established, and the QFD quality house is established. Design the information framework, interactive prototype, interface vision, and operation experience of the leisure agriculture APP, and verify the feasibility of the model and design practice with the SUS scale. The comprehensive application of the Kano-QFD model establishes a demand framework for leisure agriculture APP with high accuracy and objectivity and proposes a reasonable and usable innovative design scheme, which provides direction and reference for solving similar design problems. Taking the design of the leisure agriculture APP as an example, the effectiveness of the integration of Kano and QFD is verified, and an optimization idea is provided for the design of the leisure agriculture APP.

Keywords: QFD quality function deployment · Kano model · leisure agriculture · rural revitalization

1 Introduction

With the deepening of urbanization, the attractiveness of traditional rural culture is increasing day by day. Rural tourism, agricultural sightseeing, farming experience, fruit and vegetable picking, etc. have attracted a large number of urban residents. Rural tourism is an important strategy for rural development. It can not only increase the income of rural residents, and solve the "three rural" problems to a certain extent, but also meet the psychological needs of urban residents to experience rural life. Rural land construction is an important part of promoting the development of rural tourism, and it is also a solid

© The Author(s), under exclusive license to Springer Nature Switzerland AG 2023
G. Salvendy and J. Wei (Eds.): HCII 2023, LNCS 14052, pp. 29–39, 2023.
https://doi.org/10.1007/978-3-031-35921-7_3

foundation for promoting rural revitalization. Rural land has the characteristics of low land cost, original ecology, and large area. It is a unique feature of villages. Developing rural abandoned or idle land and realizing the effective use of land resources is conducive to promoting the coordinated development of urban and rural economies.

At present, most studies on land are from the perspective of economics and management, and there are few kinds of literature on land from the perspective of design. Wang Chunjie et al. [1] analyzed the impact of local governments' differentiated investment attraction on urban innovation and pointed out that industrial structure, environmental pollution, and industrial agglomeration are important factors for the government's differential investment attraction. Ma Hongxuan [2] pointed out that rural land circulation is conducive to improving the scattered and extensive land management model, optimizing the allocation of land resources, and promoting the rapid development of the local economy. In the same way, Zhang Xi [3] discussed the improvement of the land transfer transaction mechanism and the protection of the legitimate rights and interests of farmers' land. Zhang Zhanlu et al. [4] proposed that land development rights transactions should be encouraged and properly promoted, the market-oriented allocation of land resources should be promoted, the channels for the flow of land elements between urban and rural areas should be opened up, and the integrated development and synergy of land, capital, and labor should be promoted.

2 Kano-QFD Design Method Explanation and Research Process

The Kano model was proposed by Japanese scholar Kano Noriaki in order to improve satisfaction with products and services. It is used to mine user needs and core problems that need to be solved, and solve similar problems by analyzing the relationship between quality characteristics and user satisfaction [5]. As a qualitative research method, this model first obtains the functional requirements of the leisure agriculture APP through user research, distinguishes the priority and type of requirements, and divides the requirements into must-have requirements M, expected requirements O, and attractive requirements A. There are five types of indifferent demand I and reverse demand R. Second, analyze the influence value of the demand and construct an influence matrix. Finally, obtain user needs through market research and user research, fill in the questionnaire data into the evaluation form, calculate the Better-Worse value, construct a quadrant map, and clarify the design requirements and function priorities.

QFD (Quality Function Deployment Theory, also known as House of Quality) was proposed by Japanese scholar Yoji Akao. It is a research method for quantitative analysis of needs [6], which uses diagrams to quantify the degree of correlation between user needs and functional attributes. Through the scoring of the demand technology matrix by the expert group, the impact value of product functions on user satisfaction is calculated in detail, the user needs are transformed into product functions, and the design scheme is derived.

The combination of the Kano model and QFD helps to visualize and parameterize the user needs to be obtained from the research, and to clarify the design entry point. Use the Kano model to preliminarily classify user needs, use QFD to quantitatively analyze the classified user needs and transform the design direction, and build a quality house. Design requirements – output design scheme process (see Fig. 1).

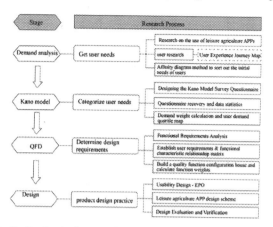

Fig. 1. Design and research process of leisure agriculture APP

3 Demand Acquisition Based on Kano Leisure Agriculture APP

3.1 Acquisition of User Needs

The mining of user needs is the design entry point for the innovative design of leisure agriculture apps. The purpose of the Kano questionnaire survey is to understand the real needs of users. Through in-depth research on target users and user interviews, fully understand the user's operation process for leisure agriculture apps, and disassemble each stage, behavior, and scene of user use in detail, design a user experience journey map, discover user pain points and convert them to design opportunity points, the user experience journey map is shown in Fig. 2.

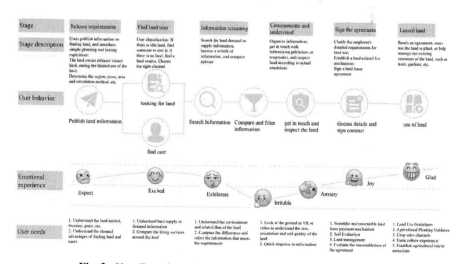

Fig. 2. User Experience Journey Map of Leisure Agriculture Apps

3.2 Kano Research

There are two main types of questionnaire surveys for leisure agriculture APPs: looking for land and looking for tenants. Since urban users are usually busy at work, few people live in rural areas for a long time, mainly to experience agricultural culture or learn rural planting knowledge. General short-term rental. Another type of tenant mainly wants to contract land, plant or manage fruit trees or vegetable gardens, etc., and needs to rent for a long time. However, landowners often have idle land or orchards due to travel or work and need to find someone to manage them so as not to be abandoned. Through in-depth interviews with the target users of the leisure agriculture APP, the first-level needs of users are sorted into information authenticity, soil quality assurance, land survey, agricultural guide, agricultural product sales, life sharing, quick screening, peripheral services, and cultural experience.

First, design the Kano questionnaire based on the above-mentioned first-level needs, and ask the respondents about the individual needs of users from the forward and reverse directions to determine the weight of the needs. Set the corresponding scores as 4, 2, 0, – 2, and –4 through the five dimensions of satisfaction, desire, indifference, tolerance, and disgust to measure the impact of different needs on user satisfaction. Secondly, classify the interactive needs of the respondents on the leisure agriculture APP, construct the user demand influence matrix.

A total of 324 questionnaires have been released, and the targets are rural users who need to rent land and urban users who need to rent land. Among them, 234 people have experience in land planting and 100 people have no experience in land planting. If the information is excluded and the incomplete questionnaire is filled out, it is valid. 315 copies were recovered, with an effective recovery rate of 97%. The questionnaire has 9 measurement dimensions and 19 questions, including a question about whether there is land planting experience. It meets the requirement of the Kano model that the sample size is 5–20 times the number of questions (Table 1).

3.3 Calculation of the Importance of User Needs

The quantitative parameters of the Kano model were designed through the leisure agriculture APP questionnaire:

$$W_j = \sqrt{\overline{X}_j^2 + \overline{Y}_j^2} \tag{1}$$

In $\overline{X}_j$ represents the user satisfaction score when the requirement is not met, and $\overline{Y}_j$ represents the user satisfaction score when the requirement is met, W_j Indicates the importance of the function. Combine Better-Worse Taxonomy divides user needs according to Kano need types, expected needs ($X > 2, Y > 2$), necessary needs ($X > 2, Y < 2$), Charisma needs ($X < 2, Y > 2$), neutral demand ($X < 2, Y < 2$), neutral requirements have no impact on users.

Table 1. Average satisfaction of leisure agriculture APP users

User needs	Satisfaction without functionality $\overline{X}_j$	Satisfaction with functionality $\overline{Y}_j$	Importance W_j	Sequence
True information	1.72	4.22	4.56	2
Soil quality assurance	1.85	4.61	4.97	1
Land inspection	1.74	3.55	3.95	6
Agricultural guide	2.53	3.63	4.42	4
Farm for sale	1.26	4.32	4.50	3
Life sharing	2.42	2.51	3.50	9
Quick filter	2.13	3.64	4.22	5
Peripheral services	1.98	3.31	3.86	8
Cultural experience	1.54	3.57	3.89	7

4 Analysis of APP Functional Requirements Based on QFD

4.1 Mapping and Analysis of Functional Requirements

Based on the analysis of user needs and the Kano model, the user demand weight and first-level demand element indicators of leisure agriculture APPs are obtained, and the first-level functional requirements of QFD are mapped, and the first-level functional requirements are refined and decomposed to obtain the second-level functions. Requirements to ensure maximum satisfaction of user needs, as shown in Table 2.

4.2 Correlation Matrix of User Needs and Functional Characteristics

User requirements and quality characteristics are the core components of the QFD House of Quality, which can intuitively and effectively reflect the relationship between requirements and functions, and realize user requirements to the greatest extent. The left side of the House of Quality is user demand elements, the roof is functional characteristics, the ceiling is the relationship between functional characteristics, the room is the relationship between demand and function, and the right wall is the market competitiveness index comparison between this product and competing products, and the floor is the importance of engineering measures. In the house of quality of leisure agricultural APPs, the degree of correlation between requirements and functions is recorded as strong correlation 5, moderate correlation 3, weak correlation 1, and irrelevance 0 from high to low, and is scored by the expert group (Table 3).

Table 2. Expansion of functional elements

Primary demand elements	Level 1 Functional Requirements	Secondary Functional Requirements
C_1 True information	F_1 Certification Information	F_{11} Data review
		F_{12} Information Release
C_2 Soil quality assurance	F_2 Soil identification	F_{21} Intelligent Recognition
		F_{22} Soil Science
C_3 Land inspection	F_3 Broker	F_{31} Remote viewing
		F_{32} Site visit
C_4 Agricultural guide	F_4 Interface navigation	F_{41} Operation navigation
		F_{42} Agricultural Encyclopedia
C_5 Farm for sale	F_5 Online store	F_{51} Sell online
		F_{52} Business cooperation
C_6 Life sharing	F_6 Circle friends social	F_{61} Online dating
		F_{62} Agricultural dynamics
C_7 Quick filter	F_7 Personalized recommendation	F_{71} Recommendation
		F_{72} Credit Rating
C_8 Peripheral services	F_8 Land surrounding	F_{81} Market traffic
		F_{82} Hydropower management
C_9 Cultural experience	F_9 Book an experience	F_{91} Service package
		F_{92} Learning experience

4.3 Functional Requirements Weight Calculation

The weight of functional requirements is an important indicator to reflect the priority level of functions. By calculating the degree of correlation between a single functional requirement and a requirement element, the weight value of the functional requirement is obtained. The formula for calculating the weight value of each functional requirement is:

$$H_j = \sum_{i=1}^{n} W_i R_{ij} (j = 0, 1, 2, 3, \ldots\ldots m) \qquad (2)$$

Table 3. Matrix of relationship between requirement elements and functional requirements

Elements of demand		Functional requirements																		
		F1		F2		F3		F4		F5		F6		F7		F8		F9	
user need	Importance	F_{11}	F_{12}	F_{21}	F_{22}	F_{31}	F_{32}	F_{41}	F_{42}	F_{51}	F_{52}	F_{61}	F_{62}	F_{71}	F_{72}	F_{81}	F_{82}	F_{91}	F_{92}
C_1	4.56	●	○			○	●			●	●	●		○	●			○	
C_2	4.97	○		●	●	○	●			△	○				○				
C_3	3.95	○	○		●	○	●		△				△	●	●				
C_4	4.42				△					△									
C_5	4.50	○	●						●	●	●	△	○	○	○				●
C_6	3.50		●						●	○	○	○	○			●			
C_7	4.22							○		●	△								○
C_8	3.86												●	●	○	●	○	○	●
C_9	3.89		○						○	○	○							●	●
Weights H_j		63.06	65.63	22.80	63.92	40.44	71.29	12.66	61.24	81.08	98.90	37.80	68.68	77.96	82.63	41.95	11.67	44.71	71.35
sequence		10	8	16	9	14	6	17	11	3	1	15	7	4	2	13	18	12	5

Note: ● means strong correlation, ○ means moderate correlation, △ means weak correlation, and blank means no correlation, scoring 5, 3, 1, 0 respectively

The importance of the functions is sorted by the weight values required by the functions, as shown in Table 3 above. The sale of agricultural products, quick screening, certification information, cultural experience, and land inspection are important parts of the APP information architecture design.

5   Leisure Agriculture APP Design Practice

5.1   Information Architecture Design

Based on the analysis and data of Kano-QFD preliminary research, the functional characteristics in QFD are transformed into the core functions of the leisure agriculture APP, and the abstract functions are concretized. Designed the usability of the information architecture from three aspects: environment, process, and operation, classify and cluster the functions, and use the nodes of the tree diagram as the basic unit of the information architecture to facilitate users to quickly find specific functions. Improve the efficiency and satisfaction of APP use. The information architecture design of the leisure agriculture APP is shown in Fig. 3.

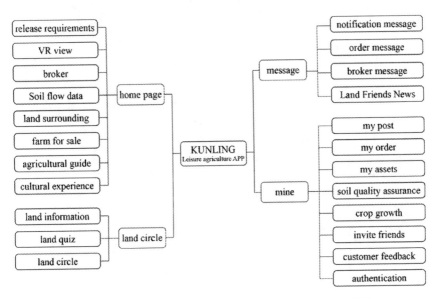

Fig. 3. Information architecture design of leisure agriculture APP

5.2   Interface Visual Design

Based on the interactive prototype of the leisure agricultural APP, analyze the usability of the product in terms of use environment, task process, and operation behavior, and improve the satisfaction of user operation. By analyzing the user's psychology and the nature of the APP, the color matching of the APP is positioned in a fresh, bright, simple, and eye-catching green flat design style, and the main function buttons are highlighted, the secondary information is weakened, the user's visual burden is reduced, and the physical area of the button is strengthened, increase fault tolerance and function feedback, and ensure the effectiveness of function clicks. The visual design of some leisure agriculture APP interfaces is shown in Fig. 4.

Fig. 4. Visual Design of the Leisure Agriculture APP—Kunling Interface

5.3 Design Evaluation

Design evaluation is an all-around evaluation of the scientific interaction logic, interface design aesthetics, and user operation fluency of leisure agriculture apps. Through the SUS scale, 5 positive questions and 5 reverse questions are set [7], and the testers rate the product from 1 to 5. By selecting 20 typical users to test Kunling APP and completing the SUS scale, the test questions and scoring results are shown in Table 4.

Through the base item X_i-1, the even item 5-X_i, the conversion scores of all items are added and then multiplied by 2.5 for calculation, the total score of the SUS scale is 77.75, and the grade is B + in the SUS score curve, which shows that the system has good usability.

Table 4. Appraisal on Interface Design of Leisure Agriculture APP—Kunling

Measurement items	Strong disagree	Different meaning	Generally	Agree	Firm agree	Average Score
1. I am willing to use leisure agriculture APP frequently	0	3	3	8	6	3.85
2. I don't think the system needs to be this complicated	5	10	3	1	1	2.15
3. I think the system is easy to use	0	4	2	5	9	3.95
4. I need help from others to use the system	8	7	3	2	0	1.95
5. I found that the different functions of the system are well integrated	1	1	2	4	12	3.90
I think there are too many inconsistencies in the system	9	4	3	4	0	2.10
I think most people can quickly learn to use this system	0	1	2	6	11	4.35
I found the system very clumsy to use	12	6	1	1	0	1.55
I feel confident using the system	0	0	3	6	11	4.40
I need to learn a lot to use the system	9	5	4	2	0	2.15

6 Conclusion

This study proposes to apply the Kano model and QFD house of quality in the interface design of a leisure agriculture APP. By transforming user needs into functional requirements and then into design requirements, and carrying out the design practice of the leisure agriculture APP, the Kano-QFD model is verified in the interactive usability of interface design. In the demand mining stage, use research interviews and user experience journey maps to initially extract user needs. In the requirements classification stage, user requirements are refined and classified based on the Kano model, and the importance of requirements is distinguished. In the functional requirements stage, based on the QFD house of quality, the functional requirements are quantitatively analyzed and the relationship matrix between user requirements and technical functions is established to calculate the weight indicators of functional characteristics. In the design practice stage, the functional requirements are built as an information framework, the main functional structure of the leisure agriculture APP is controlled, and the interactive prototype design and visual interface design of the leisure agriculture APP is carried out. In the design evaluation stage, the SUS scale is used to evaluate the satisfaction of the leisure agriculture APP, and the interface design is further improved.

Acknowledgement. Guangdong Province Philosophy and Social Sciences "14th Five-Year" Plan 2022 Regular Project: Digital Inheritance and Innovation of Cantonese Culture—Taking the Design and Development of Cantonese Dialect Emoji Package as an Example (GD22YYS03); Guangdong Technology College 2023 university-level science and technology project and "innovation and strong university project" scientific research project (2023YBSK085) (2023YBSK083) (2023YBSK084).

References

1. Wang, C., Huang, J., Zou, W.: Research on the impact of differentiated land investment on urban innovation—based on the investigation of land market transaction data. Finance Econ. **288**(8), 29–36 (2022)
2. Hongzhen, M.: Research on the economic problems of rural land transaction based on the ecological environment. Agric. Econ. Issues **11**, 146 (2020)
3. Xi, Z.: Research on the problems and improvement suggestions of the mechanism and system of rural land transfer transactions. Agric. Technol. Econ. **02**, 146 (2021)
4. Zhang, Z., Li, P.: The influence and mechanism of land development right transactions on urban-rural income gap——taking the practice of land tickets in chongqing as an example. Chin. Rural Econ. **447**(3), 36–49 (2022)
5. Wei, Y., Li, A., Xu, X., Jiang, X.: Research on Usability Design of Cloud Raising Pet APP Based on Kano-QFD. Packag. Eng. **43**(2), 378–386 (2022)
6. Xiao, J., Wang, X., Zhang, H.: Coping with diversity ratings in prioritizing design requirements in quality function deployment: a consensus-based approach with minimum-maximum adjustments. Comput. Ind. Eng. **163**, 107799 (2022)
7. Bangor, A., Kortum, P.T., Miller, J.T.: An empirical evaluation of the system usability scale. Intl. J. Hum.-Comp. Interact. **24**(6), 574–594 (2008)

Research on the Communication Mode of Mobile Applications Under the Human-Computer Interaction Mode

Jiaying Huang[1] and Wenhua Li[2(✉)]

[1] Guangzhou Academy of Fine Arts, Guangzhou 510000, China
[2] No. 168, Waihuan West Road, Panyu District, Guangzhou 510000, China
vivian.lee8686@gmail.com

Abstract. This article intends to sort out and analyze the model types and current status of human-computer interaction in mobile applications and explore and discuss the communication methods of human-computer interaction in mobile applications. Today's mobile applications, accompanied by the anthropomorphic and immersive design of the system, have built a bridge of communication and interaction between the sender and the receiver, making it possible for users to build social relationships in the virtual field, bringing users and the media closer. At the same time, it also provides the possibility to shorten the distance between users, users and communities in the virtual field. For users, mobile applications are no longer machines or tools. Driven by the human-computer interaction mode, mobile applications have become personal and emotional "partners", participating in various life scenes and emotional connection activities of users. The human-computer interaction mode of mobile applications based on emotional communication has comprehensively improved the user's sense of immersion, participation, and experience, and also puts forward higher requirements for the design of future mobile application products. New technologies generate and realize new interaction modes, and new technologies better enhance the user experience of mobile application human-computer interaction. New technologies also provide more possibilities for the down-spreading of mobile application human-computer interaction modes. At the same time, the communication effect in the human-computer interaction mode of mobile applications has been improved.

Keywords: mobile application · dissemination · human-computer interaction · method

1 Introduction

1.1 Modes and Types of Human-Computer Interaction in Mobile Applications

With the rise of mobile applications, people have undergone unprecedented changes, whether it is the blowout growth that is currently presenting, or the online and offline social participation and interactive activities through it. The important role has made the

G. Salvendy and J. Wei (Eds.): HCII 2023, LNCS 14052, pp. 40–52, 2023.
https://doi.org/10.1007/978-3-031-35921-7_4

user participation of mobile applications the focus of today's media research. Openness, immersion, and sharing are undoubtedly the most significant features that distinguish the mobile communication era from the traditional media era. Throughout the evolution and development of the human-computer interaction mode of mobile applications, the human-computer interaction from the simple task feedback of "user button-machine response" in the past has evolved into a more humanized and intelligent emotional communication [1]. In view of this, human-computer interaction is no longer a one-way, straight-line, and fixed communication, but a two-way, complex, and changing interaction. It is necessary to make extensive use of cognitive science, psychology, computer science and other disciplines for interdisciplinary research to achieve innovative development of communication methods [1].

The human-computer interaction modes of mobile phone applications include:

1. Graphical interaction: users can understand the functions of the application program more clearly through image means such as icons, pictures and titles, and disseminate content through picture display, so that users can obtain more comprehensive information.
2. Sound-based interaction: it provides user instructions and feedback information in the form of voice, making it easier for users to identify and receive information more conveniently and quickly.
3. Touch-type interaction: you can operate applications by touching or click menus and icons on the screen with fingers, and carry out man-machine communication in an easier way. The content is disseminated through the user's touch or click, and the form is concise and unified.
4. Voice-based interaction: users can easily control the application program through voice commands, allowing users to perform interactive operations without touching the screen.
5. Action-based interaction: Through input methods such as actions and gestures, users are allowed to operate applications to achieve an interesting interaction mode [2].

There are three types of mobile application human-computer interaction modes: command-based interaction, direct operation, and dialogue-based interaction [3].

Command-based interaction is a mobile application human-computer interaction mode that uses a series of command line instructions to enable users to interact with computers. This mode allows users to enter instructions and let the computer execute instructions and then return results. Usually, this mode uses a text interface, but there are also some mobile applications that can interact using voice commands.

Direct operation is a mobile application human-computer interaction mode, referring to users operating applications by touching the screen, pressing buttons, rotating wheels or other operation devices without needing to control the application through text input or input instructions. Users only need to operate simply to complete an operation. This mode makes it easier for users and is more accepted.

Dialogue-based interaction is a type of mobile application human-computer interaction mode, which is a text-based interaction mode. Users can communicate with the computer system through text input, and the system will also reply to user commands or inquiries in the form of text. The biggest advantage of this mode is that users can input any information they want through text input without the restriction of verbal commands, and they can still communicate with the computer system when they are not familiar with the system [4].

1.2 The Importance of Research on Human-Computer Interaction Models in Mobile Applications

Mobile applications rely on mobile networks and other emerging media technologies (such as 5G, cloud technology, AI, etc.), combined with mobile hardware terminals (such as mobile phones, tablet computers, etc.), to provide users with knowledge, content, and other functional services. Style [1]. The importance of mobile applications lies in their ability to help businesses better understand customers, provide services more effectively, and optimize customer experience. Mobile applications can provide real-time information updates, customized services and interactive experiences, thereby enhancing client engagement, increasing customer satisfaction, and improving service efficiency. It not only provides users with timely information and services, allowing users to obtain the required information more conveniently, but also greatly improves the user experience with mobile applications, providing effective functions and interesting applications to meet the needs of users. Mobile applications can help companies expand their brand image, allow consumers to better understand the company, increase brand awareness, and attract more customers. At the same time, mobile applications can help companies better implement marketing activities, improve marketing effects, and attract more potential customers. They provide customers with better services, help customers understand the company and products more conveniently, so as to improve customer satisfaction. In short, mobile applications are of great significance to enterprises, which can greatly improve the business efficiency of enterprises, increase brand awareness, improve customer satisfaction, and thus obtain more profits.

Mobile application human-computer interaction, which is also known as HMI (Human-Machine Interface), is an interface that can interact between users and computers, and it can conduct human-computer dialogue, so that users can interact more naturally, with easier communication and control. The importance of human-computer interaction in mobile applications lies in improving user experience. Mobile application human-computer interaction can reduce the complexity of users' operations, allowing users to operate more simply and efficiently when using the apps, thereby improving user experience. It also increases user engagement. The use of mobile application human-computer interaction can achieve user participation, which plays an important role in improving user participation and usage time. And help to increase user loyalty. The use of mobile application human-computer interaction can make users closer to the apps, enable users to master the apps faster, and make it easier for them to integrate into the apps, so that users have higher loyalty in the app. The human-computer interaction of mobile applications is helpful for the promotion of the apps. Promoters will decide whether they have confidence in the app based on their experience and reputation of the apps. This depends on mobile application human-computer interaction, and only such interaction can make users more comfortable when using the apps.

In short, mobile application human-computer interaction allows users to better control and use mobile applications, thereby improving user experience. It helps users use applications more easily, greatly reducing time spent and improving work efficiency. In addition, human-machine interaction can also improve application security and reliability. By improving the user interface, making it easier for users to use while helping to achieve better accessibility of applications, it helps to integrate mobile applications more elegantly into real-world environments. Mobile application human-computer interaction can also realize the energy efficiency optimization of equipment, so that it can more effectively achieve the target task. It helps to collect user behavior data. By analyzing user behavior data, we can gain a deeper understanding of user needs, so as to provide better personalized services.

1.3 Current Research on Human-Computer Interaction Models in Mobile Applications

In recent years, the research on the human-computer interaction mode of mobile applications has received more and more attention, and researchers from different disciplines have also actively participated in it to explore more effective human-computer interaction modes. Human-computer interaction technology on mobile devices, while providing users with a better experience, also brings a series of new technical challenges.

First of all, the screen size of mobile devices is small, the display content is large, and the user interface is more complex, which puts forward higher requirements for the design of the interaction mode. Secondly, mobile devices have a variety of input devices, such as touch screen, keyboard, mouse, etc., but these devices often have their own limitations, making the design of user interface and interaction design more challenging.

In order to cope with the above challenges, the research on the human-computer interaction mode of mobile applications mainly focuses on the following points: one is the intelligent interaction mode, which uses machine learning, natural language processing and other technologies to improve the intelligent interaction capabilities of mobile devices [4]; the other is the visual interaction mode, which uses technologies such as virtual reality and augmented reality to enhance the visual interaction capabilities of mobile devices; the third is the cognitive interaction mode, which uses technologies such as cognitive computing and intelligent perception to enhance the cognitive interaction capabilities of mobile devices [4].

At present, more and more researchers are paying attention to the research of human-computer interaction mode in mobile applications, and some progress has been made, but there are still many technical problems to be solved. For example, how to achieve efficient human-computer interaction on mobile devices? How to design a better human-computer interaction mode for different types of users? How to deeply study the integration of various technologies to improve the quality of human-computer interaction?

2 Research Content

2.1 Content and Communication Mode of Human-Computer Interaction Mode in Mobile Application

Human-computer interaction mode refers to the interaction mode between users and electronic devices in the development of touch screen mobile applications [5]. It is an interaction mode based on touch operation and visual interface, which allows users to interact with software systems more naturally and simply. The content of the human-computer interaction mode includes: designing scalable visual elements; providing navigation menus; responding to various terminal devices; designing to adapt to user operations and instructions; setting shortcut keys for complex operations; providing visual feedback for touch operations.

The communication modes of mobile application human-computer interaction mode are divided into four categories. Visual communication: graphical design enables users to understand the functions of the application more intuitively, such as icons, animations and texts, as well as clear buttons or graphical interfaces, to achieve visual communication. Language communication: man-machine dialogue makes users understand each function of the application and how to operate them. Tactile communication: it makes users feel its functions through various gestures and haptic feedback of the devices. Mixed communication: it combines visual communication, language communication, tactile communication and other communication methods to make users more intuitive understanding of user experience and other content.

2.2 Communication Methods in the Human-Computer Interaction Mode of Mobile Applications

In the current human-computer interaction mode of mobile applications, speech recognition technology is widely used. Speech recognition technology, also called speech recognition or speech processing, is a robotics technology from speech to computer recognition. It mainly completes speech recognition by converting speech into text, which usually includes voiceprint recognition, language recognition and interference intervention suppression and many other technologies [6]. It allows mobile applications to use voice to interact with users to perform various tasks such as users place orders, perform search queries, etc. For example, many devices can be controlled by voice dialogue. Users can use intelligent audio assistants to query weather, location and time information, and can also use voice to search and browse content such as news, music, etc., and to help users perform a series of operations, such as send messages etc. For optimal recognition accuracy, there are many factors to consider to ensure that users can easily access voice features, including hardware constraints (handset, mic or other device), voice quality, and more. It also requires a rigorous speech recognition process to ensure real-time, high accuracy, such as custom wake-up sentences, recognition rate inspection, automatic correction, etc. Today, many large companies, such as Baidu, Google, etc., are providing services for users to improve the accuracy of speech recognition.

Virtual button technology is an emerging human-computer interaction technology, which is mainly used in mobile applications. It uses touch technology to make the interaction between the user and the device faster and more convenient, and the user can realize the button function with a single tap or swipe in the application [7]. The main application of the virtual button technology is when the space of the mobile device is limited, the virtual button can enable the user to complete the button function in a very small space, without losing too much space without real buttons. In addition, the virtual keys usually have more functions, and can be displayed on the screen in a visual form, making the operation more convenient. In addition, virtual button technology can also

provide users in different fields with more convenient and intuitive operation procedures, greatly improving user experience. Of course, virtual buttons can also provide
other functions, such as enhancing security and performance, and improving interactive
experience and performance through a flexible hierarchical structure.

At present, the visual recognition technology in the human-computer interaction
mode of mobile applications refers to the application of visual information (such as
image or video information) to identify and identify objects in the scene, so as to achieve
information access and effective operation. These technologies primarily use machine
learning to analyze large amounts of image data in order to better recognize and manipulate objects [2]. At present, visual recognition technology is gradually being applied to
fields such as smart home, smart security, automatic driving, and virtual reality, and has
become an increasingly popular interaction mode for human-computer interaction. For
example, in the application of smart home scenarios, users can use visual recognition
technology to enable smart homes to recognize objects in the home and perform operations and services. In autonomous driving technology, visual recognition technology
is an indispensable core component. It can interpret the environmental information in
front of it and better control the direction and speed of the vehicle. Visual recognition
technology allows mobile applications to realize intelligent interaction. Through visual
recognition technology, eye movements and entire facial movements can be tracked,
eye tracking, object recognition and other functions can be realized, so that users can
communicate intelligently with devices through mobile applications.

2.3 Characteristics of Human-Computer Interaction Modes in Mobile Applications

At present, the human-computer interaction mode of mobile applications must be limited
by the size of the mobile phone screen to achieve a smoother and more efficient user
experience. For the screen size, the mobile application designer should grasp the size,
it should not be too large or too small, save the screen space as much as possible,
reduce the size of the control as much as possible, grasp the space ratio, maintain a good
interface layout, and use small icons and fonts to save screen space. At the same time, it is
necessary to adopt simple and clear controls, simplify the user operation process, reduce
the number of user operations, minimize user input with technologies such as automatic
input and voice input to reduce user input operations and improve user experience [7].

For mobile applications, touch operation has become one of the most important operation modes. Touch operation can greatly improve the convenience of human-computer
interaction. Users can operate through an easy and fast shouting symbol, thereby enhancing user experience. Some well-designed mobile applications can realize one-step operation, and the operation can be easily completed with one finger operation, which greatly
saves the user's operation time and makes the user experience more convenient; on the
other hand, some interactions such as sliding to zoom and scrolling slide technology also
brings great convenience to users. Users no longer need to click buttons or select menus.
Users only need to swipe the screen to operate, which greatly improves the operation
speed and efficiency of mobile devices.

Mobile application human-computer interaction mode has become an important
part of mobile application development, aiming to provide users with a more convenient

operating experience. After continuous technological improvement, the adaptability of mobile phone applications is getting better and better. The adaptability of mobile applications is reflected in the fact that users can adjust the size or style of the operation interface according to their own preferences, so that users can have a better experience. For example, in the Alipay APP, users can adjust different user interfaces according to their preferences for better browsing and operation. Users can also adjust the position of the buttons to make the interface layout more reasonable. In addition, the adaptability of the mobile phone application is also reflected in its optimization for different systems to ensure smoother use. For example, in the Android system, the application can intelligently switch between different screen sizes to support different models of mobile phones, and adaptive network environment to ensure that the application can be used in a low-speed network environment.

2.4 Influence of Human-Computer Interaction Mode in Mobile Application

The downward communication mode of mobile application human-computer interaction mode can help designers better understand the user behavior of mobile applications, and help them better design software interfaces that meet user habits and needs; it can help developers better understand mobile applications. It can help them design more efficient applications; it can help companies discover business opportunities related to the effective way of disseminating mobile applications, which can effectively improve the economic benefits of enterprises; it can help the government to adjust consumer behavior, in order to achieve more effective dissemination of mobile products, improve consumer satisfaction and consumption levels.

In short, the research on the communication mode of mobile application human-computer interaction mode is of great significance, and it has a positive effect on improving the economic benefits of enterprises, helping the government to adjust consumer behavior and improving consumer satisfaction.

3   Research Methods

3.1 Factors Affecting the Communication Effect of Mobile Application Human-Computer Interaction Mode

There are many factors that affect the communication effect of mobile application human-computer interaction mode, including the advantages of mobile application products; the formulation and implementation of market activities; the choice of mobile application promotion opportunities; the relationship between users and mobile application products. There are a large number of products in the mobile application market, especially social applications. Marketing activities are an important channel of communication, such as social media, search engine promotion, etc. If the formulation and execution of marketing activities are in place, the communication effect can be effectively improved. In different seasons, there are different consumption and purchase characteristics, and the promotion timing of high-quality mobile applications will affect the communication effect to a certain extent. High-quality mobile application products will have a high-quality user experience, and there will be good word-of-mouth communication among users, thereby greatly improving the communication effect.

3.2 Ways to Improve the Communication Efficiency of Mobile Application Human-Computer Interaction Mode

First, the usability and ease of use of human-computer interaction modes need to be improved. Use simple, intuitive, and easy-to-understand operating procedures to improve user experience; use the intelligence of mobile applications to provide personalized services; use interactive guidance, combined with graphics and images, to make it easier for users to understand and operate; use multiple languages to improve the penetration rate of mobile applications; combine user behavior, mine user preferences, and increase application usage; combine the characteristics of mobile applications to improve application visibility and communication efficiency.

Second, take full advantage of social media advocacy. Use social media platforms to disseminate and publicize mobile applications and take advantage of social communication effects; use social media platforms to promote mobile applications to increase the exposure of mobile applications; use the characteristics of social media platforms to formulate marketing strategies to improve the spread of mobile applications efficiency; actively participate in discussions on social media platforms, provide users with effective after-sales service and technical support, and improve user experience; track hot spots on social media platforms, adjust marketing strategies in a timely manner, and improve the communication efficiency of mobile applications.

3.3 Methods to Improve the Communication Effect of Mobile Application Human-Computer Interaction Mode

a) To improve the communication effect of the human-computer interaction mode of mobile applications, new interaction modes can be adopted, such as designing more touch controls, adding voice recognition, visual recognition and new intelligent controls, improving the human-computer interaction experience and enhancing the user's sense of immersion. Immersion means that the system connects all the morphological environments selected and used by the participants across domains and media, and finally forms a participant-centered, ubiquitous media scene that breaks the sequence of time and space, so that users can be more focused and selfless in the chain of communication activities. In this process, the participants "wholeheartedly" enter the media field, and this process is affected by three factors: space, authenticity, and participation [8]. At this stage, the human-computer interaction of mobile applications based on emotional communication has comprehensively improved the user's sense of immersion, participation, and experience with full-scenario, multi-channel, and strong arousal, and it also puts forward higher requirements for the design of future mobile application products.

b) Improve the application interface: adopt a more concise and intuitive interface, and add more animations to provide users with a better operating experience. Adopt smooth animation to ensure the appearance of mobile products is generous and simple; eliminate redundant operations, simplify the operation process, and improve the operation experience; provide intelligent prompts to provide users with a convenient operation experience. Design a clear menu to facilitate users to perform visual hierarchical inspection; improve gesture operations according to some interaction modes, so that users can get rid of intermediate steps and complete the operation process faster. The visual design of mobile applications should be simple and refined. The selection of icons and the processing of pictures should have friendly value-added services, such as color pattern, interface size and logo, etc. In addition, Colors should also be coordinated, otherwise it will degrade the overall user experience. The color selection should be related to the function of the application in a graphical form to convey information.

c) Improve user experience: provide timely feedback on user operations, provide more personalized services, and allow users to have more functions to choose from. Reasonably organize the operation process to reduce user operation steps as much as possible; ensure the quality of network connection, improve the form of expression, and improve the response speed; adopt multi-screen adaptation technology to ensure that the new functions are naturally coordinated with the original functions, allowing users to operate more easily and freely; optimize module and component design, enrich user experience, and continuously improve product quality.

d) Improve application usability: provide users with more functions, improve the usability of applications, and make it easier for users to master usage methods. Use multi-terminal cross-platform hybrid development technology to realize the interaction between the client and the server, making the user experience smoother.

e) Increase application promotion efforts: through social media, advertising, film and television and other channels, increase application promotion efforts to improve communication effects.

3.4 Communication Strategy of Mobile Application Human-Computer Interaction Mode

The strategy of the human-computer interaction mode of the mobile application must be precise and accurate, answer the user's questions in a timely and accurate manner, and reduce the user's waiting time. The strategy of mobile application human-computer interaction mode must have strong usability, including operation friendliness, cross-device/network adaptability, etc. The strategy of mobile application human-computer interaction mode should be able to improve and optimize the interaction between users and applications, and strengthen the interaction between users and applications. The strategy for the human-computer interaction mode of mobile applications should try to protect the security and privacy of users' personal data, and use users' personal information in a reasonable and legal manner. The strategy for the human-computer interaction mode of mobile applications should be highly customizable, and can be personalized according to different user needs to provide better services.

3.5 Optimization of Communication Strategy of Mobile Application Human-Computer Interaction Mode

The optimization of the optimization strategy for the dissemination of mobile application human-computer interaction mode should focus on improving user experience. Optimize user experience, research through systematic analysis of user behavior habits, improve user experience of mobile applications, improve application fluency, set up more intelligent voice and image interaction design, strengthen user cognition, etc. By optimizing the design, it is easier and more enjoyable for users to use mobile applications, and the user experience is improved, so that it is easier for users to accept and spread the application. At the same time, the content of the application will be strengthened, so that users will have more surprises when using the application, making it more interesting and meaningful to use, thereby stimulating users' desire to spread the application [1]. Provide interactive functions as much as possible: By providing interactive functions, enrich the social elements of the application, so that it is easier for users to discover new content and interactive functions when using the application, and it is easier to trigger spreading behaviors. And by optimizing the application promotion channels, the application can be spread to more users more effectively, so that the application can be known by more users in a shorter period of time, and it is easier to trigger the spread behavior.

3.6 Optimization of User Interaction Experience in Mobile Application Human-Computer Interaction Mode

The human-computer interaction mode of the mobile application should ensure that the interface design of the application is simple and easy to use, which is convenient for the user to operate better, so that the user can obtain a better experience. In the application design, add interactive functions as much as possible, such as voice interaction, touch interaction, etc., so that users can better control the application. Strengthen the intelligence of applications, such as intelligent search, to make it easier for users to find the information they need, or to implement the function of dynamic recommendation, so that users can obtain information more usefully. Strengthen the security of mobile applications, prevent user privacy leakage and information loss, and ensure user safety. Methods are as below:

a) Optimize the interaction design of mobile applications: adopt a more concise user interface design and use an interaction mode that is closer to the user, such as using simpler interaction methods such as sliding and clicking, which are easier to operate.
b) Optimize the user experience of mobile applications: Make the user experience of mobile applications as close to users as possible, such as adopting more friendly prompts, richer animation effects, and more complete search functions, etc., all help to reduce user operations Difficulty, improve user experience.
c) Optimize the functions of mobile applications: realize mobile application functions more comprehensively, such as adding more functional modules, more complete security policies, more flexible user processes, etc., to provide users with richer functions and more convenient user operations.

d) Optimize user services of mobile applications: provide more comprehensive user services, such as providing more convenient customer service, continuously optimize and improve applications, and better meet user needs.

In short, a simple and clear menu structure, friendly prompt information, simple operation, easy-to-operate interface, and rich animation effects can make the human-computer interaction experience of mobile application interface design better. The interface design of mobile applications should be as simple as possible, highlighting the main functions, minimizing menu clutter, so that users can quickly find the functions they want. Provide timely and friendly operation prompts to users, such as prompts for input errors, prompts for login failures, prompts for success, etc., to help users better understand and master operations, and improve user experience. Minimize cumbersome operations as much as possible, so that users can complete operations quickly and effectively. For example, providing functions such as one-click login and one-click registration can effectively improve user experience. The interface design of mobile applications should be as simple as possible, and complex dialog boxes should not be present, otherwise it will confuse users and affect operation efficiency. Use as few controls as possible and present functionality in a concise manner to improve user experience. Rich animation effects: Appropriate animation effects can make the mobile application interface more beautiful, more interesting, and improve user experience.

3.7 New Technologies Improve the Experience of Communication in Mobile Applications in the Human-Computer Interaction Mode

a) Using multi-touch technology: multi-touch technology allows users to use multiple fingers to touch the phone interface. In this way, complex operations can be completed more easily and the operating experience can be improved.
b) Augmented reality technology: Augmented reality technology can be used to display virtual elements in 3D form, and users can operate the 3D graphics of augmented reality with their fingers just like manipulating real objects to realize the interactive mode of touch. Through virtual reality technology, users can experience the thrilling 3D virtual environment, allowing users to have a better and more profound experience. Research multimedia technology, carry out more efficient codec processing for multimedia content on mobile devices, integrate virtual reality technology, build a more realistic environment simulation, better improve mobile application performance, and enhance user experience and immersion.
c) Using voice technology: develop a voice recognition system, and users can use oral instruction technology to issue instructions, which can complete tasks more quickly and realize intelligent human-computer interaction. Through intelligent voice interaction technology, users can greatly simplify the operation process of using mobile phones, reduce the burden on users, and increase users' sense of immersion when using mobile phones.
d) Using visual technology: It can provide a virtual camera similar to a camera, and show the image captured by the mobile phone to the user. In this way, the user can use his own vision to obtain information in the virtual reality, and more directly understand the relevant information of the mobile phone application. For example,

mobile users can use their own photos as avatars when using apps provided by some partners, thereby improving the interaction with the app and enhancing the user's sense of immersion.

e) Using somatosensory technology: The accelerometer can make mobile users more interesting and meaningful when using their mobile phones, and make the user experience more immersive. Through somatosensory technology, users can directly control mobile devices, enhance their interaction with devices, and enhance immersion.

3.8 New Technology Emerges to Realize New Interaction Mode

Develop new interactive designs, such as faster touch mode and mouse sliding, which can allow users to complete operations faster; use machine learning to provide users with personalized content: use machine learning and deep learning technology, according to user behavior habits and preferences, recommend targeted content; use existing technologies to implement new mobile applications: provide users with a good sense of experience through language recognition, AR, VR and other technologies; use intelligent robots to enhance user experience, based on voice, vision, etc. Technology allows intelligent robots to interact with users, enhance empathy, and realize new interaction modes.

1. Augmented Reality (AR) and Virtual Reality (VR): AR and VR can provide users with interactive and real-time natural user experience, allowing users to enter a more coherent virtual world [9]. They help mobile users take advantage of the virtual environment for understanding and learning, as well as for simulation and imitation practice.
2. Intelligent Recommendation Systems: Intelligent recommendation systems can accurately recommend relevant content based on users' historical browsing records, as well as based on their portraits, behavior analysis and neural networks [10]. It can provide users with more personalized services and faster search results, thereby greatly improving the user experience.
3. Motion Interfaces: Motion interfaces can be operated by shaking and gestures, allowing users to control the device more freely, further reducing the operating threshold and improving user experience.
4. Natural Language Processing (NLP): Natural language processing allows users to search and query through natural language dialogue [11], making user interaction with OnLine more natural and realizing true virtual reality.
5. Speech Recognition/Automation: Speech recognition and automation technologies allow users to use text, pictures, videos, and voice on mobile devices to complete tasks more quickly and efficiently, improving mobile user experience.

4 Conclusion

Based on the analysis of the existing human-computer interaction mode, combined with the user experience requirements of mobile applications, the human-computer interaction mode required for the communication mode of the mobile application is determined, and the improvement measures of the communication mode are proposed to improve the communication efficiency. The down-communication method of the mobile application human-computer interaction mode can effectively improve the user experience, and can also improve the flexibility and usability of application functions. It is a faster and more effective way to disseminate information and provide services to meet the needs of users. The communication mode of mobile application human-computer interaction mode can improve the communication effect according to the methodology provided in this paper, improve and optimize the interaction between users and applications, and strengthen the interaction between users and applications, but it needs to be optimized according to the actual situation. Different ways of dissemination of human-computer interaction in mobile applications eventually produce different products and services that consumers want on mobile applications.

Acknowledgement. This article is for the 2022 Guangdong Province General Universities Youth Innovative Talent Project (Philosophy and Social Sciences) – Guangdong-Hong Kong-Macao Greater Bay Area Cultural and Creative Cross-media Design Research (No.: 2022WQNCX034), Guangzhou Academy of Fine Arts 2021 Guangzhou Academy of Fine Arts "Academic Improvement Plan" scientific research project – Guangdong-Hong Kong-Macao Greater Bay Area intangible cultural heritage creative cross-media design and communication research (No. 21XSC52) phased results.

References

1. Liang, S.: From "stimulus-feedback" to "emotional communication" – the evolution and development of mobile application human-computer interaction models. Young Journalist J. https://doi.org/10.15997/j.cnki.qnjz(2021)
2. Adam, M.T.P., et al.: Design science research modes in human-computer interaction projects. AIS Trans. Hum.-Comp. Int. **13**(1), 1–11 (2021)
3. Oviatt, S., et al.: Designing the user interface for multimodal speech and pen-based gesture applications: state-of-the-art systems and future research directions. Hum. Comp. Int. 15(4), 263–322 (2000)
4. Huang, K.-Y.: Challenges in human-computer interaction design for mobile devices. In: Proceedings of the World Congress on Engineering and Computer Science, vol. 1, no. 6 (2009)
5. Dix, A., Finlay, J., Abowd, G., Beale, R.: Human-Computer Interaction, 3rd edn. Prentice Hall, New York (2003)
6. Lv, Z., et al.: Deep learning for intelligent human–computer interaction. Appl. Sci. **12**(22), 11457 (2022)
7. Koskinen, E., Topi, K., Pauli, L.: Feel-good touch: finding the most pleasant tactile feedback for a mobile touch screen button. In: Proceedings of the 10th International Conference on Multimodal Interfaces (2008)
8. Schubert, T., Friedmann, F., Regenbrecht, H.: The experience of presence: factor analytic insights. Presence Teleop. Virt. **10**(10), 266–281 (2001)
9. Love, S.: Understanding mobile human-computer interaction. Elsevier (2005)
10. Volokha, V., Derevitskii, I., Bochenina, K.: Intelligent Recommender System with Online Generation of Model-Based Initial Interviews for Poi Recommendations. Int. J. Artif. Intell. **21**(1), 132–153 (2023)
11. Liddy, E.D.: Natural language processing (2001)

LoomoRescue: An Affordable Rescue Robot for Evacuation Situations

Denys J. C. Matthies[1(✉)], Sven Ole Schmidt[1], Yuqi He[1,2], Zhouyao Yu[1,2], and Horst Hellbrück[1]

[1] Technical University of Applied Sciences, Lübeck, Germany
denys.matthies@th-luebeck.de
[2] East China University of Science and Technology, Shanghai, China

Abstract. Rescue robots can play an important role in disaster situations, such as locating people for evacuations. This paper demonstrates how to transform an affordable consumer robot, such as the Loomo Segway, into an intelligent rescue robot. Our proof-of-concept shows how LoomoRescue can autonomously browse offices to locate people and how to detect their vital signs through posture and heart rate detection in real-time. Our indoor localization is a SLAM approach based on an external UWB position system plus a movement correction with an ultrasound sensor in combination with an IMU. The accuracy of linear movement showed minor deviation with an average error of 1.65%, while the angular movement showed an error of 2.43%. We classify three types of critical postures with an average detection rate of 78.33% within a distance of 1–20 m. Our optical heart rate detection is 87.3% accurate to the ground truth. We envision that such an affordable robot can be used for evacuation purposes as it may be part of the standard inventory in the future.

Keywords: Rescue Robot · Computer Vision · Optical Vital Sign Detection · Posture Recognition · SLAM · Autonomous Navigation

1 Introduction

Throughout the past decade, the use of rescue robots in disaster scenarios has been increasing [1]. These robots especially provide a benefit in scenarios that pose a threat to humans. Rescue robots play an important role in searching and locating trapped survivors. Different form factors have been developed for these purposes, such as robot dogs, drones, and other wheeled robots [2]. These devices can be crucial in searching for victims or merely supporting us with understanding conditions in inaccessible areas.

The current state-of-the-art in rescue and assistive robots demonstrate that significant research exists concerning assistance robots. However, particularly rescue robots are usually expensive and demand high robustness, speed, versatility, and ease of use for the piloting human in accordance to an extensive review by Delmerico et al. [1]. Ways to enable an affordable and consumer-available robot that already matches many of these requirements becoming a rescue robot

© The Author(s), under exclusive license to Springer Nature Switzerland AG 2023
G. Salvendy and J. Wei (Eds.): HCII 2023, LNCS 14052, pp. 53–73, 2023.
https://doi.org/10.1007/978-3-031-35921-7_5

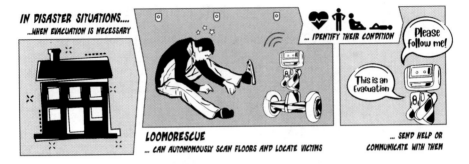

Fig. 1. LoomoRescue can be useful for disaster situations, such as when evacuation is necessary. The robot is fully autonomous and can systematically navigate through a floor, looking for possible victims. Further, LoomoRescue is able to understand whether the person may be in a critical condition by detecting vital signs through posture and heart rate. Finally, LoomoRescue can communicate with the victim or send a notification to a rescue team.

that acts autonomously to identify victims' health status in real time remains an unanswered question. We envision low-cost rescue robots to be a part of public facilities to enable support in disaster situations, such as building evacuations (Fig. 1).

To demonstrate this, we developed a rescue robot based on an affordable consumer robot, the Loomo Segway[1]. We posed two research questions. Firstly, how can we enable an autonomous navigation? Secondly, we sought to investigate whether it was possible for Loomo to understand a human's critical activity?

We developed a proof-of-concept that transforms an affordable consumer robot into a rescue robot by enabling:

- Simultaneous Localization and Mapping (SLAM) [3] and path planning using a multi-sensor fusion approach incorporating an IMU, Ultrasonic sensors, and an additionally equipped Ultra Wide Band (UWB) based multi anchor localization system [4],
- Optical vital sign detection using a posture recognition approach by using Google's ML kit [5], as well as a heart rate detection by using an Eulerian Video Magnification (EVM) approach [6] to magnify subtle changes in skin colour.

Our main contribution is to integrate these different techniques into an affordable consumer robot that demonstrates that it can be converted into a rescue robot. According to Wobbrock this concerns an artifact contribution [7].

2   Related Work

There is a great body of related work, as this project intersects multiple areas. We selected some exemplary projects from the field of search-and-rescue robotics and human activity recognition that somewhat represent the state-of-the-art.

---

[1] https://www.segway.com/loomo/.

2.1 Search-and-Rescue Robots

Over the past few decades, several kinds of rescue robots have been developed. Though, research on rescue robots mainly focuses on localization and control systems. In 2019, Delmerico et al. [1] conducted an extensive review on the current state and future outlook of rescue robotics. Delmerico et al. categorized rescue robots into Ground Robots (e.g., Legged robots [8], Tracked and wheeled robots [9]), Aerial Robots (e.g., Drones [10,11], Swarms [12]), and Marine and Amphibious Robots (e.g., Snake-like Design [13]). In the following, we will discuss some related work in more detail.

Kiyani et al. [14] developed a prototype of a search-and-rescue robot that has the ability to locate itself in a known environment and to locate victims and transport them to safe zones. This is at least a proof-of-concept of an Arduino-driven mini-robot in a lab environment, but which is far away from reality.

A system that has been tested in an actual fire container house was proposed by Young-Duk in 2009 [15]. Here, a fire rescue robot is remotely controlled using Bluetooth and RF communication. Firefighters may deploy the robot in a hazardous fire scene through a remote control guiding the robot for a possible evacuation. The controlling firefighter receives information from the robot in the form of image feedback and sensor data. Additionally, the firefighter can communicate with the victims through the robot's speaker, and thus, guide them out of the scene. The robot relies on explicit control and is not autonomous.

Another search-and-rescue robot system for underground coal mine rescue is proposed by Zhao et al. [16]. Here, the robot is remotely controlled using Wifi and a fiber-optic cable and used to explore a coal mine shaft and to collect environmental information. The operating control unit incorporates an electronic compass, a gyroscope, two wheel encoders, and four infrared sensors. The infrared sensors are used to measure the distance of the robot to the wall to prevent unwanted crashes. The other sensors are used to deduce the motion trajectory and form part of the positioning function. Further, the authors use the image information from a camera to correct the position of the robot manually. Still, the robot is mainly piloted by a human and not fully autonomous.

Another remotely guided control system for rescue robots is developed by Mano et al. [17]. Depending on the tasks and working environment, it can switch efficiently between remote control mode and auto-detect mode to take full advantage of the robot's functions using a SLAM-based map building. Functioning-wise this project comes closest to ours.

There are also researchers using the same type of robot used in this research, the Segway Loomo. For instance, Gollasch et al. [18] extended the Segways software API, and Steiner et al. [19] developed a ROS framework to improve Loomo's navigation for greater stability and speed.

To summarize this subsection, we would like to look at two comprehensive overviews by Murphy et al. [20] and Delmerico et al. [1]. Both point to the need for rescue robots, demanding that they be robust, fast, versatile and, above all, highly user-friendly in use. Many rescue robots are prototypes, not consumer-ready and of high expense. Furthermore, these robots are to be piloted by a trained user. In our research, we aim to demonstrate how to convert a highly developed consumer-ready robot, which is affordable and stable into a rescue robot that can even work autonomously, not requiring trained pilots.

2.2   Human Activity Recognition

The research field of human activity recognition is broad and incorporates a vast variety of approaches to detect the human's activity [21], such as through wearables [22], and other distance sensing techniques and technologies, such as camera-based sensing [23]. As Loomo has a camera, which we utilize for sensing posture and heart rate, we focus on these two aspects in the following subsections.

Posture Recognition. Human posture detection is one of the important application in human activity recognition. Often, machine learning approaches are utilized to recognize the posture of the entire body via camera/image sensing. Accurate recognition has shown to be a fundamental problem in computer vision in recent years [24]. There is extensive literature on this topic, as evidenced by the works of Bissacco et al. [25] and Dimitrijevic et al. [26].

Human posture detection and comprehensive analysis are required in different applications, such as motion analysis, monitoring, human-robot interaction, and medical rehabilitation. Anitha and Priya [27] build an automatic monitoring system for the elderly by sending an alert when an unusual posture is detected. Hernández [28] used posture detection in monitoring the exercises and providing useful information for Robotic-Assisted rehabilitation therapies.

Cao et al. [29] present the first real-time multi-person system, named Open-Pose, that collectively identifies key points of the human body, arms, face, and feet (a total of 135 key points) in an individual's image. The main functionalities of 2D and 3D real-time multi-person keypoint detection, single-person tracking, and calibration toolbox are used. Bazarevsky et al. [30] developed a lightweight neural network to estimate human pose detection, which can also be used for real-time mobile devices. Their development has been integrated into Google ML Kit [5] and can be utilized by any mobile device via ML Kit's API. The API's high reliability rendered it an optimal choice for our research.

Heart Rate Recognition. Heart rate recognition is vital to understand the user's condition and thus is an objective in human activity recognition. Optical recognition of heart beats is possible as blood circulation creates a periodic change in the human body, although it is not perceivable to the eye. In 2011, Poh [31] used this weak signal captured by an ordinary RGB-camera to design a "magic mirror", which can reveal the user's heart rate. The theory of Poh's magical mirror is to use the change of light when blood flows in the human body [32]. The greater the amount of blood passing through the blood vessels, the more light is absorbed by the blood, and the less light is reflected from the surface of the human skin. Therefore, the heart rate can be estimated by time-frequency analysis of the images. This is the main idea also denoted as Photoplethysmography (PPG).

However, this change of color in the skin is subtle and hard to capture by most cameras. In this case, can have to "magnify" these unobservable changes in the image to a magnitude sufficient to be observed by the naked eye. In 2012, Wu et al. [6] started from this perspective and proposed an algorithm called Eulerian Video Magnification (EVM) to reveal temporal variations in difficult or impossible videos to see with the naked eye.

Several works are developed based on this algorithm to detect heart rate successfully. Bosi et al. [33] used this algorithm to estimate heart rate using Microsoft device Kinect^{TM} version 2.0. Similar to Gambi et al.' work [34], which also develop a heart rate detection on Kinect 2.0 camera, but further validated this method and compared it to classical wearable systems. Chambino et al. [35] developed an Android-based application for real-time monitoring of vital signs. We adopted this implementation for our research.

3   LoomoRescue

3.1   Concept

Robots that assist humans is an age-old vision and still an ongoing trend in human-robot interaction research. In this work, we would like to research whether current state-of-the-art consumer technology, the Segway Robot Loomo, can be utilized as a rescue robot. Therefore, our research is guided by two overarching research questions:

RQ1: How can we enable Loomo to autonomously navigate through an environment?

RQ2: How can we enable Loomo to understand human's critical activity?

3.2   Requirements

To answer our research questions, we set out certain requirements that Loomo should be able to provide.

Requirement 1: To answer the first question on autonomous navigation, we need to teach the rescue robot to understand its location in an environment. To fulfil this requirement, the robot provides a number of embedded sensors that can be utilized, such as the ultrasonic sensor, hall sensor, and inertia measure unit. Combining these sensor will, in theory, enable the robot to navigate without crashing and possible to organized a structure, such as a floor plan, once the robot explores an indoor-environment. The feasibility of that has already impressively demonstrated by Chen et al. [36]. In a hazardous scenario, there may not be time for time-expensive exploration and thus, a floor plan might already be provided to the rescue robot. In this case, the robot is required to exactly locate itself in that floor plan.

Requirement 2: To answer the second research question, we need to enable Loomo to find a person and understand the physical condition of a person. There are several ways to incorporate such functions, such as by listening (microphone), or looking (camera) through an environment. To judge on whether a person's status is critical, the robot requires to have an understanding of typical human activity and anomalies. Loomo may be required to understand whether a person lies on the floor and whether the emitted vital signs, such as heart rate, respiration, and micro-vibrations, are abnormal. This is required to work instantaneously in real-time.

3.3   Design Decisions

To match the requirements, we need to make certain design decisions.

Decision 1: LoomoRescue needs to be effective and thus we decide to provide the robot with a floor plan. The problem of any robot is that it cannot locate itself in this environment without a positioning system. This results in robots not being fully autonomous. To overcome this, we equip Loomo with an external UWB position system, which consists of a tag carried by Loomo and tags distributed all over the floor.

Decision 2: The posture of the human body is an obvious sign to understand physical wellness. Therefore, we found it important to dynamically detect and analyze the posture of the human body. This should be performed visually by Loomo's camera. Loomo should be able to classify dangerous postures, such a person lying on the floor. Therefore, an advanced posture detection will be implemented in this work. Further we decided to enable Loomo to detect heart rate, which is an important vital sign.

3.4   Implementation

Loomo Device. Loomo, firstly released in November 2016 and also known as the Segway Robot, is a combination of a self-balanced vehicle (SBV) and a companion robot. Loomo is 640 mm in height, weights 17.5 kg and has a battery capacity of 310 Wh. In programming mode, the robot and can go up to 8 km/h, otherwise it can go faster. Loomo uses an Intel quad core CPU with 2.4 Ghz, and 4 GM RAM. The OS is based on Android that is programmable, movable, and expandable by Segway Robotics – a Mobile Robot Platform Kit [37]. The developer version enables to create a fully functional, stable, reliable, convenient, and easy-to-use robot development platform.

The provided Software Development Kit (SDK) enables developers to control the base functions at an abstract level, which include: the control, initialization, and configuration of the Intel RealSense camera; Speech recognition including pre-defined commands, base locomotion commands, the access to sensors, a connectivity package to enable linking a mobile device, and an emoji library that contains pre-defined "human-like" sounds and eyes that will be drawn on Loomo's display. On top of that there is the possibility for a hardware extension that allows mechanical and electrical engineers to design and attach additional components to the robot. Since Loomo is ran by an Android System, we can also access a number of raw sensor data, such as the IMU, which is important in this project.

Loomo's Sensors. Loomo provides a number of sensor, which are essential for its functioning and for further development. These include: a RealSense RGB-Depth camera (30 FPS), a HD camera (1080p, 104° wide-angle), a microphone array composed of five mics, a touch sensors on the head, ultrasound sensor, hall sensors embedded in the wheels, two IMUs in the robot body and head. For our implementation, we particularly processed the raw data of the Ultrasound sensor and the IMU.

Ultrasound Sensor: An ultrasonic sensor converts sonic signals into electrical signals. Ultrasound is a sound wave with a frequency of more than 20 kHz, which travels at 343 m per second in air at 20 °C. It is usually designed to measure the distance between an object and the transreceiver that emits ultrasonic waves at 40 kHz [38]. The principle is to measure the latency between the emitted and received echo signal. This is also denoted as time of flight (ToF), which enables us to calculated the exact distance [39].

Inertial Measurement Unit (IMU): The IMU is a compound sensor, which usually consists of three linear accelerometers which measure acceleration, three gyroscopes which measure angular velocity rate [40]. Such type of IMU is also denoted as a 6-axis/DoF IMU. To encounter sensor drifts, a 9-axis/DoF includes a three-axis geomagnetic sensor, which can be used to correct the angular velocity sensor by the absolute pointing of the geomagnetic field to give accurate readings [41].

Reference Localization System and Communication via the MQTT Protocol. To ensure reliable self-localization of Loomo, we resort to a multi-anchor localization system based on Ultra Wide-Band signals (UWB), which

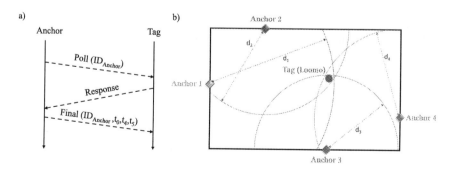

Fig. 2. Position estimation of the reference localization system applying two-way ranging and multilateration.

can be easily integrated in an office building. Such multi-anchor system is based on the *two-way ranging* methodology (TWR) for distance estimation between a given *tag* connected to the Loomo and each anchor node installed static in the room geometry.

By using TWR, the anchors do not need to be synchronized in time, which decreases the amount of hardware interconnection between them. For each anchor separately, the transmission delay τ_{tag} between tag and anchor is estimated as shown in Fig. 2a). For establishing TWR between one anchor and the tag, this anchor sends a *Poll*-message to the tag at time t_0 to initialize the TWR. The message includes an ID indicating the anchor unambiguously. The message is received at the tag at time t_1. After a certain processing time, the tag sends at time t_2 a *Response*-message to the anchor, which is received at time t_3. After processing this message, the *Final*-message is sent at time t_4 including the stored time stamps t_0, t_3 and t_4 in the message's payload. The tag received this message at t_5. The transmission delay, which is calculated at the tag's microcontroller results to:

$$\tau_{tag} = \frac{(t_3 - t_0) - (t_2 - t_1) + (t_5 - t_2) - (t_4 - t_3)}{4} = \frac{2t_3 - t_0 - 2t_2 + t_1 + t_5 - t_4}{4} \tag{1}$$

Due to the constant transmission velocity, namely the speed of light with $c_0 \approx 3 \cdot 10^8$ m/s, the distance results as multiplication of delay τ_{tag} and c_0. Since only the distance to the tag is known, but not the direction, an distance radius for each anchor node returns.

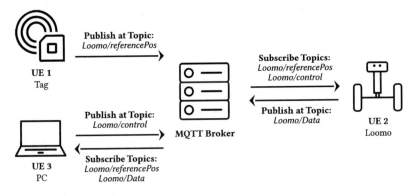

Fig. 3. User Equipments (UE) communicating via MQTT protocol.

As shown in Fig. 2b), a position where the object is most likely to be located is obtained by *multilateration*, the iterative overlay of the different distance radii in the tag's microcontroller. Since the exact position of the anchor nodes is known by the tag, the overall position of the tag is calculable. Overall, the system results in an estimation accuracy of ±20 cm in the currently installed state, which is why we use it without hesitation as a reference value for Loomo similarly as shown by Leugner et al. [42]. Built-in sensors from Loomo can further be used to increase accuracy.

To connect the Loomo with the tag's position estimation, we establish a connection including the *Message Queuing Telemetry Transport* protocol (MQTT). The MQTT is from the field of IoT-applications and enables the wireless data exchange of two or more User Equipments (UE) without initializing the communication between the UEs itself.

The general structure of the MQTT is shown in Fig. 3. It consists of a MQTT Broker in the center, which serves as a data hub. If a UE *publishes* data to the broker, the data itself is stored at the broker with a corresponding topic, consisting of a head topic and subtopics, which are ordered hierarchically. So, the data is indicated unambiguously. If new data with a topic is published by the same or another UE, the older data is deleted. So, no long term data storage including storage management is needed. Every UE connected to the MQTT broker is able to *subscribe* to specific head topics or subtopics. Then it receives all data stored at the MQTT with the specific topic close directly after storage. With MQTT connection of the tag, the Loomo and a remote PC, we are able to integrate the UWB multi-anchor system as reference to the Loomo.

Feature Extension 1: Localization and Movement. The localisation system is key to guide the robot traverse the map, where the participation of sensors plays an important role. For the localization, there is an ultrasound sensor, IMU, and UWB, which was explained above. Given the 9-axis IMU may only have accurate and stable angle data we need to find a way to fuse it with the ultrasonic sensor and the UWB positioning system, creating a correction method for Loomo's positioning. Previous works have showed how to impressively correct GPS by adding an IMU [43] in real-time. Other works demonstrated positioning correction with acoustic sensing using the Doppler-Shift [44] and utilizing acoustic sensing under device motion from a robot [45]. Another technology to accomplish indoor navigation and localization is using radar, as nicely showcased by Yue et al. [46].

3.4.4.1 Internal Localization and Move Control: The original control command in the Loomo SDK API provides ultrasound data, which are as accurate as even reflecting wheel movement for instance. This inference of movement, however, creates a large error when processing it in this form. Therefore, we also utilize the IMU in combined to improve the PID algorithm for the movement control (see Fig. 5). Both, the ultrasound sensor and the IMU have a quick update rate of 50 milliseconds. This is a high response rate and thus suitably to meet the demand of real-time movement control.

3.4.4.2 External Localization: It would be sufficient to control robot's movement though the method explained above. However, there is a problem: the calculation of current position heavily depends on the former position. Since sensors present drifts and inaccuracies, the errors will accumulate with time and show too great deviation after a while. Thus an external positioning system is introduced to improve the positioning accuracy and to correct the error. The UWB

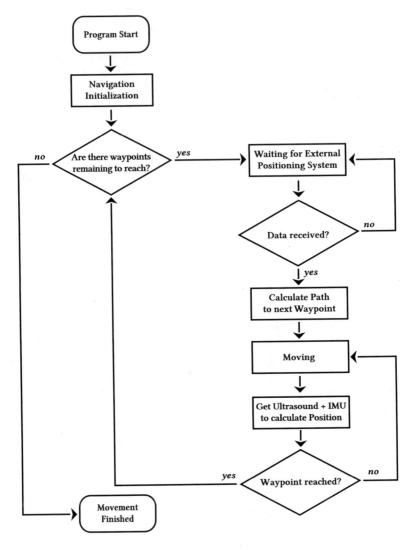

Fig. 4. Flow diagram depicting the decisions while moving through a floor.

positioning system, as mentioned above, can be used as an additional source of information that provides coordinates, while it supports full map navigation functionality. In this setup we have two independent localization systems working respectively. The external UWB system will guide the robot traverse the floor through waypoints. However, entering a room, for instance, requires higher accuracy than ±20 cm and therefore, we fall back on internal sensors to avoid LoomoRescue bumping against the door frame. Figure 4 shows a flow chart on how our navigation is designed.

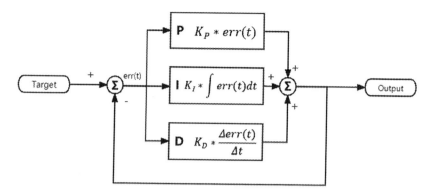

Fig. 5. PID Block Diagram: The PID algorithm is to utilize the feedback of position data to fix the input of Loomo's motors. There are three elements for the feedback calculation. The P element can simply multiply the error with a coefficient, which gains a quick response value. The I element mean the integral errors in a time period, so it enables fine-tuning of the robot over short distance. The element of D estimates the trends of movement and thus can perform an adjustment of the speed.

Feature Extension 2: Human Activity Recognition. To fulfil our requirements set out, we are required to develop an addition function for Loomo, so it can understand the human activity. As discussed earlier, to identify a critical vital state, we decided to include a detection of posture as well as a heart rate detection. With these features, Loomo Robot would be enabled to estimate the condition of the person.

Since Loomo is unable to touch the person, we decided to use a vision-based approach. To not re-invent the wheel, we will rely on established machine learning libraries: OpenCV [47] and the ML Kit by Google's to enable on-device machine learning [5]. Both libraries offer android packages, which can be integrated with Loomo. To get OpenCV properly running, we required to included an additional Java Native Interface (JNI) that would execute C++ code.

Fig. 6. Showing three classified of the implemented posture detection. The skeleton is colored in accordance to the criticalness, when the video feed is displayed at the Loomo device. (Color figure online)

3.4.5.1 Posture Detection: Google's ML kit's pose detector provides us with up to 33 landmarks that are generation from an image at which a human is identified. The implementation works in real-time once provided the video feed from the HD camera. To classify postures, which is the main objective of our pose detector, the relative placements of these landmarks are calculated in a plane rule-based manner similarly as demonstrated in the PhD Thesis of Rithik Kapoor [48]. This way, we categorized three critical stages of postures, as illustrated in Fig. 6:

- **Normal**: Representing a category of posture that is usually not considered as dangerous, such as standing straight on the ground.
- **Warning:** Representing a category of posture which might mean this person needs additional help in an emergency scenario. As "warning" we classified someone that remains sitting in an emergency scenario such as an event of a fire.
- **Danger:** Representing a category of posture that is usually considered as dangerous. We classified any postures as "danger" at which a person is somewhat lying on the ground, including any postures the person shows an awkward horizontal posture.

3.4.5.2 Heart Rate Detection: Our heart rate detection contains three major steps: A) Face detection, B) Eulerian Video Magnification (EVM) magnification, and C) Photo-Plethysmography (PPG) signal processing.

Fig. 7. Heart rate detection on Loomo when toggled on the video feed.

In step A, we use the OpenCV library to detect the face as the Region of Interest (ROI) from each video frame. We initialize a cascade classifier to identify faces based on a pre-trained model (*lbpcascade_ frontalface.xml*) that can be obtained through the official OpenCV website. The application basically extracts a rectangle area that contains the ROI.

In step B, we look at these sub-frames, which will be processed by the EVM algorithm. The EVM performs a spatial filter to decompose the frames by blurring, differentiating, and down sampling the image with a Gaussian pyramid. After obtaining the different spatial bands, a temporal filter is implemented on each spatial band to select bands of interest by frequencies. In our case, we want to amplify the heart rate signal and select $f_L = 0.4$ to f_H 4 Hz (24 to 240 bpm) for bandpass filtering, which is approximately the range of human heart rate. This seems to be the appropriate cutoff frequencies as shown in related work [6]. Finally, we amplify the change in color and add the magnified result to the origin frame.

In step C, the raw Photo-plethysmography (PPG) signal that was obtained by the color-magnified result, will be sent to further processing, which includes signal smoothing and a peak detection.

We utilize the average green channel from the magnified video frame sequence, which is smoothed by a moving average filter aiming to reduce random noise while retaining its peaks as follows

$$y\,[i] = \frac{1}{n} \sum_{n-1}^{j=0} x\,[i+j] \tag{2}$$

where $\boldsymbol{y}$ is the output signal, x is the input signal, n is the length of queue. The moving average filter views the successive sampled data as a queue of fixed length n. After inserting a new data, the first data of the above queue is removed, the remaining $n\text{-}1$ data are moved forward in turn, and the newly sampled data are inserted as the tail of the new queue. Then the arithmetic operations are performed on this queue and obtain the ith output result. The Loomo robot has a self-balance movement, which is a periodical forward and backward movement. This makes the relative position of the light source to change constantly in a certain interval, which needs to be considered and removed from the data. Finally, the estimated heart rate is calculated by finding the peaks of the smoothed PPG signal. Assume the number of series of frames is L, the frame rate is calculated in *FPS*, and there are N peaks detected in this series of frames. The heart rate in beats per minute (*BPM*) is computed as follows:

$$BPM = 60\frac{N \times FPS}{L} \tag{3}$$

The result of implemented heart rate detection is displayed in Fig. 7.

4   Evaluation

To quantify the effectiveness of our implementation, we ran an evaluation on our added features: Localization and Human Activity Recognition (posture & heart rate detection).

4.1   Feature Extension 1: Localisation

In terms of localisation, we have two parts in total. The UWB positioning system is used for global positioning and navigation on the map, while each movement in the local area is controlled using the robot's built-in ultrasonic sensor in combination with the IMU using the PID algorithm. The UWB system has already been experimentally determined to have a mean error of ± 20 cm in an indoor environment following studies by Leugner et al. [42] and Schmidt et al. [49]. Therefore, the performance of the robot's internal navigation will be evaluated here.

Test of Linear Movement. In the test of linear movement, we have two conditions. First we let the robot travel 1 m along a straight line and afterwards 2 m. For both conditions, we measured the distance from its starting point and calculated the error. The purpose is to test the accuracy of a single move and the effect of different distances on the accuracy.

As shown in Table 1, through eight trials, when the robot advances 1 m, with the help of our sensor approach, its endpoint difference averages at 2.01 cm. At the second condition, the average difference was at 2.58 cm when advancing 2 m. A paired t-Test $T(7) = -0.64$, $p = 0.27$, showed the deviations occurring at 1 m ($M = 2.01$ cm; $SD = 1.16$ cm) and at 2 m ($M = 2.58$ cm; $SD = 1.69$ cm) to be not statistically different. The average error of 1.65 % is substantially smaller than that of the UWB positioning system. However, the UWB system does not accumulate errors over time.

Test on Angular Movement. Since the UWB positioning system does not measure angles, the global and local angle indications are all dependent on the IMU, which require high accuracy. In our angular movement test, we let the robot rotate $45°$ and $90°$ on the ground, while we marked the starting and ending positions in order to calculate the errors.

Table 1. Linear Movement Test

Trial	Expected Distance: 100 cm			Expected Distance 200 cm		
	Actual (cm)	Delta (cm)	Error (%)	Actual (cm)	Delta (cm)	Error (%)
1	99.6	0.4	0.4	197	3	1.5
2	98.2	1.8	1.8	202.8	−2.8	1.4
3	100.6	−0.6	0.6	195.4	4.6	2.3
4	96.4	3.6	3.6	198.7	1.3	0.65
5	102.8	−2.8	2.8	194.9	5.1	2.55
6	101.4	−1.4	1.4	202.6	−2.6	1.3
7	97.0	3	3	200.5	−0.5	0.25
8	97.5	2.5	2.5	199.3	0.7	0.35

Table 2. Angular Movement Test

Trial	Expected Angle: 45°			Expected Angle: 90°		
	Actual (°)	Delta (°)	Error (%)	Actual (°)	Delta (°)	Error (%)
1	44.23	0.77	1.71	88.85	1.15	1.28
2	43.36	1.64	3.64	90.46	−0.46	0.51
3	41.34	3.66	8.13	89.8	0.2	0.22
4	44.19	0.81	1.80	91.45	−1.45	1.61
5	43.33	1.67	3.71	91.55	−1.55	1.72

As shown in Table 2, through five trials, the average difference of the robot was 1.71° at 45° of rotation. When Loomo rotates 90°, the average difference is at 1.07°. A paired t-Test $T(4) = 1.002$, $p = 0.18$, showed the deviations occurring at 45° ($M = 1.71°$; $SD = 1.17°$) and at 90° ($M = 0.96°$; $SD = 0.6°$) to be not statistically different. We consider the overall deviation of 1.34° of angular movement to be quite high. Even if the error of angular measurement accumulates over an extensive time period of use, we have the UWB system to correct the location.

4.2 Feature Extension 2: Human Activity Recognition

Posture Detection. As we used a related work, namely Google's ML kit, to extract the feature points and human skeleton, there is no point in evaluating their trained model, which seems sophisticated to us. The implementation runs stable and in real-time. Our rule-based classification also showed great accuracy, but which showed difficulties at different distances between human and robot. Therefore, we measured the detection accuracy with four different distances. Each posture was executed in four distances. This was repeated 20 times, which resulted in 240 trials in total. The result is displayed in the Table 3.

Table 3. Successful detection rate by distance in percent (20 trials each).

Distance d (m)	Normal (%)	Warning (%)	Danger (%)
d <1	75	15	25
1 ≤ d < 5	85	75	70
5 ≤ d < 10	90	85	80
10 ≤ d < 20	70	75	75

From the table, we can obtain that the probability of getting an accurate pose within a certain measurement distance seems to be different. However, there is no statistical detection difference between all three postures ($F_{2,6} = 1.71$; $p = 0.26$)

following a one-way ANOVA for correlated samples. The average success rate is 68.3% ($SD = 23.5\%$) among all distances. Not considering distances shorter than 1 m, the average detection rate raises to 78.33% ($SD = 7.1\%$).

It is striking that the successful detection seems to be compromised with distances below 1 m. This is indicated by a one-way ANOVA for correlated samples ($F_{3,6} = 1272.22$; $p = 0.039$) and finally evidenced by a post-hoc analysis using a Tukey HSD Test. The detection rate is significantly lower in distances < 1 m than distances between ≤ 5 m and < 10 m ($p < 0.05$). No further differences were found.

Generally, it become obvious that sufficient detection with too close distances may not be guaranteed. The reason is that the identification of the posture is accomplished by calculating the relative position of the detected landmarks. Therefore, this detection and identification work well when the needed body landmark is included in the frame. However, if some of the body landmarks are not captured by the input frame, the information about his landmark will be missing. Thus, reducing the success rate of the obtained results. The detection error caused by missing landmarks is particularly noticeable at short distances because the camera cannot capture the whole body of the inspector well.

Heart Rate Detection. To gain insights into the performance of Loomo's newly acquired heart rate detection, we ran a study with 13 participants (Computer Science students aged between 21 and 26). As ground truth of heart rate, we used a Pulse Oximeter and the Apple watch Gen. 5, which showed almost no difference and is in line with the findings from Pipek et al. [50]. For each user we conducted a single measurement. The study results are shown in Table 4.

Table 4. Study results: Showing the calculated heart rate by Loomo against the ground truth [in bpm]

Participant	P1	P2	P3	P4	P5	P6	P7	P8	P9	P10	P11	P12	P13
Loomo (bpm)	83	65	74	78	69	67	75	68	70	74	61	73	67
Ground Truth (bpm)	110	81	75	96	81	72	88	82	80	80	66	78	76
Difference (bpm)	−27	−16	−1	−18	−12	−5	−13	−14	−10	−6	−5	−5	−9

The study results show a mean deviation of -10.84 heart beats per minute. Loomo's calculated heart rate is 87.3% accurate to the ground truth. We ran a Bland-Altman analysis, which ensured no bias to exist. This is confirmed by a Pearson correlation, which showed a positive correlation coefficient, with an average of $r = .83$ ($SD = .69$). All participants demonstrated a statistically significant positive relationship ($r > .7$, $p < .05$). However, it must also be stated that the heart rate sometimes showed wide range, differing of up to 27 beats, which is almost 25% (P1). Also striking is that Loomo provided a constantly lower heart rate than the actual ground truth. We suspect our noise filter to have canceled out the rather weak heart beats. Although this heart rate detection method is not able to extract the exact pulse signal, Loomo still achieves the goal of identifying vital signs, which is the overarching goal in this research.

5 Discussion

In this section, we would like to critically discuss the limitations of our work and to provide possible approaches to overcome these:

Classifying Critical Postures: Currently, we drove a quick'n dirty approach to classify three critical stages of posture by calculating the relations of the pose landmarks to each other. Although this approach showed to be fine, one could employ a training a simple ML-model, such as using a simple C4.5 decision tree.

Coping with Loomo's Self-balancing Movement: Since Loomo is standing on two wheels only, it deployes a bouncing back and forward movement to avoid the robot to fall over. These periodic movements impact all sensor data. There are several approaches that can be used to eliminate these signal in the sensor data, such as deploying a butterworth filter, a principle component analysis, etc.

Valid Vital Signs: Collecting accurate vital signs, such as the correct heart rate, is a challenge. For a remote PPG signal detection, like ours, we see a variety of environmental factors, such as changing ambient light, shadows, natural movement of user, etc. that can impact the measurement significantly. In our use case clinical valid data is not required, however, it is desirable.

Improving Heart Rate Detection: The simple moving average filter seems not to be the perfect choice to handle the raw PPG signal. This is because rather weak heart beats might be smoothed to much this way. A better approach might be the signal peak detection algorithm, such demonstrated by Jang et al. [51].

Increasing Number of Add-ons: Loomo already provides rich functionality with the standard sensors provided. Adding a variety of unique sensors to Loomo might open up new application field or enhance Loomo's capabilities to make autonomous decisions. For instance, attached gas sensors may provide crucial information on the environment. Moreover, using electric field sensors can help deciding whether danger by electric dives occurs or whether human body activity is present.

Deployment in Reality: In this research, we provided a proof-of-concept implementation, showcasing future opportunities. In reality, however, a greater number of studies and development is required. For instance, it is unclear how the form factor of a dual-wheeled robot like Loomo can overcome obstacles. In a disaster situation, such as when a certain gas like carbon monoxide is released, Loomo could help in finding survivors. However, in an earth quake situation when a building structure is destroyed, Loomo is likely to fail in making its way through rough terrain. Further it is unclear how false-positives and true-negatives are handled, such as missing out on finding an immobilized person, because a body part might be covered. Another problem is finding the face in unconventional positions. Therefore, it is at least questionable whether a future robot can yet to be fully autonomous or whether human remote control is required for support.

Robust Infrastructure: A future implementation is required to have a robust communication system that needs to be put in place, on a software and hardware level. High bandwidth seem to be a basis for video-streaming that may be essential in a disaster scenario, so the robot can also be remotely controlled by a rescue team. Further some type of position system is required to be in place, which may account to as an additional cost as well as being another source of potential error.

Intelligent Path Planning Algorithm: What is the quickest way? Advanced path planning may be required to enable to robot to make intelligent decisions on its own without being remotely controlled, such as when a network connection broke down. Is there a safe area? Where is the robot going once followed?

Improving Navigation by SLAM: In this project, the effects and possibilities of multi-sensor fusion are tried in the direction of a fire-fighting robot. However, because of the involvement of external position system. There is high requirement of deployment environment. Plus, a receiver mounted makes the robot too large in size. So a better substitution of UWB position system is visual SLAM. With the help of in-built camera, visual SLAM can decrease the demand of environment and make robot more flexible during task.

Feature Point Extraction: The feature points are extracted between frames by ORB method, which is an algorithm that can figure out the same points in two pictures continuously taken [52]. Feature point extraction matters both in SLAM and posture recognition that when doing image processing we can only take feature points in account, and thus reduce computation burden greatly.

6 Conclusion and Future Work

The Loomo Segway is one of the few consumer robots that offer high mobility, increased computing power, and sensing capabilities. Unfortunately, Loomo is only used for entertainment purposes and does not make use of its potential. Yet, in addition to a follow function that works questionably well, the device is only controlled manually, while it cannot understand a persons condition. In this paper we showcased a new application, a proof-of-concept of an affordable rescue robot that may be deployed in evacuation scenarios. We demonstrated how to instrument Loomo, in order to navigate autonomously through an indoor space. Further, we showed how to estimate a victims activity state, by classifying their posture and detecting their heart rate, both by using an optical RGB camera approach. We evaluated the detection quality of our approach and conclude as follows to our research questions. RQ1: We can enable Loomo to autonomously navigate through a known environment by equipping it an external UWB position system and driving a SLAM-approach. RQ2: We can we enable Loomo to understand the human's critical activity by extracting posture and heart rate information from the RGB-camera feed.

By combining these two techniques, in future rescue robots can be improved by not only reducing the cost but also enhancing their ability to recognize the victim's health condition. Particularly the application of SLAM algorithms allow robots to autonomously perceive and explore their environment, which is a future direction for investigation. Combined with path planning algorithms, unmanned autonomous search-and-rescue robots seem promising. We see the application in evacuation scenarios where the robot sends the location of injured people to the rescue team. Its unmanned nature means that it can be deployed in hazardous environments and with multiple units to effectively increase search and rescue.

References

1. Delmerico, J., et al.: The current state and future outlook of rescue robotics. J. Field Robot. **36**(7), 1171–1191 (2019)
2. Ventura, R., Lima, P.U.: Search and rescue robots: the civil protection teams of the future. In: 2012 Third International Conference on Emerging Security Technologies, pp. 12–19. IEEE (2012)
3. Durrant-Whyte, H., Bailey, T.: Simultaneous localization and mapping: part I. IEEE Robot. Autom. Mag. **13**(2), 99–110 (2006)
4. ND with Us: UWB minutes: Ranging technics (2020)
5. G. M. Kit. Google (2022)
6. Wu, H.-Y., Rubinstein, M., Shih, E., Guttag, J., Durand, F., Freeman, W.T.: Eulerian video magnification for revealing subtle changes in the world. In: ACM Transactions on Graphics (Proceedings of the SIGGRAPH 2012), vol. 31, no. 4 (2012)
7. Wobbrock, J.O., Kientz, J.A.: Research contributions in human-computer interaction. Interactions **23**(3), 38–44 (2016)
8. Kuindersma, S., et al.: Optimization-based locomotion planning, estimation, and control design for the atlas humanoid robot. Auton. Robot. **40**(3), 429–455 (2016)
9. Schwarz, M., et al.: Nimbro rescue: solving disaster-response tasks with the mobile manipulation robot momaro. J. Field Robot. **34**(2), 400–425 (2017)
10. Falanga, D., Kleber, K., Mintchev, S., Floreano, D., Scaramuzza, D.: The foldable drone: a morphing quadrotor that can squeeze and fly. IEEE Robot. Autom. Lett. **4**(2), 209–216 (2018)
11. Wojciechowska, A., Frey, J., Mandelblum, E., Amichai-Hamburger, Y., Cauchard, J.R.: Designing drones: factors and characteristics influencing the perception of flying robots. Proc. ACM Interact. Mob. Wearable Ubiquit. Technol. **3**(3), 1–19 (2019)
12. Ruiz, C., et al.: Idrone: robust drone identification through motion actuation feedback. Proc. ACM Interact. Mob. Wearable Ubiquit. Technol. **2**(2), 1–22 (2018)
13. Wright, C., et al.: Design of a modular snake robot. In: 2007 IEEE/RSJ International Conference on Intelligent Robots and Systems, pp. 2609–2614. IEEE (2007)
14. Kiyani, M.N., Khan, M.U.M.: A prototype of search and rescue robot. In: 2016 2nd International Conference on Robotics and Artificial Intelligence (ICRAI), pp. 208–213 (2016)
15. Kim, Y.-D., Kim, Y.-G., Lee, S.-H., Kang, J.-H., An, J.: Portable fire evacuation guide robot system. In: 2009 IEEE/RSJ International Conference on Intelligent Robots and Systems, pp. 2789–2794 (2009)

16. Zhao, J., Gao, J., Zhao, F., Liu, Y.: A search-and-rescue robot system for remotely sensing the underground coal mine environment. Sensors **17**(10), 2426 (2017)
17. Mano, H., et al.: Treaded control system for rescue robots in indoor environment. In: 2008 IEEE International Conference on Robotics and Biomimetics, pp. 1836–1843 (2009)
18. Gollasch, D., Engel, C., Branig, M., Weber, G.: Applying software variability methods to design adaptive assistance robots. In: Proceedings of the 12th ACM International Conference on PErvasive Technologies Related to Assistive Environments, PETRA 2019, pp. 313–314. Association for Computing Machinery, New York (2019)
19. Steiner, M.: ROS navigation stack on a Loomo Segway robot. Ph.D. thesis, B.Sc. thesis, Vienna University Munich Vienna (2018)
20. Murphy, R.: Human-robot interaction in rescue robotics. IEEE Trans. Syst. Man Cybern. Part C (Appl. Rev.) **34**(2), 138–153 (2004)
21. Jobanputra, C., Bavishi, J., Doshi, N.: Human activity recognition: a survey. Procedia Comput. Sci. **155**, 698–703 (2019)
22. Lara, O.D., Labrador, M.A.: A survey on human activity recognition using wearable sensors. IEEE Commun. Surv. Tutor. **15**(3), 1192–1209 (2012)
23. Ke, S.-R., Thuc, H.L.U., Lee, Y.-J., Hwang, J.-N., Yoo, J.-H., Choi, K.-H.: A review on video-based human activity recognition. Computers **2**(2), 88–131 (2013)
24. Rogez, G., Rihan, J., Ramalingam, S., Orrite, C., Torr, P.H.: Randomized trees for human pose detection. In: 2008 IEEE Conference on Computer Vision and Pattern Recognition, pp. 1–8 (2008)
25. Bissacco, A., Yang, M.-H., Soatto, S.: Detecting humans via their pose. In: Advances in Neural Information Processing Systems, vol. 19 (2006)
26. Dimitrijevic, M., Lepetit, V., Fua, P.: Human body pose detection using Bayesian spatio-temporal templates. Comput. Vis. Image Underst. **104**(2–3), 127–139 (2006)
27. Anitha, G., Baghavathi Priya, S.: Posture based health monitoring and unusual behavior recognition system for elderly using dynamic Bayesian network. Cluster Comput. **22**(6), 13583–13590 (2019)
28. Hernández, Ó.G., Morell, V., Ramon, J.L., Jara, C.A.: Human pose detection for robotic-assisted and rehabilitation environments. Appl. Sci. **11**(9), 4183 (2021)
29. Cao, Z., Hidalgo, G., Simon, T., Wei, S.-E., Sheikh, Y.: OpenPose: realtime multi-person 2D pose estimation using part affinity fields. IEEE Trans. Pattern Anal. Mach. Intell. **43**(1), 172–186 (2021)
30. Bazarevsky, V., Grishchenko, I., Raveendran, K., Zhu, T., Zhang, F., Grundmann, M.: BlazePose: on-device real-time body pose tracking. arXiv preprint arXiv:2006.10204 (2020)
31. Poh, M.-Z., McDuff, D.J., Picard, R.W.: Non-contact, automated cardiac pulse measurements using video imaging and blind source separation. Opt. Express **18**, 10762–10774 (2010)
32. Verkruysse, W., Svaasand, L.O., Nelson, J.S.: Remote plethysmographic imaging using ambient light. Opt. Express **16**, 21434–21445 (2008)
33. Bosi, I., Cogerino, C., Bazzani, M.: Real-time monitoring of heart rate by processing of Microsoft Kinect^{TM} 2.0 generated streams. In: 2016 International Multidisciplinary Conference on Computer and Energy Science (SpliTech), pp. 1–6 (2016)
34. Gambi, E., et al.: Heart rate detection using Microsoft Kinect: validation and comparison to wearable devices. Sensors **17**(8) (2017)
35. Chambino, P.B.: Android-based implementation of Eulerian video magnification for vital signs monitoring (2013)

36. Chen, W., Zhang, F., Gu, T., Zhou, K., Huo, Z., Zhang, D.: Constructing floor plan through smoke using ultra wideband radar. Proc. ACM Interact. Mob. Wearable Ubiquit. Technol. **5**(4), 1–29 (2021)
37. Segway Robotics. Segway Robotics | Developer (2022)
38. Arun Francis, G., Arulselvan, M., Elangkumaran, P., Keerthivarman, S., Vijaya Kumar, J.: Object detection using ultrasonic sensor. Int. J. Innov. Technol. Explor. Eng. **8**, 207–209 (2020)
39. Koval, L., Vaňuš, J., Bilík, P.: Distance measuring by ultrasonic sensor. IFAC-PapersOnLine **49**(25), 153–158 (2016). 14th IFAC Conference on Programmable Devices and Embedded Systems PDES 2016
40. Zhang, P., Gu, J., Milios, E., Huynh, P.: Navigation with IMU/GPS/digital compass with unscented Kalman filter. In: IEEE International Conference Mechatronics and Automation, vol. 3, pp. 1497–1502 (2005)
41. Zhang, Y., Fei, Y., Xu, L., Sun, G.: Micro-IMU-based motion tracking system for virtual training. In: 2015 34th Chinese Control Conference (CCC), pp. 7753–7758 (2015)
42. Leugner, S., Hellbrück, H.: Lessons learned: indoor ultra-wideband localization systems for an industrial IoT application. Technical report, Technische Universität Braunschweig, Braunschweig (2018)
43. Saha, S.S., Sandha, S.S., Garcia, L.A., Srivastava, M.: TinyOdom: hardware-aware efficient neural inertial navigation. Proc. ACM Interact. Mob. Wearable Ubiquit. Technol. **6**(2), 1–32 (2022)
44. Chen, X., Chen, Y., Cao, S., Zhang, L., Zhang, X., Chen, X.: Acoustic indoor localization system integrating TDMA+ FDMA transmission scheme and positioning correction technique. Sensors **19**(10), 2353 (2019)
45. Liu, J., Li, D., Wang, L., Zhang, F., Xiong, J.: Enabling contact-free acoustic sensing under device motion. Proc. ACM Interact. Mob. Wearable Ubiquit. Technol. **6**(3), 1–27 (2022)
46. Yue, S., He, H., Cao, P., Zha, K., Koizumi, M., Katabi, D.: CornerRadar: RF-based indoor localization around corners. Proc. ACM Interact. Mob. Wearable Ubiquit. Technol. **6**(1), 1–24 (2022)
47. Bradski, G., Kaehler, A.: Opencv. Dr. Dobb's J. Softw. Tools **3**, 120 (2000)
48. Kapoor, R.: Creating and comparing seated posture classification models using machine learning and computer vision. Ph.D. thesis (2022)
49. Schmidt, S.O., Hellbrück, H.: Detection and identification of multipath interference with adaption of transmission band for UWB transceiver systems. In: IPIN-WiP (2021)
50. Pipek, L.Z., Nascimento, R.F.V., Acencio, M.M.P., Teixeira, L.R.: Comparison of SpO2 and heart rate values on apple watch and conventional commercial oximeters devices in patients with lung disease. Sci. Rep. **11**(1), 1–7 (2021)
51. Jang, D.-G., Park, S., Hahn, M., Park, S.-H.: A real-time pulse peak detection algorithm for the photoplethysmogram. Int. J. Electron. Electr. Eng. 45–49 (2014)
52. Gao, X., Zhang, T., Liu, Y., Yan, Q.: 14 Lectures on Visual SLAM: From Theory to Practice. Publishing House of Electronics Industry, Beijing (2017)

Developing Interface Designs with Personality Types: Self-management Application – Luvlife

Yun Rou Tan, Kasthuri Subaramaniam$^{(\boxtimes)}$ ⓘ, and Raenu Kolandaisamy ⓘ

Instiute of Computer Science and Digital Innovation UCSI University, Kuala Lumpur, Malaysia
kasthurisuba@ucsiuniversity.edu.my

Abstract. In this era of digital technology, the use of technology in daily life has increased the amount of time spent in front of screens. Time and timing issues have become important for all of us. This project aims to develop a self-management application that allows users to customize their user interfaces based on their personality preferences. In this project, the Myers-Briggs Type Indicator (MBTI) personality test will be used to measure and evaluate users' personality preferences. A survey questionnaire was conducted to understand users' preferences. This project managed to determine the user interface preferences of the MBTI users.

Keywords: User interface · MBTI · Human personality types

1 Introduction

In this age of information technology, people are becoming increasingly connected to the world around them. The adoption of technology in our daily activities increased the time that people spend in front of the screen. The mobile phone has changed the way people communicate and work. Time and timing issues have become more and more important to all of us. In these last two decades, people have had a faster pace of life. They make things faster, reducing their time spent and compressing actions such as eating faster, sleeping lesser, or making a phone call while having lunch. It shows that people have a limited way to deal with time at work – poor time management. There are several methods of time management like tips and techniques to determine which goals to pursue in the short term, how to translate these goals into immediate tasks, how to plan and prioritize tasks daily, and how to focus on completing tasks without any interruptions.

Besides, there are so many things that people can do or work with only using their mobile phones. These had become a day-to-day routine for the people. While they are doing a task or studying, people will receive updates and notifications from different applications such as social media from the mobile phone which may be caused an overwhelming distraction. They spend a lot of time on social media which can divert their concentration and focus from some tasks [1]. People easily get attracted by other applications instead of the teaching or working application tools. This may have caused them to form poor time management and procrastination habits. Based on the journal by

Häfner and Stock [2], good time management can lead to an increase in perceived control of time and a decrease in perceived stress. Hence, there is plenty of time management, task management, and productivity applications launched to help people manage their time and task well.

2 Literature Review

2.1 Mobile Application

In recent years, the mobile phone is no longer only a communication tool but has also become an essential part of people's communication and daily life. A mobile application is a set of programs that runs on the mobile phone to perform certain tasks for the mobile user. There is a global positive impact of the mobile application. Mobile applications are running on mobile phones which are moveable and easy to use. Mobile application not only benefits users but also plays an important role in the business field. Many business companies started to use mobile applications to earn revenue. Software developers develop applications with different programming language codes such as Java for the android platform and Switch for the iOS platform.

There are many mobile applications developed for people in different areas use like communication, entertainment, utilities, e-commerce, etc. Some of the applications downloaded by users are task manager, notepad, social networking, diary, translators, etc. At first, people only used a mobile application to receive a call, do simple calculations, set alarm clocks, etc. As technology becomes more and more advanced, more applications were developed and are designed to help people in their daily life. For example, people can turn on their air conditioner using their mobile application before they reached home. Most people from developed countries can't imagine leaving without a mobile phone [3]. There are many similar mobile applications developed every year. People begin to compare those applications by their features, UI designs, price, etc. Developers begin to receive bad reviews from the users due to the ugly UI designs or bad features. Therefore, developers nowadays should focus more on their application's UI designs to satisfy users' requirements.

2.2 Human-Computer Interaction (HCI)

Human-computer interaction (HCI) researchers have been paying attention to mobile platforms, and touchscreens have changed mobile user interface and interaction design [4]. HCI was founded in 1982. It is the interaction between humans and computers and become an important component of Information Technology (IT). This interaction is mainly done at the user interface. It is a practice of understanding the differences in how humans use technology. The goals of HCI are to achieve functionality, usability, enhanced user experience, and how to design and implement IT systems that satisfy human users [5]. It helps to make interfaces that increase productivity and enhance user experience.

The core terminology in HCI is usability. Usability is known as "user-friendly". It ensures that the products meet the three outcomes which are: (1) the product is easy for users to become familiar with while using the first time, (2) the product is easy for users to use, (3) the product is easy for users to remember the user interface and how to use it [4]. It helps products to improve users' performance and achieve their goals. Interaction between users and computers occurs at the user interface. Interaction design means designing interactive products like software to support people in their daily and working lives. Designing a user interface needs to know both human and machine sides because the HCI is concerned with the interaction of humans and computers [6]. Hence, user interface design is very important in developing technology such as mobile applications.

2.3 User Interface Design (UI)

As digital technology keeps developing at a rapid speed, the human-computer interface is becoming more and more complicated in its operation. A human-computer interface is also called a user interface (UI). UI is the main key of the HCI and communication in a device. UI represents the software to the user. It communicates with the user on behalf of the software application. It is more advantageous for an application that has these interface design concepts such as attractive, clear, concise, familiar, and efficient [7]. According to Guntupalli [8], a UI design should be tested across several platforms to make sure that it displays all the information as originally designed when it is seen by the users. Users should be given clear and familiar help instructions so that the new users of the system can be used it easily. Besides, the interface should be nice-looking and easy to be used as users may use this application daily. For example, introverted personality person prefers to have a design that is seen as comfortable, or insecure [9]; they prefer a cooler background color display on the application. Users will use the application more frequently if it matches their preferences.

Therefore, it is necessary to create a suitable UI that can match the user's preference. As Wartiningsih from [10] claimed humans with different personalities especially extroverts or introverts, will prefer different learning styles that might influence their learning activities. The same goes for UI designs, different users with different personality types will prefer different UI designs that might improve their efficiency [20]. Due to the increasing number of electronic products, the work of UI designers is more comparable to the work of the artist today, UI interface design is not just beautifying the applications. A beautiful UI interface allows users to have a great experience and bring more benefits to the company. UI interface designers need to consider more from users' perspectives like how to design a user-satisfied and comfortable UI interface to provide a more satisfying experience for users [11].

2.4 The Myers-Briggs Type Indicator (MBTI)

The personality test was trending these few years. By doing personality tests, people tend to know more about themselves and can know which situations are ideal for them. The Myers-Briggs Type Indicator (MBTI) is one of the most famous personality tests that is constructed by two Americans, Katharine Cook Briggs and her daughter Isabel Briggs Myers [11]. It is derived from Carl Jung's theory of psychological types.

16 personality types assigned have a four-letter acronym that represents the appropriate set of preferences which are "E" for extroversion and "I" for introversion; "S" for

sensing and "N" for intuition; "T" for thinking and "F" for feeling; "J" for judging and "P" for perceiving. For example, INFJ stands for Introverted, Intuition, Feeling, Judging. Figure 1 shows the 16 types of MBTI personality.

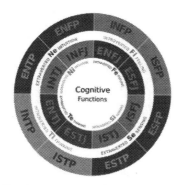

Fig. 1. 16 Types of MBTI Personality

Many companies conduct these personality tests while interviewing new workers. The company can understand an employee's true character after doing the personality tests [12]. They are able to assign the employee to a suitable position or determine whether they are suited for this company. It helps the company to reduce employee turnover and increase productivity. The MBTI has been widely used and validated in the education field also. Students are able to know themselves more after doing this personality test. They can choose their preferred field based on their personality results.

Therefore, this project aims to develop a self-management application that allows users to customize their user interfaces based on their personality preferences. In this project, the Myers-Briggs Type Indicator (MBTI) personality test will be used to measure and evaluate users' personality preferences. A survey questionnaire was conducted to understand users' preferences. The goal of this project is to determine the user interface preferences of MBTI users.

3   Problem Statement

In this technology-based world, rapid technological advancement is happening so quickly. The use of technology has become essential for humans in their daily lives. Technology has changed the way humans used to communicate in the workplace. People can use smartphones to do many works. For example, the arrival of smartphones and mobile chat applications has brought communication to a new level. Users are able to communicate with others anytime instead of wasting time going to a place to meet their customers. There are many productivity applications available such as project management, time management, and task management that help users to organize their things well. However, there are some issues faced by users in these existing applications.

The problem with the existing application is some of the applications are not free to use. Users need to pay before downloading and using the application. Also, some applications can only allow users to use for three months for free, after that, users must purchase to continue using the application [13]. Thus, many people will decide not to use these kinds of applications. Without these 'helpers', it may lead users have poor productivity and poor time management for their daily work.

Another problem with the existing application is there are no existing applications that provide a personality-based user interface. As from the journal by O. Nov and O. Arazy (2013) [14], user interface (UI) is not only personalized across users but also tailored to a user's particular attitude at a point in time. For instance, extroverts prefer warm (yellow-red) colors as their background color; introverts prefer cool (green-blue) colors as their background color [15]. These personality traits may affect users' interface design preferences and their productivity [19].

Besides the problem above, some existing applications are dissatisfied with users. The reasons are the poor design of the user interface and the complexity to use [16]. As we discussed before, UI interface designers need to consider more from users' perspectives like how to design a user-satisfied and comfortable UI interface to provide a more satisfying experience for users [17]. For example, users are dissatisfied with the UI design of the application, which may reduce users' productivity. Users who do not have the motivation to use the application to do the task may lead to procrastinating [18]. Therefore, user interface design plays a very important role while developing an application to meet users' needs.

4 Analysis and Synthesis

A survey about interface design with personality types of self-management systems is conducted for collecting data. Google Form is used for this survey to collect data from respondents. The survey's google form link is shared with colleagues, and friends and will be posted on social media platforms like Course Networking, and Facebook. All respondents will answer the survey through the google form. The purpose is to understand end users' requirements so that the product will meet their needs. A total number of 80 respondents completed the survey through Google Form. There are two sections to this survey. The first section is the demographic section. This section will be collecting respondents' age, gender, education level, and MBTI Type. The second section is the main section where the respondents will be required to select features and user interface design such as font type, font size, theme color, and layout based on their preferences. The data collected from the respondents were analyzed and discussed below:

The results show that there are 67 out of 80 respondents (83.8%) from the age group of 18–23, 10 respondents (12.5%) from the age group of 24–29, and followed by 3 respondents (3.7%) from the age group of 30 & above. Besides, there are 54 female respondents (67.5%) and 26 male respondents (32.5%) who answered the survey. Most of the respondents are from the undergraduate level. There are 53 out of 80 respondents (65%) who hold a Bachelor's Degree.

Figure 2 shows the MBTI personality types of each respondent. There are a total of 16 types of MBTI personality types. The pie chart is then converted into a table for better understanding and analysis.

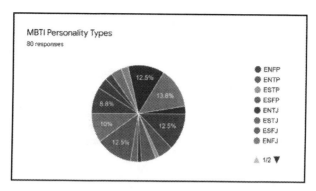

Fig. 2. MBTI Personality Types of Respondents

Table 1. Number of Respondents in each MBTI Personality Types

MBTI Personality Types	Number of Respondents
ENFJ	8
ENFP	10
ENTJ	1
ENTP	4
ESFJ	10
ESFP	4
ESTJ	2
ESTP	1
INFJ	10
INFP	7
INTJ	2
INTP	3
ISFJ	11
ISFP	3
ISTJ	2
ISTP	2
Grand Total	**80**

Table 1 shows the number of respondents in each MBTI personality type. The highest number of respondents comes from the ISFJ personality group type which has 11 respondents (13.8%). The second-highest number of respondents in personality group types are ENFP, ESFJ, and INFJ which have the same number of respondents. Each of them has 10 respondents (12.5%) in their personality group type. Besides, there are 8 respondents

(10%) who come from the ENFJ personality type which has the third-highest number of respondents.

Table 2. Number of Respondents in Preference Font Type

Font Type	Number of Respondents
Inconsolata (Monospaced)	7
Just Another Hand (Script)	31
Playfair Display (Serif)	30
Roboto (Sans Serif)	5
Yeseva One (Display)	7
Grand Total	**80**

Table 2 shows the preferred font type by respondents. There are 31 respondents (38.7%) who prefer to set their font type as Script family font (Just Another Hand). The second-highest font type that respondents preferred is from Serif family font (Playfair Display) which has 30 respondents (37.5%).

Table 3. Number of Respondents in Preference Font Size

Font Size	Number of Respondents
12 pt	15
14 pt	24
16 pt	28
18 pt	10
20 pt	3
Grand Total	**80**

Table 3 shows the number of respondents who preferred font size in the application. As the table has shown above, there are 28 respondents (35%) who prefer a font size of 16 pt which is the highest number of respondents in preference font size. The next preferred font size is 14 pt which has 24 respondents (30%). On the other hand, there are only 3 respondents (3.7%) who prefer a font size of 20 pt.

According to Fig. 3 and table 4, there are 30 respondents (37.5%) who prefer to have palette 1 as the application's theme color. Next, 26 respondents (32.5%) prefer to have a palette 5 as the theme color.

Based on Fig. 4 and Table 5, there are 44 respondents (55%) preferred to set the layout of the application as layout 1. There are 14 out of 80 respondents (17.5%) who voted for layout 2 and followed by layout 3, layout 4, and layout 5, which has 8 respondents (10%), 7 respondents (8.8%), and 7 respondents (8.8%) respectively.

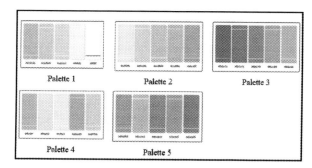

Fig. 3. Theme Color Palettes

Table 4. Number of Respondents in Preference Theme Color

Theme Color	Number of Respondents
Palette 1	30
Palette 2	13
Palette 3	5
Palette 4	6
Palette 5	26
Grand Total	**80**

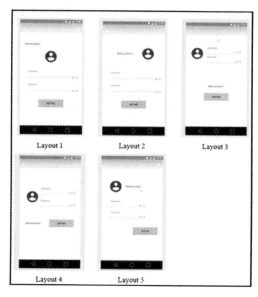

Fig. 4. Layout Design

Table 5. Number of Respondents in Preference Layout

Type of Layout	Number of Respondents
Layout 1	44
Layout 2	14
Layout 3	8
Layout 4	7
Layout 5	7
Grand Total	**80**

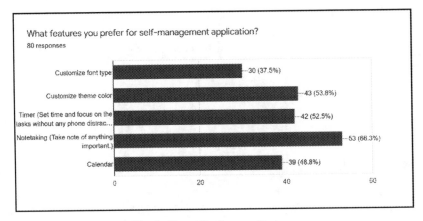

Fig. 5. Users' Preferences Features

Figure 5 shows the features that users would like to have in the application. The top three features will be implemented into the application. The most voted features are notetaking which allows users to take note of anything important to them. There are 53 responses (66.3%) who voted for this feature. Next is customized theme color that allows user to choose their own preferred color which has 43 responses (53.8%) and followed by a timer that allows users to set time and focus on the tasks without any phone distraction which has 42 responses (52.5%).

Based on the overall results and findings from the survey, the highest number of respondents are come from ENFP, ESFJ, ISFJ, and INFJ. Thus, these 4 personality types will be chosen for the development of the application. Each user interface will be designed based on their preferences which are font type, font size, theme color, layout, and features.

5   System Design

5.1   Use Case Diagram

Figure 6 shows the use case diagram of the application. It shows that the application has only one actor which is the user, and what activities can be performed in the application. Users need to log into their accounts in order to perform all the activities in the application.

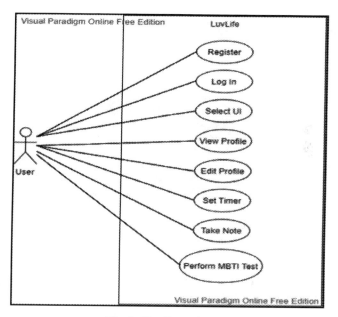

Fig. 6. Use Case Diagram

5.2   Application Design

Figures 7, 8, 9, and 10 show the user interface of the sign-up and sign-in screen from different personalities. For example, the INFJ user interface will be palette 1 in color, layout 5, 16pt font size, and serif font family. The design from each MBTI type is designed based on users' preferences.

When users have chosen their personality type, it will go to the sign-up page. Users can register an account here. Their information will be saved into the firebase database. If the user already has an account, the user can click on the yellow text below the sign-up button, it will go to the sign-in page.

Fig. 7. ENFP User Interface

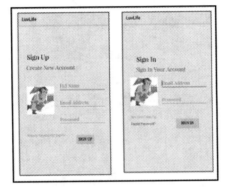

Fig. 8. ESFJ User Interface

Fig. 9. ISFJ User Interface

Fig. 10. INFJ User Interface

6 Evaluation

User Acceptance Testing (UAT) is known as beta testing. It is done by the end-user to verify or accept the application before launch. In this project, there are 4 end users from different educational backgrounds and different MBTI personality types which will be represented as User A, User B, User C, and User D to protect their confidential information. There are 25 features for users to test. The result shows that all users can run all the features in the application.

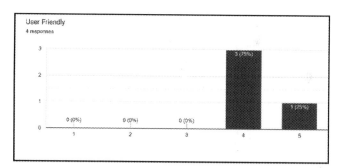

Fig. 11. Results of User-Friendliness of The Application

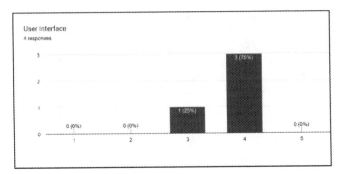

Fig. 12. Results of The User Interface of The Application

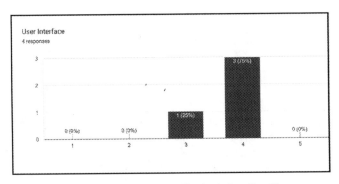

Fig. 13. Results of The Application's Loading Time

Figures 11, 12, and 13 show the results of the user-friendliness, user interface satisfaction, and loading time of the application. Overall, the results show that the users felt the application is easy to use, the user interface is quite satisfactory, and the loading time is quite fast from page to page. Besides that, the users are asked to give some feedback and suggestions after testing the application. The results were shown in the table below (Table 6), with each row considered as a user.

In summary, all features in the application are runnable. The users are satisfied with the user interface, loading time, and easy to use. There are some suggestions from the users which will be considered in the further improvements of the application to develop a more user-satisfying application.

Table 6. Feedback and Suggestions on Each Application's Page

Login page	Register page	Profile page	Note page	Timer page	Customize page
Good	Can ask for more information	Cannot change profile image	Cannot edit or delete the note	Good	Can add a 'back' button
Good	Good	Can show more information	Cannot delete or edit the note	Cannot set my own time	The other page didn't change the color I chose
Nice	Nice	Can add 'upload profile image' function	Unable to delete note	Cannot set my own time	Can add more color choices
Nice, suggestion: can put our own profile image	Nice	Can add upload profile image function	Unable to edit/delete note	No comment	The tab color didn't change on the other pages

7 Conclusion and Future Work

7.1 Conclusion

In conclusion, this project managed to determine the relationship between user interface design and personality type based on MBTI, to design and develop a self-management mobile application with users' preference user interface design, and to evaluate the existing application. The aim of this project is to develop a self-management application based on MBTI users' preferences and user interface. Literature reviews and studies of existing applications have been conducted to determine their issues. A survey has been conducted to determine and analyze the user interface preferences of MBTI users. The proposed application – Luvlife is implemented using the Android Studio platform and it is suitable for Android-based mobile devices. It has managed to achieve all objectives in this project and managed to solve all the existing application problems. The app is free to use, has a personality-based user interface, and a user-friendly user interface. But the application is not perfect enough, there are still a lot of parts that need to be improved. It can be further improved in the future based on the users feedback who participated in the user acceptance test (UAT).

7.2 Future Work

In future work, all recommendations and feedback by users will be considered for further improvements and enhancements. The application can be supported not only on Android-based mobile devices but also on IOS-based mobile devices. Besides, the application will be supported in multiple languages so all users from different countries can use the app. The application will also add more features in the future. Some of the examples are users able to upload their profile image in the application, users able to delete, edit, and view the note, and users able to set the timer's time. Last but not least, the application will be improved by allowing users to have more choices while customizing their user interface such as more selection in background or toolbar color, being able to change another similar font type, and able to select other layouts designs.

References

1. Siddiqui, S., Singh, T.: Social media its impact with positive and negative aspects. Int. J. Comput. Appl. Technol. Res. **5**(2), 71–75 (2016). https://doi.org/10.7753/ijcatr0502.1006
2. Häfner, A., Stock, A.: Time management training and perceived control of time at work. The J. Psychol. **144**(5), 429–447 (2010). https://doi.org/10.1080/00223980.2010.496647
3. Islam, R., Islam, R., Mazumder, T.: Mobile application and its global impact. Int. J. Eng. Technol. (IJEST) **10**(6), 72–78 (2010)
4. Punchoojit, L., Hongwarittorrn, N.: Usability studies on mobile user interface design patterns: a systematic literature review. Adv. Hum.-Comput. Interact. **2017**, 1–22 (2017). https://doi.org/10.1155/2017/6787504
5. Draganova, A., Doran, P.: Use of HCI components into IT courses. Int. J. Inform. Educ. Technol. **3**, 245–248 (2013). https://doi.org/10.7763/IJIET.2013.V3.273
6. Jalil, A.B., Kolandaisamy, R., Subaramaniam, K., Kolandaisamy, I., Khang, J.Q.G.: Designing a mobile application to improve user's productivity on computer-based productivity software. J. Adv. Res. Dyn. Control Syst **12**(03), 226–236 (2020)
7. Yellin, B.: Human-computer interaction and the user interface, Education.dellemc.com. https://education.dellemc.com/content/dam/dell-emc/documents/en-us/2018KS_Yellin-Human-Computer_Interaction_and_the_User_Interface.pdf (2018)
8. Guntupalli, R.C.C.: User interface design: methods and qualities of a good user interface design (2008)
9. Karsvall, A.: Personality preferences in graphical interface design. In: Proceedings of the second Nordic conference on Human-computer interaction – NordiCHI'02 (2002). https://doi.org/10.1145/572020.572049
10. Wartiningsih, H.D.S.: Adaptive e-learning model in learning personality characters (2020)
11. Lei, J.: The application research of "Chinese style" elements in UI Interface Design (2019)
12. Hendriks, F.: Jung Personality Types. Toolshero. https://www.toolshero.com/psychology/jung-personality-types/#:~:text=Jung%20first%20introduced%20his%20personality,life%20attitudes%3A%20introversion%20and%20extraversion (2018)
13. Evernote Reviews & Product Details. https://www.g2.com/products/evernote/reviews
14. Adewale, O., Osajiuba, O., Agbonifo, O.: Development of a myers-briggs type indicator based personalised e-learning system. Int. J. Comput. (IJC) **35**, 101–125 (2019)
15. Choungourian, A.: Introversion — extraversion and color preferences. J. Projective Techniques Pers. Assess/ **31**(4), 92–94 (1967). https://doi.org/10.1080/0091651X.1967.10120401
16. Sunsama Reviews & Product Details: https://www.g2.com/products/sunsama-sunsama/reviews#survey-response-5025276
17. Subaramaniam, K., Ern-Rong, J.L., Palaniappan, S.: Interface designs with personality types: an effective e-learning experience. Evergreen **8**(3), 618–627 (2021). https://doi.org/10.5109/4491654

18. Huang, K.-Y.: Challenges in human-computer interaction design for mobile devices. In: Proceedings of the World Congress on Engineering and Computer Science, vol. 1, pp. 1–6 (2009)

19. Subaramaniam, K., Ern-Rong, J.L., Palaniappan, S.: Interface designs with MBTI personality types. In: Proceedings of Mechanical Engineering Research Day. Melaka, Malaysia. pp. 178–179, 16 Dec 2020

20. Subaramaniam, K., Palaniappan, S.: Learners' perception on integration of human personality types on mobile learning platform. In: Salvendy, G., Wei, J. (eds.) HCII 2021. LNCS, vol. 12796, pp. 329–343. Springer, Cham (2021). https://doi.org/10.1007/978-3-030-77025-9_27

Auto-Tagging User Traits in the Context of Smartphones

Srija Sistla, Nikitha Jayakumar[(✉)], Smrithi K., G. B. S. Akhil, and Nitin V. Pujari

PES University, Banashankari Stage III, Bangalore 560085, India
nikithajayakumar311@gmail.com, nitin.pujari@pes.edu

Abstract. In the past few decades research has been done on the prediction of personality traits of users from social media to enhance users experience while using social media applications. Most often we tend to be more upfront with our smartphones and personalise it to suit our daily moods and emotions. These sensor-rich devices can easily be repurposed to collect rich and extensive records of their users' behaviour. Questionnaire based personality tests pose certain challenges as test takers may not be able to accurately answer the questions due to various personal or professional reasons on a survey. Employing a methodology based in the context of smartphone application usage data is an attempt to increase the accuracy in identifying the user's personality traits as this data will be more closely related to the user's changing behavioural pattern over a set of time periods.

Keywords: Human Behaviour · Machine Learning · App Usage · Usage Stats · Big Five Personalities · Personality Traits · Recursive Feature Elimination · Decision Trees · Random Forest · Gradient Boosting

1 Introduction

Over the past decade, novel methods of collecting data have opened up more opportunities for research on human behaviour. Personal mobile devices and online social networks provide real-time data to study human behaviour and interaction. Data-driven inferences regarding individuals' personality traits provide vast opportunities for research.

The data collected from smartphones provide more information about an individual than what can be retrieved from an individual's social media presence. The wide range of sensors on a smartphone coupled with the device's logging abilities, for example, app-usage logs, location, communications, screen activity, website tracking can all be lucratively captured via an application to record users' behaviours on a daily basis not only on the devices that belong to the individuals but also those individuals' devices that are in close proximity to them. This kind of data has much potential for psychological research to the extent that such research has already yielded valuable findings. The findings include studies relating communication data and physical activity to an individual's mental wellness and emotion. However, behavioural data obtained from smartphones also contain private and personal information. Thus, this data must be collected, processed and analysed responsibly after getting informed consent from the smartphone

© The Author(s), under exclusive license to Springer Nature Switzerland AG 2023
G. Salvendy and J. Wei (Eds.): HCII 2023, LNCS 14052, pp. 90–105, 2023.
https://doi.org/10.1007/978-3-031-35921-7_7

user. The data collected has to be minimal without violating the privacy of the user. Here, a model is developed that can identify and tag users' traits based on the users' application usage on their An-droid smartphones. It only gathers the statistics of the application usage without monitoring the user's activity within the application. The data once collected from smartphone users with their permission is analysed and annotated to a certain personality trait. To this effect, the classification considered is the Big Five personality classification.

One of the most widely used and proven questionnaire-based studies is the Big Five Personality traits. The Big Five traits are a classification for personality traits used reliably and extensively in many fields to capture personality description. The theory identifies five factors: conscientiousness, agreeableness, neuroticism, open-ness to experience and extraversion. Each trait represents a continuum. This means that an individual can fall anywhere on the continuum for each trait. To determine the traits, an individual will be asked to agree or disagree, on a scale of 1 to 5, to each phrase that is presented as a question. Based on the answers provided, results show where the individual lies on the spectrum for each trait. For example, the result can show a high score in conscientiousness and low score in extraversion.

Research has also shown that about half of the variation of traits amongst individuals results from their genetic inheritance and the other half from their environment. Studies have also found that conscientiousness, extraversion, openness to experience and neuroticism are traits that are relatively stable from childhood through adulthood. These traits are shown to be able to predict a variety of life outcomes: health, relationships, political participation, purchasing behaviours, academic performance and job performance.

However, the results of these questionnaire-based tests are directly proportional to the honesty levels of the users' answers and the effectiveness of the questions in capturing users' behaviour. Often, it is considered disappointing as these tests only rephrase the users' answers and are entirely dependent on how self-reflective the users are. [5] Thus, this work is our attempt at accurately predicting the Big Five personality traits of the users from their smartphone usage data without having to fill any questionnaires unless preferred to by the user.

2   Related Work

The individuals' personality dimensions in this paper can be predicted from 6 classes of behaviour: communication, social behaviour, music consumption, app usage, mobility, overall phone activity, day and night time activity, etc. The results are cross-validated to show which of the Big Five personality dimensions are predictable and which patterns of behaviour are indicative of which dimension. The models for prediction used are Nonlinear Random Forest and Linear Net Elastic. The results after performing the analysis show that the nonlinear random forest model outperformed the linear elastic net models on average in both prediction performance and the number of successfully predicted criteria which clearly indicates that there is a non-linear correlation. The proposed models in this paper are able to predict personality for openness, conscientiousness, and extraversion. It is seen that the scores for agreeableness could not be predicted at all.

The class of communication and social behaviour is very important for the prediction of personality trait dimensions, but app usage details and day and night time activity are also deemed to be important [1].

In this paper, they analyse smartphone usage data based on application categories and use it to predict the personality traits that are determined using the IPIP 50-item Big Five questionnaire. It enables them to observe that communication-oriented applications and games have a direct relation to a person's traits. Their dataset originates from Carat, which is an open source mobile data gathering platform. It ensures the anonymity of the volunteers worldwide who are interested in partaking in citizen science. Principal component analysis is used by them to pick out the apps contributing well to the generalisation capacity of their model. Random Forest Regression turned out to give the best accuracy for apps and app categories, though DNN and SVR gave comparable results. The prediction model is built using application categories instead of just applications and is found to reduce the level of aggregation and make it more robust. Besides achieving a great goodness fit result of 86–91%, they are also able to study the effect of individual categories on each of the big five traits, establishing a deeper understanding. [2].

This paper works on a scalable machine-learning approach to predict personality traits based on seven different categories of applications like social media apps, messaging apps, gaming apps, music and video apps, shopping apps, photography apps, mobile finance apps and mobile personalization apps. The relationship be-tween behavioural factors and personality traits are mostly non-linear. The Random Forest algorithm is used in the modelling due to its ability to capture both linear and non-linear relationships and it usually performs better than other models in terms of prediction accuracy. In addition, Random Forest provides insights on what factors are more important in model generation and it does not overfit, which makes this model less sensitive to variance. [3].

Using the information available in smartphones, such as web usage, music, vid-eo, maps and proximity information along with SMS and call logs, they have devised an automatic method using supervised learning to classify user traits based on the big five personalities, with an accuracy of about 80%. They analyse the correlations between the big five traits as well as the values of the individual traits to obtain the central tendencies. For feature selection, they only consider the features that show strong correlations to a degree of $p < 0.1$. All the variables are then de-correlated and the principal component analysis is being used to preserve only the dimensions that contributed to 99% of the variance. The results obtained by them regarding the correlations reinforced the results obtained in the past work, like showing that internet usage is correlated with introversion. They achieved an accuracy of 75.9% in classifying the user traits. They use a shorter version of the self-perceived personality questionnaire, consisting of only 10 items which seem to be more viable in preserving the volunteer's interest, data collection model being passive and non-intrusive further helps in gaining more of the volunteers' interest and acceptance [4].

3   Methodology

An application to collect data of the user and display the results was built which consists of three functionalities. The three functionalities implemented as modules were personality test module, allow data collection module and the personality pre-diction module.

3.1 Personality Test Module

The personality test module administered a questionnaire that aligns with the standard Mini-IPIP test. It comprised 20 questions with 5 options for each question. The questions were framed in the context of the problem statement. The personality predicted for each user is part of Big Five personality traits. Four questions of the questionnaire corresponded to a trait. Each of these questions were assigned positive keyed or negative keyed values. The results of the questionnaire were a percentage value determining each of the five traits. The personality test results were stored in a Firestore database. The test results were used as a target variable to only train the personality prediction model since supervised machine learning models were used as the prediction models.

3.2 Data Collection Module

The data collection module collected information regarding the application name, package name, access counts, usage time and event type of all the apps used by the user on their devices. The device usage data was collected for the duration of a month and it was stored in the Firestore database. Only details relevant for personal-ity prediction like the access counts, usage time and application name were extracted to be sent to the pre-processing phase. The app was allowed to extract device usage data only if the user gave permission to allow usage tracking on their devices. This step was necessary to collect usage data from the user. Each time the user wants the data to be updated, such that the personality prediction will be based on their current usage data, the users will have to click on the allow data collection button again. This would prompt the user to allow usage tracking if the permission had been revoked by the user at an earlier stage.

3.3 Dataset

The data was collected from 140 users out of which 108 users provided information about the personality test and app usage data. 32 users were not comfortable with sharing their app usage data. Since the volunteers were mostly based out of college there was a possibility that the data might be biased towards the ages be-tween 18–30.

There were 950 distinct apps from all users. Of these, 70 apps did not have a pre-defined category. For such apps, a category had been allotted to it manually.

The results obtained from the personality test were assigned classes based on their quintile ranges for the purpose of classification (Table 1).

$$For\ each\ trait: \quad (Sum\ of\ scores) * 5$$
$$The\ score\ above\ is\ normalised\ as(score - 4)/(20 - 4) * 100.$$
$$Categorised\ according\ to\ the\ quintile\ range.$$

The app usage statistics dataset was then merged with the personality test dataset and anonymized by removing the sensitive data (Fig. 1).

Table 1. Quintile Ranges and Labels for Extraversion.

Label	Quintile
E1	0–20
E2	20–40
E3	40–60
E4	60–80
E5	90–100

SHOPPING	SOCIAL	SPORTS	TOOLS	TRAVEL_AND_LOCAL	VIDEO_PLAYERS	WEATHER	CONSCIENTIOUSNESS	AGREEEABLENESS	EXTROVERSION	OPENNESS	NEUROTICISM
620	421756	413986	560927.4545	55777	18334660		c3	a3	e4	o5	n3
192898.4	11189646		444888.7692	1241387	12063210		c5	a4	e4	o3	n2
226631	3414882		1607345.375	1129283.9	35458914		c2	a5	e2	o4	n3
348128	16381865.3		255224.8462	108596	36136005		c3	a3	e3	o5	n3
	9568837.33		851718.0909	47995	1336251.5		c4	a4	e4	o3	n3
8074	4428958		692401.1429	258152	25836		c4	a5	e4	o3	n3
	31938418		103211.5	183743	36955705		c5	a5	e2	o3	n3
	13144592		477363.625	3576462	18404235		c3	a4	e4	o3	n4
	1446951		1137776.8		3142531		c3	a4	e2	o2	n4
161237	5445530.8		757725.1	430682	1680246		c3	a3	e3	o4	n4
57239	23905613	1066121	1665725.857	3920858	487291	68589	c2	a4	e4	o3	n3
	1103		3661806.167	534606	2148249		c4	a4	e4	o3	n2
27376.2	144544.2	3707	2243985.333	1703302			c3	a3	e3	o2	n2
	15507550		373910.5556	953533	5798	1527	c4	a5	e3	o3	n2
230734.83	32511003		1020884.667	2209846	21578144		c2	a5	e5	o4	n3
	19249185.5		977405.5	37853	4324235		c4	a5	e4	o4	n3
	10936000.6		610352.6667	383307	6872204.667		c4	a3	e3	o3	n2
			20705				c3	a3	e3	o5	n3
1334899.5	1483939		304359.1	1719959	5608		c4	a3	e2	o3	n2
86620.5	6966804.75		351787.8	440592	316892		c5	a4	e3	o3	n3
707949	2841474.5		638657.3333	701722.5	29572831		c4	a5	e1	o3	n1
57382	920251.5		454386	13180032	1349		c4	a5	e4	o4	n2
	2252886		918206.5		3743583		c3	a4	e2	o3	n3

Fig. 1. Merged dataset

3.4 Personality Prediction Module

The third functionality is the personality prediction module. A supervised machine learning model was trained to predict personality traits of a user based on their de-vice's app usage data. As part of the pre-processing, the applications used by all users in the dataset were categorised into 42 distinct categories as recognised by Google Play Store. A Python package by the name 'play-scraper' was used for categorization of the apps. For exploratory data analysis (EDA), graphs were plotted to under-stand the correlation between each of the personality traits and the various app categories.

For every app, there were 2 attributes recorded – total usage time and access count. Using these two attributes a third attribute was derived.

Average usage time = Total usage time/Access counts

For feature selection, two different methods were tested: filtering based and wrapper-based methods. Here, the features being selected were the categories of the apps. Under filtering-based methods, the k-best algorithm using f-values and mutual information gain methods was explored. Under wrapper-based methods, RFE (Re-cursive Feature Elimination) was implemented. As the dataset is relatively smaller, wrapper-based methods gave better accuracy and hence was chosen as the method for feature selection.

Every trait had 6 different sets of best features based on the aggregate values, the aggregate values considered were – mean of total usage time, sum of total usage time, mean of usage counts, sum of usage counts, mean of average usage time which was defined as total usage time divided by the usage counts, sum of average usage time.

After finding the best category – aggregate for each trait, that is the most relevant aggregates for each category, the features were then combined and another round of RFE was performed to find the overall best features for each trait. A graph of accuracy vs number of features was plotted for each trait.

For the classification model, each of the Big 5 traits were assigned 5 labels based on their quintile range. A classification model was then designed for each trait independently. As the features were non-linear, a non-linear random forest was used with a gradient boosting algorithm to improve the accuracy. To find the optimum number of trees for each trait, we iterated through a loop and a graph of accuracy vs number of trees was plotted.

Before training the model, the data was first oversampled using Random Oversampler to balance the classes in order to avoid the bias. After oversampling, the data was then normalised by passing it through the Standard Scaler model as the ranges for each attribute were different. Once the data was normalised, it was then sent through a gradient boosting algorithm with n-number of decision trees to train the model.

Algorithm.

1. Create dataset where users are the rows and application aggregate statistics are columns

   For every user:

   For each app used:

   Extract total usage time

   Extract access counts

   Calculate average usage time using

   Average usage time = Total usage time / Access counts

   Identify category as defined by Google Play Store

2. Using the above dataset, create new dataset where users are the rows and aggregate statistics of the app categories are the columns

   For every user:

   Apps are grouped by their categories

   Within each category, calculate:

   Sum of usage time of all apps in the category

   Sum of access counts of all apps in the category

   Sum of average usage time for all apps in the category

   Mean of usage time of all apps in the category

   Mean of access counts of all apps in the category

Mean of average usage time for all apps in the category

3. The 6 aggregate statistics listed above are the features used to determine the features that are most relevant for each category. 2 methods were used:

Filtering based k-best algorithm

Wrapper based Recursive Feature Elimination (RFE)

As dataset is small, Wrapper based RFE gave better accuracy and thus chosen for feature selection

4. Identify the best feature for each category from the initial round of RFE.

For the second round of RFE, features are combined, to find the best features for each trait.

For each trait:

Plot graph of accuracy vs. number of features

5. Oversample data using Random Oversampler to balance classes.

Normalise data using Standard Scaler model as ranges for attributes were different

6. For each trait:

Classification model is designed as Non-linear random forest with gradient boosting algorithm

Plot graph of accuracy vs. number of trees

4   Results and Discussion

4.1   Exploratory Data Analysis

Exploratory Data Analysis (EDA) was performed with graphs that were plotted for each personality trait against certain categories to understand the categories significance on each trait.

Extraversion.
The metric used for the above analysis was the sum of all the usage time the user spent on all the apps in the given category (Fig. 2).

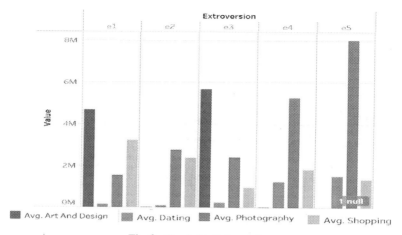

Fig. 2. Graph for Extraversion

From the above graph, it could be inferred that more extraverted people tend to spend more time on Dating, Photography apps. Less extraverted people prefer spending more time on Art and Design and online Shopping related apps.

Social gatherings and events for the week can be recommended for more extra-verted people whereas art-based events and apps can be recommended to less intro-verted people.

Agreeableness

The metric used for the above analysis was the mean of the average time spent on all the apps in a category. Average time is defined by dividing the total usage time of an app by its access counts (Fig. 3).

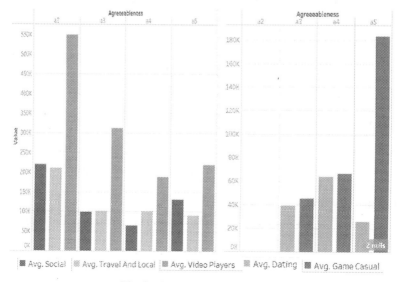

Fig. 3. Graphs for Agreeableness

From the graph below, it could be inferred that more agreeable people on average spend less average time on Social, Travel and Video player apps. More agreeable people prefer spending more time on apps in categories of Game Casual and Dating.

For users who score lower on agreeableness, more frequent suggestions can be made on Travel and Video Player apps, based on the history of their app usage.

Neuroticism

The metric used for the analysis was the mean of counts for the graph on the left and mean of total usage time for the graph on the right (Fig. 4).

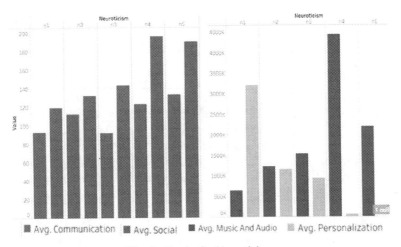

Fig. 4. Graphs for Neuroticism

Apps in categories of Social and Communication are accessed more often by people who show high neuroticism traits. They also prefer to spend more time on Music and Audio apps whereas the people showing lesser neuroticism traits spend more time on Personalization apps.

For users with higher neuroticism traits, themes with soothing colours and ringtones can be set on their smartphones.

Openness

Apps in categories of Art and Design, Entertainment, Food and Drink, are seen to be used by people who are more open and Social apps are used by less open people (Fig. 5).

Users of Food and Drink apps who score high on openness with new restaurant suggestions and for those who score less on openness, restaurants that they have visited in the past can be shown.

Entertainment apps include event ticket booking apps. People who score high on openness can be recommended events different from those they have purchased tickets

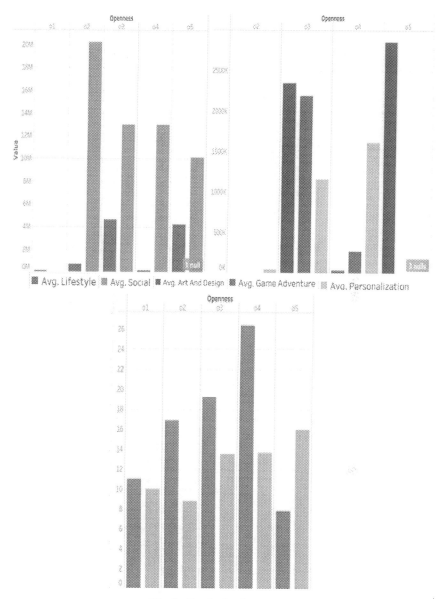

Fig. 5. Graphs for Openness

for in the past whereas people who score low on openness can be recommended events similar to the ones they have purchased tickets for in the past.

Conscientiousness
The metric used for the below analysis was the mean of the average time and mean time that the user spends on all the apps in a category (Fig. 6).

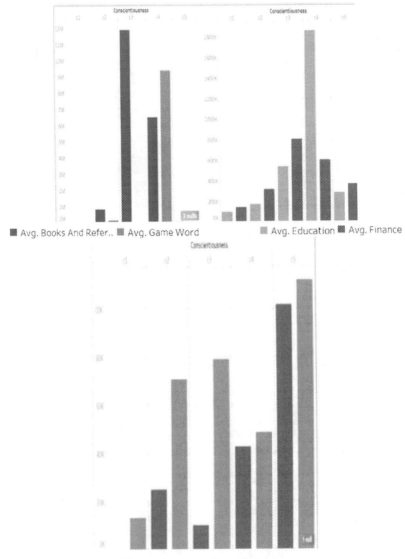

Fig. 6. Graphs for Conscientiousness

It could be inferred that the apps in categories of Education, Finance, News and Magazines, Medical are shown to be used by people who show the most conscientiousness traits.

More content about current affairs and finance can be displayed to these users with higher consciousness levels. For users with lesser conscientiousness, planners can be made based on their calendar and phone usage (Table 2).

Table 2. Results from EDA Graphs.

Trait	Level of Trait	Application Category
Extraverted	Higher	More time on Dating, Photography
Extraverted	Lower	More time on Art & Design, Shopping
Agreeable	Higher	Less time on Social, Travel, Video Player More time on Game Casual, Dating
Neuroticism	Higher	More time on Music, Audio More frequency on Social, Communication
Neuroticism	Lower	More time on Personalization
Openness	Higher	More time on Art & Design, Entertainment, Food and Drink
Openness	Lower	More time on Social apps
Conscientiousness	Higher	More time on Education, Finance, News & Magazines, Medical

4.2 Feature Selection

By plotting a graph between accuracy and number of features for each trait the following observation was noted (Table 3).

Table 3. Number of Features for Each Trait.

Trait	Number of Features
Extraverted	17
Agreeable	14
Neuroticism	34
Openness	24
Conscientiousness	46

For Extraversion the 17 features were found to be – 'Business – mean of counts, Music and audio – mean of count, Communication – sum of counts, Education – sum of counts, Game action – sum of counts, Photography – mean of time, Social – mean of time, Tools – mean of time, Tools, Tools – sum of time, Productivity – mean of average time, House and home – sum of time, Lifestyle – sum of time, Photography – mean of average time, Photography – sum of time, Travel and local – sum of time, Entertainment – mean of average time, Maps and navigation – mean of average time'.

For Agreeableness the 14 important features were found to be – 'Productivity – mean of counts, Communication – sum of counts, Music and Audio – sum of time, Business – mean of average time, Lifestyle – mean of average time, Productivity – mean of average time, Social – mean of average time, Travel and Local – mean of average time, Health and fitness – sum of average time, Lifestyle – sum of average time, News and Magazine – sum of average time, Social – sum of average time, Photography – sum of average time, Tools – sum of average time'.

For Neuroticism the 34 important features were found to be – 'Music and audio – mean of count, Photography – mean of count, Productivity – mean of count', Social – mean of count, Tools – mean of count, Travel and local – mean of count, Video players – mean of count, Art and design – sum of count, Books and reference – sum of count, Business – sum of count, Communication – sum of count, Dating – sum of count, Education – sum of count, Photography – sum of count, Shopping – sum of count, Travel and local – sum of count, Video players – sum of count, Tools – mean of time, Travel and local – mean of time, Food and drink – sum of time, Game action – sum of time, Game adventure – sum of time, Game arcade – sum of time, Game card – sum of time, Lifestyle – sum of time, Medical – sum of time, News and magazines – sum of time, Personalization – sum of time, Business – mean of average time, Finance – mean of average time, Food_and_drink – mean of average time, Game action – sum of time, Game_adventure – sum of time, Game arcade – sum of time, Game card – sum of time, Lifestyle – sum of time, Medical – sum of time, News and magazines – sum of time, Personalization – sum of time, Business – mean of average time, Finance – mean of average time, Food and drink – mean of average time, Social – mean of average time, Video players – mean of average time, Communication – sum of average time'.

For Openness the 24 important features were found to be – 'Lifestyle – mean of counts, Photography – mean of counts, Productivity – mean of counts, Social- mean of counts, Art and Design – sum of counts, Business – sum of counts, Comics – sum of counts, Dating sum of counts, Social – sum of counts, Travel and Local – sum of counts, Video Players – sum of counts, Game Sports – mean of time, Lifestyle-sum of time, Music and Audio – sum of time, Travel and Local – sum of time, Art and design – mean of average time, Communication – mean of average time, Food and Drink – mean of average time, Lifestyle – mean of average time, Music and audio – mean of average time, Travel and Local – sum of time, Art and design – mean of average time, Communication – mean of average time, Finance – sum of average time, Food and drink-mean of average time, Lifestyle – mean of average time, Music and Audio – mean of average time, Business – sum of average time, Communication – sum of average time, Entertainment – sum of average time'.

For Conscientiousness the 46 important features were found to be – 'Music and audio – sum of count, Productivity – sum of count, Travel and local – sum of count, Video players – sum of count, Business – mean of time, Communication – mean of time, Education – mean of time, Entertainment – mean of time, Finance – mean of time, Game action – mean of time, Game racing – mean of time, Health and fitness – mean of time, Lifestyle – mean of time, Medical – mean of time, Photography – mean of time, Social – mean of time, Tools – mean of time, Education – sum of time, Music and audio – sum of time, Business – mean of average time, Medical – mean of average time, Music and audio – mean of average time, Social – mean of average time, Events – sum of average time, Finance – sum of average time, Food and drink – sum of average time, Game action – sum of average time, Game arcade – sum of average time, Game board – sum of average time, Game card – sum of average time, Game Casual – sum of average time, Game educational – sum of average time, Game puzzle – sum of average time, Game sports – sum of average time, Game strategy – sum of average time, Health and fitness – sum of average time, House and home – sum of average time, Lifestyle – sum of average time, Maps and navigation – sum of average time, Medical – sum of average time, Photography – sum of average time, Productivity – sum of average time, Shopping – sum of average time, Social – sum of average time, Sports – sum of average time, Tools – sum of average time'.

4.3 Modelling Accuracies

The modelling accuracies were calculated by correlating the personality traits obtained through smartphone usage statistics with the personality traits calculated from standard personality questionnaires answered by the users (Table 4).

Table 4. Modelling Accuracies.

Trait	Number of Trees	Accuracy
Extraverted	23	72.2%
Agreeable	29	73.9%
Neuroticism	86	85.1%
Openness	45	93.5%
Conscientiousness	90	71.4%

4.4 User Interface

See (Figs. 7, 8 and 9).

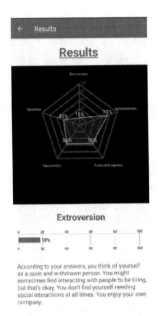

Fig. 7. Personality Test Results

Fig. 8. App Usage Statistics

Fig. 9. Personality Prediction Results

5 Conclusion

On exploring the device usage and settings of various gadgets, the data pertaining to laptops and desktops was found to be inconclusive. Thus, the scope of the problem statement was narrowed down to smartphones alone. As the most affordable and available smartphones today are Android based, such smartphones were the focus of our study.

Application usage statistics data is readily available on the smartphone and can be retrieved with minimal to no data breach which makes it the ideal for use to find the personality traits of the user. On correlating this data to the user's Big 5 Personality traits, significant trends were found. This resulted in successful prediction of the users' personality traits with an accuracy above 70%. This accuracy was calculated by correlating the personality traits obtained through smartphone usage statistics with the personality traits calculated from standard personality questionnaires answered by the users.

This research has potential applications in marketing as it automatically extracts each users' broader behaviours and preferences for personalised experiences. It could also over time replace the conventional questionnaire-based personality tests. This work represents an initial step and substantial research work in this field remains.

6 Future Work

This research project can be extended by collecting the data over longer periods of time, as it could give more accurate temporal representation of users' behaviour. Further, we could expand our dataset to include a more diverse population in terms of age, gender as well as iOS users. The features can be extended to include the age, gender and geographic location of the user for better understanding and prediction. The prediction model would be trained better if a larger sample size is used.

References

1. Stachl, C., et al.: Predicting personality from patterns of behavior collected with smartphones. Proc. Natl. Acad. Sci. **117**(30), 17680–17687 (2020)
2. Peltonen, E., Sharmila, P., Asare, K.O., Visuri, A., Lagerspetz, E., Ferreira, D.: When phones get personal: predicting big five personality traits from application usage. Pervasive Mob. Comput. **69**, 101269 (2020)
3. Chittaranjan, G., Blom, J., Gatica-Perez, D.: Who's who with big-five: analyzing and classifying personality traits with smartphones. In: 2011 15th Annual international symposium on wearable computers, pp. 29–36. IEEE (2011)
4. Xu, R., Frey, R.M., Fleisch, E., Ilic, A.: Understanding the impact of personality traits on mobile app adoption–Insights from a large-scale field study. Comput. Hum. Behav. **62**, 244–256 (2016)
5. Chen, A.: How accurate are personality tests, Scientific American. https://www.scientificam erican.com/article/how-accurate-are-personality-tests. 10 Oct 2018

A Study on the Usability of Handwriting Assistant for Smartphone's Lock Screen

Viktor Zaytsev[1]([✉])(iD), Dmytro Zhelezniakov[1,2](iD), Anastasiia Cherneha[1](iD), and Olga Radyvonenko[1](iD)

[1] Samsung R&D Institute, Kyiv, Ukraine
{v.zaytsev,d.zhelezniak,a.cherneha,o.radyvonenk}@samsung.com
[2] Taras Shevchenko National University of Kyiv, Kyiv, Ukraine

Abstract. Advances in the development of devices with handwritten input, and the emergence of deep learning have led to the rapid development of handwriting recognition applications, but the methods and implications of handwritten interaction on the Lock Screen of the smartphone, taking into account usability, are still not sufficiently considered in existing studies. In this paper, we propose a novel method for the quick processing of handwritten input and delivering results without explicitly starting the presumed application associated with an action. Handwritten input is processed either with or without requiring authorization, depending on the sensitivity of the implied action. The method comprises the initial handwritten input processing to locate and extract textual information, then entity extraction from the recognized text, and device context identification. The extracted entities and the current device context are analyzed to identify the action imposed by the user, to process the input, and to obtain and deliver the results in a single or a few steps. The proposed method is suitable for integration with the first screen of the device, also known as the Lock Screen, but it can also be utilized in applications based on handwriting input. The user study demonstrates that the proposed method accelerates the time to completion (TTC) of the most common actions by 20% compared to traditional input when all the necessary steps are required to be explicitly performed by the user.

Keywords: Digital Ink · Handwriting recognition · Lock Screen · User Study · Usability

1 Introduction

In recent years, mobile phone lock screens have become an important part of human-computer interaction, as they are the first interaction point between users and devices. Research in this area has been ongoing for several years and has aimed to understand the ways in which lock screens can be designed to enhance the user experience, while also considering factors such as usability, security [1], efficiency, user behaviour and preferences [12], and the effectiveness of various lock screen features [11].

© The Author(s), under exclusive license to Springer Nature Switzerland AG 2023
G. Salvendy and J. Wei (Eds.): HCII 2023, LNCS 14052, pp. 106–123, 2023.
https://doi.org/10.1007/978-3-031-35921-7_8

One key area of research has been on the use of personalization and customization on lock screens to increase user engagement [22]. This includes the use of personalized lock screen widgets to display important information such as time, date, notifications, etc. Another research area has focused on the usability and efficiency of lock screens, such as the use of different approaches for unlocking the mobile phone and accessing features. Studies have investigated the impact of an approach used for unlocking design on the speed and accuracy of accessing the functions of mobile phones. The traditional approach to accessing the function after unlocking the smartphone is when the user manually launches an application and enters the data, which meets strict formatting recommendations. Often it leads to multi-step routines to perform simple actions, such as the calculation of mathematical expressions, creating contact, and schedule management. Usually, it can take up to tens of seconds to unlock the screen, find the necessary application, and perform a simple action when the user deals with the habitual device, while up to several minutes on the device with a less known interface. Using these interfaces is sometimes frustrating and annoying [11] for the user and can lead to poor user experience.

At the same time the ubiquity and continued growth of mobile devices equipped with a stylus, and the breakthrough of advanced machine learning algorithms of handwriting recognition, have led to exploring new applications and scenarios for using handwriting input and developing new user interfaces. Previous research has shown that handwriting interfaces are preferred in many domains, especially for learning [14]. Moreover, handwriting can express the main ideas in a more concise and complete way compared to typing [18]. But the area of handwriting interfaces for lock screens is still not sufficiently considered in existing studies.

In this paper, we propose a Handwriting Assistant (HA) that allows the user to perform a set of actions directly from the smartphone's Lock Screen. The intended action is extracted from the handwritten input, thus eliminating the need to input extra information. The main goal of this study is to evaluate the proposed concept of a HA in terms of usability and compare it with other approaches, including a voice assistant and a standard approach, which involves the search and launch of the corresponding application.

2   Related Works

Recent research has advanced various aspects of both handwriting input and screen unlocking in mobile applications. Investigation in handwritten interfaces has focused on the development of advanced machine learning algorithms that can accurately recognize the handwriting of different users in different languages and scripts. Other studies have explored the use of handwritten input for tasks such as text input [26], math equation solving [24,25], and creative expression [10].

Another field of study is related to user interface design and usability. Research aimed at usability studies users' preference for pen-based interfaces for certain types of input data [6], preference for direct-writing interfaces without switching between input boxes [9], and user's request for stylus operation area to cover the whole display [13]. A number of works investigate user perception of recognition errors [3] or interface usability in special scenarios, for example, text entry by children [17], or handwriting for in-vehicle information systems [27].

Modern Lock Screens can show notifications or important information, quickly launch applications, and even manage content. But at the same time, its main function is to authenticate the user. Therefore, the main research focus is on authentication methods such as PINs, stroke-based patterns, signatures [20], biometric methods (fingerprints, face, gaze), and implicit authentication [16] (combination of contextual and behavioral authentication factors). There are well-presented studies that provide comparisons of unlocking methods from different aspects such as usability and security [1,11]. Some studies analyze the user behavior of interacting with a locked screen. In [12], the authors have analyzed contextual antecedents to Lock Screen checks and types of interaction with the locked smartphone. The authors of the paper [2] proposed the concept of interaction with the Lock Screen, in which the user can perform small actions. They showed that about a quarter of all user interaction sessions with the phone are short actions that take less than one minute. Another interface for performing microtasks on the Lock Screen has been introduced in the work [21]. The authors of the work [15] have proposed a method to perform a function from the Lock Screen using handwritten input, where each function is associated with the corresponding handwritten gesture. The "Screen off memo" function introduced a Lock Screen for entering full-fledged handwritten notes [19]. Developing this idea further, in [23] the authors proposed a method for the quick processing of handwritten input and providing results without explicitly starting the presumed application associated with an action. It is this development that formed the basis of this study.

3   Lock Screen with Handwriting Assistant

We present here a concept of a Lock Screen with Handwritten Assistant with a simple interface as a single note-taking canvas that launches when the stylus is ejected from its slot in the smartphone.

The general overview of the proposed approach is shown in Fig. 1. The system operates with a handwritten note, as an input, which is presented as an ordered set of handwritten strokes. The user can input handwritten notes that may include text and other elements such as pictures, sketches, schemes, etc. To separate text elements from other non-text strokes, at the first stage, we perform layout analysis which includes grouping and classification of the input strokes sequence into *text* and *non-text*. At this step, we utilize bi-directional gated recurrent unit neural network architecture and batch processing modes [5]. If the handwritten note does not contain text elements, it will be saved in separate storage since authentication was not performed.

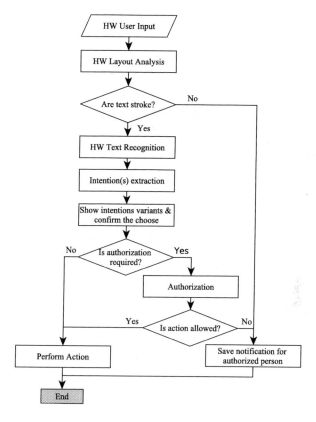

Fig. 1. An overview of the proposed approach.

Handwritten strokes that have been classified as *text* are passed to the second stage with handwritten recognition. The text recognition module is implemented using a BLSTM neural network [7] for the input sequence labelling and Connectionist Temporal Classification as a loss function [8]. In the next step, the recognized text is used to classify the message and extract information. Implementation of this step relies on named entity recognition and pattern templates [4].

Some actions require authentication before changing the user's data. Such authentication could be done in the background while the user writes a note (for example, if face authentication is supported) or implemented as a separate authentication step. Since not all personal devices support a digital pen, we used pre-provisioned prepared devices to perform tasks related to handwriting. Therefore, the branch related to authorization was disabled for this study. Making changes based on the user intent classification is the last step that utilizes the operating system API. An example of the user scenario is shown in Fig. 2.

(a) User's input.   (b)   Automatically   recog- (c) Result of user intent ex-
nized user's intention and ecution.
suggested action.

Fig. 2. Lock Screen Handwriting Assistant.

Owing to the presented approach, a prototype application for a mobile device
with an embedded stylus has been developed in order to perform the experimental study.

4   Experimental Study

Our goal was to answer the following research questions to ensure a deeper
understanding of the demand for the proposed concept of the Lock Screen HA,
as well as convenience compared to other available methods:

1. How effective is solving different tasks with the help of a HA in comparison
   with the standard approach?
2. What are the strengths and weaknesses of the HA on the Lock Screen?
3. What actions are expected to support by the HA?
4. How convenient is the use of the HA compared to voice?
5. What factors and conditions influence the choice of input type: HA, voice
   assistant, or standard approach?

In order to answer these questions we conducted a user study. At the beginning of the session, we asked participants to fill out a baseline (pretest) survey.
After completing the practical session the participants were asked to take part in
a follow-up survey. The questionnaires and tasks were prepared in the Ukrainian
language. The practical part of the study began with a brief description of the HA
but without a detailed explanation of intents structures. If participants could not
guess each intent structure or had some issues with the application, an instructor
was ready to help. The users were asked to accomplish the tasks in three ways:
standard input, voice input, and using the proposed method. Due to the Voice
assistant's limited support of the Ukrainian language, only two subtasks for

Voice input were available. The participants were provided with smartphones equipped with a built-in stylus (Samsung Galaxy S22 Ultra) and an installed application for automatically collecting detailed information about user activity during task completion. To measure TTC for the standard approach, the video screen capture is used.

4.1 Tasks

In terms of user intent, we have identified the most common types of short hand-written notes and the corresponding actions: planned/scheduled events, contacts, shopping memos, simple mathematical expressions, and To-Do lists. It was also found that most of such notes usually contain only meaningful information. For example, contact information is written in a compressed form and contains only the person or organization's name and phone number. Such a notation is usually easy to understand and can be recognized and routed to the appropriate application on the user's device for further processing.

Based on our findings, we prepared the following set of tasks in order to obtain the statistical data:

1. Calculate math expression. An example:

   ```
   The bill in the restaurant for a group of friends was 4198
   UAH (Ukrainian hryvnia), also they decided to tip 450 UAH.
   The total amount was equally divided between five people.
   How much does it cost for each person?
   ```

2. Add a new contact. An example:

   ```
   Add a new contact Viktor Meyer with a phone number
   0986479801
   ```

3. Set an alarm clock. An example:

   ```
   Set an alarm to 7:50
   ```

4. Create a schedule. An example:

   ```
   Create the event 28.01 11:30 Meeting with partners
   ```

5. Set a timer. An example:

   ```
   Set a timer for 2 minutes 10 seconds
   ```

In Fig. 3 an example of the HA task solving (Fig. 3a) and the completed HA task (Fig. 3b) are demonstrated.

 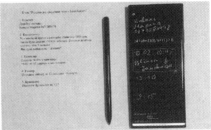

(a) The participant performs the task using (b) Example of the result of the completion
the HA.   of the task using the HA.

Fig. 3. The HA: tasks examples.

4.2 Survey

The baseline survey includes questions about demographics, how often a particular input method is used by the participant and his preferences. The follow-up survey contains questions for subjective assessments for various methods of input in terms of learnability, efficiency, reliability, security, and social comfort. These assessments were collected by offering a set of statements (e.g. "I thought the input method was easy to use"). Participants were invited to express their agreement on a 5-point scale for each statement. In addition, this questionnaire contained open-ended questions to tell us what the participant liked in the proposed method, what was uncomfortable, and what should be added, improved, or refused. At the end of the questionnaire, it was proposed to evaluate different ways of interaction depending on various circumstances (for example: at home, at work, during a meeting, etc.).

5 Evaluation and Results

Overall, 30 people took part in the user study. Questionnaires, standard input and handwritten input tasks were completed by all the participants. Whereas, voice input tasks were completed by 28 participants (one participant refused to perform the voice input task, and one participant could not complete it being offline due to the blackout). In Table 1 demographics of the participants are presented.

5.1 Efficiency

Since time is the most objective measure of efficiency for the input interface and access to the functions of a mobile phone from the point of view of the user, we consider time to completion (TTC) as the main metric of efficiency. For each task, we measured TTC in two variants: total TTC, and TTC of the best attempt. In some cases, a task is not completed in one attempt due to some errors. So, total

Table 1. Participant demographics.

Participants	30	
Age	1	16–19 years
	9	20–29 years
	9	30–39 years
	8	40–49 years
	1	50–59 years
	2	60–69 years
Gender	9	female
	21	male
Occupation	Tech	20
	Non-tech	10

TTC measures the time of all attempts, while the best TTC measures only the last, successful attempt. The main reasons for failed attempts were recognition errors or errors related to interface misunderstanding. The average total TTC for each task is shown in Fig. 4a and the average best TTC is demonstrated in Fig. 4b. The results of the Wilcoxon Signed Rank Test in Table 2 demonstrate a statistically significant difference between completion times of standard and handwritten inputs for each task. As one can see, for the best attempt, the HA is on average more effective than standard input for each task: 21.3% faster for adding a contact, 27.4% faster for a calculator, 47.5% more effective for adding an event to calendar, 60.4% and 53.2% faster for timer and alarm respectively. As for total TTC, the HA is on average still more effective for all tasks except for the calculator. That is mostly due to repetitive recognition errors for some users. Recognition errors mostly contribute to the overhead in total TTC compared to TTC of the best attempt.

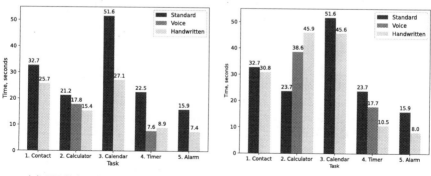

(a) TTC for the best attempt.   (b) Total TTC for all attempts.

Fig. 4. Average time to complete.

Table 2. The Wilcoxon Signed Rank Test resulting z-values and p-values for TTC of the best attempt.

	Handwritten VS Standard		Standard VS Voice		Handwritten VS Voice	
	z	p	z	p	z	p
Contact	−3.1	**0.002**	n/a	n/a	n/a	n/a
Calculator	−3.49	**< 0.001**	−1.59	0.11	−1.93	**0.05**
Calendar	−4.61	**< 0.001**	n/a	n/a	n/a	n/a
Timer	−4.53	**< 0.001**	−4.62	**< 0.001**	−1.07	0.29
Alarm	−4.68	**< 0.001**	n/a	n/a	n/a	n/a

The average TTC for voice assistant is near to the average TTC for handwriting. The Wilcoxon Signed Rank Test shows there is no statistically significant difference between handwriting and voice inputs efficiency for best attempt TTC. But there is a statistically significant difference between voice and standard input in timer-setting task.

5.2 Strengths and Weaknesses

To approach assistant usability from different aspects, we defined its usability through the following criteria: learnability, efficiency, reliability & transparency, security, and social comfort. In the final questionnaire, each criterion was represented by one to three questions. Answer options were provided on the 5-point Likert scale. To obtain scores for each usability criterion, each participant's answers related to certain criteria were averaged. A chart in Fig. 5 displays the distribution of the resulting values, with scores grouped in ranges. Detailed results of the final questionnaire, before aggregating questions to usability criteria, are summarized in Fig. 6.

Most of the participants gave positive answers regarding learnability (25/30), and only one was negative. This result is better than for voice input, but worse than for a standard one. Overall, learnability can be considered as a strength of the HA, although there is a room for improvement, such as adding support for more commands and patterns.

Efficiency. The largest number of positive scores are given to the HA: 21 compared to 17 for standard and 12 for voice. Interestingly, 40% of participants estimated the standard input efficiency as mediocre, although for all participants it was the main and most familiar input method. At the same time, the standard input received the least number of negative scores – only one, compared to four for handwriting and 11 for the voice. Still, we can consider efficiency as a strength.

Reliability and Transparency. Participants are less confident in the reliability & transparency of the HA. Only four people gave the best scores on this criterion. Looking at the detailed questionnaire results in Fig. 6, we can see that the main

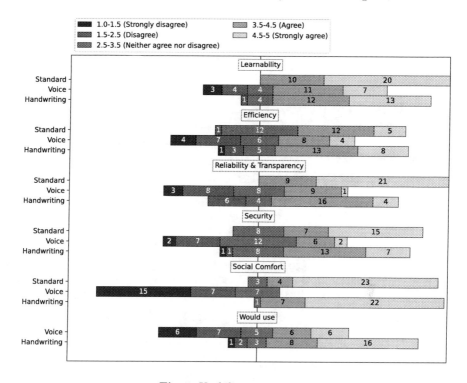

Fig. 5. Usability assessment.

weakness of the HA is recovery from error. Currently, if the result of recognition is incorrect, users have to rewrite the input.

Security. By security, in terms of usability, we mean the subjective perception of the user about how safe to use the given input type or have it enabled on a device. Most of the participants (20 out of 30) positively evaluated the security of the HA, and two participants negatively. The standard method received 22 positive scores and zero negatives. Thus, for some users, the idea of using the HA on the lock screen seems less secure than using standard input. However, the lowest security scores received the voice assistant, with nine negative and only eight positive scores.

Social Comfort. Comfort of use in the presence of other people is the strength for the HA. It received 29 positive scores, negative scores were absent. At the same time, for the voice assistant, this criterion is the main weakness, with 22 negative scores and zero positive scores.

5.3 Expectations

Among the proposed actions to expand the functionality was integration with shopping and to-do lists (for example, adding new items). One of the participants suggested adding a possibility to convert handwritten input to text and instantly

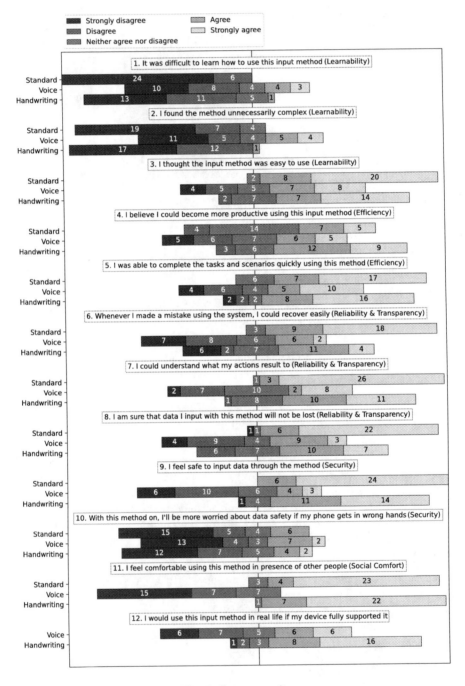

Fig. 6. Survey results.

share it. Another participant proposed adding functionality to send messages in the format 'Recipient: message text'.

5.4   Preference Factors and Conditions

At the beginning of the study, we assumed that the preference for using a lock screen assistant of a certain type may differ depending on the circumstances. So, in the follow-up questionnaire, we asked participants to evaluate from 0 to 10, how likely they would use each input type in certain circumstances: at home, at the workplace, during a work meeting, during the meetings in their personal life (with friends, family, etc.), while walking on the street, in public places (transport, restaurant, etc.), during driving. Using the obtained scores, the Wilcoxon Signed Rank Test was calculated, revealing a statistically significant ($p = 0.05$) difference between handwritten and standard input types only for usage at home and during meetings in their personal life. For these two situations, the average score and the median score are slightly higher for a standard input than for handwritten.

Substantially different from both standard and handwritten inputs is a voice input. The only circumstance where it scored higher is 'driving', for all other cases scores are significantly lower. Means and medians of participants' scores are shown in Table 3. The test results are presented in Table 4.

Table 3. Means and medians for input type in different circumstances preference scores.

	Standard		Voice		Handwritten	
	Mean	Median	Mean	Median	Mean	Median
Home	8.27	9	4.77	5	6.57	8
Workplace	8.53	10	1.0	1	7.53	9
Work Meeting	6.8	8	0.96	1	7.23	7.5
Personal life meeting	8.73	10	2.17	1	7.0	9
Walking outside	7.07	8	4.07	3.5	5.5	6
Public Places	8.47	10	1.3	1	6.47	8
Driving	1.57	1	6.1	7	1.1	1

5.5   Comparison with a Voice Assistant

As we can see from the results, the effectiveness of a voice assistant for the best attempt is comparable with the HA. However, the users rating has more negative scores for each criterion of the usability. The main weakness of voice assistants is social comfort. Analyzing the factors of preferences, we can also see the main strength of voice assistants – the ability to use them during driving. So, in the current state of the language support by voice assistants, the HA is preferred in most cases.

Table 4. The Wilcoxon Signed Rank Test resulting z-values and p-values for input type preference in different circumstances.

	Handwritten VS Standard		Standard VS Voice		Handwritten VS Voice	
	z	p	z	p	z	p
Home	-2.14	**0.032**	-2.98	**0.003**	-2.2	**0.027**
Workplace	-1.33	0.183	-4.72	**< 0.001**	-4.57	**< 0.001**
Work Meeting	-0.37	0.707	-4.56	**< 0.001**	-4.63	**< 0.001**
Personal life meeting	-2.09	**0.036**	-4.73	**< 0.001**	-4.38	**< 0.001**
Walking outside	-1.69	0.090	-2.5	**0.012**	-1.37	0.172
Public Places	-1.95	0.051	-4.8	**< 0.001**	-4.3	**< 0.001**
Driving	-1.73	0.084	-3.7	**< 0.001**	-4.3	**< 0.001**

5.6   Other Findings

We found that in general, TTC correlates with age. In Fig. 7a and Fig. 7b points distributions are shown with regression lines. For standard input, the Pearson correlation coefficient for age and total TTC is $\rho_{Age,TTC} = 0.60(p = 0.0005)$, and for age and the best TTC is $\rho_{Age,TTC} = 0.64(p = 0.0002)$. For handwritten input, the correlation is much weaker with $\rho_{Age,TTC} = 0.01(p = 0.94)$ for total TTC and as $\rho_{Age,TTC} = 0.29(p = 0.13)$ for the TTC of best attempt. So, it can be noted that the effectiveness of handwritten input is more consistent through different age groups.

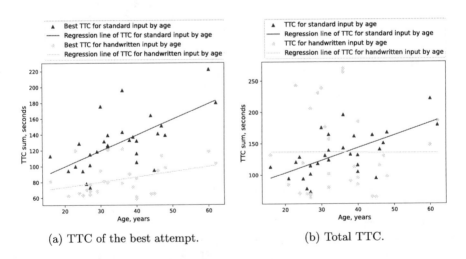

(a) TTC of the best attempt.   (b) Total TTC.

Fig. 7. Time to complete by age.

6   Users Feedback and Discussion

The presentation of our findings is focused on the practical matters of the HA concept for the lock screen. In this section, we move on to reflect on what the main advantages and disadvantages of this concept are, what can be improved, what are the limitations of the HA, and what additional use cases can be proposed. This analysis is based both in the opinion of users, which is reflected in answers to open-ended questions, and in our observations of the learning process and the performance of task.

Most of the participants noted that the proposed method provides a faster input method compared to the use of standard applications. The second main advantage that many participants highlighted is the concept of unified interface. However, the analysis of how the participants tried to use the system before training, and the mistakes made during the task completion are of the greatest interest, since they show opportunities for improving the proposed concept and directions for further research. We also believe that the suggestions or difficulties faced by individual participants are the most valuable information, since most often users cannot formulate a problem until they encounter it.

Let's consider some aspects that were discovered at the first phase when the concept of the HA was presented to the participant, but the training has not yet taken place. Nine participants tried to work with the HA similarly to the interaction with a voice assistant, when it is necessary to explicitly state what should be done. For example, the user wrote *"Create a new contact with the name ... and phone number ..."*. Three more participants tried to portray the desired action in the form of a sketch. For example, a participant drew an hourglass icon next to the time to complete the task of setting the timer (Fig. 8a). Also, participants often tried to set the date and time using the names of months or days of the week. Or they used a non-standard delimiter between the date and time. One participant tried to use the 12-hour clock time convention, which is not common in our country. Another participant specified a type of phone number (such as work, home) when creating a contact, which led to an incorrect name definition. Four participants used 2D mathematical notation to solve a calculation problem (Fig. 8b). Some users were embarrassed by the pop-up frame with the proposed action that appeared when they were distracted for some time and did not finish writing.

At the second stage, we told each participant how to write in order to perform the required action. Despite the training, some participants were still used the incorrect delimiters between parts of the date and time. This is easy to explain with a habit. However, most often, errors occurred at the recognition stage. Almost all participants who faced such errors noted this in the follow-up survey. Most often, these were seemingly minor errors, but they led to the inability to determine the intention or process it correctly. Several cases were associated with incorrect spacing between words. Often the participants tried to fit the text in one row, which resulted in very sloppy writing or some letters being written on top of others. Another type of recognition error is associated with writing of delayed characters or strokes when the user returns to the already written words and adds something. A detailed consideration of all errors associated with the recognition stage is beyond the scope of this article. Although, it should be notes that the accuracy of recognition is a key factor that affects the usability of the proposed HA concept.

Respondents in the follow-up survey noted a small number of supported actions as shortcomings. Participants also noted the need to improve the interface for faster and more convenient handwriting editing. Another wish was the possibility of gluing text written with hyphenation and supporting multi-line mathematical expressions. The fact is that the phone screen is small, and this leads to the need to use hyphenation in words (Fig. 8c). However, the system interpreted instances of the hyphenated word as two separate words.

 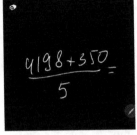 

(a) Example of the input with a sketch to specify the desired action.   (b) Example of math expression in 2D notation.   (c) Example of input with hyphenation.

Fig. 8. Examples of handwriting input.

Two participants noted the possible ambiguity of the system behavior or lack of feedback in some cases. So they raised the questions: *"What happens if a contact with that name or phone number already exists?"* or *"What happens if I already have another event scheduled for this time?"*.

One participant noted that writing with a stylus is not as familiar for him as writing with a regular pen. Another participant said that he does not like to write by hand and prefers typing.

A couple of participants expressed their thoughts on the possibility of using the HA on other devices or in other applications. One of the proposed options was integration with a Family Hub (smart fridge touch panel). One participant suggested that working with timers, reminders, and shopping lists would be in demand. Another participant indicated that he often uses note-taking applications (such as Samsung Notes, Google Keep, GoodNotes, etc.), and the HA can be useful there.

In general, the participants positively assessed the proposed concept of the HA. Some of the mentioned shortcomings can be corrected relatively easily by refining the application. Examples of these improvements include support for a wide range of date and time formats, recovery of text written with hyphens, and support for multi-line mathematical expressions. However, some elements require more significant refinement at the architecture level and user interface. So, at the architecture level, it is necessary to provide the ability to recognize such elements as sketches and mathematical expressions in 2D notation. At the level of the user interface, it is necessary to provide feedback in order to resolve certain ambiguities.

7   Limitations

The results presented in this article are limited in several ways. Firstly, due to the complexity of data collection, all our participants are from the same city. However, we tried to attract as many people with different occupations as possible. As a result, only six people had a personal mobile phone with a stylus and constantly used handwriting on their phones in their usual life. The rest of the participants either never used the stylus before or used it only a couple of times. Therefore, subjective views on interaction with the HA may differ for users who are not represented in our survey.

It would also be very desirable to test in real conditions, so that the participants could use the proposed HA for a long period of time. However, to do this it would be necessary that all participants have phones with a stylus. Because of this, user ratings of usability, efficiency, safety, and others are based on usage over a short period.

The next important limitation is a comparison with a voice assistant. Most participants do not use a voice assistant at all or use it very rarely. The main reasons were indicated by the majority of the participants, are small functionality, limited support for the Ukrainian language, and recognition errors. Only two people said that they regularly use the voice assistant. It should be noted that the main function that is used in voice interaction is making calls. Thereby, the comparison results with the voice assistant may differ significantly depending on the language.

Another important point is to use only one type of device while collecting data for the HA. Expanding the list of devices (for example, smart watches, tablets, interactive panels) may open up new requirements or limitations as well as new opportunities.

8   Conclusion and Future Work

In this work, we presented and studied a new method for inputting and processing frequent commands using short handwritten notes on the Lock Screen.

The study involved 30 people who examined user experience in aspects such as learnability, efficiency, reliability, security, and social comfort. Based on a user study, it can be argued that this approach provides TTC at least 20% faster than the standard method. In addition, the participants highly appreciated the aspects associated with social comfort. However, participants gave low marks for reliability and transparency. This is mainly due to the lacking support for error correction and insufficient feedback. Despite the existing shortcomings, the participants expressed their readiness to use this method of interaction, subject to improving the quality of recognition and expanding the functionality. They also offered several options for expanding functionality and indicated possible integration into other devices and applications.

Our further research is aimed at finding solutions to overcome the identified shortcomings, improve the recognition accuracy and take steps in the direction of the explainable AI, and apply the improved HA to other devices and applications.

References

1. Andriotis, P., Oikonomou, G., Mylonas, A., Tryfonas, T.: A study on usability and security features of the android pattern lock screen. Inf. Comput. Secur. **24**(1), 53–72 (2016)
2. Banovic, N., Brant, C., Mankoff, J., Dey, A.: ProactiveTasks: the short of mobile device use sessions. In: Proceedings of the 16th International Conference on Human-Computer Interaction with Mobile Devices & Services, pp. 243–252 (2014)
3. Bott, J.N., Laviola Jr, J.J.: The WOZ recognizer: a wizard of Oz sketch recognition system. ACM Trans. Interact. Intell. Syst. **5**, 1–38 (2015)
4. Cooper, R., Ali, S., Bi, C.: Extracting information from short messages. In: Montoyo, A., Muñoz, R., Métais, E. (eds.) NLDB 2005. LNCS, vol. 3513, pp. 388–391. Springer, Heidelberg (2005). https://doi.org/10.1007/11428817_44
5. Degtyarenko, I., et al.: Hierarchical recurrent neural network for handwritten strokes classification. In: ICASSP 2021–2021 IEEE International Conference on Acoustics, Speech and Signal Processing (ICASSP), pp. 2865–2869 (2021)
6. Forsberg, A.S., Bragdon, A., Jr., J.J.L., Raghupathy, S., Zeleznik, R.C.: An empirical study in pen-centric user interfaces: diagramming. In: Alvarado, C., Cani, M.P. (eds.) Eurographics Workshop on Sketch-Based Interfaces and Modeling. The Eurographics Association (2008)
7. Frinken, V., Uchida, S.: Deep BLSTM neural networks for unconstrained continuous handwritten text recognition. In: 2015 13th International Conference on Document Analysis and Recognition (ICDAR), pp. 911–915. IEEE (2015)
8. Graves, A., Fernández, S., Gomez, F., Schmidhuber, J.: Connectionist temporal classification: labelling unsegmented sequence data with recurrent neural networks. In: Proceedings of the 23rd International Conference on Machine learning, pp. 369–376 (2006)
9. Gu, J., Lee, G.: Towards more direct text editing with handwriting interfaces. Int. J. Hum.-Comput. Interact. **39**(1), 233–248 (2023)
10. Ha, D., Eck, D.: A neural representation of sketch drawings. In: International Conference on Learning Representations (2018)
11. Harbach, M., De Luca, A., Egelman, S.: The anatomy of smartphone unlocking: a field study of android lock screens. In: Proceedings of the 2016 CHI Conference on Human Factors in Computing Systems, pp. 4806–4817 (2016)
12. Heitmayer, M.: "It's Like Being Gone For A Second": using subjective evidence-based ethnography to understand locked smartphone use among young adults. In: Proceedings of the 23rd International Conference on Mobile Human-Computer Interaction. MobileHCI 2021, Association for Computing Machinery, New York, NY, USA (2021). https://doi.org/10.1145/3447526.3472026

13. Hsu, Y.-H., Chen, C.-H.: Usability study on the user interface design of tablet note-taking applications. In: Stephanidis, C., Antona, M., Ntoa, S. (eds.) HCII 2021. CCIS, vol. 1419, pp. 423–430. Springer, Cham (2021). https://doi.org/10.1007/978-3-030-78635-9_55

14. Ihara, A.S., Nakajima, K., Kake, A., Ishimaru, K., Osugi, K., Naruse, Y.: Advantage of handwriting over typing on learning words: evidence from an N400 event-related potential index. Front. Hum. Neurosci. **15**, 679191 (2021)

15. Kim, S.H., Kwon, M.S., Kim, D.H., Lee, D.H., Hwang, S.t.: Apparatus and method for executing functions related to handwritten user input on lock screen. Google Patents, 05 March 2015. https://patents.google.com/patent/US20150062041A1/en, US Patent 0062041

16. Koushki, M.M., Obada-Obieh, B., Huh, J.H., Beznosov, K.: Is implicit authentication on smartphones really popular? On android users' perception of "smart lock for android". In: 22nd International Conference on Human-Computer Interaction with Mobile Devices and Services, pp. 1–17 (2020)

17. Read, J.C.: A study of the usability of handwriting recognition for text entry by children. Interact. Comput. **19**(1), 57–69 (2006)

18. Roschelle, J., Tatar, D., Chaudhury, S.R., Dimitriadis, Y., Patton, C., DiGiano, C.: Ink, improvisation, and interactive engagement: learning with tablets. Computer **40**(9), 42–48 (2007)

19. Samsung: Use Screen off memo on your Galaxy Note. https://www.samsung.com/us/support/answer/ANS00080345/. Accessed 07 Feb 2023

20. Tolosana, R., Vera-Rodriguez, R., Fierrez, J., Ortega-Garcia, J.: DeepSign: deep on-line signature verification. IEEE Trans. Biometrics Behav. Identity Sci. **3**(2), 229–239 (2021)

21. Truong, K.N., Shihipar, T., Wigdor, D.J.: Slide to X: unlocking the potential of smartphone unlocking. In: Proceedings of the SIGCHI Conference on Human Factors in Computing Systems, pp. 3635–3644 (2014)

22. Wohllebe, A., Adler, M.R., Podruzsik, S.: Influence of design elements of mobile push notifications on mobile app user interactions. Int. J. Interact. Mob. Technol. **15**(15), 35–46 (2021)

23. Zaytsev, V., Zhelezniakov, D., Hirilishena, L.: Electronic device for performing operation on basis of handwriting input, and method for operating same. World Intellectual Property Organization, 02 September 2021. https://patentscope.wipo.int/search/en/detail.jsf?docId=WO2021172648. WO2021172648

24. Zhelezniakov, D., Cherneha, A., Zaytsev, V., Ignatova, T., Radyvonenko, O., Yakovchuk, O.: Evaluating new requirements to pen-centric intelligent user interface based on end-to-end mathematical expressions recognition. In: Proceedings of the ACM International Conference on Intelligent User Interfaces, pp. 212–220 (2020)

25. Zhelezniakov, D., Zaytsev, V., Radyvonenko, O.: Acceleration of online recognition of 2D sequences using deep bidirectional LSTM and dynamic programming. In: Rojas, I., Joya, G., Catala, A. (eds.) IWANN 2019. LNCS, vol. 11507, pp. 438–449. Springer, Cham (2019). https://doi.org/10.1007/978-3-030-20518-8_37

26. Zhelezniakov, D., Zaytsev, V., Radyvonenko, O., Yakishyn, Y.: InteractivePaper: minimalism in document editing UI through the handwriting prism. In: The Adjunct Publication of the 32nd Annual ACM Symposium on User Interface Software and Technology, pp. 13–15 (2019)

27. Zhong, Q., Guo, G., Zhi, J.: Chinese handwriting while driving: effects of handwritten box size on in-vehicle information systems usability and driver distraction. Traffic Inj. Prev. **24**, 1–6 (2022)

Design and Evaluation of Voice User Interfaces and Conversational AI

Exploring the Mobile Usability of Argumentative Dialogue Systems for Opinion Building

Annalena Aicher[1]([⊠])(ID), Stefan Hillmann[2](ID), Sebastian Möller[2](ID), Wolfgang Minker[1](ID), and Stefan Ultes[3](ID)

[1] Institute of Communications Engineering, Ulm University, Albert-Einstein-Allee 43, 89081 Ulm, Germany
{annalena.aicher,wolfgang.minker}@uni-ulm.de
[2] Quality and Usability Lab, TU Berlin, Ernst-Reuter-Platz 7, 10587 Berlin, Germany
{stefan.hillmann,sebastian.moller}@tu-berlin.de
[3] Language Generation and Dialogue Systems, University of Bamberg, An der Weberei 5, 96047 Bamberg, Germany
stefan.ultes@uni-bamberg.de

Abstract. Nowadays speech-driven interfaces such as mobile digital assistants and chatbots can support collaborative information seeking and are becoming increasingly commonplace. Especially, mobile dialogue assistants offer innovative approaches to deliver and access information and thus, display a promising approach to assist humans in their opinion building process. Still, due to the complexity of argumentative tasks mobile argumentative speech interfaces are still very scarce. Hence, the effect of such interfaces on a user's opinion building process is quite unexplored. In this paper, we investigate the influence of such interfaces on the interest and opinion building process of users. Both categories Therefore we introduce two (I/O) modalities (menu/speech) of the argumentative dialog system (ADS) BEA ("Building Engaging Argumentation" [2]) which enables the user to scrutinize arguments on both sides of a controversial topic. In particular, we reflect on the influence and advantages of a spoken hands-free versus a clickable drop-down menu-based ADS with regard to "mobile" dialog systems use cases. Therefore the users' expectations and experiences in a self-assessment questionnaire are evaluated and discussed in comparison to our user interest and opinion model.

Keywords: Preference Modeling · Interest Modeling · Human-Computer Interaction · Spoken Dialogue Systems · Cooperative Argumentative Dialogue Systems

1 Introduction

Conversations are a natural way for people to exchange different points of view and form opinions. However, most common virtual agents are only able to conduct simple

This work has been funded by the DFG within the project "BEA - Building Engaging Argumentation", Grant no. 313723125, as part of the Priority Program "Robust Argumentation Machines (RATIO)" (SPP-1999).

G. Salvendy and J. Wei (Eds.): HCII 2023, LNCS 14052, pp. 127–143, 2023.
https://doi.org/10.1007/978-3-031-35921-7_9

conversations, such as food orders or hotel bookings. Usually, they are unsuitable for more complex and sophisticated conversations [43]. In particular, dialog systems that can exchange arguments and converse with humans in natural language are still a major challenge in artificial intelligence.

The goal of this paper is to evaluate the mobile usability of an artificial argumentation system in interaction with humans by comparing two different interaction modes. In contrast to persuasion systems, our interaction aims not to persuade the user but to cooperatively explore the pro and con arguments of a given topic.

Complex tasks like argumentation require flexible natural language understanding (NLU), argumentative dialogue structures, and commonsense knowledge integration. The speech-driven argumentative dialog system (ADS) we introduce in this paper combines these components and enables the user to scrutinize arguments on both sides of a controversial topic. By adopting the approach of Aicher et al. [2] our ADS aims to cooperatively engage the user to explore arguments in natural language in order to support a critically reflected opinion-building process.

In order to evaluate the usability of our ADS for this aim, we compare two configurations of our system, which only differ in their input/output (I/O) modality. In the speech system, the user's spoken utterances are processed and answered in natural language, whereas in the menu system, the input is via mouse click and the corresponding system answer is displayed on the system's GUI. We investigate the impact of these different I/O modalities in an extended user study with 202 participants. Especially as the speech-driven version displays a preliminary mobile, hands-free interaction system, we analyse its impact on the user interest and opinion. Therefore, to continuously track the user interest the users self-rated their interest on a 5-point Likert scale before, during, and after the interaction. Likewise, the users self-rated their opinion on the topic of the discussion before and after the interaction and were able to state their opinion by giving explicit feedback during the interaction. This feedback in form of a preference/rejection of a currently presented argument was mapped onto the user's opinion on the overall topic considering weighted Bipolar Argumentation Graphs (wBAGs) [3,4]. Thereby changes in the user's opinion could be detected without explicitly asking and lets the user take the initiative to express their current opinion, indicating a certain engagement in the discussion.

The results show that our ADS in both modalities has a significant influence on both "categories", user interest and opinion, giving also an insight in the change of both aspects during the interaction.

The remainder of the paper is as follows: Sect. 2 gives an overview of related work and Sect. 3 describes the architecture of our ADS, the respective dialogue model, and framework and opinion preference model. Section 4 describes the experimental setting of the online user study and the results of the study are presented and discussed in Sect. 5. We close with a conclusion and a brief discussion of future work in Sect. 6.

2   Related Work

In the following, a short overview of existing literature is given on the main aspects of the herein presented work, namely argumentative/mobile Dialogue Systems, Opinion modeling based on user preferences, and methods to determine the user's interest.

2.1 Argumentative/Mobile Dialogue Systems

Unlike most approaches to human-machine argumentation, we pursue a cooperative exchange of arguments. Thus, our system does not try to persuade or win a debate against the user and does not model the interaction in a competitive scenario. In contrast, Slonim et al. [44] use a classical debating setting. Their IBM Debater is an autonomous debating system that can engage in a competitive debate with humans via natural language. Another speech-based approach was introduced by Rosenfeld and Kraus [42], which based on weighted Bipolar Argumentation Frameworks. Arguing chatbots such as Debbie [38] and Dave [25] interact via text with the user. A menu-based framework that incorporates the beliefs and concerns of the opponent was also presented by Hadoux and Hunter [21]. In the same line, Chalaguine and Hunter [13] used a previously crowd-sourced argument graph and considered the concerns of the user to persuade them. A persuasive prototype chatbot is introduced by Chalaguine and Hunter [12] to convince users to vaccinate against COVID-19 using computational models of argument. Furthermore, Fazzinga et al. [18] discuss an approach towards a dialogue system architecture using argumentative concepts to perform reasoning to provide answers consistent with the user input.

In contrast to all aforementioned ADS we aim for system that cooperatively engages the users to explore arguments and state their preferences in natural language. Therefore a menu-based argumentative dialogue system introduced by Aicher et al. [2] was modified and extended. It provides a suitable basis as it engages in a deliberative dialogue with a human user providing all con and pro aspects to a given argument.

With regard to mobile dialogue systems many applications are focused rule-based approaches [39] to assist a user, e.g. responding to queries or helping in easy tasks. Sonntag et al. [46] demonstrated how the speech-based annotation system "RadSpeech" can be used for radiology images with the help of an ontology-based knowledge representation. Furthermore, Johnston et al. [24] describe a multimodal application MATCH (Multimodal Access To City Help) tailored to provide a mobile multimodal speech-pen interface for restaurant and sub-way information for New York City. Similarly, MUMS (Multimodal Route Navigation System) Hurtig [23] allows users of a mobile device to present public transportation route queries with any preferred combination of speech and pen input. Furthermore, Tsourakis [49] extended the open source platform "Regulus" which supports the construction of rule-based medium-vocabulary spoken dialogue applications (used e.g. in a calendar application, a medical speech translator and a second language learning system) to the mobile area. Another architecture named "Asgard" is presented by Liu et al. [26] which shall support the expert-free development of multilingual dialogue systems and seamless deployment to mobile platforms.

2.2 Opinion Modelling Based on User Preferences

Our approach to model the user opinion on the discussed topic via explicit feedback (preference utterances of the user) is based on wBAGs [3,4,7,10,37]. In this context Amgoud et al. [5] discuss how to compute and justify a preferred decision choice considering the strength of arguments. Carenini and Moore [11] devised and implemented an evaluation framework in which the effectiveness of evaluative arguments can be measured with real users. Other approaches handle conflicting user preference within arguments in Ambient Intelligence environments e.g. smart homes [29]. Exemplary they use preference criteria to make decisions based on inhabitants' preferences on lighting, healthy eating, and leisure.

The collection and modelling of user preferences, which are either explicitly expressed, e.g., as ratings for products, or are inferred by interpreting user actions [40], are crucial for decision support [30] and recommender systems. Most decision making support systems [6,41] as well as recommender systems [27] are clearly focused on the application concerning specific items, like, e.g., movie recommendations [9]. Thus, most existing research in this area is based purely on quantitative aspects such as indices of popularity or measures of similarity between items or users. However, those systems are focused on quantitative decision support problems only and do not involve an immediate user interaction via dialogue. In contrast, the herein discussed approach includes a domain-independent opinion model that is developed during the active involvement of the user via dialogue which enables us to directly access the user's preferences and opinions. Furthermore, we do not aim for a decision or recommendation but only keep track and analyze the user's current opinion and respective changes.

2.3   Methods to Determine User Interest

To provide personalized applications that fit user needs, it is common to build user profiles, e.g., from heterogeneous information associated with an individual user or a group of users showing similar interests [16,19,48]. In order to determine the interest of a single user, existing research distinguishes between explicit and implicit user feedback [19]. For example, Amazon.com uses customer history records to recommend books, and the movie streaming provider Netflix recommends movies to different users according to their individual browsing and watching records, as well as explicit ratings of seen movies/TV shows [22,40]. In general, two types of filtering mechanisms can be distinguished based on explicit user ratings regarding recommender systems. First, collaborative filters [15,20,32] which use the user-user similarity principle stating that if a user highly rated an item, similar users would probably highly rate that item. Second, content-based filters [33,45] which recommend items based on the item-item similarity principle stating that if users highly rated an item, they would highly rate similar items.

Commonly used in e-commerce [14], most research deals with user interest in website content, based on the browsing history (e.g., [34,54]). Yi et al. [52] correlate user interest with the user's browsing time on webpages and the length of their content. Furthermore, Zeng et al. [53] captures temporal aspects of user interests in online conversation recommendation.

The scarce existing research on user interest in dialogue systems depends on explicit user feedback, likewise to aforementioned approaches in other research areas. For example, Rach et al. [36] asked users to evaluate dialogue content during an ongoing conversation[1]. In contrast to their binary approach we integrated an explicit interest rating on a 5-point Likert scale after every turn of the interaction. Thus, specific content-related interest and also rather general interest of the user in the interaction is continuously tracked, as well as a possible loss of one or another.

---

[1] Rating categories: (not) interesting, (not) convincing, (not) comprehensible and (not) related.

3   System Framework and Architecture

In the following, the architecture of our ADS is outlined. After describing the dialogue framework and model, the interface and NLG/NLU architecture are introduced.

3.1   Dialogue Framework and Model

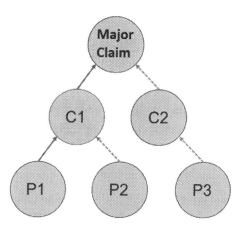

Fig. 1. Visualization of argument tree structure. The major claim is the root node, which is supported by the claim C2 (green dotted arrows) and attacked by claim C1 (red arrows). The respective leaf nodes are the premises P1, P2 and P3. (Color figure online)

In order to be able to combine the presented system with existing argument mining approaches to ensure the flexibility of the system in view of discussed topics, we follow the argument annotation scheme introduced by Stab and Gurevych [47]. It distinguishes three different types of components (Major Claim, Claim, Premise), which are structured in the form of bipolar argumentation trees as depicted in Fig. 1. The overall topic of the debate is formulated as the *Major Claim* Φ_0 representing the root node in the graph. *Claims* (C1 and C2 in Fig. 1) on the other hand are assertions that formulate a certain opinion targeting the *Major Claim* but still need to be justified by further arguments, *premises* (P1 and P2) respectively. We consider two relations between these argument components (nodes), *support* (green arrows), or *attack* (red arrows). Each component apart from the Major Claim Φ_0 (which has no relation) has exactly one unique relation to another component. This leads to a non-cyclic tree structure, where each parent node (C1 and C2) is supported or attacked by its child nodes. If no child nodes exist, the node is a leaf (e.g. P1, P2, and P3) and marks the end of a branch.

The interaction between the system and the user is separated in turns, consisting of a user action and the corresponding answer of the system. Table 1 shows the 13 possible actions (moves) the user is able to choose from. In general, we distinguish three main types of moves: preference moves, information-seeking moves, and others (navigation moves, status quo moves, exit). The determiners show which moves are available depending on the position of the current argument φ_i (root/parent/leaf node).

Table 1. Description of the thirteen moves with corresponding determiners.

Move	Description	Determiners
$why_{pro}(\varphi_i)$	Ask for a pro argument on current φ_i	If supporting child exists
$why_{con}(\varphi_i)$	Ask for a con argument on current φ_i	If attacking child node exists
$level_{up}$	Returns to previous φ	Except for $\varphi_i \neq \Phi_0$
$jump\_to(\varphi_i)$	Jump to φ_i	
$prefer(\varphi_i)$	Feedback to prefer φ_i	Except for $\varphi_i \neq \Phi_0$
$prefer(\varphi_i > \varphi_j)$	Feedback to prefer φ_i over φ_j	If siblings of φ_i are preferred
$reject(\varphi_i)$	Feedback to reject φ_i	Except for $\varphi_i \neq \Phi_0$
$indifferent(\varphi_i)$	Feedback to be indifferent about φ_i	Except for $\varphi_i \neq \Phi_0$
$stance(\varphi_i)$	Ask for stance on current φ_i	
$stance(\Phi_0)$	Ask for stance on current φ_i	
$number_{visited}$	Ask for number of heard arguments	
$moves_{available}(\varphi_i)$	Ask for available moves depending on φ_i	Speech I/O setting
$exit$	End conversation	$number_{visited_i} = 10$

We use explicit user feedback ($prefer(\varphi_i)$, $indifferent(\varphi_i)$, $reject(\varphi_i)$) to estimate the (overall) preference considering wBAGs [3,4], which is explained in more detail in Subsect. 3.2.

In the herein presented study, a sample debate on the topic *Marriage is an outdated institution* is chosen [35] is used. It serves as a knowledge base for the arguments and is taken from the *Debatabase*[2] website. It consists of a total of 72 argument components (1 Major Claim, 10 Claims, and 61 Premises) and their corresponding relations are encoded in an OWL ontology [8] for further use. Due to the generality of the annotation scheme, the system is not restricted to the herein-considered data. In general, every argument structure that can be mapped into the applied scheme can be processed by the system.

3.2 Opinion Preference Model

We determine the user opinion by utilizing wBAGs in which a *weight* is assigned to each argument. Weighted Bipolar Argumentation Graphs are graphs whose arguments have basic weights and may be supported and attacked by each other [4]. Therefore, a change in the weights will lead to an iterative update of the graph structure. We overtake their

---

[2] https://idebate.org/debatabase (last accessed 23th June 2021). Material reproduced from www. iedebate.org with the permission of the International Debating Education Association. Copyright © 2005 International Debate Education Association. All Rights Reserved.

approach to determine the *strength* of an argument from its weight and the strength of its attackers and supporters. If the user states a preference/indifference/rejection towards argument i, its weights are updated such that:

$$\text{preference:} \quad \omega_i = \omega_{i,\max} + \frac{n_v}{n_a}\left(1 - \omega_{i,\max}\right) \tag{1}$$

$$\text{rejection:} \quad \omega_i = 0 \tag{2}$$

$$\text{indifference:} \quad \omega_i = 0.5 \tag{3}$$

where $\omega_{i,\max}$ denotes the maximum strength of all siblings of argument i. n_v describes the number of sibling arguments of argument i which have already been presented to the user and n_a denotes the total number of all sibling arguments. According to Wilcock and Jokinen [50], in scenarios that do not adhere to a clear structure regarding speaking time and turn-taking (like debates), extensive utterances presented by synthetic speech are hard to follow and understand. To prevent the user from being overwhelmed by the amount of information, in contrast to Aicher et al. [2], we introduce the available arguments incrementally depending on the user's request. Thus, the user can state their preference[3] before all sibling arguments have been presented. The preference update takes into account how many sibling arguments have already been heard in relation to the ones available. The nodes are updated recursively until the root node is reached.

3.3 Interface and NLU Framework

The system's graphical user interface (GUI) is illustrated in Fig. 2. The interface can either provide a drop-down menu or speech input as needed. In the drop-down system users can choose their action by clicking, whereas in the speech system, an NLU framework based upon the one introduced by Abro et al. [1] processes the spoken user utterance. This input is captured with a browser-based audio recording that is further processed by the `Python` library `SpeechRecognition`[4] using the Google Speech Recognition API. Its intent classifier uses the BERT Transformer Encoder presented by Devlin et al. [17] and a bidirectional LSTM classifier. The system-specific intents are trained with a set of sample utterances from a previous user study. After a user intent is recognized, the system response is presented using the speech synthesis provided by Google Web Speech API.

In the speech-based system, instead of the drop-down menu displayed in Fig. 2, a button with the label "Start Talking" is shown. The button is pressed to start and stop the speech recording. Except for this difference, both systems share the same architecture. The visualization of the dialogue history shows the system's responses left-aligned and the corresponding user moves right-aligned (see Fig. 2). A progress bar above the dialogue history shows the number of arguments that were already discussed and how many are still unknown to the user at each stage of the interaction. This provides a visual cue of the length of the ongoing conversation to the user. Furthermore, on the left side, the sub-graph of the bipolar argument tree structure (with the displayed claim as root)

---

[3] Here preference denotes the following options: preference, indifference and rejection.
[4] https://pypi.org/project/SpeechRecognition/, last accessed 17.02.2022.

is shown. The current position (i.e., argument) is displayed with a white node outlined with a green line. Already-heard arguments are shown in green and skipped arguments in red. Grey nodes are still unheard.

The natural language generation is based on the original textual representation of the argument components. The annotated sentences form stand-alone utterances serving as a template for the respective system response. Additionally, a list of natural language representations for each type of system move was defined. During the generation of the utterances, the explicit formulation and introductory phrase are randomly chosen from this list.

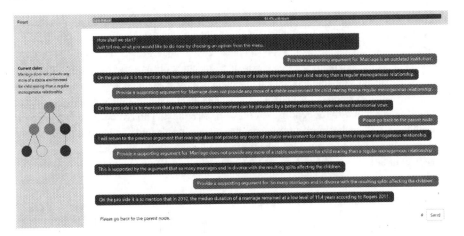

Fig. 2. GUI of the menu system with folded drop-down menu. Above the drop-down menu, the dialogue history is shown. On the left side, the sub-graph of the current branch is visible. (Color figure online)

4   User Study Setting

In the following presented user study was conducted online via the crowdsourcing plat-form *Crowdee*[5] with participants from the UK, US, and Australia in the period 12–29th November 2021. All 292 participants were non-experts without a topic-specific back-ground or experience with dialogue systems. Before the interaction started, the user were given an introductory text, explaining the argument structure, possible user moves and in-between interest ratings and a demo video (menu: 1:11 min, speech: 1:33 min) showing a sample interaction starting with the system's greeting and selected user moves which are most important for a fluent interaction (information-seeking, pref-erence statements, navigational moves). Afterwards, the users were given the task to "listen to enough arguments to build a well-founded opinion on the topic". The end of the interaction could be chosen freely as soon as at least ten (to collect sufficient data for modeling) arguments were heard. The first 139 participants interacted with our ADS via drop-down menu input, and the other 153 via speech. Each participant did the study completely online without supervision by an experimenter.

---

[5] https://www.crowdee.com/.

Before and after the conversation the participants had to rate statements on a 5-point Likert scale regarding the interaction. A part of these questions was taken from a questionnaire according to ITU-T Recommendation P.851[6] [31]. As these questions are primarily investigated within the framework of another research and are not the focus of this work, we will concentrate only on relevant aspects, in particular implications for data exclusion and some general findings which might influence the herein-discussed results. Analyzing the questionnaire answers and feedback, the data of 90 participants showed anomalies. Thus, their data was excluded according to previously defined exclusion criteria: Contradictory answers in control questions in the questionnaire, taking less than 30 s to read through the introduction and watch the introduction videos, taking less than 120 s to answer the 40+15 questions in the final questionnaire and feedback indicating that problems occurred during the interaction or participants reported that they did not know what to do. This leads to a total number of data records of 202 participants (menu: 104, speech: 98) which were included in the further analysis.

During the dialogue after each move (except concerning moves addressing the major claim) the participants had to rate their interest in the currently discussed aspect on a 5-point Likert scale (see **Interest** in Sect. 5). The first claim[7] is presented after the user asks for a pro/con argument. It is the only claim which is chosen randomly as afterward the participants have to choose from the remaining claims whenever they navigated back to the major claim. After that, the user selects the most interesting claim and the ADS continues the dialogue by presenting the chosen argument.

5   Results and Discussion

Table 2. Participants' ratings of the speech system, the menu system and the combined data. M_{pre} denotes the mean before and M_{post} after the interaction. Statistically significant ($p < 0.01$) differences are marked with *.

	Opinion					Interest				
	M_{pre}	SD	M_{post}	SD	$|\Delta_M|$	M_{pre}	SD	M_{post}	SD	$|\Delta_M|$
Menu	2.62	1.16	**2.89**	1.26	**0.27***	3.31	1.03	**3.48**	1.01	0.17
Speech	2.68	1.18	**3.00**	1.20	**0.32***	3.49	0.88	3.14	1.20	**0.35***
Speech and Menu	2.65	1.17	**2.94**	1.23	**0.29***	3.4	0.96	3.32	1.12	0.06

On average, participants spent 31.45 min interacting with the system (speech: 35.34 min; menu: 27.57 min). In the speech(menu) system 17(10) of 98(104) participants and thus, 17.3% (9.6%) only heard the minimum number of arguments. A total of 27 participants (13.4%) quit the interaction after the minimum number of ten presented arguments was reached. In line with the assumption of Yi et al. [52], this suggests that

---

[6] Such questionnaires can be used to evaluate the quality of speech-based services.

[7] Due to the argument tree structure described in Sect. 3 the respective argument component is a root node of the corresponding branch.

the other 175 participants were still interested in the topic and continued the interaction. Most of the participants (speech: 44.3%; menu: 50.9%) heard 20–30 out of 72 available arguments. One participant in the speech and 35 participants (33.6%) in the menu system listened to more than 30 arguments. Thus, the interaction with the speech-based system was slower as people on average spent more time with it compared to the menu-based system, even though they considered fewer arguments than in the menu-based system during that time. This might be explained by the fact that spoken user and system utterances take more time, than clicking on an option and reading the displayed answer, which makes the menu-based system more efficient by presenting more arguments in a shorter time.

Before and after the interaction the participants had to rate the following two questions concerning the major claim of the discussion ("Marriage is an outdated institution"):

Opinion: *What is your current opinion about this claim ?* on the scale: 5 (strongly agree), 4 (agree), 3 (neutral), 2 (disagree), 1 (strongly disagree).
Interest: *How interesting is this claim for you?* on the scale: 5 (extremely interesting), 4 (very interesting), 3 (moderately interesting), 2 (slightly interesting), 1 (not at all interesting).

Table 2 shows the results of the participant's self-ratings regarding these two questions. A non-parametric Wilcoxon signed rank test [51] for paired samples ($\alpha = 0.05$), shows for both systems a significant change of the user **opinion** during the interaction. This change is bigger in the speech system condition. Moreover, taking the ratings of both systems together the change in opinion is highly significant with $p < 0.01$, which indicates that the interaction had an influence on the users' opinions. This increase can be explained by the fact that the participants became more neutral when considering arguments that contradicted their own stance. During the interaction, it could be perceived that the more often users listened to arguments contradicting their previously stated opinion, the more likely they stated a preference with regard to these arguments, which led to a more neutral stance. These findings match the expectation that our argumentative dialogue system is able to engage in a more balanced exploration of both sides of a controversial topic. By listening to counter-arguments users were not considered before their stance shifted to a more balanced, neutral[8] one.

Regarding the user **interest** a discrepancy between the two modalities is perceivable. Whereas the interest of the participants using the menu system increased from 3.31 to 3.48, the interest of the ones using the speech system decreased from 3.49 to 3.14 significantly (cf. right part of Table 2). This can be explained by the influence of the difference in the (perceived) usability of both systems. The menu system outperformed the speech system regarding the user ratings in the questionnaire based on the ITU-T Recommendation P.851. It contains, e.g., the category "Overall Quality" ("What is your overall impression of the system?") which is rated on a different 5-point Likert scale[9]. We found a highly significant ($p < 0.01$) difference between the menu system (with a rating of 3.49 for overall quality) and the speech system (rated 2.66). This difference

---

[8] Neutral indicates that the participants' opinion towards the Major Claim is neutral. This does not mean that participants' positive and negative opinions cancel each other out.
[9] 5 = Excellent, 4 = Good, 3 = Fair, 2 = Poor, 1 = Bad.

points to a lower user satisfaction in the speech-based system compared to the menu-based system which is underpinned by the fact that content- but not modality-dependent items are rated significantly better in the menu system than the speech system. The correlation between these item ratings and the before/after interest rating indicates, that the latter is induced by the difference in the overall perception.

Especially, we noticed, that the participants seemed to have a certain expectation towards the speech system. Especially for mobile usage, the robustness of the automated speech recognition (ASR) in the speech system must be ensured, since noise occurs even more easily when moving from one place to another.

To determine whether the difference in user interest and opinion between the two systems means Δ_M is significant, we used the non-parametric Mann-Whitney U test [28] for two independent samples with no specific distribution. Still, even though the means of the two modalities show differences, they are statistically not significant w.r.t a significance level of $\alpha = 0.05$.

Table 3 displays the percentage of performed moves depending on the move type and modality. Interestingly, 53% (speech) and 43% (menu) of the performed moves are concerned with the argument exploration (why con/pro). About 27% (speech) and 42% (menu) of the moves expressed a preference[10]. Thus, in the menu system, users expressed their opinion (preference) nearly as often as they asked for a new argument. In contrast, in the speech system participants requested arguments about twice as often as they stated their opinion/preference. One explanation for this could be that in the menu system, all possible moves (especially the preference/indifference/rejection towards an argument) were displayed in the drop-down menu. In contrast, this visual support did not exist in the speech system, except in the event that the users asked for the available options. As shown in Table 3 the available_ options move was rarely requested, which might also explain some problems the participants had with the speech system.

Interestingly, users of the speech system stated over 90% of their preferences while descending the argument branches and thus, as a direct response to the currently presented argument. In 60% of their preference moves, users of the menu system had already heard the respective argument and were revisiting the argument while ascending the respective branch. This might be explained by the fact, that users are more likely encouraged to express a preference directly in the speech system analogous to a real conversation with a human interlocutor. In such conversations, it is not common to revisit already discussed arguments if no new point is made. In contrast, in the menu system users are enabled to navigate fast through the argument tree by jumping forth and back with one click. Therefore, the menu system displays a rather game-like situation than a natural one.

In both systems, the user opinions calculated by the system based on the preference modeling described in Sect. 3.2, matched the self-ratings of the users except for 4 speech system users. These exceptions can be explained by errors made by the ASR which did not transcribe the user utterance correctly, resulting in a wrong intent mapping and thus, incorrect calculation of the users' opinions.

Hence, we verified that the herein-presented preference model based on explicit user feedback is able to track and detect user opinions correctly.

---

[10] For better readability we refer to all preference-related moves (indifferent, reject, prefer, prefer_current, prefer_old, equal) as preferences.

Table 3. The percentage of performed moves dependent on the move type. The higher percentages for the respective system are marked in bold.

	move type	moves performed (%)	
		speech	menu
other	available_options	**3.66**	0
	exit	**2.71**	0.06
	show_preferred	**0.95**	1.17
	stance	**1.89**	1.12
	stance_overall	1.37	**3.88**
	number_visited	1.90	**2.72**
	level_up	**7.54**	6.29
	$\sum_{other}$	**20,01**	15.24
preference	indifferent	1.91	**5.42**
	reject	8.59	**10.05**
	prefer	11.22	**18.98**
	prefer_current	1.39	**2.22**
	prefer_old	0.63	**2.51**
	equal	**3.19**	2.55
	$\sum_{preference}$	26.93	**41.73**
why	why_con	**22.67**	14.58
	why_pro	**30.93**	28.47
	$\sum_{why}$	**53.06**	43.05

In both systems, the interposed interest ratings were higher when descending the argument tree than ascending it. We perceive that the users lose interest when they received enough information on the topic. This indicates that during the argument exploration, a saturation effect occurs. The findings for both, the menu and the speech system, show that especially after a preference statement the interest in the current argument is rated low (menu: 2.02 (SD: 0.87); speech: 1.96 (SD: 0.53)). In contrast, when users requested more information their interest ratings were very high (menu: 3.75 (SD: 1.01); speech: 3.89 (SD: 0.96)). Thus, we conclude that there is a strong correlation between information-seeking moves and high interest, as well as between "preference/level up"- moves and low interest. Thus, the presented argumentative dialogue system seems to be able and suited to track the user interest continuously and influence the latter.

In conclusion, the presented findings show that even though navigational moves have to be performed, they still play a minor role compared to all performed moves. It can clearly be seen that the main functionalities of the system which are to explore arguments and state a preference towards them are used in both modalities. In the menu system, the ratio of information-seeking moves to preference moves is equal and in the speech system, the former is twice as high. Still, in both systems, the users show an opinion-building process and they both show a shift from a rejecting towards a rather neutral position towards the Major Claim. Likewise, the influence of the ADS on the user interest is strongly perceivable with regard to the interposed interest self-ratings. A significant change in the latter can be perceived in the before/after user interest ratings which strongly correlates with the general impression of the system.

Furthermore, we perceived that a further improvement of the technical issues, especially with regard to the ASR is necessary to increase user satisfaction. Since mobility entails more flexibility, a free exchange with the speech system is more appealing to users than the predefined responses in the menu system. Still, since a speech interface a priori will take more time to interact with, it would be reasonable to choose the modality according to the user's expectations and motivation. In case they prefer a natural, mobile chat-like interaction which might take longer but is more interactive and where they can express themselves freely, the speech-based system would be suitable. In case they prefer an efficient interaction with as much information as possible during a short time, the menu-based system would be suitable. In general, a possible solution to both aspects (technical issues and long interaction time) might be a text-input modality (input via typing and output on the screen without spoken language), where the users are able to express their thoughts and requests in their own words but still do not have to deal with an erroneous ASR and can scan the system's response quickly and still allow for a more natural, mobile interaction.

6   Conclusion and Future Work

In this work, we have evaluated the influence of two different I/O modalities on the users' interest and opinion in an argumentative dialogue system by conducting a crowdsourcing study with 202 participants. We described changes in the user's exploration behaviour, in particular, with regard to individual user expectations of a mobile application depending on the respective modality.

The self-ratings of the user opinion clearly show a significant influence between before and after the interaction with the herein presented ADS. Moreover, we showed that our ADS is able to continuously track and detect the user opinion correctly based on the introduced preference model. This is underpinned by the fact that the results of the opinion self-ratings before and after the interaction, fit the findings regarding the results obtained during the ongoing interaction.

Regarding user interest, it is crucial to differentiate between the before/after ratings and the ones given during the interaction. Whereas during the interaction significant changes in the user interest can be perceived, the before/after comparison is mainly influenced by the general perception of the system. The ratings about the interest in the interaction indicate a strong relationship between the high interest and information-seeking moves as well as low interest and preference/level_up moves. This points towards a saturation effect if the user has heard enough arguments on certain aspects of the topic. Therefore, we could show that the ADS has a strong influence on the user's exploration behavior and thus, interest.

In future work, we will incorporate our findings about the relation between user moves and user interest into an implicit model to detect and use an appropriately trained

ANN classifier to adapt to the user interest. Furthermore, by implicitly detecting a potential loss of user interest, the system will be able to proactively suggest new arguments and, e.g., engage the user in hearing additional arguments. By incorporating the user opinion and preference estimation in the system's choice of new arguments we will investigate how users react to arguments that are in line as well as contrary to their already established opinion. As we aim for a cooperative but unbiased and well-founded opinion-building process, we will explore approaches like Reinforcement Learning to establish the optimal strategy which maintains the user's motivation to talk to the system. Finally, we will evaluate the above-mentioned extensions of the system in a broad crowd-sourcing study and investigate if we can improve user satisfaction and motivation to engage in an argumentative discussion.

By showing the fundamental functionality of our interest and opinion model and its consistency with the self-assessment ratings, this work provides important implications for the design of future mobile (ubiquitous) interactive applications.

References

1. Abro, W.A., Aicher, A., Rach, N., Ultes, S., Minker, W., Qi, G.: Natural language understanding for argumentative dialogue systems in the opinion building domain. Knowl.-Based Syst. **242**, 108318 (2022)
2. Aicher, A., Rach, N., Minker, W., Ultes, S.: Opinion building based on the argumentative dialogue system BEA. In: Marchi, E., Siniscalchi, S.M., Cumani, S., Salerno, V.M., Li, H. (eds.) Increasing Naturalness and Flexibility in Spoken Dialogue Interaction. LNEE, vol. 714, pp. 307–318. Springer, Singapore (2021). https://doi.org/10.1007/978-981-15-9323-9_27
3. Amgoud, L., Ben-Naim, J.: Evaluation of arguments from support relations: axioms and semantics. In: Proceedings of the 25th International Joint Conference on Artificial Intelligence, IJCAI-16, pp. 900–906 (2016)
4. Amgoud, L., Ben-Naim, J.: Weighted bipolar argumentation graphs: axioms and semantics. In: Proceedings of the Twenty-Seventh International Joint Conference on Artificial Intelligence, IJCAI-18, pp. 5194–5198 (2018)
5. Amgoud, L., Bonnefon, J.-F., Prade, H.: An argumentation-based approach to multiple criteria decision. In: Godo, L. (ed.) ECSQARU 2005. LNCS (LNAI), vol. 3571, pp. 269–280. Springer, Heidelberg (2005). https://doi.org/10.1007/11518655_24
6. Amgoud, L., Prade, H.: Using arguments for making and explaining decisions. Artif. Intell. **173**, 413–436 (2009)
7. Baroni, P., Romano, M., Toni, F., Aurisicchio, M., Bertanza, G.: Automatic evaluation of design alternatives with quantitative argumentation. Argument Comput. **6**(1), 24–49 (2015)
8. Bechhofer, S.: Owl: Web ontology language. In: Liu, L., Özsu, M.T. (eds.) Encyclopedia of Database Systems, pp. 2008–2009. Springer, Boston (2009). https://doi.org/10.1007/978-0-387-39940-9_1073
9. Briguez, C., Budán, M., Deagustini, C., Maguitman, A., Capobianco, M., Simari, G.: Argument-based mixed recommenders and their application to movie suggestion. Expert Syst. Appl. **41**(14), 6467–6482 (2014)
10. Budán, M., Simari, G., Simari, G.: Using argument features to improve the argumentation process. In: Computational Models of Argument - Proceedings of COMMA 2016, Potsdam, Germany, 12–16 September, 2016, pp. 151–158 (2016)
11. Carenini, G., Moore, J.D.: Generating and evaluating evaluative arguments. Artif. Intell. **170**(11), 925–952 (2006)

12. Chalaguine, L., Hunter, A.: Addressing popular concerns regarding covid-19 vaccination with natural language argumentation dialogues. In: Vejnarová, J., Wilson, N. (eds.) ECSQARU 2021. LNCS (LNAI), vol. 12897, pp. 59–73. Springer, Cham (2021). https://doi.org/10.1007/978-3-030-86772-0_5

13. Chalaguine, L.A., Hunter, A.: A persuasive chatbot using a crowd-sourced argument graph and concerns. In: COMMA (2020)

14. Chalyi, S., Pribylnova, I.: The method of constructing recommendations online on the temporal dynamics of user interests using multilayer graph. EUREKA Phys. Eng. (3), 13–19 (2019)

15. Chien, Y.H., George, E.I.: A Bayesian model for collaborative filtering. In: AISTATS (1999)

16. Das, R., Farrell, R.G., Rajput, N.: Social recommender system for generating dialogues based on similar prior dialogues from a group of users. US Patent 8,275,384 (2012)

17. Devlin, J., Chang, M.W., Lee, K., Toutanova, K.: BERT: pre-training of deep bidirectional transformers for language understanding. In: Proceedings of the 2019 Conference of the North American Chapter of the Association for Computational Linguistics: Human Language Technologies, vol. 1, pp. 4171–4186. Minneapolis, Minnesota. Association for Computational Linguistics (2019)

18. Fazzinga, B., Galassi, A., Torroni, P.: An argumentative dialogue system for COVID-19 vaccine information. In: Baroni, P., Benzmüller, C., Wáng, Y.N. (eds.) CLAR 2021. LNCS (LNAI), vol. 13040, pp. 477–485. Springer, Cham (2021). https://doi.org/10.1007/978-3-030-89391-0_27

19. Gauch, S., Speretta, M., Chandramouli, A., Micarelli, A.: User profiles for personalized information access. In: The Adaptive Web, pp. 54–89 (2007)

20. Gazdar, A., Hidri, L.: A new similarity measure for collaborative filtering based recommender systems. Knowl.-Based Syst. **188**, 105058 (2020)

21. Hadoux, E., Hunter, A., Polberg, S.: Strategic argumentation dialogues for persuasion: framework and experiments based on modelling the beliefs and concerns of the persuadee. Argument Comput. **14**, 1–53 (2022). https://doi.org/10.3233/AAC-210005

22. Hawashin, B., Aqel, D., AlZu'bi, S., Jararweh, Y.: Novel weighted interest similarity measurement for recommender systems using rating timestamp. In: 6th International Conference on Software Defined Systems (SDS), pp. 166–170. IEEE (2019)

23. Hurtig, T.: A mobile multimodal dialogue system for public transportation navigation evaluated. In: Proceedings of the 8th Conference on Human-Computer Interaction with Mobile Devices and Services, MobileHCI 2006, pp. 251–254. Association for Computing Machinery, New York (2006). ISBN 1595933905

24. Johnston, M., et al.: MATCH: an architecture for multimodal dialogue systems. In: Proceedings of the 40th Annual Meeting of the Association for Computational Linguistics, pp. 376–383 (2002)

25. Le, D.T., Nguyen, C.T., Nguyen, K.A.: Dave the debater: a retrieval-based and generative argumentative dialogue agent. In: Proceedings of the 5th Workshop on Argument Mining, pp. 121–130 (2018)

26. Liu, J., Pasupat, P., Cyphers, S., Glass, J.: ASGARD: a portable architecture for multilingual dialogue systems. In: 2013 IEEE International Conference on Acoustics, Speech and Signal Processing, pp. 8386–8390 (2013)

27. Lops, P., de Gemmis, M., Semeraro, G.: Content-based recommender systems: state of the art and trends. In: Ricci, F., Rokach, L., Shapira, B., Kantor, P.B. (eds.) Recommender Systems Handbook, pp. 73–105. Springer, Boston, MA (2011). https://doi.org/10.1007/978-0-387-85820-3_3

28. McKnight, P.E., Najab, J.: Mann-Whitney U Test. American Cancer Society (2010)

29. Oguego, C., Augusto, J., Muñoz, A., Springett, M.: Using argumentation to manage users' preferences. Futur. Gener. Comput. Syst. **81**, 235–243 (2018)

30. Öztürké, M., Tsoukiàs, A., Vincke, P.: Preference Modelling. In: Figueira, J., Greco, S., Ehrogott, M. (eds.) Multiple Criteria Decision Analysis: State of the Art Surveys. International Series in Operations Research & Management Science, vol. 78, pp. 27–59. Springer, New York (2005). https://doi.org/10.1007/0-387-23081-5_2

31. P.851, I.T.R.: Subjective quality evaluation of telephone services based on spoken dialogue systems (11/2003). International Telecommunication Union (2003)

32. Pavlov, D., Pennock, D.M.: A maximum entropy approach to collaborative filtering in dynamic, sparse, high-dimensional domains. In: NIPS, vol. 2, pp. 1441–1448. Citeseer (2002)

33. Pazzani, M.J., Billsus, D.: Content-based recommendation systems. In: Brusilovsky, P., Kobsa, A., Nejdl, W. (eds.) The Adaptive Web. LNCS, vol. 4321, pp. 325–341. Springer, Heidelberg (2007). https://doi.org/10.1007/978-3-540-72079-9_10

34. Qiu, F., Cho, J.: Automatic identification of user interest for personalized search. In: Proceedings of the 15th International Conference on World Wide Web, pp. 727–736 (2006)

35. Rach, N., Langhammer, S., Minker, W., Ultes, S.: Utilizing argument mining techniques for argumentative dialogue systems. In: D'Haro, L.F., Banchs, R.E., Li, H. (eds.) 9th International Workshop on Spoken Dialogue System Technology. LNEE, vol. 579, pp. 131–142. Springer, Singapore (2019). https://doi.org/10.1007/978-981-13-9443-0_12

36. Rach, N., Matsuda, Y., Daxenberger, J., Ultes, S., Yasumoto, K., Minker, W.: Evaluation of argument search approaches in the context of argumentative dialogue systems. In: Proceedings of the 12th Language Resources and Evaluation Conference, pp. 513–522. ELRA, Marseille (2020)

37. Rago, A., Toni, F., Aurisicchio, M., Baroni, P.: Discontinuity-free decision support with quantitative argumentation debates. In: Fifteenth International Conference on Principles of Knowledge Representation and Reasoning (KR 2016), pp. 63–73 (2016)

38. Rakshit, G., Bowden, K.K., Reed, L., Misra, A., Walker, M.A.: Debbie, the debate bot of the future. In: Advanced Social Interaction with Agents - 8th International Workshop on Spoken Dialog Systems, pp. 45–52 (2017)

39. Reithinger, N., Sonntag, D.: An integration framework for a mobile multimodal dialogue system accessing the semantic web. In: INTERSPEECH, pp. 841–844 (2005)

40. Ricci, F., Rokach, L., Shapira, B.: Introduction to recommender systems handbook. In: Ricci, F., Rokach, L., Shapira, B., Kantor, P. (eds.) Recommender Systems Handbook, pp. 1–35. Springer, Boston (2011). https://doi.org/10.1007/978-0-387-85820-3_1

41. Ricci, F., Rokach, L., Shapira, B.: Recommender systems: introduction and challenges. In: Ricci, F., Rokach, L., Shapira, B. (eds.) Recommender Systems Handbook, pp. 1–34. Springer, Boston, MA (2015). https://doi.org/10.1007/978-1-4899-7637-6_1

42. Rosenfeld, A., Kraus, S.: Strategical argumentative agent for human persuasion. In: ECAI 2016, pp. 320–328 (2016)

43. Saha, T., Saha, S., Bhattacharyya, P.: Towards sentiment-aware multi-modal dialogue policy learning. Cogn. Comput. **14**, 1–15 (2020)

44. Slonim, N., et al.: An autonomous debating system. Nature **591**(7850), 379–384 (2021)

45. Son, J., Kim, S.B.: Content-based filtering for recommendation systems using multiattribute networks. Expert Syst. Appl. **89**, 404–412 (2017)

46. Sonntag, D., Schulz, C., Reuschling, C., Galarraga, L.: Radspeech's mobile dialogue system for radiologists. In: Proceedings of the 2012 ACM International Conference on Intelligent User Interfaces, IUI 2012, pp. 317–318. Association for Computing Machinery, New York (2012). ISBN 9781450310482

47. Stab, C., Gurevych, I.: Annotating argument components and relations in persuasive essays. In: COLING, pp. 1501–1510 (2014)

48. Su, Z., Yan, J., Ling, H., Chen, H.: Research on personalized recommendation algorithm based on ontological user interest model. J. Comput. Inf. Syst. **8**(1), 169–181 (2012)

49. Tsourakis, N.: Development & evaluation of multilingual multimodal dialogue systems on mobile devices. Ph.D. thesis (2013)
50. Wilcock, G., Jokinen, K.: Towards increasing naturalness and flexibility in human-robot dialogue systems. In: Marchi, E., Siniscalchi, S.M., Cumani, S., Salerno, V.M., Li, H. (eds.) Increasing Naturalness and Flexibility in Spoken Dialogue Interaction. LNEE, vol. 714, pp. 109–114. Springer, Singapore (2021). https://doi.org/10.1007/978-981-15-9323-9_9
51. Woolson, R.: Wilcoxon signed-rank test. In: Wiley Encyclopedia of Clinical Trials, pp. 1–3 (2007)
52. Yi, J., Zhang, Y., Yin, M., Zhao, X.: A novel user-interest model based on mixed measure. In: Journal of Physics: Conference Series, vol. 887, p. 012061. IOP Publishing (2017)
53. Zeng, X., Li, J., Wang, L., Mao, Z., Wong, K.F.: Dynamic online conversation recommendation. In: Proceedings of the 58th Annual Meeting of the Association for Computational Linguistics, pp. 3331–3341. Association for Computational Linguistics (2020)
54. Zhou, G., et al.: Deep interest evolution network for click-through rate prediction. In: Proceedings of the AAAI Conference on Artificial Intelligence, vol. 33, pp. 5941–5948 (2019)

"What Can I Study at OVGU?" – An Analysis of the Applicability of Conversational Voice Assistants in Student Advisory Service

Matthias Busch, Felix Böhm, and Ingo Siegert[✉]

Mobile Dialog Systems, Institute for Information Technology and Communications,
Otto von Guericke University Magdeburg,
Universitätsplatz 2, 39106 Magdeburg, Germany
{matthias.busch,felix.bohm,ingo.siegert}@ovgu.de
http://mds.ovgu.de/

Abstract. In modern student marketing, digitalization and individualization are important key concepts to attract the attention of prospective students. Different influences both from the perspective of universities as well as possible applicants create challenges for advertising the opportunities for prospective students.

This paper explores the integration of speech-based conversational agent as a tool of the General Student Advisory Service (GSAS) for informing possible applicants about study courses at the Otto-von-Guericke-University Magdeburg (OVGU).

We present the development of the conversational Assistant "Ask Uni Magdeburg" that is available both at the Google Assistant and Alexa Platform. This voice app (VA) supports the student advisors by offering prospective students the opportunity to explore interests and strengths and get referred to either the general student guidance from the GSAS or to study course advisors of the different institutions.

Keywords: Study Course Information · Conversational Assistant

1 Introduction

The student advisors of the GSAS are first line of contact for most prospective students. The consultations at the GSAS are mostly in person at the university, at fairs or at local schools. This allows the advisor to address the individual needs of possible applicants and explore the strengths as well as interests together.

While advisors from the GSAS can give a general overview of the topics of the course of the university, they often interact with study course advisors that are part of different institutions and have a deeper knowledge about each area of specialization. In times of the COVID Pandemic, personal meetings with the advisors were a restricted resource and other means of a kind of personal interaction has to be used and established. Traditionally, digital media like website offer applicants a form of self-service. Although these websites can include a

G. Salvendy and J. Wei (Eds.): HCII 2023, LNCS 14052, pp. 144–155, 2023.
https://doi.org/10.1007/978-3-031-35921-7_10

vast amount of information, they lack the adaptability to address each individual users.

We argue that conversational voice agents [3,6] can offer prospective students a better opportunity to explore the applicant's interests and strengths in an individualized dialogue [2,4]. The digital agent can then refer the applicant to either a more general or a specialized study consultation.

1.1 Perspective of the Applicants

From the perspective of possible applicants, there are more than 400 universities, universities of applied science, and universities of cooperative education in Germany, only. These offer approx. 9,000 Bachelor's degree courses. Thus, prospective students have a huge number of options to choose from.

In the case, that prospective students already have an idea, overview pages of various study course information providers are a good starting point. But, to identify a suitable course of study, it is still necessary to work through the subsequent information websites of the respective courses of studies of the universities of interest. If prospective students do not yet have a clear idea about their study courses, various online-study course self-assessments can be used to find a suitable course of study.

These tests are available in a variety of designs by using e.g. checkboxes, text fields, or chatbots. A reputable provider who creates an individual interest profile based on 72 self-assessment questions is the "Studiuminteressentest (SIT)" of DIE ZEIT Online and the German Rectors' Conference/Hochschulrektoren-konferenz (HRK). This type of study information is very complex due to the large empirical surveys required to match the fields of study to areas of interest. However, prospective students having a wide range of personal interests barely receive concrete feedback from such online questionnaires, that sometimes can even be contradictory [1].

Furthermore, interdisciplinary study courses are hardly representable into specific interests, as they combine different competencies and needs. Therefore, it is necessary to get a subsequent study guidance.

For this use case, (prospective students who are still unsure about their choice of study, strongly interdisciplinary courses, and connection with a study guidance) the interaction with a conversational voice would be a valuable option. So far, only a few text-based applications are used at universities, while the focus of these chatbots is mostly limited to information retrieval, e.g., cafeteria menus or library information. To get optimal assistance in the selection of study courses, the GSAS would be the ideal partner. However, the GSAS is not quickly accessible or available on-site only and can only offer limited appointments. Therefore, other solutions for self-help are necessary.

1.2 Perspective of the Advisors

To get optimal assistance in the selection of study courses, the GSAS would be the ideal partner.

The GSAS usually conducts individual interviews. During these interviews, the personal interests of the prospective students are assessed and suitable courses of study at the university are identified. In the first part of the interview, it is usually determined in which direction (aka clusters) the prospective student tends (STEM, social sciences, economics, etc.). Rankings of interests can also be drawn up in the process. In the further course of the interview, specifics of the individual degree programs are then asked on the basis of the identified clusters; interdisciplinary degree programs (industrial engineering, sports and technology) are also specifically included if the prospective students are open to them.

The disadvantage of this solution is that prospective students must either come to the GSAS, but this is not always possible due to space and time limitations (limited office hours and long travel distances to the university of interest), or the GSAS has to come to the prospective students. Here, the same problems arise, as well.

Moreover, many prospective students do not realize that the GSAS is the ideal contact for them if the exact choice of study program has not yet been decided, and it is the GSAS's task to help them exactly in this situation. Furthermore, many prospective students Furthermore, many prospective students are unsure whether they should talk to the CGC if they have no idea what they want to study and also feel afraid to talk to the CGC.

However, the emergence and establishment of conversational voice can offer a good addition in order to enable a first study orientation independent of office hours and the "fear" of a personal contact.

Chatbot agents have been already introduced in the field of student counselling at various universities, but the here presented one is the first providing a common speech-based interaction via the widely used voice platforms of Google and Amazon [9]. Its aim is to engage prospective students in the university and to provide them with a straightforward first step towards the study guidance.

2   Goals for the Design

Together with experts from the GSAS the following goals for a supporting conversational agent were defined:

G-1 Guidance through an initial study counseling with the aim to identify suitable study courses.
G-2 Give information about study courses and indicate/transmit to contact persons.
G-3 Answer frequently asked questions (FAQ) about studying at the OVGU.
G-4 Allow GSAS update and adapt the conversational assistant.

3   Design of Dialogue

In order to design a suitable dialogue that on the one hand reflects the GSAS's approach as well as possible, but on the other hand can also be mapped well into the classic query scheme of voice assistants, a corresponding prototype dialogue was created with the GSAS. To this end, the general procedure of voice assistants was first introduced in a design workshop, along with their capabilities and limitations. In the process, it was first decided to only commit to an initial consultation with the conversational voice agent. This focuses on identifying suitable study courses without going into the admission requirements or specific content.

Furthermore, it was quickly determined that the initial counselling must be divided into two dialogue parts. One for the query as to which rough interests (aka clusters) come into question for the prospective student. Then one for the query about specifics that distinguish the study programs in the cluster well. Both should be implemented in a quiz-like style. Furthermore, an additional path to answer general FAQ-like questions was included.

Figure 2 depicts the general dialogue through the conversation as a result of the first design workshop. This dialog mainly serves two use cases of a course guidance service: support in choosing a study course (G-1, G-2) and answering FAQ (G-3), whereas the study course identification is solved by two parts, the "ClusterQuiz", which aims to determine one broad study cluster and the "CourseQuiz", which aim to identify 1–3 suitable study courses (Fig. 1).

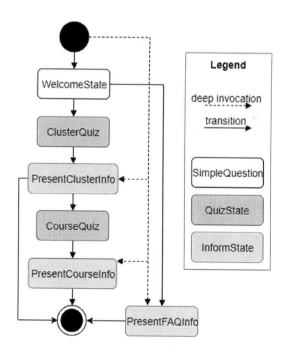

Fig. 1. Dialogue Flow Overview

3.1   Welcome and FAQ-State

At the beginning of the dialog, the assistant greets the user and asks the users if they want to explore what they would study at the OVGU. The student counselling is conducted as a quiz-like question and answer system and the prospective student will be guided through two quiz rounds. Afterwards, relevant information of the identified study course will be provided.

The FAQ feature (G-3) represents a different use case. Questions about study regulations and studying at the OVGU in general are answered. To identify topics of interest, question phrases and their variations are taken from a Whats-App study consultation, that was established by the marketing department a few years ago.

In addition, it is possible to directly acquire information using a so-called a "deep invocation" at the start of the dialog. In that sense, requests like "What are the application deadlines at the University of Magdeburg?" can be handled by the system [5].

3.2   ClusterQuiz

The aim of the ClusterQuiz is to identify the broader study clusters. The Otto von Guericke University distinguishes seven clusters, namely: 1) natural sciences/math, 2) engineering/computer science, 3) economics, 4) human medicine, 5) society/media/education 6) health/sport/psychology 7) teaching program. Each cluster comprises thematically similar study courses (study courses can be part of several clusters). The dialog with the conversational voice agent is organized in a decision-tree manner. Either "Yes/No"-Questions or questions asking for a distinct option are asked. The decision-tree is depicted in Fig. 2.

At the end of the ClusterQuiz the prospective student is guided into one cluster, with a maximum of four questions. The idea behind it was that people interested in studying could take the ClusterQuiz several times without having to answer numerous questions each time.

The final decision tree has been evaluated with experts from the GSAS in terms of clarity and comprehensibility. It was then decided that the conversational agent displays the result of the ClusterQuiz as an intermediate result and asks the prospective student whether he or she would now like to continue, in order to narrow down the possible courses of study in the identified cluster. If the prospective student agrees, the conversational agent continues with the CourseQuiz.

3.3   CourseQuiz

The aim of the CourseQuiz is to narrow down the suggestions of study courses by asking for individual preferences of the prospective student. Therefore, CourseQuiz uses a set of questions, which are evaluated using a scoring method to select the final suggestion. The questions were generated together with the GSAS and include essential distinguishing features of the study courses in the corresponding

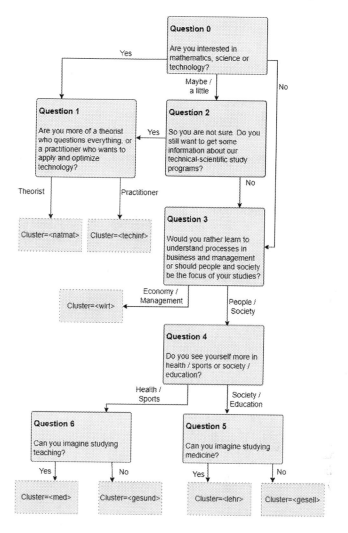

Fig. 2. Decision tree for the ClusterQuiz.

cluster. Here, in addition to the courses of study content, later career opportunities are also used.

The answers to the CourseQuiz are evaluated by a scoring mechanism; for each of the questions, points are distributed to the study programs included in the cluster and added up at the end. Figure 3 depicts some questions for the natural sciences/math cluster.

To ease the maintenance of the conversational speech agent in later operation, both the questions and scores are maintained in a table-like structure. This makes it possible for CGC staff, even without programming skills, to expand or

	A	B	C	D	E
1	question	Angewandte Statis	Biosystemtechi	Chemieingeniei	Computervisua
2	Hast du dich in der Schule für Chemie interessiert?	-1 ▾	0 ▾	0 ▾	0 ▾
3	Interessierst du dich für die Umwelt?	-1 ▾	0 ▾	0 ▾	0 ▾
4	Würdest du gerne neues Wissen erforschen?	-1 ▾	0 ▾	0 ▾	0 ▾
5	Interessierst du dich für elektrische Geräte?	-1 ▾	1 ▾	1 ▾	0 ▾
6	Kannst du dir vorstellen Verantwortung in großen F	0 ▾	1 ▾	0 ▾	-1 ▾
7					

Fig. 3. Scoring table for the CourseQuiz part.

exchange the questions, add new courses of study or even change the scores for individual answers and courses of study.

As this approach is not indented to result in a single study course having the highest score, and it is likely that 2–3 study courses have the same score, the conversational speech agent will always depict the three study programs with the highest score. After presenting the results, the prospective student can either visit the information of one of these results, by going to the university website (either manually or using the short links provided when using the conversational speech agent via mobile phone) or restart the ClusterQuiz to see how certain preferences affect the selected courses of study.

To ensure that prospective students do not lose interest in doing exploratory work here, the questions per cluster are limited to a maximum of 10 questions. However, this requires considerable effort, especially in the development of suitable questions that represent the different courses well. It is therefore recommended that the respective advisors are also involved in this process, as they usually know the individual courses better.

The course Information and the cluster information include contact details to either the specialized study course advisors or to the general study advisors. This information can be displayed on screen or sent by mail.

4   Implementation

A wide range of solutions exists, that offer chatbot or speech assistant technologies [6]. Common voice assistant platforms like Amazon Alexa and Google Assistant allow developing so-called actions or skills using their ecosystem [9]. Dialogow (DF)[1] offers Natural Language Understanding (NLU) capabilities to Google Assistant Actions. The Alexa Skill Kit (ASK) [5] does the same for Alexa Skills.

For the implementation of our conversational assistant, we use the Jovo framework[2], which serves as a wrapper to unify the communication with DF and ASK. The integration of DF[3] further enables us to add multiple chat platforms

---
[1] https://dialogflow.com/.

[2] https://www.jovo.tech/docs/.

[3] https://cloud.google.com/dialogflow/docs/integrations.

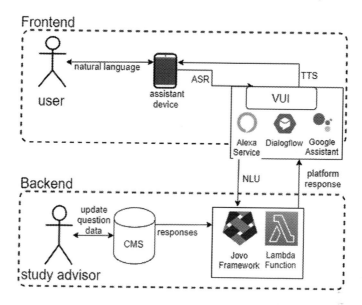

Fig. 4. Architecture Overview

like Facebook Messenger, Slack, or Telegram at a later stage. Figure 4 depicts an overview of the conversational assistants' architecture and the relation between each component.

Jovo also unifies the definition of the Language Model (LM)[4] of our voice user interface (VUI) for both DF and ASK. Both platforms define the VUI with intents. Intents define different actions or intentions a user could express towards the assistant. "YesIntent" and "faq-ApplicationDeadline" are exemplary intents defined in the LM of our assistant. Some intents can include parameters called slots. They refer to a mutable aspect in an expression. "I am interested in {course}", for example, defines an intent, that contains a slot variable called *course*. The type of *course* will then include variables such as *Mathematics, European Studies*, or *Electrical Engineering and Information Technology*.

Choosing proper training utterances for the intents and slot values is an important and challenging task during the development of VUIs applications, as it depends on multiple aspects like the domain knowledge of the user, his/her preferred language style, and the overall quality of the trained NLU component. Given an LM the NLU components like ASK or DF can then perform the NLU task, which can be understood as a mapping of the spoken text to structured data allowing the identification of the meaning of the text.

The user can at any time in the dialog express any of the defined intents. To guide the user through the dialog, it is important, that the assistant takes the initiative and suggests possible answers. For each state of Fig. 2 a set of accepted intents exists that triggers a transition to the next state, every other intent will

---

[4] https://www.jovo.tech/docs/model.

trigger a helpful response. The *QuizStates* will use the current loaded question to decide a transition to a subsequent question or the final result. The result is then presented via the *InformState*.

4.1 Adaptability

At some point, after the assistant went online, changes to the content will be necessary. This might be due to the addition of new study courses, updates to the answers of the FAQ section, or tweaks to the quiz contents (G-4).

The incorporation of these changes should be possible for non-programmers, like employees of the GSAS or the marketing department. To achieve this, the Google Sheets content management system (CMS) integration of the Jovo Framework is used. It allows accessing information in a dedicated Google Sheet at run time. In our application, the Google Sheet contains:

– the decision tree of the introductory quiz,
– the questions of the course quiz and their respective scores,
– the information about study programs,
– the answers to the FAQs, and
– the texts of general reprompts.

All of this information can be edited at any time by an authorized person.

4.2 System Output

The feedback to the users is an important aspect of the application, as the output should provide the information the users are looking for in an appropriate format. Information on clusters and study courses are provided as so-called "cards" onto the mobile phone of the user. A card is a text output that is supported by an image or a hyperlink. The text of the card briefly summarizes the main aspect of a cluster or study course. The hyperlink, which in our case usually leads to the relevant pages of the university website, is intended to allow the user to retain the gained information and to obtain further assistance. In Fig. 5 an example of such a card is given.

The answers to the FAQs are uttered and, if supported by the device, shown as written text. If services beyond the scope of our conversational assistant are required, it refers to relevant websites or the university's GSAS.

Thus, our application is not intended to replace the student counseling, but rather to serve as an introduction and to get into contact with prospective students.

5 First Results

The challenges for universities in student recruiting and counseling have continuously grown in recent years. A stagnating number of high school graduates increases the competitive pressure among universities. In addition to "classical"

Fig. 5. Example card of the Google Assistant with link on a mobile phone

ways of reaching prospective students, such as school visits, fairs, study information days, or internships, especially online marketing becomes increasingly important. The OVGU continues this strategy with the development of a conversational assistant. The GSAS, the marketing department, and the Mobile Dialogue Systems Group are working in cooperation on an implementation presented in this paper. Our assistant offers an uncomplicated first step into the study guidance and provides an initial orientation. Evaluation and validation using larger test groups are still pending and have yet to show the accessibility and adequacy of the system.

The digital course guidance is not intended to replace an individual consultation at the GSAS, but to form a bond between the university and potential students.

6   Conclusion

The challenges for universities in student recruiting and counseling have continuously grown in recent years. A stagnating number of high school graduates increases the competitive pressure among universities. In addition to "classical" ways of reaching prospective students, such as school visits, fairs, study information days, or internships, especially online marketing becomes increasingly important. The OVGU continues this strategy with the development of a conversational assistant. The GSAS, the marketing department, and the Mobile Dialogue Systems Group are working in cooperation on an implementation presented in this paper. The implementation uses the abstraction provided by the Jovo framework to be accessible for users via multiple conversational platforms without losing platform-specific features. Our assistant offers prospective students an uncomplicated first step into the study guidance through a little quiz and provides an initial orientation. Evaluation and validation using larger test groups are still pending and have yet to show the accessibility and adequacy of the provided functionality and content.

The digital course guidance is not intended to replace an individual consultation at the GSAS, but to form a bond between the university and potential students. Particularly, engaging high school graduates' attention and forwarding them to the universities wide range of courses are important for a successful student marketing. In addition, answering frequently asked questions through a conversational assistant is another way for the GSAS to offer information. The provided content can be edited by the marketing department and the GSAS themselves through a specific Google Sheet without the need for assistance.

At the moment, we have refrained from collecting further personal data on prospective students, such as school performance or interests. Although, this information enables a deeper understanding of the prospective student and may improve the counselling, the incorporation of these personal information endangers data misuse [7]. If this personal data is important for an improved counselling, further means need to be included, see [8] for initial discussions on that issue.

In the end, the proposed conversational assistant is an example of the innovative power and creativity of the Otto-von-Guericke-University Magdeburg.

Acknowledgements. We thank P. Niehoff and A. Knirbs from the GSAS for their support and consulting.

References

1. Gollub, J., Meyer-Guckel, V.: Wer bin ich - und wenn ja, wie viele? Online-Studienselbsttests als Orientierungs- und Entscheidungshelfer. In: dvb-forum 02/2014 Professionalisierung der Bildungs- und. Berufsberatung: Und sie bewegt sich doch, pp. 36–41. Wbv Media, Bielefeld (2014)
2. Kisser, L., Siegert, I.: Erroneous reactions of voice assistants "in the wild" - first analyses. In: Elektronische Sprachsignalverarbeitung 2022. Tagungsband der 33. Konferenz. Studientexte zur Sprachkommunikation, vol. 103, pp. 113–120. TUDpress, Sonderborg (2022)
3. Kotzyba, M., Siegert, I., Gossen, T., Nürnberger, A., Wendemuth, A.: Exploratory voice-controlled search for young users: challenges and potential benefits. Kognitive Syst. 1 (2015)
4. Krüger, J., Siegert, I.: das ist schon gruselig so dieses Belauschtwerden - subjektives Erleben von Interaktionen mit Sprachassistenzsystemen zum Zwecke der Individualisierung. In: Sprachassistenten - Anwendungen, Implikationen, Entwicklungen: ITG-Workshop: Magdeburg, 3. März, vol. 2020, p. 29 (2020)
5. Kumar, A., et al.: Just ask: building an architecture for extensible self-service spoken language understanding. arXiv preprint arXiv:1711.00549 (2017)
6. McTear, M.: Conversation modelling for chatbots: current approaches and future directions. Studientexte zur Sprachkommunikation: Elektronische Sprachsignalverarbeitung 2018, pp. 175–185 (2018)
7. Siegert, I., Silber Varod, V., Carmi, N., Kamocki, P.: Personal data protection and academia: GDPR issues and multi-modal data-collections "in the wild". J. Appl.

Knowl. Manage.: OJAKM **8**, 16–31 (2020). https://doi.org/10.36965/OJAKM.2020.8(1)16-31

8. Siegert, I., Sinha, Y., Winkelmann, G., Jokisch, O., Wendemuth, A.: Public interactions with voice assistant - discussion of different one-shot solutions to preserve speaker privacy. In: Identification of Sensitive Data in Language Resources within the 13th Language Resources and Evaluation Conference, pp. 44–47. European Language Resources Association, Marseille (2022). https://aclanthology.org/2022.legal-1.8

9. Tas, S., Arnold, R.: Nutzung von sprachassistenten in deutschland. In: ITG Workshop Sprachassistenten Anwendungen, Implikationen, Entwicklungen, pp. 11–12 (2020)

User Perspective on Anonymity in Voice Assistants

Matthias Haase[1], Julia Krüger[2], and Ingo Siegert[3(✉)]

[1] Department of Engineering and Industrial Design,
University of Applied Sciences Magdeburg-Stendal, Magdeburg, Germany
matthias.haase@h2.de
[2] Department of Psychosomatic Medicine and Psychotherapy,
Otto von Guericke University Magdeburg, Magdeburg, Germany
[3] Mobile Dialog Systems, Otto von Guericke University, Magdeburg, Germany
siegert@ovgu.de

Abstract. In recent years, a growing importance of voice assistants can be observed. Looking more closely at the use of voice assistants, it becomes clear that everyday users of voice assistants are still in the minority, at least in Germany. Previous empirical studies have already found a correlation between the use of voice assistants and the trust in these technologies, as well as concerns about data security. However, there is so far little evidence on whether there are correlations between individual user characteristics and both perceived trust and security concerns. Furthermore, it is also unclear to what extent these user characteristics are generally related to use or non-use. In this paper, the design of a study is presented that surveyed various user characteristics such as technical experience, Big Five personality, willingness to use and experience in dealing with digital technologies, but also the trust in voice assistants, concerns about data security and the actual use of voice assistants within the framework of an online survey. After evaluating the results, attitudes of non-users towards voice assistants will be investigated in a second qualitative survey. The insights gained from these surveys could promote the acceptance of voice assistants and especially the introduction of anonymisation methods.

Keywords: Voice Assistants · Trust · Privacy Concerns · Big-Five Personality · Technology Commitment

1 Introduction

In recent years, voice assistants have become part of our everyday lives. Especially commercial voice assistants have rapidly gained a growing user base [12,13,20] and became one of the mainstay products for private household use. One reason for this development seems to be the naturalness and simplicity of communication without using additional external periphery. But since they are entering sensitive areas, socio ethical aspects of their use are becoming more relevant.

G. Salvendy and J. Wei (Eds.): HCII 2023, LNCS 14052, pp. 156–166, 2023.
https://doi.org/10.1007/978-3-031-35921-7_11

Although voice assistants are becoming more popular in daily use, many people are concerned about the privacy of their user input data (speech data) which is stored and processed on a cloud platform. The skepticism about the potential misuse of sensitive and private user speech data for unauthorized purposes is hindering the adoption of voice assistants in public and healthcare interactions [31]. Therefore, anonymization of users' speech during speech-based interaction with these systems is becoming essential and appropriate anonymization techniques are continuously being developed and optimized, e.g., [21,26,29]. For example, the authors of [29] differentiate between noise addition, speech transformation, voice conversion, speech synthesis, and adversarial learning. In [21] presented an x-vector based anonymization using autoencoders for voice conversation. The authors of [26] present a fast speech-filter based anonymization technique that does not require an additional training phase.

Despite the increasing availability of speech-based technology, there is still a substantial number of people who use these technologies only to a limited extent or even not at all. The reason why some people do not use speech-based technologies while others do, is still not well clarified. Therefore, many studies simply differentiate between users and so-called "non-users" (e.g., [27]). Furthermore, a study from 2019 showed that the proportion of non-users of voice assistants increased rapidly over the 2-year period in Germany. The study could further trace back the non-usage to privacy concerns [28]. In order to uncover the reasons for the use and especially the non-use, it is essential to examine the users and, in particular, the non-users. So far, conducted research focussing on attitudes towards the use of voice assistants mostly mentioned a lack of trust in voice assistants or in the companies behind these technologies. However, to the best of our knowledge, a deeper understanding on how users and non-users assess and justify their mistrust, what they think about the possibility of speaker anonymization, and what may influence their attitudes and user behavior, has not been gained so far.

In 2019, one study achieving relatively high visibility was commissioned by Microsoft [19]. Based on the results, numerous researchers argue about the benefits of automated speaker anonymization. Undoubtedly, this study provides useful information, especially regarding the use of voice assistants: Summarizing, [19] indicates that individuals are quite critical about voice assistants. However, central aspects have not been considered, e.g., like potential connections between users' attitudes and actual behaviors as well as possible factors that influence users' attitudes, or at least have a moderating effect. In line with this argumentation, other studies conclude that non-use is a result of a lack of trust and or privacy/data security concerns [6,9,30]. A recent survey by Bitkom on the reasons for rejecting voice assistants in Germany stated that the main reasons mentioned by the participants were concerns about data security [4]. In this study, 59% of the participants said they were concerned about their data, 53% were afraid that a third party could eavesdrop on them and 35% did not want background-speech from their home to be transmitted over the internet. However, the survey also showed that there is a general willingness to use voice assistants. Only 22% of the participants did not want to control their devices by voice. However, the mere numbers do not allow a differentiated view on why some participants are concerned about their data and others are not. Durable findings on user perspectives and trust in voice assistants show that perceived usefulness and perceived competence have a positive impact on trust and attitudes towards voice assistants [22]. In addition, it was determined that privacy had a negative impact on attitudes, but not on trust towards voice assistants [22].

It is still unclear which factors – besides the perceived usefulness of the Technology Acceptance Model (TAM) – are related to trust and privacy concerns regarding voice assistants. In the last years, it could be observed how the companies behind the products can have influence on how trustworthy they are perceived to be. This applies to voice assistants as well as information technologies and web applications in general. As an example, consider the 2018 Facebook scandal, in which the data analytics company Cambridge Analytica was able to obtain personal data of up to 87 million users [7]. Events like this severely test the trust of users. Some studies examine how organizations deal with situations like these and how remorse leads to restoring trust [2]. Even if companies play a major role in user's perception of them, in the end it is still the individual user her-/hisself deciding to trust or mistrust whether individuals trust them or not and this decision may be connected to the user's personality. Considering, for example, trust in automation processes of information technologies in general [8] or general trust towards robotics or artificial intelligence [18]. The focus in that sense is on personality characteristics. Studies in these research areas report about correlations between Big-Five dimensions, the dominating theory in personality psychology, and trust in technologies. Especially the dimensions of conscientiousness, extroversion, and neuroticism seem to be related to trust. However, other research does also report a connection between the Big Five dimensions and the use of technology in general. For example, the authors of [1] investigated the Big Five dimension in terms of their influence on the use of quite different technologies. However, the interaction between the use of voice assistants, trust, and personality traits has not been investigated so far. Therefore, in the presented study will not only examine the influence of the Big Five personality dimensions, but will also investigate the influence of technology commitment [17] on the use of voice assistants. Technology commitment is a construct based on a personality psychological approach.

For the sake of completeness, it is necessary to mention that in literature correlations between trust, the use of voice assistants as well as specific other factors are at least discussed. These correlations are, among others, the gender of the synthesized voice [11] and the match between the voice assistant's appearance and personality characteristics of the user [24].

The aim of this study is to increase the understanding of individual reasons for the use and non-use of voice-assisted technologies by surveying users and non-users and whether anonymization of user's information and speech input helps to reduce restraints towards voice assistants. The paper is structured as follows: In Sect. 2, the procedure of the data collection, recruitment, and survey design are presented. Section 3 presents recruitment results, especially the description of the sample. Afterwards, Sect. 4 gives a final summary and an outlook regarding the data analysis of the survey data.

2   Methods

The study provides a two-fold data collection. In the first step, connections between attitudes toward voice assistants and technology commitment (technology acceptance, competence, and control beliefs), the individual personality profile, and actual usage or non-usage are examined. Therefore, data is collected using a questionnaire-based online survey. The second step examines the non-users regarding their reasons for not using voice assistants. Furthermore, whether anonymization, and in particular the anonymization of the voice, contributes to reducing possible restraints towards voice assistants.

The research design of the study follows a mixed-method approach, using quantitative as well as qualitative methods. In the first, purely quantitative research phase, the aim is to examine correlations between various user variables and the use or non-use of voice assistants. The results of the first part of the survey are required in order to proceed with the second part.

In the second, more qualitatively oriented phase, the aim is to gain a more detailed understanding of individual motivations for not using voice assistants. It is intended to offer respondents the opportunity to present individual reasons for non-use and ideas about possible changes in their attitudes and usage behavior if they are assured of voice anonymization. Usually, this kind of information is gathered by using a guideline based interview. Due to availability of subjects, we decided, however, to conduct a written survey with open response questions. The selection of the sample for the second part of the survey is done with the help of a qualitative sampling plan [10]. Qualitative content analysis [15] is used to analyze the open self-reports.

This paper only describes the first part of the survey in detail.

2.1   Recruitment

In the first part of the survey, a heterogeneous sample with regard to age (age groups of 18 to 25, 26 to 35, 36 to 45, 46 to 55, 56 to 65 and over 66) and gender was aimed at. Besides, information about the level of education, details on technology use and experience with modern information and communication technologies are collected. The target number of individuals per age group is 100 to 200 in total. Recruitment was done by students of the study programs Human-Technology Interaction and Rehabilitation Psychology at the University of Applied Sciences Magdeburg-Stendal and via different mailing lists of the involved researchers. The students were instructed to use the so-called snowball method. Following this method, the students inform other students, friends and family members about the survey and request others to do so as well. The first part of this data survey was conducted from Jan. 16 to Jan. 29, 2023.

2.2 Survey and Evaluation Methods

The survey was conducted using the SoSci survey hosted at the Otto von Guer-icke University, Magdeburg [14]. This procedure guarantees end-to-end SSL encryption and secure data storage. The servers are located in a certified and secured data center in Germany, and the General Data Protection Regulation (GDPR) is taken into account during the survey. The Ethics Committee of the Department of Applied Human Sciences at Magdeburg University of Applied Sciences endorsed the first step of the study (to date, the second step is in evalu-ation). Before taking part, subjects gave their consent after they were informed about the objectives of the study, the voluntariness of their participation, their right of revocation, and about their rights according to the GDPR. They were furthermore asked for permission to contact them regarding a possible partici-pation in the second part of the survey.

2.3 Survey Content

The 57-item survey included questions on sociodemographic variables, the cur-rent use of technology, and the perceived hedonic and utilitarian benefits [16] of voice assistants. Furthermore, questions about trust regarding voice assis-tants [19,22] and general privacy concerns [16,19] were asked. The Big-Five personality dimensions were assessed by using a brief version of the Big-Five Inventory (BFI-K) [23] and the technology commitment was assessed by using the Brief Measure of Technology Commitment [17]. A complete overview of the survey content is depicted in Table 1. The choice of short questionnaire versions should minimize the risk of premature termination of the survey.

The survey items were spread across a total of seven categories. To ensure a clear delineation, each section (see Table 1) was presented on a separate page.

Short Version of the Big-Five Inventory (BFI-K). The five factors of per-sonality (extraversion, agreeableness, conscientiousness, neuroticism, and open-ness to experience) are assessed using the 21 Item short version of the Big Five Inventory [23]. The subjects are confronted with 21 statements and have to decide what applies to them personally. The response is given on a 5-point Lik-ert scale from "very incorrect" to "very correct". To illustrate, an exemplifying item for the scale Extraversion is: "I am rather reserved, reserved" [23, p. 206]. The reliability of the BFI-K scales can be considered as acceptable to good (Cronbach's alpha = .64 to .86) and there is evidence for criterion-related valid-ity.

In particular, for the Big Five personality dimensions there is a wide vari-ety of well-established instruments with excellent test quality factors like the NEO-FFI [5]. However, this questionnaire contains 60 items, and would have almost doubled the survey completion time. Therefore, besides the construct validity and further test quality criteria, a great value was set on economy when selecting the questionnaires. This should decrease the probability for premature termination of the survey.

Table 1. Overview of the contents of the survey

Section	# Items	Content	
Sociodemographic Variables	5	age, gender, education degree, current employment, place of residence	–
Big-Five Personality	21	Short version of the Big-Five Inventory (BFI-K)	[23]
Technology Commitment	12	Brief Measure of Technology Commitment	[17]
Technology Usage	6	computer usage per week, smartphone usage per week, use of static voice assistants (e.g., Amazon Alexa), frequency of static voice assistant use, use of smartphone based voice, assistants (e.g., Amazon Alexa), frequency of smartphone based voice assistant use	–
Hedonic and Utilitarian Benefits of Voice Assistants	5	Hedonic Benefits (enjoyment, entertainment value, fun in accomplishing tasks) Utilitarian Benefits (convenience in organizing time, facilitation of tasks)	[16]
Trust	3	truthfulness of statements, trustworthiness, trust in developing companies	[19, 22]
Privacy concerns	5	doubts about confidentiality, concerns about doing business using voice assistants, concerns regarding storage of personal data, concerns regarding storage of the amount of information, unwillingness to share personal information	[19, 22]

Technology Commitment. The construct of technology readiness comprises three different aspects in dealing with technology (technology acceptance, technology competence belief, and technology control beliefs), which are assessed by using 12 items [17]. Similar to BFI-K, subjects have to decide which statement applies to them personally. The response is also given on a 5-point Likert scale from "not true at all" to "completely true". An exemplifying item from the acceptance scale is: "Regarding new technical developments, I am very curious." [17, p. 90]. Reliability can be considered as good (Cronbach's alpha = .74 to .84) and evidence for construct validity is given.

3   Initial Results Regarding the Participant Sample

A total of 765 people took part in the first part of the survey and 75.9% (581 of the 765) completed the survey. 72 subjects dropped out when they were asked for socio demographic information. Another 46 subjects dropped out while answering the questions on the Big Five personality dimensions, and 38 subjects while answering questions on Technology Commitment. Lastly, the remaining 29 subjects dropped out during the last four sections. Of course, it is not possible to figure out whether the persons dropped out on their own or if there were technical problems, e.g., regarding the Internet connection.

Table 2 shows that the intended equal representation of the defined age groups could not be achieved:The age group "18 to 25" is clearly over-represented and the age groups "56 to 65" and "66 to 75" are clearly underrepresented. Not surprising, the average age of the participants (M = 34.5 years) is relatively young. In terms of gender distribution, the majority is female (55.6%, n = 323) and 43.5% (n = 253) is male while the remaining 0.7% (N = 4) reported to be diverse. There is also a clear bias in terms of education: 75.4% of the participants (n = 438) had a higher level of education, such as a secondary school-leaving or a university degree. Just 23.6% of the subjects reported to have a lower level of education. And only 1% of the participants (n = 6) reported that they did not have any educational qualifications or did not give detailed information about their qualification.

Table 2. Age distribution of participants

	N	Percent
18 to 25	270	46.5
26 to 35	98	16.9
36 to 45	69	11.9
46 to 55	66	11.4
56 to 65	43	7.4
66 to 75	29	5.0
Missing	6	1.4
Total	591	100.0

Regarding the actual use of static and smartphone based voice assistants, a clear trend can be observed: The minority of the participants use voice assistants. Just 23.9% (n = 139) use a static voice assistant like Amazon's Alexa (Table 3). The number of individuals using smartphone-based voice assistants (Table 4) is slightly higher with 30.3% (n = 176), but users are clearly in the minority here as well.

4   Discussion

The presented data is part of a first step of a study regarding reasons for people to restrain from using voice assistants. Of course, non-use is not a kind of flaw, however, a deeper understanding of it may help in optimizing voice assisted services and applications. This first step of the study accomplishes the basis for

Table 3. Overview over the use of a static voice assistant (e.g., Amazon Alexa)

	N	Percent
Do not own and do not use static voice assistant	389	67.0
Own a static voice assistant but do not use this	37	6.4
Do not own a static voice assistant, but consider purchasing one	16	2.8
Use a static voice assistant	139	23.9
Total	581	100.0

Table 4. Overview over the use of a smart-phone based voice assistant (e.g., Apple Siri).

	N	Percent
Do not own and do not use smart-phone based voice assistant	150	25.8
Own a smart-phone based voice assistant but do not use this	254	43.7
Do not own a smart-phone based voice assistant, but consider purchasing one	1	0.2
Use a smart-phone based voice assistant	176	30.3
Total	581	100.0

this exploration by differentiating users and non-users regarding particular user characteristics. According to recently published studies, constructs like trust or data security concerns, which were shown to be relevant in non-using voice assistants [6,9,22,30], are taken into account. Furthermore, correlations between the using behavior, trust in voice assistant technologies, experiences in using modern systems, personality dimensions as well as technology commitment, will be explored in the following step of data analysis. In the presented survey, 23.9% of the participants reported to not use "static" and 30.3% to not use smart-phone based voice assistants. These reports are comparable to a recent study, in which users made up the minority, too (47% [3]). It has to be underlined, that the equal distribution of age groups aimed at could not be reached. This bias can be attributed to the fact that 90% of all people recruiting participants for the study were aged under 25 years and consequently invited people in their age to participate. Of course, this age bias may influence the number of those participants using voice assistants, because younger people are more likely to use modern technical devices than older ones [25].

As mentioned at the beginning, speaker anonymization is becoming increasingly important on the developer side. In contrast, little is known regarding actual resentments toward voice assistants and the characteristics of the non-users. The findings enable an individual approach to the fears and obstacles of non-users and, if necessary, to reduce these with the help of appropriate anonymization methods. The second step of this study will then reveal further insights into the individual reasons of not-using voice assistants and possible arguments to reconsider this non-use, especially regarding different methods of anonymization.

Acknowledgements. One author (I.S.) of this research acknowledge funding by the Federal Ministry of Education and Research of Germany in the project Emonymous (project number S21060A) and funding by the Volkswagen Foundation in the project AnonymPrevent (AI-based Improvement of Anonymity for Remote Assessment, Treatment, and Prevention against Child Sexual Abuse).

References

1. Esmaeili, S., Tabbakh, S.R.K., Shakeri, H.: A priority-aware lightweight secure sensing model for body area networks with clinical healthcare applications in internet of things. Pervasive Mob. Comput. **69**, 101265 (2020). https://doi.org/10.1016/j.pmcj.2020.101265
2. Ayaburi, E.W.Y., Treku, D.N.: Effect of penitence on social media trust and privacy concerns: the case of Facebook. Int. J. Inf. Manage. **50**, 171–181 (2020)
3. Bitkom: Nutzen Sie die Möglichkeit, per Sprache Informationen abzufragen und Geräte zu steuern? (2022). https://de.statista.com/statistik/daten/studie/1330893/umfrage/umfrage-zur-nutzung-von-sprachassistenten/
4. Bitkom: Umfrage zu den gründen der ablehnung von sprachassistenten in deutschland im jahr 2022 (2022). https://de.statista.com/statistik/daten/studie/1330903/umfrage/umfrage-zu-den-gruenden-der-ablehnung-von-sprachassistenten
5. Borkenau, P., Ostendorf, F.: NEO-FFI: NEO-Fünf-Faktoren-Inventar nach Costa und McCrae, 2nd edn. Manual. Hogrefe, Göttingen (2008)
6. Brill, T.M., Munoz, L., Miller, R.J.: Siri, Alexa, and other digital assistants: a study of customer satisfaction with artificial intelligence applications. J. Mark. Manag. **35**(15–16), 1401–1436 (2019). https://doi.org/10.1080/0267257X.2019.1687571
7. Brühl, J., Hauck, M., Hurtz, S.: Was ist eigentlich bei Facebook los? Süddeutsche Zeitung 05 April 2018. https://www.sueddeutsche.de/digital/datenmissbrauch-was-ist-eigentlich-gerade-bei-facebook-los-1.3932349
8. Chien, S.Y., Sycara, K., Liu, J.S., Kumru, A.: Relation between trust attitudes toward automation, Hofstede's cultural dimensions, and big five personality traits. Proc. Hum. Factors Ergon. Soc. Ann. Meet. **60**(1), 841–845 (2016). https://doi.org/10.1177/1541931213601192
9. Dhagarra, D., Goswami, M., Kumar, G.: Impact of trust and privacy concerns on technology acceptance in healthcare: an Indian perspective. Int. J. Med. Inform. **141**, 104164 (2020). https://doi.org/10.1016/j.ijmedinf.2020.104164
10. Döring, N., Bortz, J.: Forschungsmethoden und Evaluation in den Sozial und Humanwissenschaften, 5th edn. Springer, Berlin (2016)
11. Habler, F., Schwind, V., Henze, N.: Effects of smart virtual assistants' gender and language. In: Proceedings of Mensch und Computer 2019, pp. 469–473. ACM (2019). https://doi.org/10.1145/3340764.3344441
12. Kinsella, B.: Nearly 90 Million U.S. Adults Have Smart Speakers, Adoption Now Exceeds One-Third of Consumers. voicebot.ai (2020). https://perma.cc/336P-2C77. Accessed 28 Apr 2020

13. Kleinberg, S.: 5 ways voice assistance is shaping consumer behavior. Think with Google (2018). Accessed Jan 2018
14. Leiner, D.J.: SoSci Survey (version 3.1.06) (2019). https://www.soscisurvey.de
15. Mayring, P.: Qualitative Inhaltsanalyse Grundlagen und Techniken, 13th edn. Beltz, Weinheim (2022)
16. McLean, G., Osei-Frimpong, K.: Hey Alexa . . . examine the variables influencing the use of artificial intelligent in-home voice assistants. Comput. Hum. Behav. **99**, 28–37 (2019). https://doi.org/10.1016/j.chb.2019.05.009
17. Neyer, F.J., Felber, J., Gebhardt, C.: Entwicklung und validierung einer kurzskala zur erfassung von technikbereitschaft. Diagnostica **58**(2), 87–99 (2012). https://doi.org/10.1026/0012-1924/a000067
18. Oksanen, A., Savela, N., Latikka, R., Koivula, A.: Trust toward robots and artificial intelligence: an experimental approach to human-technology interactions online. Front. Psychol. **11**, 568256 (2020). https://doi.org/10.3389/fpsyg.2020.568256
19. Olson, C., Kemery, K.: Voice report: from answers to action: customer adoption of voice technology and digital assistants (2019)
20. Osborne, J.: Why 100 million monthly Cortana users on windows 10 is a big deal. TechRadar (2016). Accessed 20 July 2016
21. Perero-Codosero, J.M., Espinoza-Cuadros, F.M., Hernández-Gómez, L.A.: X-vector anonymization using autoencoders and adversarial training for preserving speech privacy. Comput. Speech Lang. **74**, 101351 (2022). https://doi.org/10.1016/j.csl.2022.101351
22. Pitardi, V., Marriott, H.R.: Alexa, she's not human but. . . unveiling the drivers of consumers' trust in voice-based artificial intelligence. Psychol. Mark. **38**(4), 626–642 (2021). https://doi.org/10.1002/mar.21457
23. Rammstedt, B., John, O.P.: Kurzversion des big five inventory (BFI-K). Diagnostica **51**(4), 195–206 (2005). https://doi.org/10.1026/0012-1924.51.4.195
24. Reinkemeier, F., Gnewuch, U.: Match or mismatch? How matching personality and gender between voice assistants and users affects trust in voice commerce. In: Bui, T. (ed.) Proceedings of the 55th Hawaii International Conference on System Sciences. Proceedings of the Annual Hawaii International Conference on System Sciences, Hawaii International Conference on System Sciences (2022). https://doi.org/10.24251/HICSS.2022.528
25. Tas, S.: R.A.: Nutzung von sprachassistenten in deutschland. In: Sprachassistenten - Anwendungen, Implikationen, Entwicklungen: ITG-Workshop: Magdeburg, p. 39 (2020)
26. Siegert, I., Sinha, Y., Winkelmann, G., Jokisch, O., Wendemuth, A.: Public interactions with voice assistant - discussion of different one-shot solutions to preserve speaker privacy. In: Proceedings of the Workshop on Ethical and Legal Issues in Human Language Technologies and Multilingual De-Identification of Sensitive Data In Language Resources within the 13th Language Resources and Evaluation Conference, pp. 44–47. European Language Resources Association, Marseille, France (2022). https://aclanthology.org/2022.legal-1.8
27. Sinha, Y., et al.: Why Eli Roth should not use TTS-systems for anonymization. In: Siegert, I., Tomashenko, N., Williams, J. (eds.) Proceedings of the 2nd Symposium on Security and Privacy in Speech Communication, pp. 17–22. ISCA, Incheon, Korea (2022)
28. Splendid Research GmbH: Studie: Digitale sprachassistenten und smart speaker (2019). https://www.splendid-research.com/de/studie-digitale-sprachassistenten. Accessed (2021)

29. Srivastava, B.M.L., et al.: Privacy and utility of x-vector based speaker anonymization. IEEE/ACM Trans. Audio Speech Lang. Process. **30**, 2383–2395 (2022). https://doi.org/10.1109/TASLP.2022.3190741

30. Vimalkumar, M., Sharma, S.K., Singh, J.B., Dwivedi, Y.K.: 'okay google, what about my privacy?': user's privacy perceptions and acceptance of voice based digital assistants. Comput. Hum. Behav. **120**, 106763 (2021). https://doi.org/10.1016/j.chb.2021.106763

31. Wienrich, C., Reitelbach, C., Carolus, A.: The trustworthiness of voice assistants in the context of healthcare investigating the effect of perceived expertise on the trustworthiness of voice assistants, providers, data receivers, and automatic speech recognition. Front. Comput. Sci. **3**, 685250 (2021). https://doi.org/10.3389/fcomp.2021.685250

Design and Evaluation of Voice User Interfaces: What Should One Consider?

Andreas M. Klein[1,2]([✉]) [iD], Kristina Kölln[1,2] [iD], Jana Deutschländer[2] [iD],
and Maria Rauschenberger[2] [iD]

[1] Department of Computer Languages and Systems, University of Seville,
Seville, Spain
[2] Faculty of Technology, University of Applied Sciences Emden/Leer,
Emden, Germany
{andreas.klein,kristina.koelln,jana.deutschlaender,
maria.rauschenberger}@hs-emden-leer.de
https://www.hs-emden-leer.de

Abstract. Voice user interfaces (VUI) come in various forms of software or hardware, are controlled by voice, and can help the user in their daily life. Despite VUIs being readily available on smartphones, they have a low adoption rate. This can be attributed to challenges such as the misunderstanding of voice commands as well as privacy and data security concerns. Still, there are intensive VUI users, but they also raise concerns that may be independent of culture. Hence, we will discuss in our paper the various areas that should be considered when developing VUIs to increase user acceptance and foster a *positive* user experience (UX). We propose exploring the context of use and UX aspects to understand users' needs while using VUIs. All of our suggestions can help VUI developers to design better VUIs.

Keywords: Voice User Interfaces · Voice Assistants · Design · Evaluation · User Experience

1 Introduction

When talking about voice user interfaces (VUI) [13], voice assistants [27], or smart personal assistants [41], we consider the so-called *general-purpose assistants* that belong to the *adaptive voice/vision assistants* [41]. Popular examples include Amazon's Alexa, Apple's Siri, and Google Assistant. The different terms have, to some degree, different meanings; however, for simplicity, we will use the term VUI because all voice-controlled systems include a VUI, whether they are software systems (*e.g.,* Dragon speech recognition software) or hardware devices (*e.g.,* smart speakers such as the Apple HomePod).

VUIs are becoming increasingly popular as a way for users to interact with technology through voice commands. As more and more devices are equipped with voice recognition technology, the importance of designing effective VUIs becomes increasingly clear. Positive VUI design can improve user experience (UX) and make the technology more accessible to a wider range of people.

G. Salvendy and J. Wei (Eds.): HCII 2023, LNCS 14052, pp. 167–190, 2023.
https://doi.org/10.1007/978-3-031-35921-7_12

VUIs have developed into a leading-edge technology with a wide range of applications in corporate and consumer sectors. Such areas include, *e.g.*, healthcare, the automotive industry, voice commerce, and customer service [91]. ChatGPT, which was recently released by OpenAI [63], will improve VUIs in terms of natural speaking commands and communication as well as answer accuracy.

Although users like to use the comfort functions of VUIs (switching lights on with voice commands instead of going to the light switch), the adoption rate is low. This is often due to data security and privacy concerns [88], but it is also due to VUIs' frequent failure to understand voice commands. UX quality measurement, which is central to the human-centered design (HCD) process [29], can also be a valuable tool for VUI improvement, especially regarding the low adoption rate [38]. We must address users' concerns with *acceptance by design* [72] to overcome these barriers.

In this paper, we will cover the key principles of VUI design and evaluation to offer practical tips and best practices for creating better VUIs. Whether you are a designer, developer, or product manager, this guide will provide valuable insights into designing VUIs that are intuitive, user-friendly, and functional. VUI design plays a critical role in the success of voice-based technology. Thus, we hope the design increases the acceptance of future VUIs.

The rest of this paper is structured as follows: In Sect. 2, we briefly explain what VUIs are and what the HCD process is. We then provide an overview of current guidelines for VUI design in Sect. 3. We go on to detail what we currently know about VUI users (Sect. 4) to understand the current challenges (Sect. 5). We then describe our proposal for how to design and evaluate VUIs in Sect. 6. Finally, the paper concludes with a few closing remarks in Sect. 7.

2   Background

In this section, we define VUIs using a commonly accepted and succinct definition. We then provide a brief overview of the human-centered design (HCD) process and its interrelated activities [29].

2.1   VUI Definition

Voice user interfaces (VUI), also called voice assistants or speech-based technology, come in various systems or devices controlled by voice but can also provide voice/vision assistance [41]. We refer to software, devices, and systems that include a VUI based on the following definition:

"A voice user interface (or VUI) is what a person interacts with when communicating with a spoken language application" [13].

VUI system designations used in existing literature vary greatly (*e.g.*, voice assistants [27], AI-based digital voice assistants [19], voice-activated personal assistants [52], smart personal assistants [40], intelligent personal assistants [50], conversational assistants [4], and voice-based conversational agents [10], as well as voice-based or personal digital assistants [55]). However, they mainly refer to systems such as Amazon's Alexa, Apple's Siri, Google Assistant, and Microsoft's Cortana. Another kind of VUI system is, *e.g.*, the speech recognition software Dragon, which is a well-known VUI alternative to the keyboard for persons with disabilities [70]. We use VUIs as a synonym for all of these VUI systems in the rest of this paper.

The collective components of VUIs are referred to as a service or device [88]. VUIs come equipped with various integrated functions, such as web search or online shopping. Additional capabilities, known as *skills* for Alexa or *actions* for Google Assistant, can also be added. We will use skills as a synonym for these additional capabilities in the rest of this paper. These skills can serve various purposes (*e.g.*, entertainment, smart home) and are often provided by third parties. In addition, there are end-user environments that allow the use of preferred online web services through voice applications [77].

2.2   Human-Centered Design Process

The human-centered design (HCD) process is used to design solutions that fulfill users' requirements, thereby providing a positive user experience (UX) when interacting with the product [29]. The HCD provides general elements to design interactive systems within an iterative process. UX is the holistic consequence of the user's interaction within the context of use (*i.e.*, before, during, and after product use). The context of use includes all details about the user's interaction with the product [16].

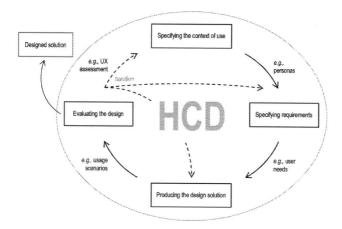

Fig. 1. HCD activities in the development process, based on [29].

The HCD process includes four elements (see Fig. 1) that should be applied during the development process: (1) *"specifying the context of use"* (*e.g.*, applying personas), (2) *"specifying the user requirements"* (*e.g.*, identifying user's needs), (3) *"producing design solutions"* (*e.g.*, developing prototypes), and (4) *"evaluating the design"* (*e.g.*, measuring UX quality) [29]. The user's interaction occurs within the context of use and results in UX being influenced by three components: the user, the system, and the context of use [23].

Although the HCD was developed with graphical user interfaces (GUIs) in mind, it can also be used to design VUIs. After we have described other proposals for how to design VUIs, we will use the HCD process and its steps to explain current challenges and solutions regarding VUI design.

3   Related Work

VUI design has been explored in the field. Cohen proposed a design process based on six VUI design principles in 2004 [13]. The main application of a VUI for his process was an automatic voice-answering telephone service. Since then, significant advancements have been made in VUI technology.

When proposing VUI design processes, researchers often focus on the differences between GUIs and VUIs and how to turn a GUI designer into a VUI developer. Using GUI heuristics as a starting point to develop VUI heuristics may enable GUI designers to easily transition into VUI development [57,58].

More recently, principles of conversational experiences have been proposed as a holistic guide for VUI design, with several methodologies and application scenarios [66]. We also want to offer a holistic view of VUI design that is based on the HCD process and updated with the latest findings regarding relevant UX aspects, evaluation methodology, and the context of use.

4   What Do We Know About Current VUI Users?

VUIs are widely available, as they have been increasingly integrated into everyday life via smart devices (*e.g.*, the internet of things, smartphones, tablets, personal computers, smart speakers, and smart home applications [85]). However, there is a high degree of skepticism about their use [34,88].

An intercultural study compared the VUI usage patterns, contexts of use, concerns, and improvement proposals of concrete user groups from Germany and Spain [38]. The research protocol provides more information if needed [39]. Despite cultural differences between the two, the study revealed similar trends and difficulties regarding speech intelligibility, correct command execution, data security, and privacy. The study revealed that about 61% of each concrete user group from Germany and Spain are intensive users. These users apply VUIs in contexts of use such as *at home* and *on the road* for typical use cases (*e.g.*, *selection of media* and *voice transmission*). The current priority in terms of VUI enhancement is improving speech recognition (*e.g.*, when users speak too fast or unclearly). Privacy is another essential improvement aspect because more than a third of Spanish and German users mentioned fear of monitoring [38].

Regarding intensive users, it has been shown that the frequency of use per day is between 76% [34,38] and 80% [43]. The research protocols provide more information if needed [35,39,44].

In Germany, a study from 2019 found that 30% of VUI users use their VUI intensively, with 11% using it daily and 19% using it several times a week [84]. We can break down the usage further into several hours a day (see Fig. 2). This is important to know when designing VUIs, as the distribution of frequency of use probably depends on the usage scenarios, meaning the task and context of the user. For example, regularly using Alexa to set a timer is a typical usage scenario that only requires a few seconds. Still, it may be done several times a day (*e.g.*, for cooking). However, if one uses a VUI (*e.g.*, Dragon) to dictate emails or complete work tasks, the duration of use is much longer, sometimes hours. Hence, the frequency of use depends not only on the VUI system but also on the context of use.

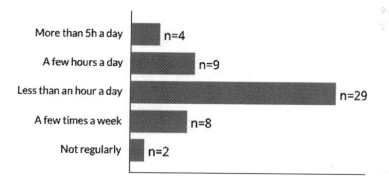

Fig. 2. Frequency of use ($N = 52$) [43].

Regarding VUI use of internet users, some European countries (*e.g.*, Denmark and Germany) lag far behind others (*e.g.*, Spain and Italy); globally, Europe ranks after the United States and Asian countries (*e.g.*, China and India) [88]. A population-representative survey in 2019 revealed that 29% of American consumers prefer chatbots for quick questions to solve customer service problems instead of, *e.g.*, phone (40%) or email (20%) [9]. An American consumer report from 2022 reveals a VUI adoption rate saturation of 50–60% for the American population. VUI use by American adults is expected to stagnate until new or improved attractive voice applications are released [30]. However, the technology of how we can interact with a system through voice has advanced greatly in recent years. That is also why every person with a smartphone has access to a VUI.

VUI use for social interaction has received little research interest and is negatively impacted by environmental factors that reduce VUI functionality (*e.g.*, background noise of other people in the same place [68] or poor internet connection

[71]). There is a demand for improvement in multi-party conversation with VUIs because VUI interaction has thus far been distinctly different from human-to-human conversation [69]. This could change with the release of the large language model ChatGPT from the company OpenAI [63], as the technology is marked by its immensely improved natural speaking and conversation abilities.

Recently, the UX aspects of VUIs have been explored using qualitative ($N = 10$) and quantitative ($N = 52$) data from intensive VUI users [43]. The two UX aspects most mentioned by users are *comprehension* (*i.e.*, correct understanding even when one does not speak clearly) and *error-free* (*i.e.*, no faults in operating and answering). The categorization of the 32 identified UX aspects, according to Kano, narrows down the relevance of the individual UX aspects for VUIs more precisely (*e.g.*, 19 UX aspects are distinct and relevant for VUI users) [46]. The research protocols provides more information on the VUI UX aspects if needed [44, 45].

It seems that many intensive VUI users have impairments, *e.g.*, visual impairment [43]. This may also have an influence on the main usage scenarios, as people with impairments report that VUIs make their daily lives easier. In contrast, intensive users with no impairments use VUIs for comfort or convenience rather than necessity. The motivations for the two are different: for example, a person with an impairment may use the VUI to dictate an email because writing it, would take a long time or may not even be possible at all without the VUI. On the other hand, a person without an impairment may use a VUI out of convenience to navigate while driving because they do not want to stop the car.

The VUI family usage reveals that the user group children playfully interact with VUIs (*e.g.*, nonsense questions for fun) while the parents make mainly goal orientated inquiries. There are content-related differences between parents (*e.g.*, weather report request) and children (*e.g.*, audio games) [31].

When designing VUIs, the duration of use, usage scenarios, and contexts of use must be addressed to foster a *positive* UX.

5   Current Challenges: Why Do We Not Have More VUI Users?

Despite the great popularity and growing adoption of automated technology, there are underlying usage concerns and little insight into user motivational factors, which leads to a limited consideration of user preferences [19]. Therefore, research on human-computer interaction (HCI) regarding AI-based voice technology is necessary because, *e.g.*, VUIs are not trusted much for service problem-solving; people prefer to interact with service employees instead of VUIs [19].

There are many examples of barriers that present when interacting with VUIs, which could lead to harmful or decreased interaction [14, 38, 72, 88].

As we pointed out previously, VUIs are available to every smartphone owner, yet the adoption rate remains very low in some countries (*e.g.*, Spain and Germany [38]). This seems to be due to various reasons we address in the following.

5.1   Context Sensitivity

The example shown in Fig. 3 illustrates the challenges users face when interacting with VUIs, which could result in less interaction [34]. In this case, Siri lost the conversational context after the first answer, resulting in an inaccurate answer to the follow-up question (*i.e.,* negative UX). Context-sensitive interaction is a necessary VUI quality feature [41,88].

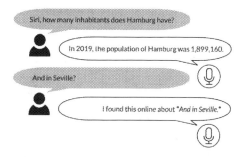

Fig. 3. VUI interaction example with a follow-up question

Follow-up questions aside, there are many other situations in which the VUI should be aware of the context. Imagine a person sitting on a train, using a VUI, and the VUI audibly confirms their credit card security code. This is just one example of sensitive information that should not be shared in public. However, there are other usage scenarios in which people might not want to share what they are doing with others. This presents a problem, as VUIs' auditory feedback is mainly through speakers (although there are VUIs with visual feedback). In addition, users are concerned not only about potential eavesdroppers in their surroundings but also about the company that provides the VUI. Users worry that VUIs are listening 24/7 and will eavesdrop on private conversations [51].

Depending on the context of the task, goal, or environment, users may not be willing to share personal information (*e.g.,* bank details).

5.2   User Needs

The VUI should be able to adapt to the user's abilities and needs. This can be due to a variety of reasons. For example, children who are not able to read yet may want to use VUIs for fun or queries, but at the same time, parents are concerned about what information children can access. Talking to VUIs as an English native or non-native speaker can be problematic, *e.g.,* when using proper names, non-English words, or pronunciations with strong accents [71]. When a person with an impairment depends on the auditory feedback and cannot use their device without it, that can be problematic if the VUI is not error-free or does not provide further help. In such cases, visual control may be the only way to interact. If a person has an impairment, it is important that they have an assistant VUI that always works. Assistive technology is one of the nine main research topics in HCI [50], and thus, the user's needs play a huge role. VUIs are beneficial for persons with disabilities and increase their independence in daily life, but they must be accessible [52].

Although VUIs are widely available, their use is limited due to challenges such as speech intelligibility, correct command execution, context-sensitive interaction, data security, and privacy [14,38,72,88]. Level of trust and privacy risks influence VUI adoption behavior. Users who expect a higher benefit from VUI technology tend to ignore privacy issues, in contrast to skeptical users [93]. Therefore, VUI adoption rates vary widely globally and are influenced by multiple factors. These include technical or cultural factors regarding, *e.g.*, various languages and accents [38,88] as well as motivation for use and empathetic aspects [19].

Regarding privacy concerns, a distinction must be made between non-users, potential users, and users. Users and potential users tend to trust large companies to protect their privacy, while non-users tend to feel uneasy and more concerned about privacy [48]. Trust directly influences VUI adoption behavior, while privacy risks indirectly impact it [93]. Privacy concerns and discomfort also occur when using VUIs in public spaces [5] or in the presence of others (*e.g.*, family members [10]). Users weigh privacy concerns against the benefits of VUIs and determine that the usefulness of the VUI outweighs their privacy concerns [93]. A study on always-listening VUIs revealed that users are willing to disclose sensitive data if it results in VUI use advantages, such as personalized and context-sensitive services [87]. Further, changing the environment for the same VUI use case (*e.g.*, weather report requests in private or public places) can lead to non-use because of discomfort when surrounded by other people.

A long-term survey in the United States investigated the integration of Alexa into people's lives. They identified that users tested Alexa in three main ways: personality, knowledge, and intelligence. They quickly realized the limits of Alexa, which resulted in decreased use in their daily routines. The interaction frequently aborts due to misinterpretation or misunderstanding of user commands [81].

VUI usage includes a wide range of use cases integrated into daily life, such as VUIs on smartphones as a standard feature, car navigation, and home automation. This results in multiple application environments, *e.g.*, *mobile, in the car*, and *at home* [14,34,71]. The identification and use of contextual information are essential for classifying VUIs as *smart* or *intelligent* [40].

5.3   Biases

The voice recognition technology of VUIs is not immune to biases regarding aspects such as gender, race, or ethnicity [86], which is a problem for facial recognition technology as well. Research has shown that accuracy gaps exist in voice recognition between genders [1,6,89], dialects [1,2,90], and other sociolinguistic variations [11,18,90]. These biases, although unintentional, are nonetheless problematic. Among American native English speakers, error rates are lowest for white subjects and higher for black and mixed-race subjects [89,90]. This is particularly troubling because these demographic groups also face discrimination in other areas of life. *Sociophonetics* [86] examines the impact of social elements on the way speech is both produced and understood.

There is a multitude of variations in the human voice, such as speaking rate, vocal effort, regional accent, pronunciation, or speaking style. To date, there is no consensus in the research community as to which of these are responsible for the unwarranted differences in accuracy and word error rate for different user groups. For example, gender differences are sometimes thought to have physical causes, such as the differences in pitch between male and female speakers [20,97], the high fundamental frequency of female voices [21,24], or the lower signal-to-noise ratio of female speakers, who tend to speak more softly than their male counterparts [90]. However, the difference in accuracy between genders could also be due to the fact that speech is analyzed differently by males and females [60]. A better understanding of the differences in analysis could increase the accuracy of speech recognition systems, but the differences also highlight that systems designed for one demographic group may not work well for another.

Methods for mitigating biases in speech recognition are only beginning to emerge. Biases may be present in several areas of a speech recognition system, including training data, resources, pretrained models, and the algorithms themselves. For example, it is well known that the performance of speech recognition systems declines in mismatched conditions in which the speaker population differs significantly between the training and target test data [17]. To address the problem of variation, it is recommended to select more diverse training data [17] and to use additional models that include demographic variations such as gender, ethnicity, and dialect [3].

Another concern is that the voices of VUIs themselves amplify gender stereotypes, with popular VUIs such as Siri, Alexa, and Cortana having female-gendered names and voices. This can be problematic when combined with submissive language, as it perpetuates harmful gender stereotypes [12,22,92]. The existence of race and gender biases in voice recognition technology is a serious issue that must be addressed and solved. Addressing these biases requires taking a closer look at the training data and algorithms used in voice recognition technology and ensuring that they are inclusive and unbiased.

5.4   GUI *vs.* VUI

VUIs describe the auditory command and response between a user and a system. They are often accompanied by graphical user interfaces (GUI). Figure 4 presents two examples of voice/vision assistants [41] after a weather request: *"How is the weather in Hamburg?"*. On the left side, Apple's Siri GUI is in the English language version, and on the right side, Microsoft's Cortana GUI is in the German language version.

There are various approaches for how to design GUIs, *i.e.,* processes (*e.g.,* HCD process [29]), artifacts (*e.g.,* personas [82]), or guidelines (*e.g.,* the law of proximity [15]). Some of these approaches (*e.g.*, the HCD or personas) can also be applied to VUI design since they address all interactive systems or users in general.

However, VUI developers should be aware throughout the design process that VUIs are different from GUIs in many ways. Not only is the input method different, but the output is too. Since the information is processed differently, auditory perception must also be considered when designing VUIs.

For example, we know that GUI elements that are placed next to each other are perceived as a group, even if they have different shapes [15]. Since a VUI does not necessarily have anything the user can see, this rule may not be applicable to VUIs at all.

Voice/vision assistants combine VUI and GUI (see Fig. 4), where speech remains the primary interaction mode and supports the user, *e.g.*, with additional visually processed information [41]. However, the multi-modal processing of different sensory stimuli can also be disadvantageous (*e.g.*, listening and reading simultaneously) [78].

Fig. 4. Example of a weather report request via voice/vision assistant of Apple's Siri GUI in English (left), and Microsoft's Cortana GUI in German (right).

There are many more rules for designing interactive systems, such as the eight golden rules of interface design [83], or the ten usability heuristics for user interfaces design [61], which were initially written with GUIs in mind and are only partially applicable to VUI design.

Design approaches have already been developed for VUIs, such as the six design principles for VUIs [13], the different usability heuristics for speech-based interfaces [47,94], or the UX aspects for VUIs [43]. The design approaches for VUIs overlap with those for GUIs, as the design principles for the two overlap. However, any time voice is considered (*e.g.,* pleasant voice), it is not applicable to a GUI unless it has an additional voice input or output.

5.5 Technical Challenges

Current technical challenges when using VUIs include correct command execution, speech intelligibility, and context-sensitivity [38,72,88]. Also, environmental aspects reduce VUI functionality [31], such as background noise of others talking in the same place [68] or poor internet connection [71]. VUIs are only intelligent if they perceive the context of use [40]. For example, when one searches for a restaurant by voice command, the context information, such as user preferences (*e.g.,* price category, favorite dishes), location (*e.g.,* driving in the car), and time limit (*e.g.,* during the lunch break), should be incorporated to fulfill the user's request. A VUI that combines artificial intelligence (AI) and natural language processing can realize voice-verbal interaction [64], but it cannot have a natural conversation as with a human [52] because of the lack of context-aware interaction [4, 40].

ChatGPT uses methods of learning from human dialogues, *e.g.,* by recording and evaluating conversations between the AI trainer and chatbot (*i.e.,* conversational context information is collected and assessed) [63]. This new release has gained attention not only from researchers but also society. ChatGPT has significantly altered the public's view of the existing capabilities and potential of AI tools for different contexts such as higher education [59]. By extension, this has also affected the view of VUIs, since the quality of task execution of VUIs depends on their ability to understand the context of use. The more context-related data available, the more accurate the VUI's response, which conflicts with protecting users' privacy [38]. ChatGPT [63] also uses a major data set, not from the microphone directly, but from previous sources. Hence, the users' concerns about the tool, the company, or anybody else listening in to answer a context-dependent query may no longer be relevant.

6 How Should VUIs be Designed?

A well-designed VUI can provide a smooth and intuitive UX, making it easier for people to interact with the technology. Thoughtful VUI design can also help to reduce frustration and minimize errors, which can lead to a better overall UX.

Interactive systems have traditionally been designed with the HCD process. The focus in standard HCD has thus far been on GUI. However, the design of VUIs is different from traditional GUIs. It requires an HCD approach that considers the unique capabilities of speaking and hearing, which are distinct from seeing.

For example, a VUI design also needs VUI UX assessment. Although there have been efforts to assess the UX of VUIs through methods such as questionnaires, interviews, and mixed methods [28,42], there is still a lack of reliable and validated methods for UX assessment [33,42]. This means we cannot fully understand or measure UX, and that the missing aspects are not considered for the next design iteration. This leads to lower usage and adoption rates.

Therefore, it is important for VUI developers to carefully consider VUI-specific artifacts or methods when designing VUIs to increase the acceptance of voice-based technology (*i.e., acceptance by design* [72]). Based on our experience and existing literature, we provide recommendations for VUI developers on how to improve the design of VUIs.

6.1   VUI Design Process

The HCD process provides recommendations for the HCD of computer-based interactive systems in which GUI dominates. From the VUI design perspective, the existing literature describes basic and advanced VUI design methods [66] as well as key principles [13]. Examples of design methods are conversational design (*i.e.,* considering context-sensitive interaction), identifying users' expectations, applying design tools (*e.g.,* prototyping tools), and usability testing [66]. Examples of prototyping tools are wizard of oz tools (*e.g.,* Woz Way), dialogue management systems (*e.g.,* SUEDE), and natural language understanding platforms (*e.g.,* Alexa skills kit) [8]. A *fundamental methodology* [13] is available with key principles such as requirements definition, context, design, development, testing, and evaluation (*e.g.,* usability tests) [13]. The HCD process, with its four steps ([1] specifying the context of use and [2] requirements, [3] producing, and [4] evaluating the design), considers the key principles of the fundamental VUI design methodology (see Fig. 1), as these steps influence the UX immensely.

We see a demand for relevant UX aspects and context-dependent UX assessment for VUIs because these areas strongly affect UX. This means that we see a demand for a VUI design based on the VUI UX aspects [43], the VUI context of use, and the context-dependent VUI UX assessment [33] to combine the *fundamental methodology* [13] and the HCD process [29]. As evaluation is very often the core of a further design iteration, we give an example of a possible VUI evaluation area (Fig. 5, left) that can be addressed with methods or artifacts (Fig. 5, right).

We will describe the examples of the VUI evaluation area and the support it can bring to VUI design in the following sections.

6.2   Specifying the Context of Use and Requirements for VUIs

In the HCD process, the first two steps are to define the context of use and the user requirements. We argue that if the existing VUI UX aspects are used within the HCD process [43], they can help VUI developers to understand the users' needs and their preferences for the current VUI task or system. To improve UX and *acceptance by design* [72], we need to address the current challenges (as described in Sect. 5), such as *sociophonetics* [86].

To increase the acceptance of the user (and stakeholders), we need to address their skills, competencies, and needs regarding the use of the VUI. These multiple user aspects could be but are not limited to a person with special needs [98]

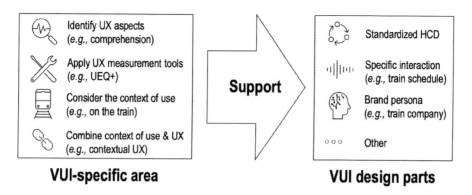

Fig. 5. VUI evaluation supports VUI design

such as dyslexia [75]. The following is an example of how to approach user aspects with the HCD process and a focus on VUI UX aspects. We can do this by identifying the target users (*e.g.,* children) for the VUI or stakeholder groups (*e.g.,* parents). We then learn about the characteristics of the users. For example, parents are concerned about the unlimited access their child may have to information that is not appropriate for children. Children, on the other hand, are less anxious about interacting with a VUI and would try everything, but they may not speak clearly or may have limited reading skills. Therefore, VUI developers must find a way to protect the child's well-being when designing commands, voice recognition, or responses. We can identify user requirements with user profiles, personas, and task scenarios that focus on VUI aspects [43]. In the first step, UX experts recommend identifying and considering the user's important UX aspects for product development. The second step should include UX aspects such as marketing, and product placement [96].

The context is relevant for all VUI design decisions; therefore, a differentiation is needed, such as consideration of the user context (*e.g.,* various linguistic expressions) and persona context (*e.g.,* formal VUI answers because of the company's image – a *brand persona vs.* user persona). Or the context of the usage scenario, such as *on the road* or *at home* [34].

A VUI persona offers high-quality UX options [65]. It includes the characteristics of the VUI's personality, thus conveying the corporate image via VUI [13]. This also depends on the usage scenarios [43]. For example, a request about train times sent to a railroad company via VUI should lead to a short answer that provides clear, detailed, and reliable information about the train timetable. These are characteristics of the train company's brand persona. VUI developers apply brand personas to realize VUIs' mental image as well as user stories to depict the interaction's context of use [56]. VUIs should, like GUIs, address the different characteristics of a person. Since there are currently many VUI users with impairments, their needs should be specifically addressed. A collection of different needs has already been summarized for web accessibility [98] and can be easily integrated into a user persona to be considered when they use a VUI. However, there are other characteristics that play a role and should be addressed. For example, children and people who are illiterate may lack reading skills, elderly people may be more resistant to speaking out loud with a device, and others may be concerned about VUI use by their children and dependents.

Another aspect to consider about the context is that an identical VUI interaction can lead to a different perception. For example, a request about an illness via a VUI may be done in private places (which leads to positive UX) but may not be done (*i.e.*, most negative UX) in public places (*e.g.*, on the train). People have privacy concerns and discomfort when utilizing VUIs in public places [5] or in the presence of others (*e.g.*, friends) [10].

To sum up, the user's needs, skills, and competencies, as well as the context or the usage scenario, must be considered in the VUI design in order to create a positive UX.

6.3   Producing the Design Solution

Prototyping techniques for VUIs help test and refine the UX and functionality before the final product is released. For GUI, we know how to produce low- and high-fidelity prototypes with, *e.g.*, paper prototypes, wireframes, or click prototypes. Due to the nature of hearing, a paper prototype is not meaningful. We do the prototyping for early assessment because speech-based technologies can benefit from additional assessment tools to incorporate usability and UX feedback early in the development process of VUIs. Hence, we need to focus on other existing evaluation methods, such as the *wizard of oz*, or we need to design new methods. Existing techniques can include storyboards, wizard of oz prototyping, low-fidelity prototyping, high-fidelity prototyping, simulation and testing, and iterative design. These techniques have different levels of detail, complexity, and purpose, and can be used alone or in combination to achieve the desired outcome. Existing guidelines from other output devices can also serve as inspiration for communication with the user, such as guidelines for ambient light systems [53,54]. These guidelines propose ways to inform the user unobtrusively, which could be adapted for VUI design. The goal of prototyping is to identify and resolve issues early in the development process, improving the overall UX and quality of the final product [8].

We also suggest designing *voice-user storyboards* or *voice-user canvases* that are similar to a regular storyboard but include additional comic elements, the goal of the user, and a possible conversation between the user and the VUI. An example (see Fig. 6) of a context and the request may be visualized as a story with different scenes or places. In an other example, a canvas is used to visualize different contexts and the same query. This depends on the VUI developer's needs and the VUI's goal. The attributes of the VUI brand persona could also be described [56].

Overall, there is a need for specific VUI prototyping tools, as the current variety is limited.

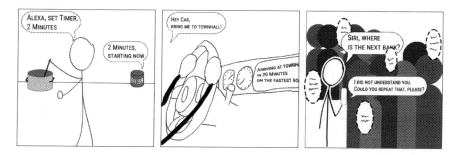

Fig. 6. Various scenarios for VUI usage in a basic storyboard: left, a cooking context when setting a timer; the middle, context of car navigation asking for directions; right, context of public spaces asking for directions.

6.4 VUI Evaluation

VUI evaluation can be done using different methods and tools for the fourth step of the HCD process [29]. This step is especially important if we design something very new, as the outcome is hard to predict. Therefore, the measurement and evaluation of early prototypes (early assessment), even with smaller groups, is as crucial for VUIs as it is for GUIs. This is especially true since VUIs are a new technology that is still evolving quickly, and it allows us to learn about the interaction.

It is essential precisely to define the context of use when evaluating VUIs [38]. Therefore, we propose considering the context of use as well as combining the concepts of UX, *e.g.,* by applying the *contextual user experience* method [62] in the HCD. Applying contextual UX can lead to a matrix consists of VUI context-of-use categories and factors mapped to relevant UX qualities [31]. This matrix helps towards a more abstract view and capturing of the VUI context of use, which is needed to realize context-dependent UX assessment for VUIs. The research protocol provides more information if needed [32]. As previously described, the user, the system, and the context of use [23] influence the interaction between the user and the system. Hence, to be able to measure the context-dependent UX to make a system *accepted by design* [72], we need different evaluation methods, depending on, *e.g.,* low-/high-fidelity prototypes, the context of use, or the number of users we have for the evaluation.

It is difficult to collect user data in general [73,74,95]. However, it is especially challenging for VUIs due to various factors. For example, users already have concerns about data collection, which is a reason for not using VUIs. For the same reason, recruiting a person for a VUI user study is challenging as well. Another factor is the cost that comes with preparing the data collection itself. There is, of course, no open access API like Twitter has for Tweets, where developers can access the data for research. This is mainly due to the fact that Twitter users publish their tweets publicly on the WEB. VUIs, however, are often in private spaces of users, so that data should not be publicly available. This means that companies storing big data from VUIs for their own analyses and developers not affiliated with these companies have the disadvantage that they have to collect data manually, which is costly in terms of time and resources.

Therefore, VUI developers with no access to these big data sets have to make the best of the limited data they can collect, which will often be small or tiny data. For example, machine learning techniques can be used even in small imbalanced data sets when design considerations or recommendations are followed, such as avoiding overfitting, using repeated measures, using cross-validation, or use of Bonferroni-Correction if multiple testing is used [73]. Another way to evaluate is, of course, to use different evaluation methods not connected to users. However, this is not within the scope of the HCD evaluation.

Since most VUI developers do not have access to a lot of data for the evaluation of VUIs, other methods or analyses are essential. Hence, existing qualitative data collection or studies come into play, such as a usability test, observations, or wizard-of-oz testing, as mentioned previously [8]. Other aspects also need to be considered when evaluating VUIs with user studies. For example, users cannot "think out loud" because the VUIs could interpret commands. Users could also become overwhelmed by simultaneously performing different meta tasks (*i.e.,* giving commands to the VUI while answering questions about the VUI). Further studies must be done on how well users can cope with this challenge and how the VUI can differentiate between commands and interview answers.

Therefore, we are relying on post-evaluation methods for user feedback because, *e.g.,* thinking aloud while interacting with a VUI is difficult. We argue that evaluation and design are currently more difficult for VUIs than they are for GUIs because of the way we interact with the device, as explained previously. If we want to perform a quantitative analysis, we need specific VUI evaluations. There is a demand for VUI evaluation with reliable, valid, and consistent methods for UX quality assessment [50]. Several approaches are known for evaluating interactive systems, such as questionnaires [42], voice recording [68], interviews and diary studies [48], psycho-physiological approaches [64], and mixed methods [28,43]. However, none of these consider the VUI context of use [33]. Existing VUI questionnaires often focus on task-related usability aspects such as efficiency, controllability, or learnability [25,26,67].

For post-evaluation, we propose the UEQ+ framework [80], as it can be adapted to further dimensions depending on the context, goal, or purpose. The UEQ+ framework [80], based on the User Experience Questionnaire (UEQ) [49], provides a flexible UX assessment approach in different languages, *e.g.,* Spanish [76]. From the VUI perspective, the UEQ+ provides three specific VUI voice quality scales designed to measure the following UX aspects: *response behavior* (*i.e.,* the VUI reacts like a human conversationalist), *response quality* (*i.e.,* the user's intention is fulfilled), and *comprehensibility* (*i.e.,* the user's intention is recognized without any special formulation) [36,37]. The UEQ+ framework currently consists of 20 scales (*e.g., efficiency, dependability, trust, and trustworthiness of content*), which can be combined arbitrarily to create a product-related questionnaire that measures a variety of UX aspects [79]. This is an essential advantage compared to existing VUI questionnaires because adaption (*e.g.*, to the specific research question) and extension (*e.g.*, to measure other UX aspects) are time- and personnel-intensive [38]. The UEQ+ framework contains a handbook and Excel sheet that include information about scale selection, questionnaire creation, and data evaluation. It is available free of charge at http://ueqplus.ueq-research.org/.

The UX tool selector is a new idea for choosing the suitable tool for context-dependent VUI recommendation [33], *i.e.* the toolbox. Regarding the given context, the selector draws on a UX measurement toolbox for VUIs, which contains, among other methods, the UEQ+ modular framework [80]. The selector is not only a suggestion of one method but can also suggest a mixed-method approach, *e.g.*, such as combining an interview with a questionnaire for scalability. Mixed-method approaches in VUI research are common [7,28,43]. An example, if one wants to assess a VUI customer service response regarding train schedules (the giving context), then the selector's recommendation could be a mixed-method approach to the UEQ+ with the six appropriate scales (*e.g.*, *efficiency*, *dependability*, *perspicuity*, *response behavior*, *response quality*, and *comprehensibility* [36]) in combination with another tool (*e.g.*, interviews). Interviews provide deeper insights into users' experiences with products [28].

7 Conclusion and Future Work

This paper presents an overview of VUI design and evaluation to design better VUIs. Therefore, we first describe current knowledge about VUI users, then the challenges of VUIs, and finish with valuable proposals to develop intuitive, user-friendly, and functional VUIs.

We are still in the early stages of designing a *positive* UX for VUIs and need to know the relevant UX aspects for our VUI usage scenarios. Furthermore, in the future, technological advancements, such as the recent release of ChatGPT, can provide new opportunities for VUI development, and we expect more to come. Therefore, we should consider different existing challenges and a possible (technical) approach to overcome these challenges by focusing on context-sensitive interaction that also considers user skills and needs.

In the future, we want to investigate the assessment for VUIs to provide valuable tools for the development of VUIs.

References

1. Abushariah, M., Sawalha, M.: The effects of speakers' gender, age, and region on overall performance of Arabic automatic speech recognition systems using the phonetically rich and balanced modern standard Arabic speech corpus. In: Proceedings of the 2nd Workshop of Arabic Corpus Linguistics WACL-2 (2013)
2. Ali, A.: Multi-dialect Arabic broadcast speech recognition. Ph.D. thesis, The University of Edinburgh (2018). https://core.ac.uk/display/429725521?source=2. Accessed 09 Feb 2023

3. Alsharhan, E., Ramsay, A.: Investigating the effects of gender, dialect, and training size on the performance of Arabic speech recognition. Nat. Lang. Eng. **54**(4), 975–998 (2020). https://doi.org/10.1007/s10579-020-09505-5

4. Ammari, T., Kaye, J., Tsai, J.Y., Bentley, F.: Music, Search, and IoT. ACM Trans. Comput.-Hum. Interact. **26**, 1–28 (2019). https://doi.org/10.1145/3311956

5. Bhalla, A.: An exploratory study understanding the appropriated use of voice-based search and assistants. In: Proceedings of the 9th Indian Conference on Human Computer Interaction, pp. 90–94. Association for Computing Machinery, New York (2018). https://doi.org/10.1145/3297121.3297136

6. Bhukya, S.: Effect of gender on improving speech recognition system. Int. J. Comput. Appl. **179**, 22–30 (2018). https://doi.org/10.5120/ijca2018916200

7. Biermann, M., Schweiger, E., Jentsch, M.: Talking to stupid?!? Improving voice user interfaces. In: Fischer, H., Hess, S. (eds.) Mensch und Computer 2019 - Usability Professionals, pp. 1–4. Gesellschaft für Informatik e.V. Und German UPA e.V., Bonn (2019). https://doi.org/10.18420/muc2019-up-0253

8. Cambre, J., Kulkarni, C.: Methods and tools for prototyping voice interfaces. In: Proceedings of the 2nd Conference on Conversational User Interfaces, pp. 1–4. ACM (2020). https://doi.org/10.1145/3405755.3406148

9. CGS: Customer Service Chatbots & Channels Survey (2019). https://www.cgsinc.com/en/resources/2019-CGS-Customer-Service-Chatbots-Channels-Survey. Accessed 09 Feb 2023

10. Cha, I., Kim, S.I., Hong, H., Yoo, H., kyung Lim, Y.: Exploring the use of a voice-based conversational agent to empower adolescents with autism spectrum disorder. In: Proceedings of the 2021 CHI Conference on Human Factors in Computing Systems, pp. 1–15. ACM (2021). https://doi.org/10.1145/3411764.3445116

11. Chan, M.P.Y., Choe, J., Li, A., Chen, Y., Gao, X., Holliday, N.: Training and typological bias in ASR performance for world Englishes. In: Proceedings of the Interspeech 2022, pp. 1273–1277 (09 2022). https://doi.org/10.21437/Interspeech.2022-10869

12. Chin, C., Robison, M.: How AI bots and voice assistants reinforce gender bias (2020). https://www.brookings.edu/research/how-ai-bots-and-voice-assistants-reinforce-gender-bias. Accessed 10 Feb 2023

13. Cohen, M.H., Giangola, J.P., Balogh, J.: Voice User Interface Design. Addison-Wesley, Boston (2004)

14. Corbett, E., Weber, A.: What can i say? Addressing user experience challenges of a mobile voice user interface for accessibility. In: Proceedings of the 18th International Conference on Human-Computer Interaction with Mobile Devices and Services, MobileHCI 2016, pp. 72–82. Association for Computing Machinery, New York (2016). https://doi.org/10.1145/2935334.2935386

15. Dahm, M.: Grundlagen der Mensch-Computer-Interaktion (Fundamentals of human-computer interaction). Pearson-Studium (2006)

16. Dey, A.K.: Understanding and using context. Pers. Ubiquit. Comput. **5**, 4–7 (2001). https://doi.org/10.1007/s007790170019

17. Doulaty Bashkand, M.: Methods for addressing data diversity in automatic speech recognition. Ph.D. thesis, The University of Sheffield (2017). https://ethos.bl.uk/OrderDetails.do?uin=uk.bl.ethos.713306. Accessed 09 Feb 2023

18. Droua-Hamdani, G., Selouani, S.A., Boudraa, M.: Speaker-independent ASR for modern standard Arabic: effect of regional accents. Int. J. Speech Technol. **15**, 487–493 (2012). https://doi.org/10.1007/s10772-012-9146-4

19. Fernandes, T., Oliveira, E.: Understanding consumers' acceptance of automated technologies in service encounters: drivers of digital voice assistants adoption. J. Bus. Res. **122**, 180–191 (2021). https://doi.org/10.1016/j.jbusres.2020.08.058

20. Gelfer, M.P., Mikos, V.A.: The relative contributions of speaking fundamental frequency and formant frequencies to gender identification based on isolated vowels. J. Voice: Off. J. Voice Found. **19**(4), 544–554 (2005)

21. Goldwater, S., Jurafsky, D., Manning, C.D.: Which words are hard to recognize? Prosodic, lexical, and disfluency factors that increase speech recognition error rates. Speech Commun. **52**(3), 181–200 (2010). https://doi.org/10.1016/j.specom.2009.10.001

22. Habler, F., Schwind, V., Henze, N.: Effects of smart virtual assistants' gender and language. In: Proceedings of Mensch Und Computer 2019, MuC 2019, pp. 469–473. Association for Computing Machinery, New York (2019). https://doi.org/10.1145/3340764.3344441

23. Hassenzahl, M., Tractinsky, N.: User experience - a research agenda. Behav. Inf. Technol. **25**, 91–97 (2006). https://doi.org/10.1080/01449290500330331

24. Hirschberg, J., Litman, D., Swerts, M.: Prosodic and other cues to speech recognition failures. Speech Commun. **43**, 155–175 (2004). https://doi.org/10.1016/j.specom.2004.01.006

25. Hone, K.: Usability measurement for speech systems: SASSI revisited. In: Proceedings of CHI (2014). http://www.cs.toronto.edu/dsli2014/submissions/Hone_CHI_workshop_paper-2014.pdf

26. Hone, K.S., Graham, R.: Towards a tool for the subjective assessment of speech system interfaces (SASSI). Nat. Lang. Eng. **6**(3 & 4), 287–303 (2000). https://doi.org/10.1017/S1351324900002497

27. Hoy, M.B.: Alexa, Siri, Cortana, and more: an introduction to voice assistants. Med. Ref. Serv. Q. **37**, 81–88 (2018). https://doi.org/10.1080/02763869.2018.1404391

28. Iniesto, F., Coughlan, T., Lister, K.: Implementing an accessible conversational user interface: applying feedback from university students and disability support advisors. Assoc. Comput. Mach. (2021). https://doi.org/10.1145/3430263.3452431

29. ISO9241-210:2019: Ergonomics of human-system interaction - part 210: Human-centred design for interactive systems. https://www.iso.org/standard/77520.html. Accessed 09 Feb 2023

30. Kinsella, B.: Voice assistant adoption clustering around 50% of the population (2022). https://voicebot.ai/2022/04/15/voice-assistant-adoption-clustering-around-50-of-the-population/. Accessed 09 Feb 2023

31. Klein, A.M., Deutschländer, J., Kölln, K., Rauschenberger, M., Escalona, M.J.: Exploring the context of use for voice user interfaces: toward context-dependent UX quality testing. Journal of Software: Evolution and Process (2023). [In revision]

32. Klein, A.M., Deutschländer, J., Kölln, K., Rauschenberger, M., Escalona, M.J.: Protocol for exploring the context of use for voice user interfaces: toward context-dependent UX quality testing. Technical report (2023). https://www.researchgate.net/. [In revision]

33. Klein, A.M.: Toward a user experience tool selector for voice user interfaces. In: Proceedings of the 18th International Web for All Conference, W4A 2021, pp. 1–2. Association for Computing Machinery, New York (2021). https://doi.org/10.1145/3430263.3456728

34. Klein, A.M., Hinderks, A., Rauschenberger, M., Thomaschewski, J.: Exploring voice assistant risks and potential with technology-based users. In: Proceedings

of the 16th International Conference on Web Information Systems and Technologies - Volume 1: WEBIST, pp. 147–154. INSTICC, SciTePress, Portugal (2020). https://doi.org/10.5220/0010150101470154

35. Klein, A.M., Hinderks, A., Rauschenberger, M., Thomaschewski, J.: Protocol for exploring voice assistant risks and potential with technology-based users. Technical report (2020). https://www.researchgate.net/, https://doi.org/10.13140/RG.2.2.21473.12646

36. Klein, A.M., Hinderks, A., Schrepp, M., Thomaschewski, J.: Construction of UEQ+ scales for voice quality. In: Proceedings of the Conference on Mensch Und Computer, MuC 2020, pp. 1–5. Association for Computing Machinery, New York (2020). https://doi.org/10.1145/3404983.3410003

37. Klein, A.M., Hinderks, A., Schrepp, M., Thomaschewski, J.: Measuring user experience quality of voice assistants. In: 2020 15th Iberian Conference on Information Systems and Technologies (CISTI), pp. 1–4. IEEE, Seville (2020). https://doi.org/10.23919/CISTI49556.2020.9140966

38. Klein, A.M., Rauschenberger, M., Thomaschweski, J., Escalona, M.J.: Comparing voice assistant risks and potential with technology-based users: a study from Germany and Spain. J. Web Eng. **7**(16), 1991–2016 (2021). https://doi.org/10.13052/jwe1540-9589.2071

39. Klein, A.M., Rauschenberger, M., Thomaschweski, J., Escalona, M.J.: Protocol for comparing voice assistant risks and potential with technology-based users: a study from Germany and Spain. Technical report (2021). https://www.researchgate.net/, https://doi.org/10.13140/RG.2.2.25678.18243/1

40. Knote, R., Janson, A., Eigenbrod, L., Söllner, M.: The what and how of smart personal assistants: principles and application domains for IS research. In: Proceedings of the 52nd Hawaii International Conference on System Sciences, pp. 1083–1094. Multikonferenz Wirtschaftsinformatik 2018, Lüneburg (2018). https://www.alexandria.unisg.ch/publications/252796

41. Knote, R., Janson, A., Söllner, M., Leimeister, J.M.: Classifying smart personal assistants: an empirical cluster analysis. In: Proceedings of the 52nd Hawaii International Conference on System Sciences (2019)

42. Kocaballi, A.B., Laranjo, L., Coiera, E.: Measuring user experience in conversational interfaces: a comparison of six questionnaires. In: Proceedings of British HCI 2018, pp. 1–12. BCS Learning and Development Ltd. (2018). https://doi.org/10.14236/ewic/HCI2018.21

43. Kölln, K., Deutschländer, J., Klein, A.M., Rauschenberger, M., Winter, D.: Identifying user experience aspects for voice user interfaces with intensive users. In: Proceedings of the 18th International Conference on Web Information Systems and Technologies, pp. 385–393. SCITEPRESS - Science and Technology Publications (2022). https://doi.org/10.5220/0011383300003318

44. Kölln, K., Deutschländer, J., Klein, A.M., Rauschenberger, M., Winter, D.: Protocol for identifying user experience aspects for voice user interfaces with intensive users (2022). https://doi.org/10.13140/RG.2.2.26828.49287

45. Kölln, K., Klein, A.M., Deutschländer, J., Winter, D., Rauschenberger, M.: Protocol for categorizing UX aspects for voice user interfaces using the kano model (2023). https://doi.org/10.13140/RG.2.2.32565.55528

46. Kölln, K., Klein, A.M., Deutschländer, J., Winter, D., Rauschenberger, M.: Categorizing UX aspects for voice user interfaces using the kano model. Springer Selection, p. 17 (2023). [Accepted]

47. Langevin, R., Lordon, R.J., Avrahami, T., Cowan, B.R., Hirsch, T., Hsieh, G.: Heuristic evaluation of conversational agents. In: Kitamura, Y., Quigley, A., Isbister, K., Igarashi, T., Bjørn, P., Drucker, S. (eds.) Proceedings of the 2021 CHI Conference on Human Factors in Computing Systems, pp. 1–15. ACM, New York (2021). https://doi.org/10.1145/3411764.3445312

48. Lau, J., Zimmerman, B., Schaub, F.: Alexa, are you listening? Privacy perceptions, concerns and privacy-seeking behaviors with smart speakers. Proc. ACM Hum.-Comput. Interact. **2** (2018). https://doi.org/10.1145/3274371

49. Laugwitz, B., Held, T., Schrepp, M.: Construction and evaluation of a user experience questionnaire. In: Holzinger, A. (ed.) USAB 2008. LNCS, vol. 5298, pp. 63–76. Springer, Heidelberg (2008). https://doi.org/10.1007/978-3-540-89350-9_6

50. Clark, L., et al.: The state of speech in HCI: trends, themes and challenges. Interact. Comput. **31**, 349–371 (2019). https://doi.org/10.1093/iwc/iwz016

51. Lenhardt, S.: Wenn der Sprachassistent mitlauscht (when the voice assistant eavesdrops) (2013). https://web.archive.org/web/20221107010344/https://www.tagesschau.de/faktenfinder/kurzerklaert/kurzerklaert-sprachassistenten-101.html. Accessed 07 Feb 2023

52. Lister, K., Coughlan, T., Iniesto, F., Freear, N., Devine, P.: Accessible conversational user interfaces: Considerations for design. In: Proceedings of the 17th International Web for All Conference, pp. 1–11. Association for Computing Machinery (2020). https://doi.org/10.1145/3371300.3383343

53. Matviienko, A., et al.: Towards new ambient light systems: a close look at existing encodings of ambient light systems. Interact. Design Archit. **2015**(26), 10–24 (2015)

54. Matviienko, A., et al.: Deriving design guidelines for ambient light systems. In: Proceedings of the 14th International Conference on Mobile and Ubiquitous Multimedia, MUM 2015, pp. 267–277. Association for Computing Machinery, New York (2015). https://doi.org/10.1145/2836041.2836069

55. Milhorat, P., Schlogl, S., Chollet, G., Boudy, J., Esposito, A., Pelosi, G.: Building the next generation of personal digital assistants. In: 2014 1st International Conference on Advanced Technologies for Signal and Image Processing (ATSIP), pp. 458–463. IEEE (2014). https://doi.org/10.1109/ATSIP.2014.6834655

56. Morawin, E., Paul, K., Uhlenbrock, J.: Voice personas (2020). https://wudos.de. Accessed 09 Feb 2023

57. Murad, C., Munteanu, C., Cowan, B.R., Clark, L.: Revolution or evolution? Speech interaction and HCI design guidelines. IEEE Pervasive Comput. **18**(2), 33–45 (2019). https://doi.org/10.1109/MPRV.2019.2906991

58. Murad, C., Munteanu, C., Cowan, B.R., Clark, L.: Finding a new voice: transitioning designers from GUI to VUI design. In: Proceedings of the 3rd Conference on Conversational User Interfaces, CUI 2021. Association for Computing Machinery, New York (2021). https://doi.org/10.1145/3469595.3469617

59. Neumann, M., Rauschenberger, M., Schön, E.M.: "We need to talk about ChatGPT": the future of ai and higher education. In: Proceedings of the 2023 IEEE/ACM 5th International Workshop on Software Engineering Education for the Next Generation (SEENG) to be Held 14–20 May 2023 in Melbourne, Australia, p. 4 (2023). https://conf.researchr.org/details/icse-2023/seeng-2023-papers/3/-We-Need-To-Talk-About-ChatGPT-The-Future-of-AI-and-Higher-Education

60. Newman, L.M., Groom, C.J., Handelman, L.D., Pennebaker, J.W.: Gender differences in language use: an analysis of 14,000 text samples. Discour. Process. **45**, 211–236 (2008). https://doi.org/10.1080/01638530802073712

61. Nielsen, J.: 10 usability heuristics for user interface design (2013). https://www.designprinciplesftw.com/collections/10-usability-heuristics-for-user-interface-design. Accessed 07 Feb 2023

62. Obrist, M., Tscheligi, M., de Ruyter, B., Schmidt, A.: Contextual user experience: how to reflect it in interaction designs?, pp. 3197–3200. Association for Computing Machinery, New York (2010). https://doi.org/10.1145/1753846.1753956

63. OpenAI: ChatGPT: Optimizing language models for dialogue (2022). https://openai.com/blog/chatgpt/. Accessed 07 Feb 2023

64. Le Pailleur, F., Huang, B., Léger, P.-M., Sénécal, S.: A new approach to measure user experience with voice-controlled intelligent assistants: a pilot study. In: Kurosu, M. (ed.) HCII 2020. LNCS, vol. 12182, pp. 197–208. Springer, Cham (2020). https://doi.org/10.1007/978-3-030-49062-1_13

65. Papież, D.: Conversational commerce: creating brand personas for the age of Voice Assistance (2019). https://www.thinkwithgoogle.com/intl/en-cee/future-of-marketing/emerging-technology/conversational-commerce-creating-brand-personas-age-voice-assistance/. Accessed 09 Feb 2023

66. Pearl, C.: Designing Voice User Interfaces: Principles of Conversational Experiences. O'Reilly Media, Inc. (2016)

67. Polkosky, M.D., Lewis, J.R.: Expanding the MOS: development and psychometric evaluation of the MOS-R and MOS-X. Int. J. Speech Technol. **6**, 161–182 (2003)

68. Porcheron, M., Fischer, J.E., Reeves, S., Sharples, S.: Voice interfaces in everyday life. In: Proceedings of the 2018 Conference on Human Factors in Computing Systems CHI, p. 1–12. Association for Computing Machinery (2018). https://doi.org/10.1145/3173574.3174214

69. Porcheron, M., Fischer, J.E., Sharples, S.: "Do animals have accents?": talking with agents in multi-party conversation. In: Proceedings of the 2017 ACM Conference on Computer Supported Cooperative Work and Social Computing, pp. 207–219. Association for Computing Machinery (2017). https://doi.org/10.1145/2998181.2998298

70. Pradhan, A., Mehta, K., Findlater, L.: "Accessibility came by accident": use of voice-controlled intelligent personal assistants by people with disabilities. Association for Computing Machinery (2018). https://doi.org/10.1145/3173574.3174033

71. Pyae, A., Joelsson, T.N.: Investigating the usability and user experiences of voice user interface: a case of google home smart speaker. In: Proceedings of the 20th International Conference on Human-Computer Interaction with Mobile Devices and Services Adjunct, pp. 127–131. Association for Computing Machinery (2018). https://doi.org/10.1145/3236112.3236130

72. Rauschenberger, M.: Acceptance by design : voice assistants. In: 1st AI-DEbate Workshop: Workshop Establishing an InterDisciplinary pErspective on Speech-BAsed TEchnology, 27 September 2021. OvGU, Magdeburg (2021). https://doi.org/10.25673/38476

73. Rauschenberger, M., Baeza-Yates, R.: How to handle health-related small imbalanced data in machine learning? i-com **19**(3), 215–226 (2020). https://doi.org/10.1515/icom-2020-0018

74. Rauschenberger, M., Baeza-Yates, R.: Recommendations to handle health-related small imbalanced data in machine learning. In: Hansen, C., Nürnberger, A., Preim, B. (eds.) Mensch und Computer 2020 - Workshopband (Human and Computer 2020 - Workshop proceedings), pp. 1–7. Gesellschaft für Informatik e.V., Bonn (2020). https://doi.org/10.18420/muc2020-ws111-333

75. Rauschenberger, M., Rello, L., Baeza-Yates, R.: Technologies for dyslexia. In: Yesilada, Y., Harper, S. (eds.) Web Accessibility Book, 2 edn., vol. 1, pp. 603–627. Springer, London (2019). https://doi.org/10.1007/978-1-4471-7440-0, https://www.springer.com/us/book/9781447174394

76. Rauschenberger, M., Schrepp, M., Cota, M.P., Olschner, S., Thomaschewski, J.: Efficient measurement of the user experience of interactive products. How to use the user experience questionnaire (UEQ). Example: Spanish language. Int. J. Artif. Intell. Interact. Multimed. (IJIMAI) **2**(1), 39–45 (2013). https://doi.org/0.9781/ijimai.2013.215

77. Ripa, G., Torre, M., Firmenich, S., Rossi, G.: End-user development of voice user interfaces based on web content. In: Malizia, A., Valtolina, S., Morch, A., Serrano, A., Stratton, A. (eds.) IS-EUD 2019. LNCS, vol. 11553, pp. 34–50. Springer, Cham (2019). https://doi.org/10.1007/978-3-030-24781-2_3

78. Robinson, C., Moore Jr, R., Crook, T.: Bimodal presentation speeds up auditory processing and slows down visual processing. Front. Psychol. (2018). https://doi.org/10.3389/fpsyg.2018.02454

79. Schrepp, M., Sandkühler, H., Thomaschewski, J.: How to create short forms of UEQ+ based questionnaires? In: Philipp, Carolin, W.B.W., Wintersberger (eds.) Mensch und Computer 2021 - Workshopband, pp. 1–6. Gesellschaft für Informatik e.V., Bonn (2021). https://doi.org/10.18420/muc2021-mci-ws01-230

80. Schrepp, M., Thomaschewski, J.: Design and validation of a framework for the creation of user experience questionnaires. Int. J. Interact. Multimed. Artif. Intell. **5**(7), 88–95 (2019). https://doi.org/10.9781/ijimai.2019.06.006

81. Sciuto, A., Saini, A., Forlizzi, J., Hong, J.I.: "Hey Alexa, what's up?": a mixed-methods studies of in-home conversational agent usage. In: Proceedings of the 2018 Designing Interactive Systems Conference, DIS 2018, pp. 857–868. Association for Computing Machinery, New York (2018). https://doi.org/10.1145/3196709.3196772

82. Sedeño, J., Schön, E.M., Torrecilla-Salinas, C., Thomaschewski, J., Escalona, M.J., Mejías, M.: Modelling agile requirements using context-based persona stories. In: Proceedings of WEBIST the 13th International Conference on Web Information Systems and Technologies, pp. 196–203. SCITEPRESS - Science and Technology Publications (2017). https://doi.org/10.5220/0006220301960203

83. Shneiderman, B.: The eight golden rules of interface design (2016). https://www.cs.umd.edu/users/ben/goldenrules.html. Accessed 09 Feb 2023

84. SPLENDID RESEARCH GmbH: Digitale Sprachassistenten (Digital Voice Assistants) (2019). https://www.splendid-research.com/de/studie-digitale-sprachassistenten.html. Accessed 09 Feb 2023

85. Statista: Absatz von intelligenten Lautsprechern weltweit vom 3. Quartal 2016 bis zum 1. Quartal 2022 (Global Smart Speaker Sales from Q3 2016 to Q1 2022) (2022). https://de.statista.com/statistik/daten/studie/818982/umfrage/absatz-von-intelligenten-lautsprechern-weltweit-pro-quartal/. Accessed 09 Feb 2023

86. Sutton, S.J., Foulkes, P., Kirk, D., Lawson, S.: Voice as a design material: socio-phonetic inspired design strategies in human-computer interaction. In: Proceedings of the 2019 CHI Conference on Human Factors in Computing Systems, CHI 2019, pp. 1–14. Association for Computing Machinery, New York (2019). https://doi.org/10.1145/3290605.3300833

87. Tabassum, M., et al.: Investigating users' preferences and expectations for always-listening voice assistants. Proc. ACM Interact. Mob. Wearable Ubiquit. Technol. **3**, 1–23 (2019). https://doi.org/10.1145/3369807

88. Taş, S., Hildebrandt, C., Arnold, R.: Voice assistants in Germany (2019). https://www.wik.org/uploads/media/WIK_Diskussionsbeitrag_Nr_441.pdf. Accessed 09 Feb 2023
89. Tatman, R.: Gender and dialect bias in YouTube's automatic captions. In: Proceedings of the First ACL Workshop on Ethics in Natural Language Processing, pp. 53–59 (2017). https://doi.org/10.18653/v1/W17-1606
90. Tatman, R., Kasten, C.: Effects of talker dialect, gender & race on accuracy of bing speech and youtube automatic captions. In: Proceedings of the Interspeech 2017, pp. 934–938 (2017). https://doi.org/10.21437/Interspeech.2017-1746
91. Tractica: Voice and Speech Recognition Software Revenue by Use Cases, Wolrd Markets: 2018–2025 (2018). https://www.fierceelectronics.com/embedded/voice-speech-recognition-software-market-turning-up-volume. Accessed 31 Jan 2023
92. Tymburiba Elian, M., Bao, S., Masuko, S., Yamanaka, T.: Designing gender ambiguous voice agents. Int. J. Affect. Eng. **22**(1), 53–62 (2023). https://doi.org/10.5057/ijae.TJSKE-D-22-00021
93. Vimalkumar, M., Sharma, S.K., Singh, J.B., Dwivedi, Y.K.: 'Okay google, what about my privacy?': user's privacy perceptions and acceptance of voice based digital assistants. Comput. Hum. Behav. **120**, 106763 (2021). https://doi.org/10.1016/j.chb.2021.106763
94. Wei, Z., Landay, J.A.: Evaluating speech-based smart devices using new usability heuristics. IEEE Pervasive Comput. **17**(2), 84–96 (2018). https://doi.org/10.1109/MPRV.2018.022511249
95. Weigand, A.C., Lange, D., Rauschenberger, M.: How can Small Data Sets be Clustered? In: Mensch und Computer 2021, Workshop on User-Centered Artificial Intelligence (UCAI 2021), vol. 1. Association for Computing Machinery (2021). https://doi.org/10.18420/muc2021-mci-ws02-284
96. Winter, D., Hinderks, A., Schrepp, M., Thomaschewski, J.: Welche UX Faktoren sind für mein Produkt wichtig? (Which UX factors are essential for my product?). In: Hess, S., Fischer, H. (eds.) Mensch und Computer 2017 - Usability Professionals. Gesellschaft für Informatik e. V., Regensburg (2017). https://doi.org/10.18420/muc2017-up-0002
97. Wu, K., Childers, D.G.: Gender recognition from speech. part i: Coarse analysis. J. Acoust. Soc. Am. **90 4 Pt 1**, 1828–1840 (1991). https://doi.org/10.1121/1.401663
98. Yesilada, Y., Harper, S.: Web Accessibility: A Foundation for Research, 2nd edn. Springer, Cham (2019). https://doi.org/10.1007/978-1-4471-7440-0

Co-Designing a Conversational Agent in Health and Social Care – Perspectives of Professional Care Staff and Older Adults

Henrike Langer[✉] and Sebastian Merkel

Ruhr-Universität Bochum, Universitätsstraße 150, 44801 Bochum, Germany
henrike.langer@rub.de, Sebastian.Merkel@ruhr-uni-bochum.de

Abstract. Working conditions in health and elderly care are increasingly characterized by work intensification, high physical and psychological demands, and a shortage of skilled workers [1]. The reasons for the high workload in healthcare are manifold. Among them are an increasing demand because of demographic developments or growing documentation efforts, fueled by the rising adoption of electronic health records [2, 3]. To address these challenges, technical solutions are seen as a promising way that can support care workers as well as patients. Voice-based human-technology interaction is an increasingly important field promising many advantages: supporting staff via documentation tasks, enabling care recipients to communicate their needs via voice commands. Against this background, the project presented here, funded by the German Ministry for Research and Education, follows a co-design process of a smart speaker with care workers and patients. The main aim of the project is to define use cases with the target groups and to disclose the potential users' assessments of the device within those. Therefore, the co-design process covers separate workshops with the two target groups, i.e., professional caregivers and potential patients.

Keywords: Nursing Care · Smart Speakers · Qualitative Research

1 Introduction

The recent debates on ChatGPT have brought already existing discussions on the potentials but also dangers of artificial intelligence (AI) to a new level. Long before these debates, dialogue systems – or conversational agents (CA) – have been intensively debated in various fields and scenarios, including healthcare [4–6] and more recently in social care [7]. In health care, CA are used for diagnosis and therapy, but also in health care service support or education [5] while in social care the main areas of use are very divers and cover general use such as entertainment but also monitoring [7, 8].

In recent years there is a growing body of literature on CA in various disciplines such as human-computer interactions, sociology or science and technology studies studying the use of CA in multiple settings and use cases but also on human-computer interaction and the conversation with CA [9]. A systematic review by Laranjo et al. comes to the conclusion that studies included in the review were mainly "quasi-experimental, and

G. Salvendy and J. Wei (Eds.): HCII 2023, LNCS 14052, pp. 191–202, 2023.
https://doi.org/10.1007/978-3-031-35921-7_13

rarely evaluated efficacy or safety." [4]. Another systematic review by Tudor Car et al. [5] concludes that "research should focus on assessing the feasibility, acceptability, safety, and effectiveness of diverse conversational agent formats aligned with the target population's needs and preferences".

The analysis of the state of research shows that many of the studies conducted so far are rather experimental in nature and long-term observations on the use of CA in healthcare are still largely pending. The requirements for CA are of increased importance, especially in the healthcare domain, where sensitive data is handled and the correct documentation and processing of information can be vital. In addition to a perfectly functioning technology, it must also fit optimally into the care processes and support the work of the nursing staff in the long term, rather than becoming an additional task in an already very tightly scheduled daily work routine. The technology must also be easily accessible for other target groups, which is often elderly patients. To ensure this, an early integration of the user groups into the development process would be beneficial in order to involve them as experts of their own circumstances. So far, hardly any co-design studies are available, as in most cases off-the-shelf products have been used. The aim of this paper is to provide a first exploratory introduction to the topic of CA in healthcare and to map the perspectives of future user groups on both sides on the potentials and challenges associated with the introduction of such technologies.

2 Background

First attempts to develop CA for healthcare date back to the 1960s [10] and since then multiple CAs have been developed specifically for this field [5]. The term CA is not clearly defined and used interchangeably with other terms like virtual assistants, AI-driven digital assistants, voice-based assistants, voice-controlled intelligent personal assistants, etc. For the sake of simplicity, we will stick to CA as an umbrella term for various types of AI-driven dialogue systems. CA come in various forms and functions: They can be rule based or smart, implemented into websites or robots, as a chatbot that needs written input or as voice-controlled digital assistant on a smartphone such as Apple´s Siri, to provide a few examples. A similarity of all CA is that they cannot only recognize and process natural language but also respond automatically using human language. The type of CA that this paper will concentrate on are in-home devices such as Amazon´s Echo or Apple´s HomePod, which are also referred to as smart speakers. A smart speaker is a technical artefact that was designed for commercial use in private living environments. The first device was introduced to the US market by Amazon in 2015. Since then, other companies such as Google or Apple have released their own products and some models come with a screen and/or cameras. Usually, one or more smart speakers are placed somewhere in the home environment and are connected to the wireless network. After an initial set-up, users can prompt commands such as asking for the weather forecast using a wake word, "Alexa" for Amazon´s Echo or "Hey Siri" for Apple´s HomePod, followed by a prompt. Besides weather forecast, smart speaker usage covers a broad range of scenarios and intentions [11, 12]. One central feature of most devices is the ability to use them to control other devices such as light bulbs or the heating in case those are compatible. Based on semi-structured interviews with early adopters of the technology, Brause and Blank [13] identified six use genres in addition to convenience and entertainment: companionship, self-control and productivity, sleep aid, peace of mind, accessibility, and health care. To this regard, the devices can be personalized by downloading applications provided by third parties using an online store. Since their market launch, the devices have become increasingly widespread in private households: e.g. market research estimates that 35% of the total US population above twelve years owned a smart speaker in 2022 [14].

The increasing uptake of smart speakers and the progress made in natural language processing and machine learning have resulted in various attempts to use the devices in healthcare. Clemente et al. summarize that "virtual assistants can be considered as a valid support for the health selfeducation [15] of people and for adherence to therapies, offering several services in a way that is immediate, simpler than other technologies [16], directly in the person's home, low cost [17] and without risk of stigmatization." [18].

These potentials and particularly that users can interact with smart speakers hands-free and without being accustomed to a visual interface, have drawn attention to the user group of older adults [19–25] and the use of smart speakers in the field of elderly care [7, 26, 27]. Against the backdrop of demographic developments resulting in a rising number of people the sector of elderly care is put under pressure. Intensified by the shortage of care workers, e.g. due to challenging working conditions [27], new possibilities are being sought to support elderly care workers and their clients/patients. In the discourse on the use of digital technologies in this field, different focal points can be identified. For example, a great deal of research and development work is being done in the area of care robotics, although this has not yet achieved any relevant market success [28]. In contrast, smart speakers are already being widely adopted, easy to purchase for comparatively low-costs, and easy to use. There are, however, also challenges associated with the devices. Most notably, this concerns the privacy and safety of smart speakers particularly regarding the protection of health data [4, 30, 31]. In an implementation study on smart speakers in social care, Edwards et al. [7] found several challenges concerning internet connectivity, the capacity of the staff, but also skills of the staff and clients/patients. Furthermore, smart speakers might distress users with mental health needs such as dementia [7]. Despite these challenges, the Echo, HomePod and co. are receiving increasing attention in the field of social care – not at least fueled by the pandemic, and the need to avoid contact with vulnerable clients/patients, smart speaker received additional attention [8]. For instance, the aforementioned study by Edwards et al. [7] comes to an overall positive conclusion of smart speaker use in this field. The authors found that the devices were mainly used for various purposes similar to the use of the general population. These cover listening to music, information-seeking, etc. Moreover, they found that the devices provided companionship to the clients/patients.

In this project, which is funded by the German Federal Ministry of Education and Research, an AI-based smart speaker is being developed for explicit use in elderly care facilities, hospitals as well as in private home care. The system is composed of a physical speaker, similar to the devices commonly available on the market, and a smartphone app to be installed on the phones of caregivers. Some of the planned functions run independently of the app, while others, such as documentation or a general memo function, rely on the voice-to-text principle. In this way, information that has been recorded can be read by the caregivers afterwards, after they have performed patient care tasks. For this purpose, the app offers a patient overview with the corresponding assignment to the rooms and the option of adding the information stored there verbally to the patient file. The system prototype will be developed further with the help of the research taking place in this project.

3   Methodology

This paper is based on data collected during co-creation workshops with caregivers and older adults. The goal of this study was the general exploration of the topic with the two predominant target groups and the collection of their impulses and interpretations. In addition, it was of interest to identify application scenarios and concrete use cases and to discuss them in terms of their prospects and challenges. Since the Smart Speaker is intended to improve communication between caregivers and care recipients, it was essential to gather the perspectives of both groups and analyze them in comparison with each other. To this end, the workshops were conducted in two waves, first with healthcare professionals and then with older adults. The structure, the duration of 1.5–2 hrs and the contents of the workshops were similar, but adapted to the target groups in each case. Healthcare workers for the workshop were recruited through a collaboration with a local health college and by approaching a provider of elder care facilities. In order to reflect the patients' point of view, contact was made with two self-organized senior citizens' groups in the area.

Initially, possible application scenarios and use cases were to be identified in co-creation workshops with three different groups of healthcare professionals. The first two groups of participants were healthcare students, who had predominantly previously completed training in nursing and for the most part continued to work in this profession alongside their studies. The third workshop was conducted with facility and nursing service managers as well as practice-oriented experts from the research community. After introducing the project and the Smart Speaker, participants discussed the potential uses of such technologies in everyday nursing care. Different contexts of formal and informal care were considered, such as hospitals, nursing homes and private care arrangements. After the general possible uses had been identified, concrete potentials, but also risks and possible obstacles to implementation were addressed. Some of these use cases were then to be further explored in a new session and discussed from a different perspective. For this purpose, co-creation workshops were held with seniors aged 60+, in which the project and the smart speaker were presented and the use scenarios from the previous workshops were discussed. In the second workshop, a stronger focus was placed on home care at the request of the older adults, as many of those present were themselves caring for relatives and were interested adopting this technology or were already using it in this context. Although all workshops followed the same structure, it was ensured that enough room was left to address not only positive aspects but also fears and possible challenges, and to discuss these in the group as well. The workshops were recorded and then partially transcribed and paraphrased. The data were analyzed using an inductive-deductive approach according to Kuckartz's qualitative content analysis [31].

4 Results

A total of three workshops were conducted between March and May 2022, with a total of 59 registered nurses and other health professionals participating. Participants' backgrounds were somewhat diverse, both in terms of specialty and the position in which they held. The students at the health college included mostly nurses, but also a few special education speech-language pathologists, physician assistants, and a health insurance clerk. The group at the third workshop included nursing directors and practice-oriented experts in gerontological and health science research. The age composition of the groups also varied somewhat. The first two groups, who were participating in postgraduate studies in nursing, were slightly younger on average than the other group, averaging between their mid-20 s and 40 s, while the third group of nursing leaders averaged around 55 years of age. The educational level of the participants was comparable between the groups on average, as the majority of the participants had both traditional nursing or provider training and experience with a practical job, as well as an additional academic qualification (postgraduate studies) or other further training (nursing service management).

As an introduction, the participants were asked to explain what the term "smart speaker" meant. This question was intended to ensure that the participants were all on the same level and that there would be no misunderstandings about the technical solution and its functions in the further course. The participants already reacted to this question with varying degrees of enthusiasm or reluctance. In the first group of students, numerous people came forward directly and were able to give examples of their own experiences with smart speakers from other manufacturers and list a range of functions. In the second group of students, there were also several people who could spontaneously explain what a smart speaker is and how it is usually used. In the group of care managers, the participants were more reserved at first and connected the definition of the device with a hesitant question: "That's something like this Alexa… Isn't it? I don't know exactly what it can do… Check the weather?". The participants were then asked to report whether they would use a smart speaker professionally or privately and, if so, for which application purposes. In the two groups of students, there was some positive feedback for private use, especially voice input on the cell phone for Internet research, but dictation in chat programs such as WhatsApp was also frequently used. Smart speakers were present in some households in the context of smart home concepts. The most frequently mentioned models were Amazon's Echo Dot and Echo Show. Many reported that they had not purchased the technology themselves, but that their significant other had introduced it to the household. Others had tested smart speakers in the past and were not satisfied with the functionality, so they returned the device. From the group of care managers, the fewest people had smart speakers themselves in their private households, but also had not yet gained any professional experience with such devices. One person reported that there was such a speaker in her household, but that only her children used it. The most common use case in private households was listening to music for all respondents. Even though the response was mostly positive, there were also some immediate critical reactions to the question about owning such a device in all three groups: "I don't think much of it," or "I wouldn't know what to do with it." These comments were initially taken note of and addressed at a later stage in the course of the workshops so as not to limit the discussion to criticism from the outset and to allow all options to be openly reflected upon.

The first group of students were then asked to draw on their practical experience in their daily work and to identify the most prevalent challenges in the everyday life of nurses. In this way, participants were asked to focus on possible solutions to problems. The most frequently mentioned problems were lack of time, shortage of skilled workers and documentation workload. The participants were then asked to consider whether and to what extent a smart speaker, could be of use in these areas. The participants could imagine that smart speakers could simplify communication between patients and caregivers. The speaker would enable patients to communicate their wishes directly to the nurse without the nurse having to come into the patient's room. This makes it possible to prioritize real emergencies over other, less dangerous scenarios and, for example, to provide help quickly in the event of a fall. The nurse can also better assess the situation on site in advance and bring all the necessary utensils directly with them without having to run back to the kitchen or laundry room. Furthermore, it would be a great relief if the smart speaker could also be used for documentation purposes, as this would save a lot of time. However, the students also expressed concern that this time gain would not necessarily benefit the nursing staff in the long term.

After this initial brainstorming session, participants were asked to come up with other possible use cases for the smart speaker. The examples of use cases mentioned here related to various areas, some of which focused more on the care recipients and others more on the caregivers and their processes. For example, various use cases were mentioned for increasing the independence of care recipients by operating equipment and infrastructure via voice control. One commonly mentioned use was light regulation by voice, which could contribute to fall prevention, among other things. The use of the speaker for entertainment purposes, for example for games, puzzles, but also for listening to podcasts or music was also suggested. The students could see further added value in the use of reminder functions. For example, care recipients could be motivated to drink or to take small exercise sessions via voice. In addition to this promotion of Activities of Daily Living (ADL), the smart speaker could also be used for specific therapeutic goals. The speech therapists in particular saw a need here, as patients would often need guidance in carrying out their daily exercise, for which, however, there was too little time in the daily routine of the clinic. A smart speaker could remind patients of the exercises and accompany them. The students also saw potential for automating logistical processes, such as ordering meals. Here, for example, a smart speaker could present the available menu options for the day in the morning and ask which of the options the patient would like to order. This feedback could be automatically fed into an ordering system. But the students also identified a number of advantages for communication between caregivers and recipients. In addition to the prioritization of real emergencies over less urgent tasks, such as ordering a coffee, other urgent requests could also be communicated more concretely (e.g., help with going to the toilet). In this way, tasks can be distributed differently and more efficiently among nursing staff if, say, they can be handled by a cleaner or a nursing assistant and do not require a certified specialist to do so. According to the students, the smart speaker has the potential to be used like an intercom system, for example, and enable direct consultation among the nursing staff without them having to physically visit each other for this purpose, which could lead to further time savings. If the smart speaker were equipped with a translation function, communication between nurses and patients, but also between nurses of different native languages, could also be improved. Nurses who worked in hospitals, particularly in the emergency room, also saw great potential for use in the context of process control. For example, the smart speaker could be used to assist staff in stressful emergency situations, such as providing instructions on how to operate a defibrillator or even during surgical preparations. By far the greatest benefit, however, was seen by students in the area of documentation. The possibility of entering important information into the smart speaker directly at the patient's bedside, such as the blood pressure or body temperature just measured, without having to take off the gloves or have pen and paper ready for this, was perceived as very attractive and received strong approval from the participants.

The students were then asked to vote on the use cases they had mentioned and their potential, and to rank them in terms of importance and potential for success. This clearly showed that the emergency call and documentation use cases were rated as the most promising by the participants. In the lower ranks, the functions entertainment and operation of infrastructures (e.g. lighting), translation, and reminders for medication and exercises were named. Meanwhile, in the final discussion, the two most popular functions were also named for the greatest risk, a possible technical failure. Here, it became apparent that the students would have little trust in a foreign and potentially error-prone technology, especially in life-critical contexts.

The second workshop with the healthcare students and the workshop with the nurse managers were identical in structure. Here, too, the concept of the smart speaker was first explained and the groups' prior knowledge of the technology as well as their private and professional experience with it were queried. Then the possible use cases were collected in the group and compared with the results of the first group of students. These were largely consistent between all three groups and could thus be used as a basis for the next exercise. The application scenarios that had been classified as the most promising up to this point were given greater focus in the following task. With the help of mind maps, the positive and limiting aspects of the use case were collected and discussed in the group on a digital whiteboard. For the emergency function, it was positively emphasized that communication via voice enables hands-free alerting from anywhere in the room and that a button on the bed does not have to be reached first, which could be problematic especially in the event of a fall. Further help can also be requested via the smart speaker while the person in distress is being cared for. In the hospital context in particular, it would also be much easier to triage between the individual requests, since an emergency can be recognized as such directly, even outside the intensive care unit. For the assisted living sector, the emergency system would be a useful addition to the currently much-used home emergency call systems, which require care recipients to wear an emergency call trigger around their neck or on their wrist. If this is out of reach in the event of a fall, it is often not possible to call for help. The caregivers mentioned the use in connection with cognitively or linguistically impaired persons, who occur more frequently in the geriatric context, as challenging. Particularly in the case of postoperative delirium or dementia, patients not only have difficulty articulating clearly, but also have problems retaining new information about unfamiliar procedures and equipment. This could cause confusion and anxiety in patients. Particularly in the case of confused patients, it would also be more common for the bell to be pressed permanently without there being an actual need for care. In the context of the Smart Speaker, it could be difficult to distinguish between these activations and prioritize them accordingly via the technology. Impatient patients could also verbally trigger an unwarranted emergency alert via the smart speaker if they learn that they are being given priority by staff. In turn, the smart speaker could become a burden to caregivers if, for example, it contacts caregivers on its own to inquire about their well-being. Here, the caregivers would like to see a distinction between the patient's sleeping and waking states. Furthermore, the integration into existing processes was discussed controversially. For example, the question arose as to how to deal with it when the orders received by the nurse through the technology do not fit in with the professional's practiced and sensible routines. Constantly interrupting the workflow to complete other tasks in between could be perceived as an additional burden, especially if additional pressure is built up via an app through a function declared as an "emergency." Artificial pre-structuring by the smart speaker could thus become a conflict between lived and learned practice. Coordination among the team could also be disturbed by the interruptions of the Smart Speaker if it is unclear who takes which order. Nurses therefore wished for a function to be able to manually check off completed orders in the app. A major issue in connection with emergencies was the technology's susceptibility to errors. Possible power failures, network disruptions or hacker attacks were rated as a major threat.

With the other target group, older adults, two workshops were conducted in the fall of 2022. The older adults, like the caregivers before them, were also asked to define smart speakers and to describe the fields of application in which they can be used. In both groups, there was a clear division into two groups: while half of them already use smart speakers as a matter of course in their everyday lives, the other half were more dismissive. Compared to the younger workshop participants from the nursing school and the somewhat older nursing service managers, the ambivalence was more pronounced here. Both groups included people who were very tech-savvy, either because they had previously worked in technical jobs or because they were retired technology consultants helping other seniors equip their homes. Because of this characteristic, the participants were only somewhat representative of their age group.

When asked about possible use cases, the older adults named almost the same as the groups before them. However, they also suggested using the smart speaker for memory training, having the device read aloud to them, or making phone calls. Particularly for the very old, the possibility of making phone calls to relatives via audio command would be very useful. However, this group also agreed that neurodegenerative diseases such as dementia were not compatible with the use of the device. In contrast to the previous groups, the seniors saw the greatest potential for rehabilitation and spa clinics, as well as in providing care for relatives via the smart speaker. Occasionally, participants were able to report on their own experiences in a nursing context. One participant impressively demonstrated her home care arrangement with her bedridden very old mother, whom she cares for together with her sons in their apartment. To do this, she made a call to the Amazon Echo Show, which is positioned in the bedroom so that the camera is pointing at her mother in bed and she can see her even when she is away. She reports that this is how she reminds her mother, for example, to drink enough from the sippy cup she also has positioned in view on the table in front of the camera, "That's how I keep track of everything, you know?".

When asked about the potential challenges that a smart speaker might pose, seniors pointed to the same issues that caregivers had already raised: potential problems with data security, power outages, unstable or even nonexistent Internet (especially in nursing homes), but intrusions into privacy from the constantly activated microphones. Overall, there was a high level of knowledge about data security and data protection in the groups; there were no fears in this regard.

5 Discussion and Conclusion

Smart speakers were predominantly perceived by the nursing staff surveyed as a potential everyday aid or supplementary support. The technology, which most have had little contact with, at least in their everyday work, primarily aroused curiosity among healthcare employees and the hope of modernizing cumbersome analog documentation processes and an emergency call system that can help prioritize tasks. But even beyond that, it was apparent that the nursing students could see potential for many other use cases. The operation of infrastructures, such as lights or beds in the patient's room, translations and reminder functions, ordering coffee, listening to the radio, requesting the time and date, help with going to the toilet, painkillers and requesting the weather, but also the specific use in accompanying logopedic therapy were identified by the experts as possible areas of application. Challenges were seen above all for the area of use by very old people, especially people in postoperative delirium or with a neurodegenerative disease such as dementia, as well as for the care of people with voice or speech problems. Privacy and data security were also critically discussed in relation to the technology. In addition, skepticism emerged regarding the reliability of the system in life-threatening scenarios.

The older adults interviewed, who were invited as the representatives of the patient group, were also interested in the technology and, for their part, had further suggestions, especially for the home care of relatives. Privacy and data security, as well as the reliability of the technology, were also issues in these groups. Overall, however, the older adults were open to using the innovation – both as potential patients and as supportive and caring family members, and some people from this group had already had their own experiences with smart speakers in care.

It is to be expected that as smart speakers become more widespread in society, openness to such systems will also increase in the healthcare sector. It is apparent that there is a great desire in the healthcare sector for a perfectly functioning system, as life-threatening situations can arise in the event of failure. There is little room for technical failure, as the data clearly show, especially in the healthcare context.

While the research presented in this paper focuses primarily on caregivers' experiences and lessons learned with smart speakers, it fails to address one of the major shortcomings of most studies published to date: Collecting longitudinal data on the adoption and use of smart speakers by both caregivers and their patients. Although this was not our original goal and we are focused on the development and design of a device, more insights from long-term observations of commercial off-the-shelf devices could help in the co-design of new technologies. Another limitation of this study is its exploratory nature. The target groups chosen are composed of diverse healthcare professionals, which was an advantage for the open-ended approach used to explore the field. In the further course of the project, there will be a stronger focus on the concretization and a more detailed evaluation of the use cases, which is why the study participants will have to be more closely matched to the future target group in the further co-design process. The study participants also had an above-average education for the nursing field due to the dual qualification of practical training and work experience and studies or training. The advantage of this particularity was that the participants could thus discuss from different perspectives, that of the nurse as well as the management level. At the same time, this group is only representative of the nursing staff as a whole to a limited extent.

The analysis of the studies carried out so far shows that in particular long-term studies in the field of CA in the health care sector are still outstanding. It would be of particular interest to find out to what extent intelligent smart speakers fulfill their intended purpose and actually make everyday care easier and help save time. In this context, the effects on the relationships between patients and caregivers, patients and relatives, and also caregivers among themselves would also be relevant. At the meso level, the structural implementation of smart speakers in existing processes in institutions, but also in family care concepts, would have to be investigated.

References

1. Merkel, S., Holman, D., Ruokolainen, M., Hess, M.: Working longer in the professional HCS sector? In: Naegele, G., Hess, M. (eds.) Alte und neue soziale Ungleichheiten bei Berufsaufgabe und Rentenübergang: Ergebnisse des EXTEND-Projektes, pp. 177–186. Springer Fachmedien Wiesbaden, Wiesbaden (2020). https://doi.org/10.1007/978-3-658-31663-1_10
2. Moy, A.J., et al.: Measurement of clinical documentation burden among physicians and nurses using electronic health records: a scoping review. J. Am. Med. Inform. Assoc. 28(5), 998–1008 (2021). https://doi.org/10.1093/jamia/ocaa325
3. Pérez-Francisco, D.H., Duarte-Clíments, G., del Rosario-Melián, J.M., Gómez-Salgado, J., Romero-Martín, M., Sánchez-Gómez, M.B.: Influence of workload on primary care nurses' health and burnout, patients' safety, and quality of care: integrative review. Healthcare 8(1), 12 (2020). https://doi.org/10.3390/healthcare8010012
4. Laranjo, L., Dunn, A.G., Tong, H.L., et al.: Conversational agents in healthcare: a systematic review. J. Am. Med. Inform. Assoc. 25, 1248–1258 (2018). https://doi.org/10.1093/jamia/ocy072
5. Tudor Car, L., Dhinagaran, D.A., Kyaw, B.M., et al.: Conversational agents in health care: scoping review and conceptual analysis. J. Med. Internet Res. 22, e17158 (2020). https://doi.org/10.2196/17158
6. Ermolina, A., Tiberius, V.: Voice-controlled intelligent personal assistants in health care: international delphi study. J. Med. Internet Res. 23, e25312 (2021). https://doi.org/10.2196/25312
7. Edwards, K.J., Jones, R.B., Shenton, D., et al.: The use of smart speakers in care home residents: implementation study. J. Med. Internet Res. 23, e26767 (2021). https://doi.org/10.2196/26767

8. Davitt, J.K., Brown, J.: Using voice and touchscreen controlled smart speakers to protect vulnerable clients in long-term care facilities. Innov. Aging **6**(4), igac024 (2022). https://doi.org/10.1093/geroni/igac024

9. Kuckartz, U.: Qualitative Inhaltsanalyse. Methoden, Praxis, Computerunterstützung, 4. Auflage, Weinheim. Beltz Juventa, Basel (2018)

10. Kim, S.: Exploring how older adults use a smart speaker-based voice assistant in their first interactions: qualitative study. JMIR Mhealth Uhealth **9**, e20427 (2021). https://doi.org/10.2196/20427

11. Weizenbaum, J.: ELIZA—a computer program for the study of natural language communication between man and machine. Commun. ACM **9**(1), 36–45 (2012)

12. Lopatovska, I., Rink, K., Knight, I., Raines, K., Cosenza, K., Williams, H., et al.: Talk to me: exploring user interactions with the Amazon Alexa. J. Librariansh. Inf. Sci. **51**(4), 984–997 (2018)

13. Bentley, F., Luvogt, C., Silverman, M., Wirasinghe, R., White, B., Lottridge, D.: Understanding the long-term use of smart speaker assistants. In: Proceedings of the ACM Interact. Mob. Wearable Ubiquitous Technol. 2018 Sep 18 Presented at: ACM on interactive, mobile, wearable ubiquitous technologies; September 18, 2018; New York p. 1–24 (2018)

14. Brause, S.R., Blank, G.: Externalized domestication: smart speaker assistants, networks and domestication theory. Inf. Commun. Soc. **23**(5), 751–763 (2020). https://doi.org/10.1080/1369118X.2020.1713845

15. Speakergy: Smart Speakers Statistics: Report 2022. https://speakergy.com/smart-speakers-statistics/#:~:text=The%20United%20States%20Smart%20Speaker,a%206%25%20increase%20from%202020 (2022). Accessed 9 Feb 2023

16. Gupta, I., et al. (ed.): IEEE International Conference on Healthcare Informatics (ICHI). IEEE (2018)

17. Meier, P., Beinke, J.H., Fitte, C., Behne, A., Teuteberg, F.: Feelfit – Design and evaluation of a conversational agent to enhance health awareness. https://osnascholar.ub.uni-osnabrueck.de/handle/unios/17711 (2019). Accessed 9 Feb 2023

18. Davis, C.R., Murphy, K.J., Curtis, R.G., et al.: A process evaluation examining the performance, adherence, and acceptability of a physical activity and diet artificial intelligence virtual health assistant. Int. J. Environ. Res. Public Health **17**, 9137 (2020). https://doi.org/10.3390/ijerph17239137

19. Clemente, C., Greco, E., Sciarretta, E., Altieri, L.: Alexa, How Do Feel Today? Smart Speakers for Healthcare and Wellbeing: an Analysis about Uses and Challenges (6th edn.). Sociology and Social Work Review (2022)

20. Choi, Y., Demiris, G., Thompson, H.: Feasibility of smart speaker use to support aging in place. Innov. Aging **2**, 560 (2018). https://doi.org/10.1093/geroni/igy023.207

21. Pradhan, A., Findlater, L., Lazar, A.: "Phantom Friend" or "Just a Box with Information": Personification and Ontological Categorization of Smart Speaker-based Voice Assistants by Older Adults. Proc. ACM Hum.-Comput. Interact. **3**(CSCW), 1–21 (2019). https://doi.org/10.1145/3359316

22. Nimrod, G., Edan, Y.: Technology domestication in later life. Int. J. Hum.-Comput. Interact. **38**, 339–350 (2021). https://doi.org/10.1080/10447318.2021.1938395

23. Brewer, R.N.: "If Alexa knew the state I was in, it would cry": Older Adults' Perspectives of Voice Assistants for Health. In: Extended Abstracts of the 2022 CHI Conference on Human Factors in Computing Systems (CHI EA'22). Association for Computing Machinery, Article 442, pp. 1–8. New York, NY, USA (2022). https://doi.org/10.1145/3491101.3519642

24. Martin-Hammond, A., Vemireddy, S., Rao, S.: Exploring older adults' beliefs about the use of intelligent assistants for consumer health information management: a participatory design study. JMIR aging **2**(2), e15381 (2019). https://doi.org/10.2196/15381

25. Chen, C., et al.: Understanding Barriers and Design Opportunities to Improve Healthcare and QOL for Older Adults through Voice Assistants (2021). https://doi.org/10.48550/arXiv.2111.03756
26. Park, S., Kim, B.: The impact of everyday AI-based smart speaker use on the well-being of older adults living alone. Technol. Soc. **71**, 102133 (2022). https://doi.org/10.1016/j.techsoc.2022.102133
27. Wright, J.: The alexafication of adult social care: virtual assistants and the changing role of local government in England. Int. J. Environ. Res. Public Health **18**, 812 (2021). https://doi.org/10.3390/ijerph18020812
28. Merkel, S., Ruokolainen, M., Holman, D.: Challenges and practices in promoting (ageing) employees working career in the health care sector – case studies from Germany, Finland and the UK. BMC Health Serv. Res. **19**, 918 (2019). https://doi.org/10.1186/s12913-019-4655-3
29. Hergesell, J., Maibaum, A., Meister, M.: Genese und Folgen der Pflegerobotik – Die Konstitution eines interdisziplinären Forschungsfeldes. Beltz Juventa, Weinheim (2020). 9783779952435
30. Guarda, P.: (2019): "Ok Google, am I sick?": artificial intelligence, e-health, and data protection regulation. BioLaw J. **15**(1), 359–375 (2019)
31. Hoy, M.B.: Alexa, siri, cortana, and more: an introduction to voice assistants. Med. Ref. Serv. Q. **37**, 81–88 (2018). https://doi.org/10.1080/02763869.2018.1404391

Uncertain yet Rational - Uncertainty as an Evaluation Measure of Rational Privacy Decision-Making in Conversational AI

Anna Leschanowsky[1]([✉]) [ID], Birgit Popp[1] [ID], and Nils Peters[2] [ID]

[1] Fraunhofer IIS, Erlangen, Germany
{anna.leschanowsky,birgit.popp}@iis.fraunhofer.de
[2] International Audio Laboratories Erlangen, Erlangen, Germany
nils.peters@fau.de

Abstract. In today's connected world, privacy decision-making is crucial for people to maintain control over their personal information and effectively manage their privacy. However, people's decisions on privacy are likely to be subject to bias and can lead to frustration and regret. Privacy strategies in Conversational AI can aim at debiasing peoples' choices by drawing from dual-process theory and triggering a more rational thinking process. Previous research on evaluation measures for such strategies has focused on minimizing regret or aligning user behaviour with their attitudes. In this paper, we propose a subjective measure of uncertainty to evaluate the effectiveness of debiasing strategies in a Conversational AI privacy scenario. We investigate two different scales of uncertainty - an adapted privacy uncertainty scale consisting of four subscales and the PANAS-X scale on the affective state of fear. We find that only one of the adapted subscales and the scale on fear showed sufficient reliability and validity results. Moreover, we did not find differences in uncertainty between our tested strategies. Finally, we propose alternative measures to investigate uncertainty and evaluate privacy strategies that promote rational thinking in the future.

Keywords: Conversational AI · System 1 and 2 · Debiasing · Uncertainty · Privacy

1 Introduction

With numerous connected devices deployed in peoples' homes, cars and public spaces, privacy decision-making becomes increasingly frequent and inevitable. Previous research on privacy decision-making has shown that people often rely on heuristics and biases when deciding whether to disclose personal information or adjust privacy settings [1]. Consequently, judgements can be suboptimal

The International Audio Laboratories Erlangen are a joint institution of the Friedrich-Alexander-Universität Erlangen-Nürnberg and Fraunhofer IIS.

and lead to frustration and regret [1,22]. Debiasing strategies can be a means of supporting people in making choices that are better aligned with their attitudes [23]. They are theoretically grounded in the dual-process theory that distinguishes between System 1, fast and intuitive thinking, and System 2, slow and analytical thinking [17]. As biased judgements usually originate from System 1, debiasing strategies that promote transitioning towards System 2 are one way to promote more rational judgements. Such strategies can aim at producing competing intuitions, e.g. by presenting alternatives, which can induce a feeling of uncertainty during decision-making. Therefore, based on theoretical and experimental research on the dual-process theory and debiasing strategies, we argue that a subjective measure of uncertainty could provide insights into System 2 activity.

We evaluate the level of perceived uncertainty in the context of privacy decision-making in Conversational AI (CAI). While various debiasing strategies have been investigated for traditional user interfaces to support users in making more optimal choices [1,4,34], similar controls for CAI systems have not yet been analyzed. Because traditional privacy controls in CAI require unfavorable modality switching and were found insufficient and cumbersome to use [21], an increasing stream of research argues for conversational privacy [6,16,28]. Our conversational privacy strategies are based on previous research on debiasing strategies and are designed to induce a controlled level of uncertainty. They aim at triggering System 2 activity and at supporting people in overcoming their biases and making better judgements. Previous research on privacy nudges proposed evaluation measures that focus on minimizing regret or aligning user behaviour with their attitudes [1]. However, such measures do not necessarily allow drawing conclusions about peoples' underlying thinking process. Therefore, we show how a subjective measure of uncertainty can provide insights on System 2 activity in Sect. 2. We describe our experimental setup and the conversational privacy strategies used to induce uncertainty in a Conversational AI privacy scenario in Sect. 3. Lastly, we show that only two subjective scales have proven reliable and propose alternative measures for assessing uncertainty and evaluating conversational privacy strategies that promote analytical thinking in Sects. 4 and 5.

2   Uncertainty as an Evaluation Measure

Situations of privacy decision-making are influenced by uncertainty and risks [2]. While uncertainty and risk are closely related, economic research describes them as two distinct constructs [19]. The distinction is based on whether probabilities of possible outcomes are known. In situations under uncertainty, probabilities are unknown, while they are knowable in situations under risks [19]. Individuals are often subject to uncertainty when making judgments about their privacy. First, information asymmetry, the fact that the user has less information available compared to the provider of a service, is a critical driver for uncertainty [2,3]. Moreover, individuals face difficulties in predicting outcomes and consequences

of their actions not only because of insufficient information but because technological developments may be unknowable and difficult to predict [2].

Considering uncertainty as a factor in privacy decision-making can be
informed by research in the behavioural economics field. Here, characteristics
of judgments under uncertainty and their underlying theory have been studied for almost five decades [32]. In uncertain scenarios, people are likely to rely
on mental shortcuts, i.e. heuristics, to reduce complexity and the need to correctly assess probabilities of possible outcomes. While these techniques can be
useful in our daily lives, they can lead to privacy choices that are biased and
unaligned with peoples' attitudes. Heuristics and biases that have been identified
as relevant hurdles for privacy choices include the availability heuristic, repre-
sentativeness heuristic and optimism bias and overconfidence [1]. Explanations
about judgments under uncertainty are primarily based on the dual-process theory or System 1 and 2 reasoning [17]. While decision-making under System 1 is
fast, automatic and effortless, choices under System 2 are slower, more controlled
and effortful. It is assumed that impressions that are created by System 1 are
mostly adopted by System 2 without further intervention. Only in situations that
are surprising or violate the mental model, System 2 and with this, analytical
reasoning, is activated [17]. This activation can be accompanied by uncertainty.

Debiasing strategies have been extensively researched in the medical field
to reduce diagnostic errors resulting from cognitive biases [20]. Similarly, they
can be applied in privacy decision-making to support people in overcoming their
biases [1,23]. Thereby, debiasing strategies can induce a controlled level of uncertainty often by producing an internal conflict or competing intuitions. Consequently, System 2 activation is likely to be triggered. For example, in a study
on the effectiveness of debiasing strategies, it was shown that the Socratic procedure, i.e. posing thought-provoking questions, and the Devil's advocate approach, i.e. encouraging people to consider an opposing point of view, led to an
increase of subjective uncertainty [8]. In particular, the authors focused on overconfidence bias and availability heuristics, both of them also prevalent in privacy
decision-making. It is important to note that we are not interested in people's
perceptions of general uncertainty in privacy decision-making settings. Instead,
we focus on the uncertainty that was induced by debiasing strategies and can be
seen as a possible result of an internal conflict. This distinction will be critical
when defining our experimental setup.

While the dual-process model has been subject to criticism and has been
adapted and modified over the years, uncertainty has remained a crucial factor.
For example, criticism regarding the dichotomy of the two systems has led to
further development of the dual process model that relies on a component to
monitor uncertainty [27]. Thereby, competing intuitions are monitored for their
similarity. Uncertainty increases the more similar competing intuitions are until
a certain threshold is reached and System 2 is activated. In the medical field,
Croskerry [10] developed a universal model of diagnostic reasoning based on pattern recognition and the dual-process theory. Again, uncertainty plays a crucial
role in the activation of System 2. If a patient's symptoms do not match previous

situations or cannot be directly assigned to a certain illness, uncertainty increases and calls for analytical thinking. In addition, behavioural, electrophysiological and neuroimaging studies have shown evidence for a relationship between uncertainty and cognitive control [26]. In particular, there is evidence that uncertain environments lead to increased monitoring activity of one's behavior [26].

Given this theoretical basis and evidence from experimental research, we hypothesize that uncertainty can be used as an evaluation measure for analytical decision-making in the privacy context. Therefore, we construct a privacy scenario in which uncertainty can be induced and varied using debiasing strategies. Moreover, while a majority of previous studies have relied on behavioural and physiological measures to assess uncertainty, we aim to investigate subjective measures of uncertainty. A subjective measure could preferably complement already established objective measures and is less time-consuming and burdensome for participants.

3   Experimental Design

3.1   CAI System, Scenarios and Experimental Conditions

We will investigate the perceived level of uncertainty in two different chatbot scenarios and five varying conditions. We use a text-based CAI system and will refer to the implementation as chatbots which use natural language to interact with a human via text [29]. We use Chatbot Language (CBL) [29] to implement the chatbot on Amazon Mechanical Turk (Mturk). As information sensitivity can impact perceived uncertainty, we investigate two chatbot scenarios – a banking chatbot asking for permission to access users' credit card information and a location chatbot asking for permission to access users' location. These two scenarios were chosen based on previous studies where credit card numbers and location data were perceived significantly different with respect to information sensitivity [30].

Our privacy strategies are designed to provide transparency in interactions with CAI based on the principle of conversational privacy [6,16]. Moreover, we aim to make the "right to deletion" required by the GDPR easily accessible by proactively presenting users with an offer to delete their data [13]. Table 1 gives an overview of control and privacy conditions. The first control condition resembles a common interaction with a CAI system nowadays, is unrelated to data privacy and thus, serves as a baseline for people's perceived level of uncertainty. As mentioned above, we are interested in the level of uncertainty induced by the debiasing strategies rather than the general uncertainty experienced in situations of privacy decision-making.

Our second control condition gives people the opportunity to actively control their privacy while at the same time nudging them into disclosing behaviour. Similar strategies, called "dark patterns" are used in interface design, e.g., when designing cookie banners [5]. Here, interfaces are designed such that individuals make decisions that favour data collectors rather than themselves [5]. Despite the fact that the second control condition is related to data privacy and might

Table 1. Overview of conditions and their questions asked by the CAI system, including two control conditions and three privacy strategies.

Condition	Question
Control 1	Is there anything else I can help you with?
Control 2	I will save your data for future interactions now, okay?
Slow Down	I will save your data for future interactions now, okay? I'll give you 20 s to think about it.
Alternative	Do you want me to delete your data from this interaction or have it saved for future interactions?
Deletion	Do you want me to delete your data from this interaction now?

lead to an increased level of general uncertainty, we expect most people to choose intuitively and therefore, rely on System 1 activity. Therefore, their perceived level of uncertainty should remain relatively low compared to the one experienced by participants who are exposed to the debiasing strategies.

We implement three different privacy strategies based on the idea of debiasing, in particular on cognitive forcing [7,23]. The privacy strategies are applied at the time of decision-making to disrupt heuristic reasoning. They are designed to induce a controlled level of uncertainty, make users engage in System 2 thinking and thereby, support the process of rational cost-benefit analysis. Drawing from previous studies on privacy nudges and cognitive forcing, we implement 1) a slow-down condition to give users time to reflect and possibly reconsider their decision [7,34], 2) an alternative condition that requires an active choice [20] and 3) an option to delete their data from the interaction [6]. The slow-down and alternative options aim at producing an internal conflict and may consequently lead to an increased level of perceived uncertainty. The option to delete data allows people to reconsider their previous disclosure to the chatbot. Similarly to the other privacy strategies, reconsideration could produce competing intuitions. On the other hand, this offer might come surprising to participants as it is not frequently used in real-life scenarios. Based on the theory, surprise is likely to trigger the activation of System 2 [17]. Moreover, surprise has been shown to be accompanied by the feeling of uncertainty and thus, could be assessed via the subjective uncertainty scale [31].

After granting or denying access to their data, participants were exposed to one of the three privacy strategies or to one of the two control conditions. Our experiment follows a between-subject design and conditions were randomly assigned to participants. We used CBL to inform participants about data protection regulations, to provide a task description and to display a survey on the chatbot interaction after the experiment.

3.2   Survey Design

We make use of subjective scales from previous research to investigate whether uncertainty can serve as an evaluation measure for our privacy strategies. We measure uncertainty retrospectively after the interaction was carried out. To the best of our knowledge, subjective measures of uncertainty have not yet been used in the context of CAI. Therefore, we adopt a privacy uncertainty scale that was used in the context of mobile applications [3]. Their study showed that privacy uncertainty was positively influenced by uncertainty regarding the collection, use and protection of users' data. Relying on this distinction allows us to validate the established scale in the context of CAI and to get a more detailed picture of possible subdimensions that induce uncertainty and may be involved in the System 2 activation process. While the original scale was used to measure privacy uncertainty before and after purchasing a mobile app, we only rely on the post-purchase scale as we are assessing uncertainty retrospectively after the use of the service. Furthermore, we removed the last three items of the post-purchase protection uncertainty scale as these items seem not relevant [3]. Lastly, we rephrased the items to match the context of the chatbot interaction (see Table 6 in the Appendix for the rephrased items).

Our second scale is based on the relationship between affective states and uncertainty. As fear was found to be significantly influenced by uncertainty [31], we assess participants' affective state on fear using the PANAS-X scale [35].

3.3   Ethical Considerations

In the following, we discuss the ethical considerations of our experimental design and describe the measures taken to ensure that participants were treated ethically. First, participants were not told prior to participating that we evaluated data-saving practices as this might have affected their behaviour and perceptions. However, our task description clearly stated that participants will be asked personal questions by the chatbot system and are free to what extent they respond truthfully. Moreover, the two scenarios were designed to ask only for information that was required to fulfil the task and thus follow current best practices of privacy design [13,22].

While our experiment made participants believe that we could access their data, our system was not able to access any personal information other than the text users shared during the interaction. This deceptive design choice was based on lessons learned from a previous study [6]. There, participants were provided with an artificial credit card number and asked to check the corresponding balance. Checking the balance for an artificial bank account did limit the interpretability of the results as it does not represent a real-life scenario in which users enter personal data. Thus, users' perceptions and behaviour may differ as they may be more concerned when disclosing real personal information. We fully disclosed our practices by debriefing participants after the study and highlighting that no personal data was accessed if they had not entered personal information during the interaction. Finally, we paid participants 2$ for their participation

Table 2. Summary of demographic and experimental data for the banking and location scenario

Demographic and experimental data	Banking	Location
# conditions	5	5
# participants	315	330
# excluded participants	33	53
# accepted participants in the different conditions (Control 1/ Control 2/ Slow Down/ Alternative/ Reconsider)	58/56/51/56/61	63/55/53/51/55
# accepted participants' disclosure behaviour (Granting Access/ Denying Access)	228/54 (81%/19%)	245/32 (88%/12%)
Mean (SD) age of workers in years	34 (10)	35 (10)
# Gender (female/male/diverse/not provided)	151/131/0/0	114/163/0/0

which calculates to an average hourly wage of 17\$ for the banking scenario and 20\$ for the location scenario.

4   Results

We show experimental and demographic data in Table 2. We excluded participants who failed at least one out of three screening questions from our analysis. Based on the results of a power analysis, we ensured that each of the groups yielded more than 50 accepted participants. The disclosure behaviour of participants was similar between scenarios with more than 80% granting access to their personal information. This is an essential prerequisite for our conditions as they rely on users sharing information in the first place.

4.1   Evaluation of the Adapted Privacy Uncertainty Scale

Evaluation Using Structural Equation Modelling. Evaluation of the privacy uncertainty scale is based on covariance-based structural equation modelling (CB-SEM). This is different to the original study where privacy uncertainty was part of a larger structural model evaluated via partial least squares SEM [3]. We do not aim for comparability but for an evaluation of the uncertainty scale in the context of CAI and rational privacy decision-making. We rely on CB-SEM as we include only reflective constructs and like to assess global goodness-of-fit measures [15]. Our structural model is based on the assumption that collection, use and protection uncertainty positively influence overall privacy uncertainty [3]. Therefore, we assume that these three constructs, i.e. collection, use and protection uncertainty, load on overall privacy uncertainty, while all four constructs are treated as a cause of their corresponding indicators. We evaluate the

CB-SEM using R and the package *lavaan*. As privacy uncertainty was measured on an ordinal 5-point Likert-Scale, we use the robust estimator Weighted Least Squares with Adjustments for Means and Variances (WLSMV) [18]. The model is built on participants' data who passed the screening questions (N = 559).

In SEM one distinguishes between the measurement model and the path analysis [11]. First, the measurement model is tested on reliability and validity by performing a confirmatory factor analysis (CFA) on the latent variables, i.e. collection, use, protection and overall uncertainty [11]. Second, the structural relationship between latent variables is evaluated by performing a path analysis [11]. To evaluate the CB-SEM measurement model, we constrain the loading of the first indicator on each latent factor to unity. We assess item reliability by investigating the standardized loadings of the individual items on their constructs (see Table 6 in the Appendix). Standardized factor loadings vary between 0.5 and 0.8 for the individual uncertainty items. All factor loadings were above the generally recommended lower limit of 0.4 with most of them exceeding factor loadings of 0.7. Thus, indicating sufficient item reliability.

Further, we analyze internal consistency reliability, convergent validity and discriminant validity of the CB-SEM measurement model. The results are shown in Table 3. A scale is generally considered reliable for Cronbach's $\alpha \geq 0.7$ and composite reliability ≥ 0.7 [15]. Moreover, we check whether convergent validity could be established with an average variance extracted (AVE) of > 0.50. Lastly, we investigate discriminant validity using the heterotrait-monotrait correlation ratio (HTMT) which has been recommended over the Fornell-Larcker criterion [15]. As we are working with conceptually similar concepts, we apply a more relaxed cut-off value of 0.9 for discriminant validity to be present [15]. While the use and overall uncertainty scale showed sufficient reliability and convergence validity scores, Cronbach's α, composite reliability and AVE were equal to or below the recommended cut-off thresholds for the collection and protection uncertainty scale. Lastly, discriminant validity could not be established for any of the scales as the HTMT yielded values ≥ 0.95.

In addition to these weaknesses in reliability and validity, the model showed a poor global model fit (see Table 4). We analyze the global model fit by using the chi-square test, Root Mean Square Error of Approximation (RMSEA), Comparative Fit Index (CFI), Tucker-Lewis-Index (TLI) and Standardized Root Mean Square Residual (SRMR) in their robust versions. We rely on commonly applied cut-off thresholds, i.e. close or below 0.08 for RMSEA, close or above 0.95 for CFI and TLI and close or below 0.08 for SRMR [18]. The chi-square test shows significant results. However, it is known to be sensitive to sample size and should therefore be assessed together with other global model fit indices. In addition, we find that the robust RMSEA is well above the recommended cut-off threshold indicating a poor fit of the model. Similarly, CFI and TLI do not show satisfactory global fit values.

Evaluation Using CFA for Individual One-Factor Models. Given that the CB-SEM measurement model showed weaknesses in reliability and validity,

Table 3. Reliability and convergent validity results based on Cronbach's α, Composite Reliability (CR) and Averaged Variance Extracted (AVE). Common cut-off thresholds are above or equal 0.7 for Cronbach's α and CR and above or equal 0.5 for AVE.

Construct	Cronbach's α	CR	AVE
Adapted Privacy Uncertainty - CB-SEM			
Collection Uncertainty	0.70	0.69	0.41
Use Uncertainty	0.81	0.82	0.50
Protection Uncertainty	0.70	0.71	0.49
Overall Uncertainty	0.81	0.79	0.54
Adapted Privacy Uncertainty - Individual One-Factor Models			
Collection Uncertainty	0.70	0.72	0.42
Use Uncertainty	0.81	0.81	0.50
Protection Uncertainty	0.70	0.71	0.51
Overall Uncertainty	0.81	0.79	0.54
PANAS-X Fear - One-Factor Model			
Fear	0.95	0.94	0.79

we could not confirm the hypothesized model structure. However, we are interested in whether people's perception of uncertainty varies among conditions and scenarios. Therefore, we evaluate the individual scales on their reliability and validity by conducting CFA on the four one-factor models. Again we investigate item reliability based on the factor loadings (see Table 7). Similarly to the CB-SEM measurement model, factor loadings of the individually fitted one-factor models showed sufficient reliability. Moreover, Cronbach's α values, composite reliability and convergent validity scores for the four individual scales were similar to the CB-SEM measurement model with low convergent validity for the collection uncertainty scale (see Table 3). Lastly, we investigate robust global model fit measures for the four individual one-factor models (see Table 4). For the collection uncertainty, the one-factor model shows an overall poor model fit. While the one-factor model for the use uncertainty scale showed satisfactory values for CFI, TLI and SRMR, RMSEA is above 0.05 indicating a good but not close fit. Model fit indices for the protection uncertainty one-factor model are not provided as the model is based on only three items and thus, just-identified with zero degrees of freedom. Lastly, the overall uncertainty one-factor model shows a non-significant chi-square test, a close fit based on RMSEA and satisfactory results for CFI, TLI and SRMR.

Based on this analysis, we recommend the usage of the overall uncertainty scale as it has proven reliable and valid in the context of CAI. We used ordinal logistic regression to investigate differences between conditions and scenarios for overall uncertainty ratings. However, our analysis did not show any differences in people's perceived levels of overall uncertainty.

Table 4. Robust measurements of model fit for the adapted privacy uncertainty scale and the PANAS-X Fear scale.

Model	χ^2/df (p-value)	RMSEA [90% CI]	CFI	TLI	SRMR
Adapted Privacy Uncertainty Scale					
CB-SEM	1068.32/98 (0.00)	0.12 [0.11–0.12]	0.86	0.83	0.07
Collection Uncertainty					
One-Factor Model	80.9/2 (0.00)	0.27 [0.22–0.32]	0.84	0.53	0.08
Use Uncertainty					
One-Factor Model	17.4/5 (0.00)	0.06 [0.03–0.10]	0.99	0.98	0.02
Protection Uncertainty - just-identified model					
Overall Uncertainty					
One-Factor Model	4.55/2 (0.1)	0.05 [0.00–0.1]	0.997	0.99	0.01
PANAS-X Fear					
One-Factor Model	34.99/9 (0.00)	0.09 [0.06–0.12]	0.99	0.98	0.02

4.2 Evaluation of the PANAS-X Fear Scale

We evaluate the PANAS-X scale related to fear on its reliability and validity by conducting a CFA. Factor loadings were generally high with values between 0.86 and 0.90. Further, reliability and convergent validity showed satisfactory results (see Table 3). Lastly, the robust model fit indices suggest an overall good fit in accordance with commonly considered values (see Table 4). Nevertheless, the close-fit model criterion was not fulfilled as the robust RMSEA was greater than 0.05.

While the scale showed good reliability and validity values in the context of CAI and privacy decision-making, participants' ratings on this scale showed high variability, i.e. high standard variations across conditions. While subjective assessments of emotions allow inexpensive and efficient measurement, they might not correctly capture underlying psychological processes and have been discussed critically in the literature [9]. Even though the questionnaire was presented right after the interaction with the chatbot, present feelings at the time of filling out the survey might have outweighed feelings experienced during the interaction and led to inconsistent ratings. Moreover, some participants might have connected fear to specific factors, e.g., spiders or flying, while others did not. This might result in inconsistent usage of the scale. Instead of assessing a rather extreme feeling as fear, a future study could investigate feelings like discomfort or uneasiness to make assumptions about peoples' underlying thinking process.

Table 5. This table provides an overview of alternative measures that can be used to assess uncertainty. It also shows alternative measures for the evaluation of privacy strategies that aim at supporting rational decision-making.

Method	Alternative Uncertainty Measures	Alternative Evaluation Measures
Subjective	Self-assessed uncertainty based on scales not used in this study	Self-Assessed Mental Demand
		Privacy Regret
Objective	Reaction Time	Pupil Dilation
	Fixation Time	Galvanic Skin Response
	Neuroimaging	
Mixed		Attitude-Behavior Alignment

5   Alternative Measures

5.1   Alternative Measures of Uncertainty

While we did not find differences in overall uncertainty and fear ratings in the context of Conversational AI, previous research successfully applied a subjective measure of uncertainty to prove the effectiveness of debiasing strategies [8]. Therefore, other subjective scales to measure the level of uncertainty might be better suited and could be tested in future studies. On the other hand, objective measures can be used to investigate perceived uncertainty. Objective measures, e.g. physiological measures, are beneficial as they can assess uncertainty at the time of decision-making. When using subjective measures, we asked participants to report their perceived uncertainty retrospectively after the interaction with the chatbot. However, uncertainty experienced during the interaction might be difficult to recall and present feelings might outweigh the previously experienced ones. Therefore, objective measurements can provide more reliable insights. We provide an overview of objective measures that have been used to assess uncertainty in Table 5.

A study on the detection of uncertainty researched physiological as well as behavioural measurements to sense uncertainty in interactive systems [14]. They identified keyboard behaviour, in particular the time of typing and the time looking at a question, as reliable indicators for uncertainty, whereas heart rate measurements did not provide useful information. Moreover, they suggested the usage of combined measurements to enhance reliability. Other studies have used functional magnetic resonance imaging (fMRI) to research brain activity patterns associated with judgements under uncertainty. Mushtaq et al. [26] provides an extensive overview of brain areas that were shown to be activated when uncertainty was involved in decision-making. The reviewed studies used a variety of tasks to manipulate the level of uncertainty, e.g. by varying the accuracy of predictors or by changing task rules. Thereby, studies include game-like tasks based on cards or checkerboards as well as more realistic tasks such as decision-making in a flight or driving simulator. Future studies could use neuroimaging to assess the level of uncertainty in a Conversational AI privacy scenario and compare the activation of brain areas with the ones previously identified.

5.2   Additional Considerations to Measuring Rational Decision-Making

We tested uncertainty as an evaluation measure for privacy strategies that are based on the idea of debiasing and aim for System 2 activation. In addition, there might be alternative evaluation measures to gain insights into participants' underlying thinking processes (see Table 5 for an overview of alternative evalua-tion measures). In the medical field, the effectiveness of debiasing strategies has been assessed by evaluating error rates in diagnostic reasoning [20]. However, error rates do not seem to be a viable measure for debiasing strategies in the privacy context. As privacy decision-making is highly subjective and depends on the participants' attitudes, the "correct" outcome of a privacy decision remains unknown to the examiner. However, previous research on social media networks has shown that people are likely to regret the disclosure of private information as a result of intuitive thinking [12,33]. Therefore, a subjective measure of pri-vacy regret could be used for evaluating privacy strategies [1]. Moreover, privacy strategies that support people in overcoming their biases should lead to decisions that are aligned with people's attitudes. Consequently, the alignment of attitudes and behaviour could serve as an evaluation measure for such strategies [1].

In addition to uncertainty, the activation process can be accompanied by other factors, e.g. cognitive load, that can be measured either subjectively or objectively [17]. Various methods have been researched to assess cognitive load, both subjective and objective. These include self-reports on mental effort, eye-tracking and pupil dilation, or galvanic skin response [24]. Particularly pupil dilation has been investigated in various contexts to assess cognitive load with larger sizes indicating the usage of more cognitive resources [24,25]. Therefore, future research could assess pupil dilation to evaluate the effectiveness of debi-asing strategies.

While future studies can consider alternative measures to evaluate debias-ing strategies, they can also make changes to the experimental design. First, our dialogue was designed so that no service was provided to the users due to apparent technical difficulties or the closure of the restaurant. This was based on the assumption that a positive ending (e.g. providing a fake balance in the banking scenario or telling the user that the pizza is on its way) might lead to uncertainty related to the corresponding outcome. The users might be unsure whether the fake credit card balance is actually correct or whether a pizza will be delivered to their location. To control for this effect, we do not provide service in both of the scenarios. However, the negative outcome could leave users with a feeling of frustration – a feeling that can be accompanied by uncertainty [31]. This means that our negative outcome scenario could also lead to uncertainty which is not related to the effectiveness of the privacy strategies but to the outcome of the scenario. While we assessed frustration in the survey to account for it, our experimental choice might have overridden small differences between groups. Therefore, future research could avoid experimental setups where users experience frustration, e.g. by providing real-life services.

Second, future research could try to increase the expected effect of uncertainty by multiple or longer exposures to debiasing strategies in a dialogue. For example, previous research has shown that people report higher levels of uncertainty when being exposed to the Socratic procedure or the Devil's advocate approach [8]. Here, people are presented with multiple thought-provoking questions or opposing points of view. Such an experimental setup ensures that people experience competing intuitions which can lead to increased levels of uncertainty. Similarly, guided reflection – a debiasing strategy known from the medical field – could be applied to practice more critical thinking in CAI privacy scenarios and could increase the expected effect of uncertainty [23]. Thereby, CAI could function as a guide or mentor and instruct users on what to consider in their privacy decision-making. Finally, when changing the experimental setup, multiple measures to assess the effectiveness of debiasing strategies should be considered to improve reliability.

6 Conclusion

We investigated perceived uncertainty as an evaluation measure for privacy strategies in Conversational AI. Our approach is theoretically grounded on the dual-process theory and previous research on the evaluation of debiasing strategies using a subjective measure of uncertainty. Our privacy strategies aim at supporting people in their privacy decision-making based on the idea of debiasing and conversational privacy. Thereby, they were designed to induce a controlled level of uncertainty and to trigger more analytical thinking. We used two subjective scales to investigate perceived uncertainty - an adapted privacy uncertainty scale and the PANAS-X scale on the affective state of fear. Only one subscale of the adapted privacy uncertainty scale, i.e. the overall uncertainty scale, and the scale on fear showed satisfactory reliability and validity results and can be recommended for future research in the context of CAI. As we did not find differences in peoples' perceived level of uncertainty on these two scales, we propose alternative measures to investigate uncertainty and evaluate privacy strategies that promote rational decision-making in the future.

Acknowledgments. Our work is partially funded by the German Federal Ministry for Economic Affairs and Energy as part of their AI innovation initiative (funding code 01MK20011A).

Appendix

Table 6. Rephrased items for the four uncertainty subscales and parameter estimates for the CB-SEM measurement model. Parameters were estimated using WLSMV and first indicator factor loadings were set to unity. Robust standard errors are computed.

Abbr.	Construct	Estimate	Std. Err	z-value	P($> |z|$)	Standardized Loadings
Coll1	I was uncertain about what information will be collected	1.00				0.75
Coll2	I was concerned about the amount of information that was collected by the chatbot	0.77	0.04	20.54	0.00	0.58
Coll3	I was afraid the chatbot would collect more information than I was initially told	0.95	0.03	34.05	0.00	0.72
Coll4	I was concerned that I will have to provide more information than I originally thought	0.67	0.04	16.29	0.00	0.50
Use1	I was concerned about how the chatbot provider would use the information that was recorded by the chatbot	1.00				0.57
Use2	I was uncertain about who would have access to the information tha was recorded	1.28	0.06	20.54	0.00	0.73
Use3	I was worried that the information that was recorded will be shared with others	1.35	0.06	20.97	0.00	0.76
Use4	I was unsure if the information that was recorded might be misused	1.27	0.06	20.56	0.00	0.72
Use5	I was afraid that if given the chance the chatbot provider might profit by selling the information to someone else	1.33	0.06	21.73	0.00	0.76
Prot1	I was concerned that the information that was collected will not be protected	1.00				0.58
Prot2	I was uncertain about what the chatbot provider would to to ensure that the information collected was secure	1.28	0.06	23.47	0.00	0.74
Prot3	I was unsure if the chatbot provider would effectively safeguard the information that was collected	1.34	0.05	24.95	0.00	0.77
All1	Overall. I was unsure if the chatbot provider would safeguard my privacy	1.00				0.80
All2	Overall. I was uncertain if the chatbot provider would be good at managing my private information	0.92	0.03	35.12	0.00	0.73
All3	Overall. I was worried if my information would be safe with the chatbot provider	0.97	0.22	44.09	0.00	0.77
All4	Overall. I was concerned that the chatbot provider might breach formal and informal privacy agreements	0.79	0.03	24.68	0.00	0.63

Table 7. Rephrased items for the four uncertainty subscales and parameter estimates for the individual One-Factor CFA models. Parameters were estimated using WLSMV and first indicator factor loadings were set to unity. Robust standard errors are computed.

Abbr.	Construct	Estimate	Std. Err	z-value	$P(> |z|)$	Standardized Loadings
Collection Uncertainty						
Coll1	I was uncertain about what information will be collected	1.00				0.66
Coll2	I was concerned about the amount of information that was collected by the chatbot	0.96	0.06	15.02	0.00	0.63
Coll3	I was afraid the chatbot would collect more information than I was initially told	1.06	0.07	14.56	0.00	0.70
Coll4	I was concerned that I will have to provide more information than I originally thought	0.89	0.06	13.93	0.00	0.59
Use Uncertainty						
Use1	I was concerned about how the chatbot provider would use the information that was recorded by the chatbot	1.00				0.44
Use2	I was uncertain about who would have access to the information tha was recorded	1.53	0.12	12.43	0.00	0.68
Use3	I was worried that the information that was recorded will be shared with others	1.82	0.14	12.93	0.00	0.81
Use4	I was unsure if the information that was recorded might be misused	1.72	0.13	12.83	0.00	0.76
Use5	I was afraid that if given the chance the chatbot provider might profit by selling the information to someone else	1.78	0.14	12.84	0.00	0.79
Protection Uncertainty						
Prot1	I was concerned that the information that was collected will not be protected	1.00				0.50
Prot2	I was uncertain about what the chatbot provider would to to ensure that the information collected was secure	1.37	0.10	13.73	0.00	0.68
Prot3	I was unsure if the chatbot provider would effectively safeguard the information that was collected	1.81	0.17	10.48	0.00	0.90
Overall Uncertainty						
All1	Overall, I was unsure if the chatbot provider would safeguard my privacy	1.00				0.80
All2	Overall, I was uncertain if the chatbot provider would be good at managing my private information	0.94	0.04	23.09	0.00	0.75
All3	Overall, I was worried if my information would be safe with the chatbot provider	1.00	0.05	22.10	0.00	0.80
All4	Overall, I was concerned that the chatbot provider might breach formal and informal privacy agreements	0.74	0.05	16.15	0.00	0.59

References

1. Acquisti, A., et al.: Nudges for privacy and security: understanding and assisting users' choices online. ACM Comput. Surv. **50**(3), 1–41 (2018). https://doi.org/10. 1145/3054926
2. Acquisti, A., Grossklags, J.: Uncertainty, ambiguity and privacy. In: Workshop on the Economics of Information Security (2005)
3. Al-Natour, S., Cavusoglu, H., Benbasat, I., Aleem, U.: An empirical investigation of the antecedents and consequences of privacy uncertainty in the context of mobile apps. Inf. Syst. Res. **31**(4), 1037–1063 (2020). https://doi.org/10.1287/isre.2020. 0931
4. Almuhimedi, H., et al.: Your location has been shared 5,398 times! A field study on mobile app privacy nudging. In: Proceedings of the 33rd Annual ACM Conference on Human Factors in Computing Systems, pp. 787–796, CHI '15, Association for Computing Machinery, New York, NY, USA (2015)
5. Bermejo Fernandez, C., Chatzopoulos, D., Papadopoulos, D., Hui, P.: This website uses nudging: MTurk workers' behaviour on cookie consent notices. Proc. ACM Hum.-Comput. Interact. **5**(CSCW2), 1–22 (2021)
6. Brüggemeier, B., Lalone, P.: Perceptions and reactions to conversational privacy initiated by a conversational user interface. Comput. Speech Lang. **71**, 101269 (2022)
7. Buçinca, Z., Malaya, M.B., Gajos, K.Z.: To trust or to think: cognitive forcing functions can reduce overreliance on AI in AI-assisted decision-making. Proc. ACM Hum.-Comput. Interact. **5**(CSCW1), 1–21 (2021)
8. Büyükkurt, B.K., Büyükkurt, M.D.: An experimental study of the effectiveness of three debiasing techniques*. Decis. Sci. **22**(1), 60–73 (1991). https://doi.org/10. 1111/j.1540-5915.1991.tb01262.x
9. Ciuk, D., Troy, A., Jones, M.: Measuring emotion: self-reports vs. physiological indicators. SSRN Electron. J. (2015). https://doi.org/10.2139/ssrn.2595359
10. Croskerry, P.: A universal model of diagnostic reasoning. Acad. Med. **84**(8), 1022–1028 (2009). https://doi.org/10.1097/ACM.0b013e3181ace703
11. Dash, G., Paul, J.: CB-SEM vs PLS-SEM methods for research in social sciences and technology forecasting. Technol. Forecast. Soc. Chang. **173**, 121092 (2021). https://doi.org/10.1016/j.techfore.2021.121092
12. Díaz Ferreyra, N.E., Meis, R., Heisel, M.: Learning from online regrets: from deleted posts to risk awareness in social network sites. In: Adjunct Publication of the 27th Conference on User Modeling, Adaptation and Personalization, pp. 117–125. ACM, Larnaca Cyprus, June 2019. https://doi.org/10.1145/3314183.3323849
13. European Commission: Regulation (EU) 2016/679 of the European Parliament and of the Council of 27 April 2016 on the protection of natural persons with regard to the processing of personal data and on the free movement of such data, and repealing Directive 95/46/EC (General Data Protection Regulation) (Text with EEA relevance) (2016)
14. Greis, M., Karolus, J., Schuff, H., Woźniak, P.W., Henze, N.: Detecting uncertain input using physiological sensing and behavioral measurements. In: Proceedings of the 16th International Conference on Mobile and Ubiquitous Multimedia, pp. 299–304. ACM, Stuttgart Germany, November 2017. https://doi.org/10.1145/3152832. 3152859
15. Hair Jr., J.F., Hult, G.T.M., Ringle, C.M., Sarstedt, M., Danks, N.P., Ray, S.: Partial Least Squares Structural Equation Modeling (PLS-SEM) Using R. CCB, Springer, Cham (2021). https://doi.org/10.1007/978-3-030-80519-7

16. Harkous, H., Fawaz, K., Shin, K.G., Aberer, K.: PriBots: conversational privacy with chatbots. In: Twelfth Symposium on Usable Privacy and Security (SOUPS 2016), USENIX Association, Denver, CO, June 2016

17. Kahneman, D.: Thinking, fast and slow. Farrar, Straus and Giroux, New York (2011)

18. Kline, R.B.: Principles and Practice of Structural Equation Modeling. Guilford publications, New York (2015)

19. Knight, F.H.: Risk, Uncertainty and Profit (1921)

20. Lambe, K.A., O'Reilly, G., Kelly, B.D., Curristan, S.: Dual-process cognitive interventions to enhance diagnostic reasoning: a systematic review. BMJ Qual. Saf. **25**(10), 808–820 (2016)

21. Lau, J., Zimmerman, B., Schaub, F.: Alexa, are you listening? Privacy perceptions, concerns and privacy-seeking behaviors with smart speakers. Proc. ACM Hum.-Comput. Interact. **2**(CSCW), 1–31 (2018)

22. Leschanowsky, A., Brüggemeier, B., Peters, N.: Design implications for human-machine interactions from a qualitative pilot study on privacy. In: Proceedings of the 2021 ISCA Symposium on Security and Privacy in Speech Communication, pp. 76–79, November 2021. https://doi.org/10.21437/SPSC.2021-16

23. Leschanowsky, A., Popp, B., Peters, N.: Adapting debiasing strategies for conversational AI. Zagreb, Croatia, p. 74 (2022)

24. Martin, S.: Measuring cognitive load and cognition: metrics for technology-enhanced learning. Educ. Res. Eval. **20**(7–8), 592–621 (2014). https://doi.org/10.1080/13803611.2014.997140

25. Mirhoseini, M., Early, S., Hassanein, K.: All eyes on misinformation and social media consumption: a pupil dilation study. In: Davis, F.D., Riedl, R., vom Brocke, J., Leger, P.M., Randolph, A.B., Müller-Putz, G.R. (eds.) Information Systems and Neuroscience. NeuroIS 2022. LNISO, vol. 58, pp. 73–80. Springer, Cham (2022). https://doi.org/10.1007/978-3-031-13064-9_7

26. Mushtaq, F., Bland, A.R., Schaefer, A.: Uncertainty and cognitive control. Front. Psychol. **2**, 249 (2011). https://doi.org/10.3389/fpsyg.2011.00249

27. Neys, W.D.: Advancing theorizing about fast-and-slow thinking. Behav. Brain Sci. 1–68 (2022). https://doi.org/10.1017/S0140525X2200142X, publisher: Cambridge University Press

28. Pearman, S., Young, E., Cranor, L.F.: User-friendly yet rarely read: a case study on the redesign of an online HIPAA authorization. Proc. Priv. Enhanc. Technol. **2022**(3), 558–581 (2022). https://doi.org/10.56553/popets-2022-0086

29. Popp, B., Lalone, P., Leschanowsky, A.: Chatbot language - crowdsource perceptions and reactions to dialogue systems to inform dialogue design decisions. J. Behav. Res. Methods **55**, 1601–1623 (2022)

30. Schomakers, E.M., Lidynia, C., Müllmann, D., Ziefle, M.: Internet users' perceptions of information sensitivity - insights from Germany. Int. J. Inf. Manag. **46**, 142–150 (2019)

31. Smith, C., Ellsworth, P.: Patterns of cognitive appraisal in emotion. J. Pers. Soc. Psychol. **48**, 813–38 (1985). https://doi.org/10.1037//0022-3514.48.4.813

32. Tversky, A., Kahneman, D.: Judgment under uncertainty: heuristics and biases. Science **185**(4157), 1124–1131 (1974). https://doi.org/10.1126/science.185.4157.1124

33. Wang, Y., Leon, P.G., Acquisti, A., Cranor, L.F., Forget, A., Sadeh, N.: A field trial of privacy nudges for Facebook. In: Proceedings of the SIGCHI Conference on Human Factors in Computing Systems, pp. 2367–2376. ACM, Toronto Ontario Canada, April 2014. https://doi.org/10.1145/2556288.2557413

34. Wang, Y., Leon, P.G., Scott, K., Chen, X., Acquisti, A., Cranor, L.F.: Privacy nudges for social media: an exploratory Facebook study. In: Proceedings of the 22nd International Conference on World Wide Web, pp. 763–770, WWW '13 Companion, Association for Computing Machinery, New York, NY, USA (2013)
35. Watson, D.B., Clark, L.A.: The PANAS-X manual for the positive and negative affect schedule (1994)

Voice Assistants for Therapeutic Support – A Literature Review

Ingo Siegert[1], Matthias Busch[1(✉)], Susanne Metzner[2], and Julia Krüger[3]

[1] Mobile Dialog Systems, Otto von Guericke University, Magdeburg, Germany
{ingo.siegert,matthias.busch}@ovgu.de
[2] Music Therapy, Faculty of Philosophy and Social Sciences, Leopold Mozart Centre,
University Augsburg, Augsburg, Germany
[3] Department of Psychosomatic Medicine and Psychotherapy,
Otto von Guericke University Magdeburg, Magdeburg, Germany

Abstract. Voice Assistants (VAs) are becoming a popular way to perform everyday tasks. In medical contexts, VAs are being studied for their usage in areas such as medical care in rural areas, medical diagnosis, and intersession treatment during therapies. This systematic review aims to assess the usability of voice-based interaction in therapies in health care and compare technical and conversational implementations and insights on the design process. The survey followed the PRISMA guidelines. IEE-Explore, ACM Digital Library, Scopus, and PubMed, were systematically searched for relevant studies that describe the use of voice-based systems in therapeutic context. 633 studies were screened, of which 9 studies met the inclusion criteria. The literature survey reveals a high degree of diversity among the identified studies regarding therapy form and level of implementation. Also, the range of utilized VA-technology and design principles is quite broad. Following this, the field of VA-supported therapy is still in an exploratory phase and further research is necessary to establish a level of consistency among studies.

Keywords: Voice Assistants · Speech based user interfaces · therapy · medical care · usability

1 Introduction

Voice Assistants (VAs) are increasingly being integrated in everyday life and represent an easy way to perform various tasks with minimal effort. This development has led to a rapidly growing user base for commercial voice assistants [21]. Users employ their voice assistants mostly for setting up alarm clocks or reminders, controlling smart home devices, or listening to music [38].

Thereby, researchers and developers distinguish different levels of VA based on the quality of assistance [8]: For **Level 1-type** interactions simple queries (web search or weather query) or commands for device control (play music, turn devices on/off) are incorporated, hardly any dialog (management) is needed [39]. Responses from the system are often used only for confirmation or to ask

G. Salvendy and J. Wei (Eds.): HCII 2023, LNCS 14052, pp. 221–239, 2023.
https://doi.org/10.1007/978-3-031-35921-7_15

for mandatory information. Technically, the focus is on the Automatic Speech Recognition (ASR) and Natural Language Understanding (NLU) components. Depending on the use case, certain domain-specific terms have to be integrated [19].

Level 2-type VAs offer a better support for users. Therefore, they need to be able to process queries regarding the course of the conversation and to be able to take domain knowledge into account when processing the statements. This central task is enabled by the Dialog Manager (DM). In addition, external sources can be accessed and domain-specific knowledge about individual processes, goals, and substeps can be provided by knowledge graphs or ontologies [16]. Both rule-based and statistical approaches exist for implementing a DM [27].

Finally, in **Level 3-type** VAs, additional personalization takes place. This allows VAs to adapt to the corresponding user in order to individualize system statements or dialog progressions (degree of assistance, preferences, expertise) [35]. This perspective is based on the concept of *Companion Systems* [44]. The following characteristics of these systems are particularly noteworthy:

- Consideration of the superordinate goals of the users
- Users are offered information proactively.
- Preparing complex alternative solutions and negotiating them interactively.
- Incorporating users' current needs, i.e., allowing the user to lead the dialog

In medical contexts, a few studies investigate the usage of VAs in different application areas. Especially level 2 and 3 VAs arousing great interest here, e.g., for diet assistance [25], medical care in rural areas [12], or medical diagnosis [5]. Furthermore, due to the dialog-like interaction style, VAs are seen as especially useful for intersession treatment during therapies. Hereby, Solutions using VAs are easy to realize; apart from a VA and a network connection, no further hardware is needed, and no further specialized devices are needed in contrast to virtual reality and robot solutions. This literature research aims to identify studies related to the usage of voice assistants in the aforementioned application. As method for the literature survey, we utilized the Preferred Reporting Items for Systematic reviews and Meta-Analysis (PRISMA) guidelines [30], aiming to identify the therapeutic application domain, the utilized voice assistant technology, evaluation details as well as details regarding the measured effects. A comparison of the used implementation methods gives first insights into a future harmonization of the usage of VAs in the domain of medical care and therapeutic support. Finally, an evaluation regarding the limitations of the implementations and experiments in the identified studies is given.

The remainder of this paper is structured as follows: In Sect. 2, we present the structured review guidelines and our criteria. Section 3 presents the procedure to identify the resulting 9 studies and indicates some statistics regarding the publications. Furthermore, this section discusses the content of the identified studies regarding the specific therapeutic application, utilized VAs, incorporated DM features, and the evaluation procedure as well as identified limitations of studies. The survey is then concluded in Sect. 4 giving a final summary and an outlook for future research trends. Thus, this study contributes to identify experiences, current limitations and potentials for the development of specialized VA in the field of therapeutic (intersession) treatment.

2   Methods

We followed the PRISMA guidelines [30] to identify the relevant studies based on eligibility criteria.

This survey aims to identify studies that use (physical) VAs in a therapeutic context. The literature search includes all criteria that use VAs and employ to a certain extent a dialog-like interaction with patients. Therefore, it is unnecessary if the patients are children or elderly or if an automatic system or a Wizardof-Oz (WOZ)-approach is employed. During screening, we excluded studies that 1) focus on robot-assisted therapy, 2) do not employ speech-based assistants, i.e., using text-based chatbots or embodied conversational agents, or are applied within a virtual reality, 3) do not employ a therapeutic context, i.e., focus on medication/appointment or diagnosis to support professionals (e.g., doctors, nurses), 4) are pure position paper or reviews.

As search engines, we used IEEExplore, ACM Digital Library, Scopus, and PubMed, as they cover related journals and conference proceedings.

As search-terms, we utilized `voice assistant` or `virtual assistant` in combination with `therap*` or `treatment`. The search ran from the 1st to 14th of November 2022.

3   Results

Initially, 633 studies were identified from the databases. After sorting out duplicates (n = 15), records clearly identifiable as unsuitable by the title and abstract (n = 508), and records not retrievable (n = 1), 110 studies were assessed for eligibility regarding the exclusion criteria. Finally, a total of 9 studies were included in the literature survey. The PRISMA flow diagram is depicted in Fig. 1. The 9 studies finally included in this review are depicted in Table 1.

3.1   Publication Statistics

In Fig. 2 the reports assessed for eligibility are depicted according to their publication date, and it can be seen that most of the studies are published just recently. Also, most of the final selected studies are published 2022.

Regarding the type of publication, most of the studies are published on conferences, whereas especially the *ACM Conference on Human Factors in Computing Systems (CHI)* and the newly established *Joint International Conference on Digital Inclusion, Assistive Technology & Accessibility (ICCHP-AAATE)* is often chosen as platform. Only 2 publications have been published in journals. This shows that there is no established journal (section) for this highly interdisciplinary topic.

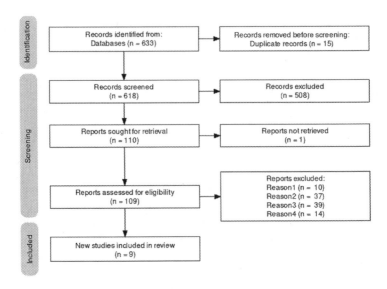

Fig. 1. PRISMA flow diagram of study inclusion and exclusion criteria for the systematic review, the detailed reasons are given in the text.

As already stated in Sect. 1, there exist many terms for speech-based interaction devices, this can be also seen in for this paper identified studies, see Fig. 3, whereas the terms *voice assistant(s)* and *conversational agent(s)* are used most often. Furthermore, it is apparent that a broad variety of therapy assistance is under investigation, as these terms are mostly occurring just once in the list of keywords. Here, the community still lacks a good, comprehensive term to indicate voice-based assistance in the therapeutic domain.

3.2 Therapeutic Application Domain and Justification for VA-Usage

As already indicated by the vast amount of keywords, the application domain for VAs in therapeutic context is quite broad and thus, also the 9 identified studies deal with different indications.

Both [31] and [9] focus on children with neurodevelopmental disorders. In [31] children with ADHD – especially those having an executive function disorder – are the targeted group. Psychological and social non-medicinal treatment is needed for them to alleviate the main symptoms and amplify the effects of drug treatment. The authors investigate whether a VAs can help children to keep the motivation high while creating 'Goal-Plan-Do-Check' course of action with self-instruction steps. The evaluation experiments are planned but not yet finished, and therefore only the design is described in the paper. On the other hand, [9] focuses on Autism Spectrum Disorder, and it is known that early and focused interventions are thought to mitigate their effect. Different types of therapy like play therapy, cognitive behavior therapy and music therapy is usually used for this. The authors of [9] state that VAs are potentially useful tools to support

Table 1. Overview of the studies included in the review.

Authors	Title
[3] Aymerich-Franch & Ferrer	Investigating the use of speech-based conversational agents for life coaching
[9] Catania et al.	Toward the Introduction of Google Assistant in Therapy for Children with Neurodevelopmental Disorders: An Exploratory Study
[11] Cheng et al.	Development and evaluation of a healthy coping voice interface application using the Google home for elderly patients with type 2 diabetes
[15] Gotthardt et al.	Voice Assistant-Based CBT for Depression in Students: Effects of Empathy-Driven Dialog Management
[31] Park et al.	Designing a Voice-Bot to Promote Better Mental Health: UX Design for Digital Therapeutics on ADHD Patients
[34] Scheible et al.	Generic Concept for Integrating Voice Assistance Into Smart Therapeutic Interventions
[41] Siegert et al.	Music-Guided Imagination and Digital Voice Assistant - Study Design and First Results on the Application of Voice Assistants for Music-Guided Stress Reduction
[43] Striegl et al.	Investigating the Usability of Voice Assistant-Based CBT for Age-Related Depression
[46] Yang et al.	Clinical Advice by Voice Assistants on Postpartum Depression: Cross-Sectional Investigation Using Apple Siri, Amazon Alexa, Google Assistant, and Microsoft Cortana

standard interventions, and in the current setting the main use of the VA is to play back music.

The authors of [46] utilize VAs to support mothers with postpartum depression. At the moment, it is analyzed how VAs responses to pre-recorded questions about postpartum depression suit scientific recommendations. The authors motivate the use of VAs by the possibility to perform a screening and clarify on misperceptions in the mothers' homes in privacy, as well as planning a treatment taking into account the special situation of the mothers.

Supporting elderly patients with diabetes 2 through VAs is the focus of [11]. Hereby, the VA especially supports in diabetes self-management by keeping track on the guidelines and assisting in the problem-solving. Unfortunately, the authors remain very vague about the exact design of the problem-solving component. Elderly patients, and age-related depression, is also focused by [15,43]. The authors motivate their experiments with the general usability of VAs for delivering psycho-educational content as one selected method for cognitive behavioral therapy (CBT) as an opportunity to replace face-to-face counseling.

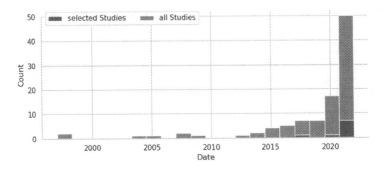

Fig. 2. Histogram plot of the 109 reports assessed for eligibility according to their publication year. The final selected studies included in the review are depicted separately.

Fig. 3. Word clouds as illustration of the used author keywords in the identified studies.

The authors of [34] focus on adults in general who need to "practice" something alone between therapy sessions and present a proof-of-concept in the home environment. Hereby, a VA can support to achieve optimal therapy results outside personal sessions. Furthermore, the authors claim that VAs could prevent misunderstandings in oral communication and a lack of motivation, identify inappropriate difficulty levels of the tasks, or allow a monitoring of the homework. As a final goal, the authors state that therapists could make ad-hoc adjustments and patients could benefit from even more individualized care. Currently, the authors concentrate on technical details and did not embrace an evaluation.

Also in [41], the authors focus on adults in general undergoing a receptive music therapy, more specially performing a music-imaginative journey in an interactive manner with a VA.

So far, all the aforementioned studies are more or less related to some professional therapy. In contrast, the authors of [3] focused more on life coaching to improve the quality of life by defining goals according to the SMART[1] principles. The VA had the role of the coach that guides the participant trough the coaching and goal definition process.

3.3   Utilized Voice Assistant Technology

Designing conversational interfaces for both health care support or therapy support requires technical and therapeutic expertise. Therefore, some voice applications were developed by an interdisciplinary team [11,31,34,41]. Also, face to face dialogues between therapists and patients [15,41,43] as well as existing survey procedures and digital tools [11] served as inspiration for the design of the systems. Moreover, different use cases and specific requirements for voice applications have been researched. The studies [9,46] give insights about the usage of voice assistants as a general tool for therapeutic support. It is furthermore highlighted in these studies that the creation of the system responses has to be carefully considered, particularly when interacting with patients having possible psychological disorders. Some studies report that an additional visual output can improve the user experience [9,11], esp. for patients with hearing or speech disabilities. However, this must be carefully weighed depending on the use case, as for example the authors of [31] have deliberately decided against using visual output as a possible distraction for their target group.

VA-Platform. Most of the identified studies utilize commercial voice assistants. Thereby, the studies in [9,46] used a Google Assistant smart speaker without any modifications or additional developed skill. In [46] the voice assistants by Amazon Alexa, Microsoft Cortana, and Apple Siri, all installed on a mobile phone, are used and evaluated without modification.

By also using commercial VAs, the authors of [11,34,41] extend the capabilities of them through self-developed skills. The Google home smart speaker[2]. is used in [11], the one from Alexa is used in [41]. The authors of [34] utilize both manufacturers.

The authors of [3] are pursuing a different path and developed their own iOS app utilizing the native iOS text-to-speech to and speech-to-text facilities. Compared to Google and Amazon, however, the possible degrees of freedom for dialogue management are severely limited.

In [31] the whole smart speaker was self-designed using a Raspberry Pi with Googles Dialogflow API.

Regarding the studies in [15,43], no further details regarding the voice assistant technology can be given, as the authors do not reveal any technical details.

Frameworks and Tools for Voice Based Systems. Regarding the utilization of already existing VA frameworks, many studies report using either

---

[1] SMART stands for Specific, Measurable, Achievable, Realistic, and Time-based.
[2] Conversational Actions for the Google Assistant platform are discontinued from 13 June 2023 on (https://developers.google.com/assistant/ca-sunset).

Dialogflow (former Api.ai)[3] or the Alexa Skill Kit (ASK) [23,34,41] for the development of their VAs-applications and/or -prototypes. These Frameworks support developers by providing a processing pipeline including pretrained ASR modules for several languages, a development console to train an application specific NLU module, and several Text to Speech (TTS) modules to generate responses in different voices. ASK [23] is tailored to develop Voice Skills for the Alexa Voice Assistant, whereas Dialogflow allows a broader integration into different platforms.

The authors of [34] highlight that in the domain of therapeutic interventions, a wide range of different VAs could be developed. In order to unify the development efforts, the authors suggest a microservice based architecture that unifies the backend for each VA. By that approach, new systems could profit from already existing solutions for common problems like monitoring for therapists as well as healthcare providers. Regarding commercial VAs, several frameworks, like RASA[4] or Jovo[5], exist that already offer the opportunity to integrate multiple voice assistant platforms as well as other voice based technology. These frameworks could serve as a basis for the suggested microservice based platform.

Dialog Management and Control Flow. Regarding the Course of interaction, most VAs take the initiative and guide the user through a predefined script. None of the presented VA was able to initiate a conversation itself without some kind of interaction by the user. For commercially available VAs, like Google Assistant, Siri and Alexa, it is not possible to implement such proactive dialogs.

The VAs of [15,41,43] always iterate over the same stages of the dialog. Apart from a state model, no further implementation details of the DMs are given within the studies. But from the description, it can be assumed that these systems are implemented with a rule based DM. Depending on the current state and the answer of the user, which are mapped to intents by the NLU module, the DM can decide to advance the conversation into the next state. Within each state, a predefined system response is then uttered towards the user.

The possible transitions between each state are defined by the developers of the system. The authors of [11] highlight the importance of a 'fallback' response that will ask the user to repeat if the answer could not be recognized, these 'fallback' responses can also be state dependent to rephrase the previous question of the system. By using a rule based approach, developers of VAs have full control over the behavior of the system. In contrast, statistical based dialog modeling promises more flexible systems that are more robust towards unforeseen flows of conversations [26], but these systems need already existing training data and can yield to conversations that are harder to interpret and explain.

As the systems of [11,31] support the users in form of a monitoring or every day tool, they do not need to follow a strict script of the dialog immediately.

---

[3] see https://cloud.google.com/dialogflow [11,31].

[4] https://rasa.com/product/rasa-platform/.

[5] https://www.jovo.tech/.

These systems are designed around some high level intents (e.g., 'I want to take the coping survey' [11] or 'I've got my bag' [31]). Based on these high level intents, the system will then proceed in a predefined dialog. In the case of reference [31], the dialog is not fully predetermined by the developers, but rather by a control app that allows parents to define tasks, subtasks, and schedules. The system of [11] also use additional intents to answer frequently asked questions.

The interaction with the VA presented in [3] is divided into different phases. Each phase spanned over one week and defined the script for the conversation. As each task builds up on the experiences of the previous phases, the VA showed a form of personalization to support users getting used to the process.

3.4   VA Evaluation Details

As already stated in previous sections, the intended application domain is quite broad and there is no standardized test procedure defined yet to evaluate the applicability of VAs in the therapy environment.

Interestingly, there are existing some definitions to evaluate the usability and chatbots/VAs [10,37] in general, but there is to the best of our knowledge no such usability evaluation description available for VAs. Moreover, the extension to measure the effectiveness of VA interventions is not standardized, yet. Therefore, in the following, we will describe the details of the identified studies regarding the overall procedure, the participants sample, the utilized survey methods, and the reported effects.

Study Procedure. Regarding the conducted studies of the reported VAs experiments, a broad variety is reported in the studies. This can be mainly explained by the different possibilities for VA-support in the therapeutic domain and by the different type of studies. Hereby it has to be stated that although all of the studies are conducted with prototype platforms, they embrace quite strict study protocols. Hereby a huge difference in the type of protocol can be seen, having just within-subject studies, randomized trials or even repeated measures crossover studies. Details can be found in Table 2.

There are studies that have been conducted only once [15,41,43,46], but there are also studies that have been repeated multiple times [3,9,31]. Two studies do not comprise evaluations and therefore, no statement can be made. But for the later real application, all studies aim that their VA can be used on a regular basis. Two studies [11,41] moreover mention that they have conducted comparison experiments against actually used treatments, i.e., mobile applications or relaxation CDs, respectively.

The same relatively inconsistent picture emerges with regard to the location of the evaluation. While the studies [3,11] are conducted at the patient's home. The studies [15,41,43,46] are conducted at the researcher's place, e.g., in a lab environment or an office environment. Hereby it has to be mentioned that the authors in [41] state that the utilized lab is a living room-like environment. But according to the motivation the researchers of these studies gave, it can be

Table 2. Overview of the experimental settings for each identified study. Studies with brackets do not yet conduct user studies. The study with a star employ a living room-like lab.

Study	Frequency		Location			Study protocol
	Once	Repeated	Home	Therapy facility	Lab	
[3]		✓	✓			within-subject
[9]		✓		✓		cohort study
[11]			✓			N/A
[15]	✓				✓	randomized trial
[31]		(✓)	✓			(repeated measures crossover)
[34]			(✓)			none
[41]	✓				✓*	repeated measures crossover
[43]	✓				✓	randomized trial
[46]	(✓)				✓	none

assumed that the later usage is also intended in the user's private households. Only the study presented in [9] is conducted at the therapy facility, as they conducted an exploratory study to investigate potentials and limitations of VA. How VA can be used regarding autism spectrum disorder treatment later was not conclusively answered by the authors.

Three studies [31,34,46] do not carry out any studies (yet). From the motivation, it can be assumed that it is planned that the later use is in a private environment. In [46], the interaction with the VA, i.e., the questions played back to the VA, are taken from a standardized questionnaire, the American College of Obstetricians and Gynecologists (ACOG) [1]. Here, patient-focused Frequently Asked Questions are mainly used. The authors of [31] state that the study is undergoing and at least present some details of the planned study, which will be used as basis for the current paper. In [34] a generic concept for therapeutic interventions by VAs is presented, and the authors mainly concentrate on the technical implementations, at the moment.

Participants' Description. Regarding the number of participants in the identified studies, it is apparent that most of the studies employ a relatively small number of participants, reaching from 4 to 21 participants with an age range in total from 4 to 83. Details are given in Table 3. From these details, it is apparent that the studies are still conducted in a prototypical manner and above all the basic functionality of the used VAs was focused on. Questions of robustness and validity of the assistance cannot be answered in such small user studies.

Additionally, most of the studies employ healthy participants only, which further underlines the prototypical character. Only three studies explicitly test their VAs using participants with a need for therapeutic support. In [9] children with low, medium, and high neurodevelopmental disorders were participating.

Table 3. Overview of participants and their age and sex distribution for each of the identified studies.

Study	# participants	Sex		Age [years]			Comments
		female	male	Min	Max	Mean	
[3]	4	3	1	24	37	31.5	
[9]	9	2	7	4	17	10.1	+ 3 therapists
[11]	10	N/A		N/A			elderly participants
[15]	10	5	5	12	30	25.6	
[31]	N/A	N/A		N/A			20 children planned
[34]	N/A	N/A		N/A			
[41]	21	9	12	19	36	24.67	
[43]	14	8	6	26	83	57.57	9 users over 60y
[46]	N/A	N/A		N/A			

In [15, 43] participants who at least partly had either been depressive and in therapy in the past, or had close relatives with depression took part.

Unfortunately most of the studies do not provide much detail about participants other than age and gender information, only two studies report on participants' previous experience with voice assistants [9, 41], and two studies provide information on participants' education levels [3, 41]. The first two studies report that at least some (2 of 9 children [9] and 8 of 21 adults [41]) had previously interacted with VAs. The latter two studies report that the users in their studies have at least a technical college entrance qualification [41], with some of them already have a university degree or even a PhD [3].

From this information, important conclusions could be drawn about the acceptance of voice assistants and the willingness to interact with them. But due to the low number of information, this is not possible regarding the actual studies.

Utilized Survey Methods. Most of the identified studies either employ (semi-structured) user interviews or some kind of questionnaires, see Table 4.

Regarding the studies that do not employ a user study (yet) [31, 34, 46], the authors of [46] at least evaluate the responses of the VA. The answers of the VA are evaluated regarding their accuracy and presence of a verbal response, as well as clinical appropriateness. This yes/no rating was conducted by the researchers themselves.

The authors of [3] used several measures before and after the study to assess the effectiveness of the VA. The Personal Growth Initiative Scale (PGI) [33] evaluates the active, intentional engagement in changing and developing as a person. A similar concept – global life satisfaction – is measured with Satisfaction with Life Scale (SLS) [14], where the authors used an adapted version with just 4 items. Also, experienced positive and negative affects using the Positive

Table 4. Overview of utilized survey methods for each of the identified study. The *
denotes a shortened version.

Study	Questionnaires	Interviews	Comments
[3]	PGI, SLS*, PANAS, usability, CSQ-8	–	
[9]	familiarity with commercial VAs, session specifics	group interview	therapists view, interaction logs
[11]	depression screening survey and user satisfaction	–	self-developed
[15]	PHQ9, TB*, SUS, CSQ-I, NPS, experience with depression and psychotherapy and experience with VAs	–	
[31]	N/A		
[34]	N/A		
[41]	sociodemographics, TA-EG, PSS-10, Stressbarometer, AttrakDiff, meCue	–	
[43]	SUS	online interview	
[46]	N/A		

and Negative Affect Scale (PANAS) [13] is measured. Furthermore, as part of the coaching experiment, the authors also measured amongst others the usability and the satisfaction with the coaching program. As usability questionnaire, an adapted version of [7] is used. For satisfaction, the authors utilized Client Satisfaction Questionnaire (CSQ-8) [2]. Additionally, participants were encouraged to comment their experience with the VA and the coaching program in general using open questions.

In [9] the experiment is evaluated at different points (before, after each session, end of study) and the authors collected the interaction logs from the Google Assistant (date, time, transcript, and response of all interactions by users). First, the therapists filled out a form on their familiarity with commercial VAs that also includes questions regarding theirs expectations about the potentials of VAs to support children with NDD during therapy. Second, after each of the three sessions, the therapists answered questions regarding the session in general and the concrete tasks supported by the VA and the experiences of children's initial engagement on a 10-point likert scale. Furthermore, open questions were asked regarding the therapeutic experience (motivation of usage as well as benefits/challenges/limitations) and technical details (technological breakdown, automatic speech recognition experience). At the end of the study, the authors interviewed the therapists remotely in a kind of semi-structured group interview regarding their experience with the VA. The interview focuses on the experience of the interviewers (main activities with VA during therapy, benefits and challenges while interacting with a VA) and to gather moments of joy and frustration with the VA, moments in which they socially interacted with the device, and also how they perceived the children with NDD interacting with it [9].

The authors of [11] used a self-developed questionnaire based on depression screening survey used by Healthy Coping application to compare the VA with and furthermore used a self-developed survey to measure the user satisfaction while using the VA.

In [15] participants had to answer Patient Health Questionnaire (PHQ9) [22] before taking part in the study to measure symptoms of depression. Furthermore, questionnaires regarding demographic information, experience with VAs, and experience with depression and psychotherapy, the subscales technology acceptance and technology competence belief of the questionnaire Technikbereitschaft (TB) [29] had to be answered. After the experiment, the System Usability Scale (SUS) [4], the Client Satisfaction Questionnaire for internet-based interventions (CSQ-I) [6], and the Net Promoter Score (NPS) [17] were utilized. The general usability was measured with SUS, while CSQ-I was intended to gain insights on the satisfaction and acceptance in the context of digital mental health interventions. NPS should extend these insights of perceived usability and acceptance.

In [41] the participants had to answer a self-developed questionnaire to gather socio-demographic information as well as previous experience with VAs [40], TA-EG [20] to capture into the affinity for technology, and PSS-10 [36] to collect information regarding the perceived stress in the past four weeks. Furthermore, a Visual Analogue Scale (VAS) rating employing a Stressbarometer [24] is done before and after each experimental condition. At the end of each condition, participants also rate their experience using Attrakdiff [18] and meCue [28]. After experiencing both conditions, open-ended, narrative-stimulating questions about their experiences with the study is posed.

In [43] the authors employ SUS to gain insights on the usability and a semi structured online interview as a formative evaluation.

3.5   Measured Effects

Although many of the studies defined a clear study protocol, the evidence on the effects analyzed is very sparse. In [11,31,34,43,46] no effects were analyzed instead the aim was to investigate exploratively of whether VAs can be used to improve education about PPD [46], to promote motivation [31], to improve medication adherence and activity [11], or to increase patients' own activity and deepen their understanding of treatment [34] or the see the usability and acceptance by the target group of CBT [43].

Studies [3,9,15,41], on the other hand, made statements about observed effects. The study in [9] was an observational study. Although support for playful activities was observed, the authors note that VAs fail to support an improvement or even address the children's poor communication and socialization skills, see technological limitations. Furthermore, the interaction was always triggered by the therapists and not by the children themselves. The authors of [3] could measure a significant increase in the development of a person (PGI) and positive affect after completing the coaching program and a moderate increase in life satisfaction (SLS) and a moderate decrease in negative affect (PANAS-N).

Additionally, the participants rated the application's usability and their satisfaction with the coaching program quite positively. The usability and acceptance of empathy-driven dialog management was measured in [15]. According to the authors, the results of the study results indicate a good level of usability and acceptance among the target group, despite the lack of benefits seen in the application of empathetic dialog management. Also, the authors of [41] reported a slightly positive evaluation as an overall assessment regarding usability (meCue) and acceptance (Attrakdiff) and observed relaxation effects. But the lack of significant differences between the control condition 'CD' and the condition 'Alexa' in both cases prevent drawing any further conclusions.

3.6   Mentioned Limitations

Different limitations of the utilized implementations are mentioned in the studies.

One very crucial drawback when using VAs is the performance of the underlying ASR. Although the overall performance of ASR-systems has been dramatically increased in the last years [45], this does not apply for all languages and use cases [42]. This issue has been reported by [31] using Korean as input, which causes problems in the proper operation of the VA. The authors solved this problem by formulating system responses with appropriate keywords that can serve as the user's response [31]. A similar issue is reported be the authors of [9]. In their study they observed that the Google Assistant has difficulties to understand children speech and that also the activation of the assistant was challenging for the children [9]. It could be assumed that children's speech in general and children with neurodevelopmental disorders in particular are challenging for ASR systems.

A further drawback in terms of technical limitations of the platforms is reported in [41]. Both Google Assistant and Amazon Alexa have a fixed waiting time after a prompt before the interaction is exited. This can interrupt the session in a disturbing way, especially during conversations in which patients are to be encouraged to speak for a longer period of time and in which longer pauses occur. Furthermore, these platforms do not support barge-in, the possibility for users to interrupt the systems' output. This limitation in combination with difficulties for a proper turn-change detection (for both system and participant) prevents a natural flow of dialogue to occur.

A further drawback, mentioned in [11] is the speed of the system's output. Especially elderly users would have difficulties following the system prompts due to the speed of narration. This issue calls for the implementation of a speed setting that would allow for the user to adjust the pace of narration based on their personal needs. Secondly, while the voice interface of Healthy Coping accommodates for a user's possibly poor vision, it is limited in its ability to assist those with hearing or speech disabilities. In order to better accommodate users with these disabilities, we would need to provide options for integrating assisting devices like hearing aids with Bluetooth functionality. Another possibility would be to have an (optional) visual interface as a support to enable a more meaningful conversational experience for elderly users as well as children [9, 11].

Furthermore, some authors also stated that it would be desirable to configure and customize already existing functionalities and contents (e.g., its replies) to meet patients' special needs. For example, the repetition of the same standardized response can cause stereotyped behaviors in some children [9] or the standardized system responses do not comply with appropriate clinical answers [46].

4 Discussion

The identified studies in the field of voice assistants are conducted in an exploratory phase. The focus of these studies is on determining the general applicability of voice assistants and evaluating the benefits of these devices for specific use cases. These benefits are often explored through the evaluation of prototypes, assessing factors such as user acceptance and the target audience.

Some studies [3, 11, 31] pointing to potentials for personalization and process support or even empathy driven dialog management [15]. However, the exact implementation needs to be further investigated, especially the connection with usability and acceptance.

Regarding the technical implementation, most studies employ cloud-services (ASK or Dialogflow). Voice Apps on Voice Assistant platforms assistants offer developers the opportunity to create voice skills or voice apps. When designing a voice app, the developer is in control of the dialog with the user. Developers can even personalize the interaction with the voice app and select a specific voice for the responses. This allows to communicate a specific corporate identity and to offer specialized solutions for a wide range of different domains. Hereby especially the authors of [34] show necessity of a unification. In contrast, an on-premise or on-device smart-speaker solution would have many advantages for the scenarios (data protection, individualization). This is also the direction of the work of [3], but it shows the strong limitation of the language model compared to available APIs, whereas current solutions, e.g. whisper [32], present good alternatives.

By utilizing smart speakers, the user has to invoke each voice app individually, that can be done by calling an app by its specific name or through an app specific invocation utterance. Although, this practice becomes more and more common for voice app users'. But at the same time, users can be overwhelmed with the broad interaction features commercial smart speakers offer and thus lose track of the specific (therapeutic) voice app.

Therefore, especially in the interaction with patients, it is still necessary to investigate in more depth which answers these systems give to the users [46] and how a good integration of specialized therapy offers can be implemented by voice assistants.

In conclusion, this research is important as it provides a deeper understanding of the potential of voice assistants and how they can be effectively integrated into various areas of life. Overall, the findings of these exploratory studies are crucial in shaping the future development of voice assistants and their applications. Especially in combination with smart speakers, voice apps can offer an easy reachable support at home. Researchers and developers can profit from a growing user base of commercially available smart speakers when creating solutions for inter-session use case, as reported in the selected studies.

References

1. ACOG Committee: COG committee opinion no. 757: Screening for perinatal depression. Obstetr. Gynecol. **132**(5) (2018). https://doi.org/10.1097/AOG. 0000000000002927
2. Attkisson, C., Zwick, R.: The client satisfaction questionnaire: psychometric properties and correlations with service utilization and psychotherapy outcome. Eval. Program Plann. **5**(3), 233–237 (1982). https://doi.org/10.1016/0149-7189(82)90074-X
3. Aymerich-Franch, L., Ferrer, I.: Investigating the use of speech-based conversational agents for life coaching. Int. J. Hum.-Comput. Stud. **159** (2022). https://doi.org/10.1016/j.ijhcs.2021.102745
4. Bangor, A., Kortum, P.T., Miller, J.T.: An empirical evaluation of the system usability scale. Int. J. Hum.-Comput. Interact. **24**(6), 574–594 (2008). https://doi.org/10.1080/10447310802205776
5. Bickmore, T., Rubin, A., Simon, S.: Substance use screening using virtual agents: towards automated screening, brief intervention, and referral to treatment (SBIRT). In: Proceedings of the ACM International Conference on Intelligent Virtual Agents (2020). https://doi.org/10.1145/3383652.3423869
6. Boß, L., Lehr, D., Reis, D., Vis, C., Riper, H., Berking, M., Ebert, D.: Reliability and validity of assessing user satisfaction with web-based health interventions. J. Med. Internet Res. **18**(8) (2016). https://doi.org/10.2196/jmir.5952
7. Brooke, J.: SUS: A 'Quick and Dirty' Usability Scale. CRC Press (1996)
8. Busch, M., Kania, M., Assmann, T., Siegert, I.: Radlogistik als anwendungsgebiet für digitale sprachassistenten - ein diskussionsbeitrag. In: Elektronische Sprachsignalverarbeitung 2023. Tagungsband der 34. Konferenz. Studientexte zur Sprachkommunikation, vol. 107, pp. 220–227. TUDpress, Munich (2023)
9. Catania, F., Spitale, M., Garzotto, F.: Toward the introduction of google assistant in therapy for children with neurodevelopmental disorders: an exploratory study. In: Extended Abstracts of the 2021 ACM CHI (2021). https://doi.org/10.1145/3411763.3451666
10. Chang, M., Michael, T., Möller, S., Schlangen, D.: The power of conversation flow in video conference tools: evaluation of speaker change cues. In: Niebuhr, O., Lundmark, M.S., Weston, H. (eds.) Studientexte zur Sprachkommunikation: Elektronische Sprachsignalverarbeitung 2022, pp. 81–88. TUDpress, Dresden (2022)
11. Cheng, A., Raghavaraju, V., Kanugo, J., Handrianto, Y.P., Shang, Y.: Development and evaluation of a healthy coping voice interface application using the google home for elderly patients with type 2 diabetes. In: 15th IEEE Annual Consumer Communications & Networking Conference (2018). https://doi.org/10.1109/CCNC.2018.8319283
12. Conde-Caballero, D., Rivero-Jiménez, B., Cipriano-Crespo, C., Jesus-Azabal, M., Garcia-Alonso, J., Mariano-Juárez, L.: Treatment adherence in chronic conditions during ageing: uses, functionalities, and cultural adaptation of the assistant on care and health offline (acho) in rural areas. J. Pers. Med. **11**(3) (2021). https://doi.org/10.3390/jpm11030173

13. Crawford, J.R., Henry, J.D.: The positive and negative affect schedule (PANAS): construct validity, measurement properties and normative data in a large non-clinical sample. Br. J. Clin. Psychol. **43**, 245–265 (2004)

14. Diener, E., Emmons, R.A., Larsen, R.J., Griffin, S.: The satisfaction with life scale. J. Pers. Assess. **49**(1), 71–75 (1985). https://doi.org/10.1207/s15327752jpa4901_13

15. Gotthardt, M., Striegl, J., Loitsch, C., Weber, G.: Voice assistant-based CBT for depression in students: effects of empathy-driven dialog management. In: Miesenberger, K., Kouroupetroglou, G., Mavrou, K., Manduchi, R., Covarrubias Rodriguez, M., Penáz, P. (eds.) ICCHP-AAATE 2022. LNCS, vol. 13341, pp. 451–461. Springer, Cham (2022). https://doi.org/10.1007/978-3-031-08648-9_52

16. Haase, P., Nikolov, A., Trame, J., Kozlov, A., Herzig, D.: Alexa, Ask Wikidata! Voice interaction with knowledge graphs using Amazon Alexa. In: Proceedings of the ISWC 2017 (2017)

17. Hamilton, D., Lane, J., Gaston, P., Patton, J., Macdonald, D., Simpson, A., Howie, C.: Assessing treatment outcomes using a single question: the net promoter score. Bone Joint J. **96-B**(5), 622–628 (2014). https://doi.org/10.1302/0301-620X.96B5. 32434

18. Hassenzahl, M., Burmester, M., Koller, F.: AttrakDiff: Ein Fragebogen zur Messung wahrgenommener hedonischer und pragmatischer Qualität. In: Szwillus, G., Ziegler, J. (eds.) Mensch & Computer 2003, Berichte des German Chapter of the ACM, vol. 57, pp. 187–196. Vieweg+Teubner, Wiesbaden (2003)

19. Hosier, J., Zhou, Y., Sharma, N., Gurbani, V.K.: Lightweight domain adaptation: a filtering pipeline to improve accuracy of an automatic speech recognition (ASR) engine. In: 4th ACAI. ACM (2022). https://doi.org/10.1145/3508546.3508641

20. Karrer, K., Glaser, C., Clemens, C., Bruder, C.: Technikaffinität erfassen - der Fragebogen TA-EG, vol. 8. VDI-Verl (2009)

21. Kinsella, B.: Nearly 90 Million U.S. Adults Have Smart Speakers, Adoption Now Exceeds One-Third of Consumers. voicebot.ai (2020). https://perma.cc/336P-2C77. Accessed 28 Apr 2020

22. Kroenke, K., Spitzer, R., Williams, J.: The PHQ-9: validity of a brief depression severity measure. J. Gen. Intern. Med. **16**(9), 606–13 (2001). https://doi.org/10.1046/j.1525-1497.2001.016009606.x

23. Kumar, A., et al.: Just ask: building an architecture for extensible self-service spoken language understanding. arXiv preprint arXiv:1711.00549 (2017)

24. Lesage, F., Berjot, S., Deschamps, F.: Clinical stress assessment using a visual analogue scale. Occup. Med. **62**, 600–605 (2012). https://doi.org/10.1093/occmed/kqs140

25. Li, J., Maharjan, B., Xie, B., Tao, C.: A personalized voice-based diet assistant for caregivers of alzheimer disease and related dementias: system development and validation. J. Med. Internet Res. **22**(9) (2020). https://doi.org/10.2196/19897

26. McTear, M.: Conversation modelling for chatbots: current approaches and future directions. In: Studientexte zur Sprachkommunikation: Elektronische Sprachsignalverarbeitung 2018, pp. 175–185 (2018)

27. McTear, M., Callejas, Z., Griol, D.: The conversational interface: talking to smart devices. In: The Conversational Interface: Talking to Smart Devices, pp. 1–422 (2016). https://doi.org/10.1007/978-3-319-32967-3/COVER

28. Minge, M.: Nutzererleben messen mit dem meCUE 2.0 - Ein Tool für alle Fälle? In: Dachselt, R., Weber, G. (eds.) Mensch und Computer 2018 - Workshopband. GI, Bonn (2018). https://doi.org/10.18420/muc2018-ws16-0485

29. Neyer, F.J., Felber, J., Gebhardt, C.: Entwicklung und validierung einer kurzskala zur erfassung von technikbereitschaft. Diagnostica **58**(2), 87–99 (2012). https://doi.org/10.1026/0012-1924/a000067

30. Page, M.J., et al.: The PRISMA 2020 statement: an updated guideline for reporting systematic reviews. PLOS Med. **18**(3), 1–15 (2021). https://doi.org/10.1371/journal.pmed.1003583

31. Park, D.E., Shin, Y.J., Park, E., Choi, I.A., Song, W.Y., Kim, J.: Designing a voice-bot to promote better mental health: UX design for digital therapeutics on ADHD patients. In: Extended Abstracts of the 2020 ACM CHI (2020). https://doi.org/10.1145/3334480.3382948

32. Radford, A., Kim, J.W., Xu, T., Brockman, G., McLeavey, C., Sutskever, I.: Robust speech recognition via large-scale weak supervision (2022). https://doi.org/10.48550/ARXIV.2212.04356, https://arxiv.org/abs/2212.04356

33. Robitschek, C.: Personal growth initiative: the construct and its measure. Meas. Eval. Couns. Dev. **30**(4), 183–198 (1998). https://doi.org/10.1080/07481756.1998.12068941

34. Scheible, J., Hofmann, F., Reichert, M., Pryss, R., Schickler, M.: Generic concept for integrating voice assistance into smart therapeutic interventions. In: IEEE 35th International Symposium on Computer-Based Medical Systems, pp. 56–61 (2022). https://doi.org/10.1109/CBMS55023.2022.00017

35. Schmidt, M., Braunger, P.: A survey on different means of personalized dialog output for an adaptive personal assistant. In: Adjunct Publication of the 26th UMAP, pp. 75–81. ACM, New York (2018). https://doi.org/10.1145/3213586.3226198

36. Schneider, E.E., Schönfelder, S., Domke-Wolf, M., Wessa, M.: Measuring stress in clinical and nonclinical subjects using a German adaptation of the perceived stress scale. Int. J. Clin. Health Psychol. **20**(2), 173–181 (2020). https://doi.org/10.1016/j.ijchp.2020.03.004

37. Schrepp, M., Thomaschewski, J.: Design and validation of a framework for the creation of user experience questionnaires. Int. J. Interact. Multimed. Artif. Intell. **7**(5), 88–95 (2019). https://doi.org/10.9781/ijimai.2019.06.006

38. Serpil Tas, R.A.: Nutzung von sprachassistenten in deutschland. In: Sprachassistenten - Anwendungen, Implikationen, Entwicklungen : ITG-Workshop : Magdeburg, p. 39 (2020)

39. Siegert: "Alexa in the wild" - Collecting Unconstrained Conversations with a Modern Voice Assistant in a Public Environment. In: Proceedings of The 12th LREC, pp. 608–612. ELRA, Marseille (2020)

40. Siegert, I., Busch, M., Krüger, J.: Does users' system evaluation influence speech behavior in HCI?-First insights from the engineering and psychological perspective. In: Studientexte zur Sprachkommunikation: Elektronische Sprachsignalverarbeitung 2020, pp. 241–248 (2020)

41. Siegert, I., Busch, M., Metzner, S., Junne, F., Krüger, J.: Music-guided imagination and digital voice assistant - study design and first results on the application of voice assistants for music-guided stress reduction. In: Salvendy, G., Wei, J. (eds.) HCII 2022. LNCS, vol. 13337, pp. 347–362. Springer, Cham (2022). https://doi.org/10.1007/978-3-031-05014-5_29

42. Silber-Varod, V., Siegert, I., Jokisch, O., Sinha, Y., Geri, N.: A cross-language study of selected speech recognition systems. J. Appl. Knowl. Manage.: OJAKM **9**, 1–15 (2021). https://doi.org/10.36965/OJAKM.2021.9(1)1-15

43. Striegl, J., Gotthardt, M., Loitsch, C., Weber, G.: Investigating the usability of voice assistant-based CBT for age-related depression. In: Miesenberger, K.,

Kouroupetroglou, G., Mavrou, K., Manduchi, R., Covarrubias Rodriguez, M., Penáz, P. (eds.) ICCHP-AAATE 2022. LNCS, vol. 13341, pp. 432–441. Springer, Cham (2022). https://doi.org/10.1007/978-3-031-08648-9_50

44. Wendemuth, A., Biundo, S.: A companion technology for cognitive technical systems. In: Esposito, A., Esposito, A.M., Vinciarelli, A., Hoffmann, R., Müller, V.C. (eds.) Cognitive Behavioural Systems. LNCS, vol. 7403, pp. 89–103. Springer, Heidelberg (2012). https://doi.org/10.1007/978-3-642-34584-5_7

45. Xiong, W., Wu, L., Droppo, J., Huang, X., Stolcke, A.: The Microsoft 2017 conversational speech recognition system. In: Proceedinbngs of the IEEE ICASSP-2018, Calgary, Kanada, pp. 5934–5938 (2018)

46. Yang, S., Lee, J., Sezgin, E., Bridge, J., Lin, S.: Clinical advice by voice assistants on postpartum depression: cross-sectional investigation using apple Siri, Amazon Alexa, Google assistant, and Microsoft Cortana. JMIR Mhealth Uhealth **11**(9), 353–360 (2021). https://doi.org/10.2196/24045

Mobile Information Systems
in Education, Healthcare, eCommerce
and Beyond

A Case Study of E-commerce Brand Evolution Based on OEM-ODM-OBM Path

Zhipeng Chu, Mengxuan Zhou[✉], and Rumeng Zhang[✉]

Ningbo University of Finance and Economics, Ningbo, People's Republic of China
chuzhipeng@nbufe.edu.cn, mengzhouzhou88@163.com,
zhangrumeng19@163.com

Abstract. Under the background of the rapid development of China's e-commerce, it is generally representative for the small and medium-sized manufacturing enterprises in Ningbo to realize the industrial upgrading based on the OEM-ODM-OBM path. In this process, some enterprises gradually independently create Electronic goods brand through e-commerce platforms and achieve success. This case study reveals the main features of the brand evolution of companies at different stages of the manufacturing path, including five aspects: product strategy, competitive strategy, market strategy, brand strategy and customer service.

Keywords: e-commerce brand · OEM-ODM-OBM path · Case Research · Evolution

1 Introduction

With the development of the Internet, there is a diversification in the way brands are created. This paper analyzes the traits needed in the evolutionary development of an e-commerce brand, etc., based on the three major stages of enterprise development. At each stage of upgrading and development of enterprises, the meaning of e-commerce branding and the elements required to be included are different. The comprehensive upgrading development process of enterprises from OEM, ODM to OBM fully demonstrates the development of China's Internet era, and also provides new development opportunities for production and sales-oriented micro and small enterprises from the perspective of brand development elements and traits. The article uses Grounded theory to further create a model of e-commerce brand development strategy to provide insights for small and micro enterprises to develop online brands to form unique competitive advantages.

2 Conceptual Definition and the Development of Assumptions

2.1 The Importance of the Internet Brand

In recent years, with the increasing improvement of the Internet online platform, the competition for the small home appliance industry is also increasingly fierce. The brand of the products sold by enterprises has gradually become the key point of development.

© The Author(s), under exclusive license to Springer Nature Switzerland AG 2023
G. Salvendy and J. Wei (Eds.): HCII 2023, LNCS 14052, pp. 243–252, 2023.
https://doi.org/10.1007/978-3-031-35921-7_16

As far as enterprise marketing is concerned, consumers' cognition of brand products is the basic content of their _ knowledge. The development of private brand is an important strategy of an enterprise. During the period, it includes the identification of enterprise products, brand introduction, and the specific actions of transforming and improving the self-brand. The sub-brands of private products need to meet the tone of the parent brand, and the parent and subsidiary brands form a synergistic effect and complement each other [1]. Based on the modeling structure, e-commerce brands and platforms are particularly important for the development of enterprises, and it can be said that brands and products promote each other[2].Enterprises need to organize and coordinate all the resources that can be used both internally and externally to further absorb and internalize the selected brand, so that it can be integrated with the enterprise resource network in various details [3]. Strengthening the brand building, learning and developing the OEM path, will be of greater help to the work of the enterprise and can increase its core competitiveness [4]. In the process of enterprise development, most of them, from the OEM production to the focus on market demand and commodity quality, adopt the operation mode of imitation, imitation, development and customization, and choose customized product development methods, which can effectively reduce the operating costs and market risks of enterprises and gain competitive advantages. The network has disappeared and started from imitation development, but now most of them have entered the stage of cost-effective positioning and developed brand products with distinctive characteristics [5].

2.2 OEM-ODM-OBM Enterprise Have Elements

The process of each stage of an enterprise is matched with its capabilities, that is, the realization of the transformation process from OEM to ODM and OBM is corresponding to its own resources and capabilities[6]. It is necessary for enterprises to enter the ODM and OBM links and achieve innovation and breakthrough in technology [7]. OEM production mode of collaboration body are not stable, the brand manufacturers of OEM enterprises too much control, at the same time OEM companies will seek in the conditions mature brand, so the interests of the foundry and entrust brand manufacturers game is very important, brand can further evolution upgrade, to some extent depends on the brand and factory game choice [8]. Under the background of Internet sales, if enterprises want to achieve leapfrog development, they need to increase the investment in enterprise digital equipment and digital technology. Digital technology is applied to the whole process of enterprise operation, such as product selection, screening and circulation in the early stage, to provide the competitiveness of enterprises [9].

2.3 Characteristics of Brand Evolution at Different Stages

The essence of the brand is to create value for the enterprise. In the process of growth, the brand needs to adjust the relevant marketing strategies according to its characteristics in different development stages, so as to ensure the development effect of the brand. In the OEM stage, the key of an enterprise is to build and improve cost advantages through large-scale production and continuous improvement of production efficiency, and shift product differentiation from OEM to ODM. When the enterprise shifts from ODM to

OBM, the key feature lies in product innovation and brand operation. The commitment and value brought by the brand is also related to the possibility of the final evolution of the enterprise. The enterprise should strengthen the importance of product quality and service for brand building [10]. Whether an enterprise can develop smoothly from OEM to ODM stage depends, to some extent, depend on the knowledge acquisition, innovation ability and the establishment of research and development team of OEM enterprises. The competitiveness of the construction of independent brand includes the competitiveness of products and the market competitiveness.

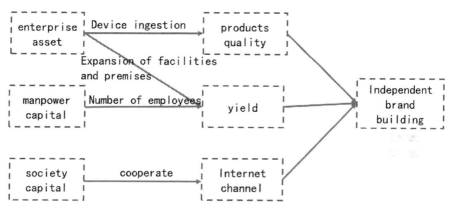

Fig. 1. Development elements of each stage of the enterprise

For enterprises in the stage of brand gestation, the main factors affecting the establishment of their independent brands include enterprise assets factors, human capital factors and social capital factors. Its risks mainly include competitive risk and financial crisis. Among them, enterprise resources are the key factors affecting the establishment of independent brands. Enterprise resources accelerate the accumulation of enterprise resources through product quality advantages, product price advantages and the construction of cooperation network, providing material guarantee for the establishment of independent brands.

3   Research Methods and Data Processing

3.1   Grounded Theory and Analysis Principle

Grounded theory is a qualitative research method that includes three stages: open coding, spindle coding, and selective coding. Small and medium-sized manufacturing enterprises in our country through the electric business platform to create e-commerce brand in the outbreak stage, independent create e-commerce brand research have not yet formed a systematic theoretical research results, so the Grounded theory as the research method, through the acquisition of you bao brand related text data analysis, extract the category and build model (Fig. 2).

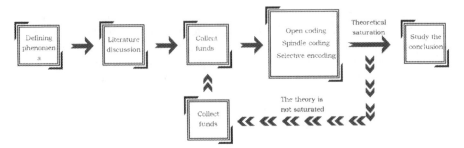

Fig. 2. Grounded Theory in the theoretical analysis process

3.2 Sample Selection

This paper selects Ningbo Ubst Technology Co., Ltd. as the object to study its independent e-commerce brand path. Ubst Technology Co., Ltd., founded in 2010, entered the small home appliance market in 2014. The company integrates research and development, production, sales as one, and its main products cover clean electrical appliances, seasonal household appliances, etc. The company has gone through the OEM stage, ODM stage and OBM stage, and finally established an independent e-commerce brand. Choosing the Ubst brand as the case sample of this study is of important reference significance for the small and medium-sized manufacturing industry to realize the independent creation of e-commerce brands through the e-commerce platform.

3.3 Data Collection and Collation

In the process of data collection, in line with the principle of "everything is data", emphasize the diversity of data resources, this paper specific collected data including the following five categories: the company website information, electric business platform opened flagship store information, network news, senior interviews, field research, a total of more than 100000 words of information.

4   Category Extraction and Model Construction

4.1   Open Coding

Open coding is the first stage of the coding process. In this stage, the collected data is deeply considered and analyzed with concepts, and the conceptual genera in the data are obtained, and the genera are named to determine the attributes and dimensions of the genera. In this paper, the original data were encoded in open, and 85 concepts were finally extracted, and the similar or repeated concepts were further refined into abstract categories, and 13 categories such as product design were extracted.

4.2 Spindle Coding

The spindle coding aims to discover and establish the potential logical relationship between the categories, and thus further develop into the main category and its subsidiary category. The categories of interrelations between different categories and logical order of similar themes are grouped into one class to constitute the main category. In the process of classification, the characteristics of Ubst brand should be taken into account, and the category that can belong to the two main categories should be attributed to the main category with the closest proximity as far as possible. This paper summarizes five main categories, such as product strategy and competition strategy. The results of open coding and spindle coding are shown in Tables 1 and 2.

Table 1. The OEM-ODM stage

fundamental category	Categorization	conceptualization
product strategy	products design	Product field, product category, product function introduction
	product life cycle	Product penetration rate, production quality, production capacity, production management
competitive strategy	competitive edge	Regional advantage, technical advantage, price advantage
	corporate strategy	Patent protection, product expansion, talent and technology, and focus on products
market strategy	pressure of competition	Competitors, the cost pressure
	Market development	Sales channels, to develop the domestic market
	business cooperation	Raw material supplier cooperation and merchant cooperation
Brand strategy	brand positioning	Brand brand, product differentiation
	brand operation	Brand rental fee, capital operation
customer service	Customer loyalty	Customer demand, product recognition, close customer relationship, repeat purchase rate

4.3 Selective Coding

Selective coding is a process of proposing "story lines" and constructing a new theoretical framework by mining core categories. Through the in-depth analysis of 90 concepts, 13 categories and 5 main categories, this paper compares the analysis results with the original materials and codes, and puts forward the core category of "Ubst independent e-commerce brand creation", so as to lead all other main categories. Story line can be expressed as: you treasure brand e-commerce brand creation strategy including product strategy, competition strategy, marketing strategy, brand strategy and customer service

Table 2. The ODM-OBM stage

fundamental category	Categorization	conceptualization
product strategy	products design	Humanized design, product quality certification, product honor, loyal consumers, product packaging
	Research and development and innovation	Rigorous product research and development, research and development innovation, design characteristics, humanized design, technology innovation
competitive strategy	competitive edge	Product advantage, price advantage, multi-platform advantage, platform recognition brand
	corporate strategy	Patent protection, product expansion, talent and technology, and focus on products
market strategy	pressure of competition	Malignant competition, negative comments, and competitors
	Market development	Sales channels, online sales, and field expansion
	business cooperation	Raw material supplier cooperation, merchant cooperation, platform cooperation
	marketing promotion	We-media promotion, live broadcast promotion, and alliance businesses
Brand strategy	brand positioning	e-commerce brand, brand spirit, consumer positioning, brand influence, brand goals
	brand operation	Brand prospect, brand purpose brand goal, operation strategy, brand concept
customer service	Customer loyalty	Brand recognition, customer demand, brand purpose, customer recognition, customer group, operation strategy, brand affirmation
	User Experience UE	Safety performance, product reviews, efficient logistics, consumer evaluation,

(*continued*)

Table 2. (*continued*)

fundamental category	Categorization	conceptualization
	after-sale service	Customer demand research, unified after-sales standards, real-time response

five meters love you, product strategy are the basis of you treasure to create independent e-commerce brand, competition strategy, marketing strategy and brand strategy is the action plan, customer service is the safeguard measures. This paper constructs the related model of Ubst independent e-commerce brand creation. As shown in Fig. 1 (Fig. 3).

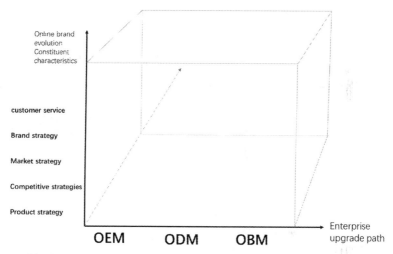

Fig. 3. Relation model of Ubst's independent e-commerce brand creation

4.4 Product Strategy

Product strategy refers to what kind of products and services that enterprises provide to meet the needs of consumers. In the OEM-ODM stage, for Ubst, the product strategy is mainly reflected in the production of the products, with the main customers of the major brands entrusting them. At this stage, Ubst needs to focus on product quality optimization and cost control, and will strive to achieve higher profitability through continuous upgrading and optimization. In the ODM-OBM stage, Ubst pays more attention to research and development and innovation. Ubst adheres to rigorous product research and development and control, and continues to invest in key technologies, product development, research and development team building and other aspects, striving to create differentiated products.

4.5 Competition Strategy

Competitive strategy refers to the establishment of competitive advantage in a specific market by formulating business strategy. The competitive strategy of Ubst products includes competitive advantage and corporate strategy. In the OEM-ODM stage, the company builds competitive advantages through technology, develops the local manufacturing advantages of Ningbo according to local conditions, and constantly produces high-quality home appliances. In the ODM-OBM stage, Ubst builds competitive advantages from the aspects of brand and user. By creating an independent electronic goods brand, Ubst establishes an online window on the e-commerce platform to realize face-to-face communication with consumers and upgrade its products. In terms of corporate strategy, Ubst has always been consistent, based on products, with talent as the starting point, to enhance the brand and corporate honor, and to form a clear product development strategy.

4.6 Market Strategy

The market strategy is mainly reflected in four aspects: competition pressure, market development, business cooperation and promotion mode. In the OEM-ODM stage, Ubst's market strategy is mainly reflected in the elimination of competitive pressure. Ubst realizes it by constantly improving the product quality and improving the production line. In the ODM-OBM stage, in terms of competitive pressure, enterprises need to avoid malicious following and selling, and malicious evaluation and other competition behaviors on the e-commerce platforms. In the face of competitive pressure, Ubst is proactive in market development, business cooperation and marketing promotion, and tries to eliminate the negative impact of malicious competition. We have continuously reached business cooperation with Tmall, Pinduoduo, Juhuasuan and other e-commerce platforms. In terms of promotion, we-media promotion, live broadcast promotion and alliance business trinity of marketing and promotion is mainly adopted to carry out brand publicity and customer traffic attraction.

4.7 Brand Strategy

With the entry of a new information age, the characteristics of the operation of small home appliance brands are mainly reflected in the value of information, network management is deeply rooted in the people, and the change of life concept brings a new consumption view of three aspects. In the OEM-ODM stage, the brand strategy is to acquire the right to use the brand, participate in product research and development, develop product technology, and provide professional production and processing. Ubst's sales also reached a new high at this stage. Later, Ubst accumulated certain products, technology, capital and other strength, after the operation of its own brand. In the ODM-OBM stage, Ubst set up its corresponding own brand according to the characteristics of the products. From the long-term development of the brand, it has the characteristics of personalization, quality, virtualization and standardization. In addition to innovation and development, for the brand operation, it is also necessary to maintain the brand by constantly conforming to the consumer needs of The Times, maintaining the brand positioning, and constantly innovating to stimulate the vitality of the enterprise.

4.8 Customer Service

For enterprises, customer service serves as a key channel to directly contact users in marketing, and the effective combination of customer service and marketing is the top priority in the development elements of Ubst. In the OEM-ODM stage, Ubst mainly provides professional consulting services and quality "three guarantees" services through high-quality reception of customers. In the after-sales stage, do a good job in product installation and debugging. Ubst has always maintained the concept of customer first, and customer service is the core competitiveness of enterprise development. Of course, Ubst in providing customer service has also achieved timely supply, grasp the best time to impress customers. In the follow-up operation, Ubst is also constantly improving its own customer service system, such as doing a good job in spare parts supply, product technology training, regular testing, door-to-door service, etc. With a series of high-quality customer service, to strengthen consumers' awareness of the brand.

5   Conclusion

Taking the brand development stage of small and medium-sized manufacturing enterprises in Ningbo as the starting point, this paper analyzes the characteristics of the brand development of different development stages with the grounded theory, and studies the influence of five brand characteristics, including product strategy, competitive strategy, market strategy, brand strategy and customer service, on the brand evolution of the enterprise. In the process of brand development, the roles of the key characteristics are also different. Through specific analysis, this paper expounds the dynamic evolution process of the key influence characteristics of the brand evolution in the enterprise development stage.

References.

1. Li, H., Ying, W., Sun, D.: The self-owned brand construction mode of chain retail enterprises from the perspective of resource orchestration: a case study of Sinopec Yijie's "Zhuomaquan" brand. J. Jiangxi Univ. Finan. Econ. (4), 35–46 (2022)
2. Mahmoud, D.K.: Review of interactions between e-commerce, brand and packaging on value added of saffron: a structural equation modeling approach. Afr. J. Bus. Manage. 6(26) (2012)
3. Li, P., Wei, H., Wang, G., Tan, D.: Research on platform opening strategy of private label retailers. China Manage. Sci. 27(3), 105–115 (2019)
4. Heron, R., et al.: Opportunities for increased collaboration to advance the development of OEM expertise internationally. Saf. Health Work 13, S75 (2022)
5. Liu, W.: A comparative study on the strategy and growth path of online retailers and traditional retailers' own brands. Bus. Econ. Manage. (1), 12–20 (2016)
6. Wang, C., Chen, J., Huang, T., Cheng, Y.: A field study on the dynamic evolution of key influencing factors of enterprises to create their own brands——A qualitative analysis based on the on-site interview data of 12 enterprises in Guangzhou. Manage. World (6), 111–127 (2013)
7. Qian, X., Lian, X.: The dynamic evolution of value commitment in the process of brand growth——Based on multiple case studies of Luolai, Gree. Shangshang and LiuGong. Enterp. Econ. 37(9), 81–88 (2018)

8. Liu, X., Yang, L.: J. Harbin Inst. Technol.(Soc. Sci. Edn.) **19**(1), 135–140 (2017)
9. Zhou, H.: Research on the path of transformation and upgrading of cross-border e-commerce enterprises under the background of digital economy. J. Xiangyang Vocat. Tech. Coll. **20**(6), 114–118 (2021)
10. Tsui, D.: OEM franchise workshops accelerate market share pull from independent workshop. Tribol. Lubr. Technol. **77**(5), 20–22 (2021)
11. dynaCERT Enters Strategic OEM Collaboration with Harold Martin. Wireless News (2021)
12. Yan, H.-D.: Entrepreneurship, competitive strategies, and transforming firms from OEM to OBM in Taiwan. J. Asia-Pac. Bus. **13**(1), 16–36 (2012)
13. Ming, T.: Research on the influence of ODM mode on consumer decision. SHS Web Conf. **96**, 04009 (2021)
14. Zhang, C., et al.: Push and pull strategies by component suppliers when OEMs can produce the component in-house: the roles of branding in a supply chain. Ind. Mark. Manage. **72**, 99–111 (2018)
15. Jia, X., Lu, D., Xu, B.: Research on the brand building path of Internet + small and medium-sized enterprises. Int. Public Relat. (03), 212 (2020)
16. Xia, S.: Research on brand building of small and medium-sized enterprises in e-commerce environment. China Small Medium-sized Enterprises **314**(1), 221–222 (2022)

Smartphones and Higher Education: Mapping the Field

Jorge Cruz-Cárdenas[1,2(✉)] 📵, Ekaterina Zabelina[3] 📵, Olga Deyneka[4] 📵,
Andrés Palacio-Fierro[1,2] 📵, Jorge Guadalupe-Lanas[5] 📵,
and Carlos Ramos-Galarza[6,7] 📵

[1] Research Center in Business, Society, and Technology, ESTec, Universidad Indoamérica,
Quito, Ecuador
{jorgecruz,andrespalacio}@uti.edu.ec
[2] School of Administrative and Economic Science, Universidad Indoamérica, Quito, Ecuador
[3] Department of Psychology, Chelyabinsk State University, Chelyabinsk, Russia
[4] Department of Political Psychology, St-Petersburg State University, St. Petersburg, Russia
[5] Quito, Ecuador
[6] Deparment of Psychology, Universidad Católica del Ecuador, Quito, Ecuador
caramos@puce.edu.ec
[7] MIST Research Center, Universidad Indoamérica, Quito, Ecuador

Abstract. Smartphones are devices widely used by the global population and are the main means by which people connect to the Internet. Smartphones are also being increasingly used in higher education, which has resulted in the generation of a large amount of academic and scientific literature. To present an ordered picture of this significant body of knowledge, the present study seeks to carry out a bibliometric analysis of the academic and scientific literature on smartphones and higher education. For this purpose, the present study uses the Scopus database from which 2,453 articles were selected. A descriptive analysis of this body of documents allows us to observe a rapid growth rate in the number of documents published annually. Additionally, it is possible to establish that the most research on the topic has been carried out in developed and emerging countries. An analysis of the co-occurrence of terms makes it possible to define three research areas: 1) technology and the applications of smartphones in higher education, 2) administrative and pedagogical considerations in the use of smartphones in higher education, and 3) negative effects of smartphone use on students. An analysis of the evolution of research priorities shows a shift of interest from a focus on smartphone technology and its applications to a focus on the negative impacts of the use of these devices and their prevention. The present study ends by presenting the most relevant conclusions and the implications of the findings for future studies.

Keywords: Smartphones · Higher Education · HEIs · Universities

---

J. Guadalupe-Lanas—Independent Researcher.

G. Salvendy and J. Wei (Eds.): HCII 2023, LNCS 14052, pp. 253–261, 2023.
https://doi.org/10.1007/978-3-031-35921-7_17

1   Introduction

Smartphones are portable devices that integrate telephony and computing functions and capabilities. Data from secondary sources demonstrate the wide penetration of these devices worldwide, both in developed and developing countries. In 2021, there were 6,259 million active users of smartphones, a number that is expected to grow to 7,690 million by 2027 [1]. In short, the vast majority of the global population already actively uses smartphones. Some of the characteristics of smartphones that have encouraged their expanding use are their mobility, light weight, ubiquity, and ability to expand our capacity for connection [2, 3].

The widespread use of smartphones and their significant capabilities have made them the subject of study in various disciplines, including education (mobile learning or m-learning). Previous studies have highlighted the advantages and disadvantages of the use of smartphones in higher education. Advantages include their connectivity capabilities, ability to provide broad access to information, and ability to increase collaboration between students and between students and teachers [4]. Disadvantages include the fact that they are seen as significant distractors [5] that can have a negative effect on student performance [6] and on the mental health of students [7].

Although the use of smartphones in higher education was already on an upward trajectory, the impact of the Covid-19 pandemic accelerated the trend. During the pandemic, there was a massive adoption of technologies by people in general [8]. Additionally, and specifically in the field of education, smartphones were one of the key devices that allowed students and teachers to remain connected and to stay on their learning and teaching paths [9].

The growing importance of smartphones in education, particularly in higher education, is generating an increasing number of studies [10]. However, the rapid growth of research in a field comes with the danger of the duplication of efforts and the fractionation of knowledge. Therefore, the present study seeks to provide an overview of the existing knowledge about the use of smartphones in higher education. The general objective of this study is to determine the characteristics and interactions of the body of academic and scientific literature in relation to the use of smartphones in higher education. Although other investigations have had a similar objective [e.g., 10], the distinctive characteristics of this study are its topicality and breadth.

2   Research Methods and Tools

The authors of the current study organized its structure based on the stages that various other authors have recommended for research oriented towards the bibliometric analysis and systematic review of literature. Therefore, the present study includes three stages [8, 11], which are to: 1) establish research objectives, 2) define document search strategies, and 3) analyze and present results. This chapter focuses on the search for relevant documents to form a database. The next chapter is devoted to the third stage, the analysis and presentation of the results.

Once the research objective was established (Introduction section), the next task was to choose the database to be searched for documents. The Scopus database was selected, as it is characterized by breadth of content, thus allowing a reliable search process. The search string used was (smartphone*) AND ("higher education" OR universit*).

The search was carried out in January 2023 in order to access content published up to and including the year 2022 without establishing any other time limit for the search. To guarantee the quality of the documents to be obtained, it was specified that these documents be articles published in journals, that is, documents that have undergone an editorial and peer review before publication. Additionally, the search was limited to documents in English. This delimitation was necessary to be able to later carry out an analysis of interrelationships between the contents of the documents. Ultimately, 2,453 documents were obtained.

3   Analysis and Results

This section seeks to analyze the body of 2,453 selected documents on smartphones and their use in higher education and does so using two approaches. The first is a descriptive approach that seeks to generate a general overview of the set of selected documents through a series of statistics. The second approach is deeper and aims to establish interrelationships between the content of the selected documents.

The evolution of documents published annually was analyzed and is presented in Fig. 1. This figure shows at least three different stages in the publication rate. Until 2009, the scientific and academic literature on smartphones in higher education was almost non-existent; in fact, the publication rate was one document per year. The year 2010 marks the beginning of the growth of scientific and academic publication in the area of interest, and this growth continues at a good pace until 2017. From 2018, the curve becomes even steeper, which indicates that publication per year grew even faster than in the second period. By 2022, there is a publication rate of 472 documents per year. This acceleration in the number of documents per year supports the perception of previous authors [3] and is a consequence of the growing interest of professionals and academics in the role of smartphones in higher education.

Another matter of interest was to determine the main areas of knowledge where the scientific and academic literature on smartphones in higher education was originating. Table 1 presents the main areas associated with the documents, using 100 documents as a cut-off point. It should be noted that the same document can be associated with more than one area of knowledge (therefore, the percentages add up to more than 100%).

Interestingly, Table 1 presents a multidisciplinary research landscape with four areas dominating the publication of studies on smartphones and higher education, Medicine, Social Sciences, Computer Science, and Engineering. The strong presence of Medicine and Social Sciences reflects both the magnitude of the impact the use of smartphones is having in our society and in higher education, as well as the nature of this impact, where positive and negative aspects come together [4, 6, 7]. However, the presence of Computer Science and Engineering is foreseeable due to the technological nature of smartphones, a technology that continues to evolve rapidly.

Another topic of interest in the descriptive analysis was that of the authors' institutions of affiliation. Table 2 presents this information, using as a cut-off point having 18 or more documents associated with an institution. As can be seen, this group is made up of

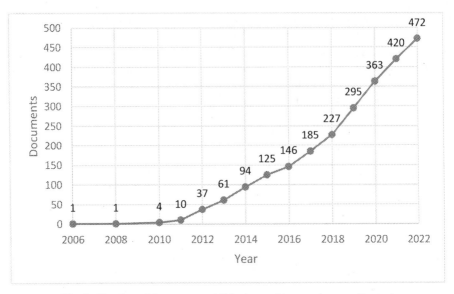

Fig. 1. Number of documents published over the years (source: Scopus)

Table 1. Main areas of knowledge

Subject area	Documents	%
Medicine	1003	40.9%
Social Sciences	760	31.0%
Computer Science	564	23.0%
Engineering	316	12.9%
Psychology	239	9.7%
Arts and Humanities	152	6.2%
Health Professions	136	5.5%
Nursing	108	4.4%

seven universities in Australia, the United Kingdom, China, and the United States. Thus, one can see the leading role of institutions in developed or emerging countries and the scarce presence of institutions or universities in developing countries. This aspect has already been highlighted in other bibliometric analyses relating to society and technology issues [12, 13].

Next, deeper analyses were carried out, this time aimed at discovering the interactions between the 2,453 documents on smartphones and higher education. For these analyses, version 1.6.18 of VOSviewer software [14] was used. The first analysis was conducted to identify the networks of the co-occurrence of terms present in the titles and abstracts of the documents. For this analysis, the software was instructed to consider only terms that

Table 2. Main institutions of affiliation

University/Institution	Associated documents
The University of Sydney	31
Nottingham Trent University	28
The University of Hong Kong	24
Deakin University	20
Harvard Medical School	18
Hong Kong Polytechnic University	18
University of Toronto	18

occurred more than 30 times. Additionally, terms with a vague or very general meaning were eliminated (e.g., "article", "baseline", "concept", and "end"), and terms with the same meaning were grouped in a thesaurus (e.g., "mobile device", "mobile", "smart phone", and "smartphone"). Once these measures were adopted, 101 relevant terms were obtained, which, subjected to analysis, formed three thematic clusters (Fig. 2).

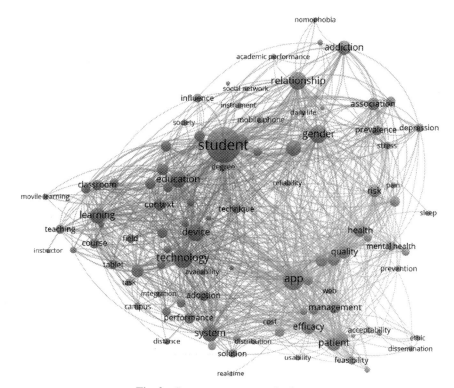

Fig. 2. Co-occurrence network of terms

Cluster 1 (42 items, red color): This is the cluster with the most elements. Terms such as "technology", "computer", "system", "device", "learning", "education", and "classroom" allow us to conclude that this cluster is oriented towards evaluating the potential offered by the use of smartphone technology in education.

Cluster 2 (35 items, green color): This is the second largest cluster. The presence of terms such as "app", "management", "quality", "health", "patient", "efficacy", "support", and "usability" lead one to deduce that this cluster focuses on the administrative and pedagogical considerations in the healthy use of smartphones in learning.

Cluster 3 (24 items, blue color): This is the third largest cluster in terms of number of items. Some of the most prominent terms in this cluster are "student", "gender", "relationship", "addiction", "nomophobia", "prevalence", "stress", and "depression". From these terms it is possible to conclude that this cluster is focused on the negative effects of the use of smartphones on university students.

A subsequent analysis focused on establishing the temporal evolution of the impact of the different terms. Figure 3 presents this evolution, presenting the oldest terms or those that had a greater presence several years ago in purple, the most current terms in yellow, and the terms located between these two extremes in green. In addition to this color coding, the size of each node shows the relative importance of the term.

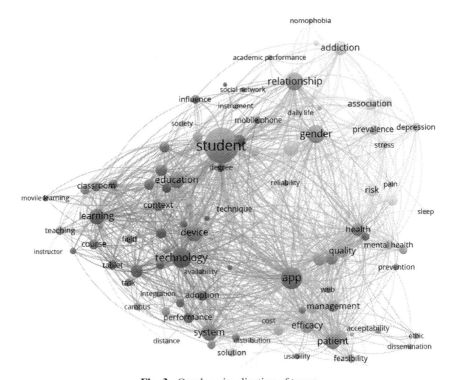

Fig. 3. Overlay visualization of terms

Figure 3 shows that years ago, the most prominent terms were "technology" and "learning". More recently, the most prominent terms were "student", "relationship", and "gender". Currently, "addiction", "risk", and "association" are used more. Based on this information, it can be stated that the study of smartphones in higher education is following a historical trajectory that began with a greater interest in the study of technology itself and its educational applications. Subsequently, studies focused on students and comparative studies (e.g., gender differences) gained more prominence. Currently, the topics of greatest interest are related to the negative effects of the use of smartphones and their prevention.

One last aspect in the data analysis is the establishment of co-authorship networks in the production of scientific literature on smartphones and higher education. For this analysis, the software was instructed to find these networks for authors with at least five documents. Thus, 33 authors qualified. In total, 10 co-authorship networks were identified, four of which were identified as having four or more authors; these are described below. The remaining six networks are not part of the analysis, as they are very small (with two authors or less).

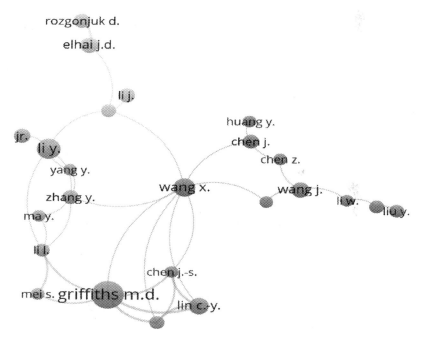

Fig. 4. Co-authorship networks

Figure 4 presents the four prominent co-authorship networks. The largest network, in red, linked 9 authors (Chen, J., Chen, Y.-C., Chen, Z., Huang, Y., Li, W., Liu, Y., Luo, Y., Wang, J., and Wang, X.). The second largest network is represented in green and had seven authors (Jr., Li, L., Li, Y., Ma, Y., Mei, S., Yang, Y., and Zhang, Y.). The third network had four authors and is represented in blue (Chen, J.S., Griffiths, M.D., Lin,

C.Y., and Pakpour, A.H.). The fourth network, also with four authors, is represented
in yellow (Elhai, J.D., Li, J., Rozgonjuk, D., and Wang, Y.). Another characteristic
of these networks is that they are multinational; that is, the authors' work institutions
are in different countries. Additionally, the institutions affiliated with these authors are
in developed or emerging countries. None of the authors are linked to institutions in
developing countries. An additional characteristic of these networks is that three of the
four include researchers from Chinese or American institutions. Finally, as can be seen
in the same figure, some authors, such as M.D. Griffiths and X. Wang, serve as liaisons
with the other networks, with M.D. Griffiths being the author with the most publications
in the area (26 associated documents).

4 Discussion and Implications

The present bibliometric study focused on the use of smartphones in higher education. To that end, it uses two data analysis techniques, descriptive and interrelationship
techniques. The descriptive techniques allow us to conclude that the study of the use
of smartphones in higher education is rapidly growing, an aspect highlighted by other
authors [10]. This situation supports the justification and objectives of this study around
presenting an orderly picture of the current situation in this area of knowledge.

Additional descriptive analyses allow characterizing the study of the use of smartphones in higher education as a multidisciplinary research field enriched by disciplines
such as Medicine, Social Sciences, Computer Science, and Engineering. Additionally,
previous studies have found a strong multidisciplinary approach in the study of technology and higher education issues [13]. This conclusion about the multidisciplinarity of
the study of smartphones and higher education allows us to recommend the formation
of multidisciplinary and interdisciplinary teams to accelerate the advancement of this
area of knowledge.

From the same descriptive perspective, the analysis of the most active institutions
in research leads to the conclusion of the strong presence of universities in developed
or emerging countries and the absence of institutions in developing countries. This conclusion is supported by the analysis of co-authorship networks carried out. Other bibliometric analyses on technology and higher education have reached similar conclusions
[12, 13]. Therefore, a recommendation of this study is the need for a greater number
of investigations in developing countries, either from the perspective of single-country
studies or from the perspective of comparative studies. A greater amount of research
in developing countries (where the majority of the world population lives) will allow a
greater generalization of the conclusions and theories that are being generated in this
area of interest.

The interaction analysis between the content of the titles and abstracts of the 2,453
articles also allows drawing interesting conclusions. Three thematic clusters emerge in
the data analysis: 1) smartphone technology applied to higher education, 2) administrative and pedagogical considerations for the use of smartphones in higher education,
and 3) negative effects that the use of smartphones have on university students. These
thematic clusters, being a good representation of the lines or areas of research [14], allow
the generation of an appropriate framework where future studies can be located.

One last topic of interest is the evolution of research priorities over the years. This evolution allows generating a good guide for future studies. Based on the results obtained, it can therefore be stated that in the thematic topic of smartphones in higher education the focus several years ago was on the study of technology itself and its potential. Subsequently, student-centered studies became important. Currently, there is a strong interest in the risks and negative effects of the use of smartphones, effects that become more significant as the use of smartphones increases [6, 7]. The picture that has been described does not mean that the other topics have been abandoned, although interest in them has declined for the time being.

References

1. Statista: Number of Smartphone Subscriptions Worldwide from 2016 to 2021, with Forecasts from 2022 to 2027 (2022), available at: https://www.statista.com/statistics/330695/number-of-smartphone-users-worldwide
2. Arain, A.A., Hussain, Z., Rizvi, W.H., Vighio, M.S.: Extending UTAUT2 toward acceptance of mobile learning in the context of higher education. Univ. Access Inf. Soc. **18**(3), 659–673 (2019)
3. Lau, K.S.N., et al.: Library and learning experiences turned mobile: a comparative study between LIS and non-LIS students. J. Acad. Librariansh. **46**(2), 102103 (2020)
4. Al-Emran, M., Elsherif, H.M., Shaalan, K.: Investigating attitudes towards the use of mobile learning in higher education. Comput. Hum. Behav. **56**, 93–102 (2016)
5. Vahedi, Z., Zannella, L., Want, S.C.: Students' use of information and communication technologies in the classroom: uses, restriction, and integration. Active Learn. High. Educ. **22**(3), 215–228 (2021)
6. Baer, S., et al.: Smartphone use and academic performance: correlation or causal relationship? Kyklos **73**(1), 22–46 (2020)
7. Lei, L.Y.-C., Ismail, M.A.-A., Mohammad, J.A.-M., Yusoff, M.S.B.: The relationship of smartphone addiction with psychological distress and neuroticism among university medical students. BMC Psychol. **8**(97), 2–9 (2020)
8. Cruz-Cárdenas, J., Zabelina, E., Guadalupe-Lanas, J., Palacio-Fierro, A., Ramos-Galarza, C.: COVID-19, consumer behavior, technology, and society: a literature review and bibliometric analysis. Technol. Forecast. Soc. Change. **173**, 121179 (2021)
9. Mella-Norambuena, J., Cobo-Rendon, R., Lobos, K., Sáez-Delgado, F., Maldonado-Trapp, A.: Smartphone use among undergraduate STEM students during COVID-19: an opportunity for higher education? Educ. Sci. **11**(8), 417 (2021)
10. Sobral, S.R.: Mobile learning in higher education: a bibliometric review. Int. J. Interact. Mob. Technol. **14**(11), 153–170 (2020)
11. Osobajo, O.A., Moore, D.: Methodological choices in relationship quality (RQ) research 1987 to 2015: a systematic literature review. J. Relatsh. Mark. **16**(1), 40–81 (2017)
12. Cruz-Cárdenas, J., Parra-Domínguez, J., Zabelina, E., Deyneka, O., Ramos-Galarza, C.: Organizational culture and digital transformation: a bibliometric approach. In: Proceedings IEEE Sixth Ecuador Technical Chapters Meeting (ETCM), pp. 1–5. Quito, Ecuador (2022)
13. Cruz-Cárdenas, J., Ramos-Galarza, C., Guadalupe-Lanas, J., Palacio-Fierro, A., Galarraga-Carvajal, M.: Bibliometric analysis of existing knowledge on digital transformation in higher education. In: Meiselwitz, G., et al. (eds.) HCI International 2022 - Late Breaking Papers. Interaction in New Media, Learning and Games. HCII 2022. Lecture Notes in Computer Science, vol. 13517, pp. 231–240. Springer, Cham (2022)
14. Van Eck, N.J., Waltman, L.: Software survey: VOSviewer, a computer program for bibliometric mapping. Scientometrics **84**(2), 523–538 (2010)

The Influence of Physician Self-descriptive Information on Patients' Decision-Making in Online Consultation Platform

Jing Fan[1] , Huihui Geng[1,2(✉)] , Fengdi Shao[1] , and Qin Ma[1]

[1] International Business School, Beijing Foreign Studies University, Beijing, China
genghh365@bfsu.edu.cn
[2] School of Economic and Management, Beijing Polytechnic, Beijing, China

Abstract. As an increasingly important application, online consultation platform allows patients to connect remotely with physicians to receive treatment advice. While bringing convenience to patients, it also provides kinds of physician's information for patients and leads them to have trouble in making online medical choice decisions. By exploring the antecedents of physician self-descriptive information on patient's decision, we hope to bridge the gap in the existing literature. Rooted in signaling theory, we study the impact of doctors' self-descriptive information, namely the richness of doctors' personal descriptive information and expertise information on patients' decision making in the specific context of an online consultation platform. Based on a dataset of 1824 observations on *Haodf*, a leading online consultation platform in China, we tested our hypotheses using text analysis methods. We find that both the richness of descriptive information and expertise information positively affect patients' choice. Moreover, patients pay more attention to physician's skills, influence as well as the coverage of physician's expertise when making decision. The research findings indicate that patient's preferences for doctors provide strong support and guidance for improving doctor-patient relationships and offer implications for medical practices and healthcare platforms improvement.

Keywords: Signaling Theory · Online Consultation Platform · Self-descriptive Information · Text Analysis

1 Introduction

Since the outbreak of COVID-19, online medical care has played an important role in providing a reliable channel for patients to access information and paid or unpaid medical services on the platform [1]. Compared with traditional medical channels, online medical platforms are not limited by space and time, which can help patients save time, reduce costs, as well as provide personalized services [2]. Therefore, online medical platform has been considered as an effective way to meet patients' needs and address information asymmetry between doctors and patients [3].

As online consultation platform plays an increasingly important role, the quality of information provided by online medical platforms and doctors directly affects patients'

G. Salvendy and J. Wei (Eds.): HCII 2023, LNCS 14052, pp. 262–275, 2023.
https://doi.org/10.1007/978-3-031-35921-7_18

experience and even patients' treatment. Previous studies have found that doctors' initiative to provide their own characteristics, such as gender, education background, personal traits and online reputation, can influence patients' decision making [4, 5].Although there is a large amount of similar information in online medical platforms, we find that there are few studies focusing on the impact of such information on patients' decision making, and there is also a lack of systematic study on physicians' personal characteristic information, such as the richness of descriptive information and expertise information.

Therefore, from the perspective of doctors' self-value realization, we attempt to conduct a classified study on doctors' personal text information in the *Haodf* online platform, and analyzes its possible impact on patients' decision-making. Based on the reading of related literature, we propose the following two research questions: (1) How does the richness of doctors' self-descriptive information affect patients' decision-making? (2) How does the representation of doctor's expertise information affect patients' decision-making? In order to answer these questions, we apply text analysis and explore how the value of doctors' self-information, as a signal, affects patients' decision-making based on signal theory.

2 Literature Review and Theoretical Model

2.1 Signaling Theory and Patients' Choice in Online Consultation Platform

Information influences people's decision making, and the more information an individual or firm has, the more likely it is to make a relatively correct decision [6]. Numerous studies have shown that signal theory can be used to explain, for example, the effectiveness of online reviews [7], the impact of ratings on product sales [8], the impact of platform itself on platform content [9] and many other scenarios.

As online medical platform is a virtual environment, how to reduce information asymmetry is a crucial issue for patients, which is well explained by signaling theory [10]. Studies have shown that patients and doctors send different signals on online medical platforms, which affects patients' cognitive ability to choose a doctor [11]. As signalers, doctors hold all their own information, both the positive and negative, which is not held by outsiders. When patients see a large amount of high-quality personal information on a doctor's personal homepage, they will be more willing to choose the doctor [12]. For example, the doctor's professional title and academic title are also reliable signals, which reflect the doctor's technical level and ability to some extent.

There are two kinds of physician's self-description information, namely descriptive information (such as education background, social position, etc.) and expertise information (such as field coverage etc.) in online consultation platform. Based on text analysis, we explore the possible influence of the two on patients' decision-making.

2.2 Physician's Descriptive Information and Patients' Choice

In *Haodf* platform, the descriptive information submitted by each doctor varies in degree of detail, and the amount of information that can reflect the doctor's ability also varies. In some studies in psychology and behavioral economics, people refer to information when making decisions even if it does not contain a lot of valuable content [13].A study found that doctors providing certain information related to their care significantly increased online engagement among patients with both diabetes and depression [14].Liang et al. found that the accuracy and completeness of online health information and other characteristics affect the quality of the information [15]. Patients hold a more cautious attitude when choosing doctors. Too little information is difficult for patients to accurately judge doctors, while rich information can help patients have a better judgment of doctors. Michal and Scott found that borrowers with different credit ratings provide different descriptions, and proposed that borrowers should choose people who express moral and trustworthy characteristics [16]. Li et al. found that for internet finance, different characteristic variables of borrowers have different influences on investment decisions. We assume that different characteristic variables of physicians have different influences on patient decisions. Therefore, the following hypothesis is proposed.

H1: Total amounts of characteristic variables in doctors' descriptive information have a positive effect on patient's choice.
H1a: Doctors' medical skill positively affects patient's choice.
H1b: Doctors' education background positively affects patient's choice.
H1c: Doctors' social influence positively affects patient's choice.
H2: Whether different characteristic variables in doctors' descriptive information have different effects on patient's choice.

2.3 Physician's Expertise Information and Patients' Choice

Good representation of doctors' expertise information can reduce the ambiguity of medical terms and help patients better understand them, thus making them easier to choose [17]. In *Haodf* platform, each doctor has a different expression quality for his or her specialty. We extract and analyze the expertise information, and determine the coverage and granularity of expertise information. The amount of expertise information refers to the total number of texts. We put forward the following hypothesis:

H3: The representation of doctors' expertise information positively affects patient's choice.
H3a: The coverage of doctors' expertise information positively affects patient's choice.
H3b: The granularity of doctors' expertise information positively affects patient's choice.

Based on the above discussion, we propose a research model, as shown in Fig. 1, to explore the impact of doctors' descriptive information and expertise information on patient decision-making.

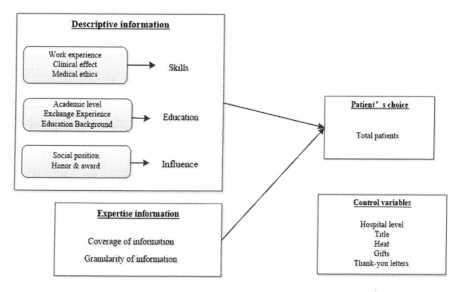

Fig. 1. Proposed research model

3 Materials and Methods

3.1 Research Setting and Data

Haodf online platform is adopted by doctors at a higher rate than other online medical platforms [18]. It provides a variety of services, including various forms of consultation, diagnosis and treatment services, disease health science knowledge and so on. By March 2021, it has registered 9,976 regular hospitals and 887,869 doctors in China. We randomly chose 2,050 doctors' descriptive information including the basic information of doctors like name and title, personal descriptive information and expertise information like work experience, academic level, honors, and awards, as well as information provided by platform, like the total number of patients, the number of thank you letters and the number of gifts. After removing the missing values, we got 1824 samples.

3.2 Measurement of Variables

In order to explore the impact of doctors' descriptive information on patients' decision-making, it is necessary to determine its features. We adopt the method of sociological qualitative analysis and text analysis, and study doctors' personal descriptive information from three aspects, namely education, skills, and influence. As a result, we classified the descriptive information into 8 categories, namely "work experience", "clinical effect", "medical ethics", "academic level", "education background", "exchange experience", "social position" and "honor & award". As for expertise information, we use coverage and granularity to describe it. Thus, summary of variables is presented in Table 1. Table 2 shows the results of descriptive statistics.

Table 1. Summary of variables

Variables		Symbols	Variable measure indicator
Dependent variable	Total patients	Total visits	Accumulative consultation number by a doctor
Independent variable-Descriptive information	Work experience	Work experience	1 if there is information about work experience, otherwise is 0
	Clinical effect	Clinical effect	1 if there is information about clinical effect, otherwise is 0
	Medical ethics	Medical ethics	1 if there is information about medical ethics, otherwise is 0
	Academic level	Academic level	1 if there is information about academic level, otherwise is 0
	Exchange experiences	Academic exchange	1 if there is information about academic exchange, otherwise is 0
	Educational background	Education background	1 if there is information about education background, otherwise is 0
	Social position	Social position	1 if there is information about social position, otherwise is 0
	Honors & awards	Honor & reward	1 if there is information about honor & reward, otherwise is 0
	Sum of characteristic variables	Sum_ch	The total number of descriptive information of a doctor, ranging from 0 to 8

(*continued*)

Table 1. (*continued*)

Variables		Symbols	Variable measure indicator
	Information of doctors' medical skill level	Skills	1 if at least one variable of the characteristic information including work experience, clinical effect, and medical ethics is assigned as 1, otherwise is 0
	Information of doctors' educational experience	Education	1 if at least one variable of the characteristic information including academic level, exchange experiences, educational background is assigned as 1; otherwise, is 0
	Information of doctors' social influence	Influence	1 if at least one variable of the characteristic information including social position, honor & award is assigned as 1; otherwise is 0
Independent variable-Expertise information	Coverage of information	Coverage	A description of the kinds of diseases the doctor specializes in. The values are 1,2,3…
	Granularity of information	Granularity	How specific the physician is in describing the individual's expertise. The value is 0 or 1
	Length of total information	Sum_exp	Text length of expertise information

(*continued*)

Table 1. (*continued*)

Variables		Symbols	Variable measure indicator
Control variable	Physician's title	Title	4,3,2, and 1 represent chief physician, associate chief physician, attending physician, and resident physician, respectively
	Heat	Heat	The heat is the index generated by the platform. The value ranges from 0 to 5
	Number of thank-you letters	Letter	After receiving a doctor's service, patients may show their recognition by writing a thanks letter to the doctor online, which is for free
	Number of gifts	Gift	After receiving a doctor's service, patients may show their recognition by giving a gift to the doctor online, which requires a fee

3.3 Econometric Methods

To explore the impact of descriptive information and expertise information on patients' decision-making, we constructed a multiple regression model. In order to eliminate multicollinearity, different independent variables and control variables are gradually added to the models.

(1)–(3) explain the impact of doctors' descriptive information on total patients, models (4)–(5) explain the impact of doctors' expertise information on total patients, and model (6) explains the impact of descriptive information and expertise information on total patients.

$$Ln(Total\ visits)_j = \beta_0 + \beta_1 Sum\_ch_j + \beta_2 Title_j + \beta_3 Letter_j + \beta_4 Gift_j + \beta_5 Heat_j + \varepsilon_j \tag{1}$$

$$Ln(Total\ visits)_j = \beta_0 + \beta_1 Skills_j + \beta_2 Education_j + \beta_3 Influence_j + \beta_4 Title_j + \beta_5 Letter_j + \beta_6 Gift_j + \beta_7 Heat_j + \varepsilon_j \tag{2}$$

Table 2. Descriptive statistics

Variable	N	Mean	Sd	Min	Max
Total visits	1824	1492.067	2520.594	1	27352
Skills	1824	0.594	0.491	0	1
Work experience	1824	0.458	0.498	0	1
Clinical effect	1824	0.321	0.467	0	1
Medical ethics	1824	0.042	0.201	0	1
Education	1824	0.904	0.295	0	1
Academic level	1824	0.744	0.437	0	1
Academic exchange	1824	0.482	0.5	0	1
Education background	1824	0.594	0.491	0	1
Influence	1824	0.768	0.423	0	1
Social position	1824	0.672	0.47	0	1
Honor & reward	1824	0.438	0.496	0	1
Sum_ch	1824	3.751	1.660	0	8
Sum_exp	1824	96.315	82.093	0	827
Coverage	1824	8.280	6.107	0	76
Granularity	1824	0.515	0.500	0	1
Heat	1824	4.139	0.308	3.4	5
Title	1824	3.344	0.722	1	4
Letter	1824	39.495	67.957	0	931
Gift	1824	128.526	302.376	0	4878

$$Ln(Total\ visits)_j = \beta_0 + \beta_1 Work\_experience_j + \beta_2 Clinical\ effect_j$$
$$+\beta_3 Medical\ ethics_j + \beta_4 Academic\ level_j + \beta_5 Academic\ exchange_j +$$
$$\beta_6 Education\ background_j + \beta_7 Social\ position_j + \beta_8 Honor\ \&\ reward_j \quad (3)$$
$$+\beta_9 Title_j + \beta_{10} Letter_j + \beta_{11} Gift_j + \beta_{12} Heat_j + \varepsilon_j$$

$$Ln(Total\ visits)_j = \beta_0 + \beta_1 Sum\_exp_j + \beta_2 Title_j + \beta_3 Letter_j + \beta_4 Gift_j + \quad (4)$$
$$\beta_5 Heat_j + \varepsilon_j$$

$$Ln(Total\ visits)_j =$$
$$\beta_0 + \beta_1 Coverage_j + \beta_2 Granularity_j + \beta_2 Title_j + \beta_3 Letter_j \quad (5)$$
$$+\beta_4 Gift_j + \beta_5 Heat_j + \varepsilon_j$$

$$Ln(Totalvisits)_j =$$
$$\beta_0 + \beta_1\,Skills_j + \beta_2 Education_j + \beta_3 Influence_j$$
$$+\beta_4 Coverage_j + \beta_5 Granularity_j + \beta_6 Title_j + \beta_7 Letter_j \quad (6)$$
$$+\beta_8 Gift_j + \beta_9 Heat_j + \varepsilon_j$$

j value ranges from 1 to 1824.

3.4 Regression Results

Model 1 explores the impact of the total number of characteristic variables of descriptive information on patient's choice. We find that the sum of characteristic variables of descriptive information has a significant impact on the total number of patients ($t = 2.72$, $p < 0.01$), indicating that the number of characteristic variables contained in the personal descriptive information submitted by doctors positively affect patient's choice. H1 is assumed to be true. Model 1 also shows the estimated results of the control variables. We find that the title ($t = 5.74$, $p < 0.001$), the number of thank you letters ($t = 4.53$, $p < 0.001$), the number of gifts ($t = 6.22$, $p < 0.001$) and heat ($t = 15.32$, $p < 0.001$) had a significant positive effect on the total patients. This indicates that the higher the doctor's title, the more thank-you letters and gifts they receive, the higher the recommendation popularity, the more visits they receive.

Further, we explored whether different characteristic information would have an impact on patients' decision making. As Model 2 shows, we found that doctors' medical skill level ($t = 2.17$, $p < 0.05$), and social influence ($t = 2.89$, $p < 0.05$) positively affected the total patients However, doctors' education experience had no significant effect on the total patients ($t = 0.57$, $p > 0.1$). To sum up, H1a and H1c are assumed to be true.

In addition, Model 3 explores whether 8 different descriptive information variables will affect patient's choice. We found that clinical effect ($t = 2.52$, $p < 0.05$), educational background ($t = 1.67$, $p < 0.1$), social position ($t = 3.52$, $p < 0.01$) had a positive impact on the total patients, while academic exchange ($t = -1.74$, $p < 0.1$) had a negative impact on the total patients. H2 is assumed to be true.

Model 4 studies whether the total amount of expertise information has an impact on patient's decision making. It is found that the text length of expertise information positively affects total number of patients ($t = 3.99$, $p < 0.001$), assuming H3 to be true.

In Model 5, it is found that the coverage of expertise information ($t = 3.72$, $p < 0.001$) had a positive effect on the choice. Doctors with higher coverage of disease are interviewed more frequently. However, the granularity has no significant effect on patients. It is assumed that H3a is confirmed, while H3b fails.

Model 6 explores the influence of personal descriptive information and expertise information on total patients. The physician's medical skill ($t = 2.17$, $p < 0.05$), social influence ($t = 2.58$, $p < 0.05$), and coverage of expertise information ($t = 3.54$, $p < 0.01$) positively affected the total number of patients (see Table 3).

Table 3. Model estimation result

	(1)	(2)	(3)	(4)	(5)	(6)
Sum_ch	0.046***					
	(0.017)					
Skills		0.125**				0.125**
		(0.057)				(0.057)
Education		0.055				0.037
		(0.096)				(0.096)
Influence		0.196***				0.175**
		(0.068)				(0.068)
Work experience			0.045			
			(0.058)			
Clinical effect			0.154**			
			(0.061)			
Medical ethics			−0.084			
			(0.137)			
Academic level			−0.032			
			(0.069)			
Academic exchange			−0.099*			
			(0.057)			
Education background			0.097*			
			(0.058)			
Social position			0.217***			
			(0.062)			
Honor & reward			0.036			
			(0.061)			
Sum_exp				0.001***		
				(0.000)		
Coverage					0.018***	0.017***
					(0.005)	(0.005)
Granularity					0.018	0.006

(*continued*)

Table 3. (*continued*)

	(1)	(2)	(3)	(4)	(5)	(6)
					(0.059)	(0.059)
Title	0.225***	0.214***	0.216***	0.257***	0.256***	0.224***
	(0.039)	(0.040)	(0.040)	(0.038)	(0.038)	(0.040)
Heat	1.719***	1.721***	1.711***	1.67***	1.651***	1.657***
	(0.112)	(0.112)	(0.113)	(0.113)	(0.113)	(0.113)
Letter	0.003***	0.003***	0.003***	0.003***	0.004***	0.003***
	(0.001)	(0.001)	(0.001)	(0.001)	(0.001)	(0.001)
Gift	0.001***	0.001***	0.001***	0.001***	0.001***	0.001***
	(0.000)	(0.000)	(0.000)	(0.000)	(0.000)	(0.000)
Constant	−1.922***	−1.99***	−1.896***	−1.783***	−1.736***	−1.875***
	(0.465)	(0.473)	(0.468)	(0.463)	(0.464)	(0.473)
Observations	1824	1824	1822	1824	1824	1824
R-squared	0.401	0.404	0.407	0.404	0.404	0.409

***p < .01, **p < .05, *p < .1

3.5 Robustness Check

For the robustness test, we excluded the top 10% and bottom 10% sample data by sorting total number of patients. It was found that the contents of different characteristic variables have different impacts on patients' decisions. Except that academic exchanges in Model 3 no longer affect patients' decisions, the rest are basically consistent with the empirical test results.

4 Discussion

4.1 Main Results

At present, there are numerous studies on online medical platforms and some information in them. Based on signaling theory, we explore the relationship between doctors' personal descriptive information and patients' choice from the perspective of doctors' self-descriptive information in the context of online medical platform. The results from this study provide generally strong and robust support for our hypotheses with 6 of 8 hypotheses finding full support.

Firstly, the number of self-descriptive information positively affects patients' choice. To supplement the views of what affects patient's choices, online reputation [19], online reviews [20] and online rating [21], we consider the richness of information represented by the doctor online.

Secondly, different descriptive information has different influences on user decision making. Clinical effect, educational background and social position positively affect patient's choice, while academic exchange has negative influence on total patients. It is obvious to know that patients value the information that can reflect doctors' professional level and doctors' social influence when choosing doctors.

Thirdly, coverage of expertise information positively affects patients' choice, while granularity has no effect. If the information provided by doctors can facilitate patients' solving of their own health problems [12], they will choose the doctor. Otherwise, they do not care about how the doctor describes their expertise.

4.2 Theoretical Implications

This study offers theoretical contributions in the following ways. First, this paper extends the research of signaling theory in the medical field. Previous studies have extensively applied signaling theory in the e-commerce and financial market, but this study focused on physicians' descriptive information as a signal in the context of online consultation platform. We find that the richness of the information provided by the doctor positively affect patient's choice.

Secondly, based on text analysis processing, this paper explores the relationship between doctors' self-worth information and patients' decision-making behavior. The physician self-descriptive descriptive information includes doctors' personal descriptive information and expertise information. Moreover, we extract physician's medical skill, social influence and education experience from doctor's self-descriptive information.

In addition, we study the representation of expertise information, which is decomposed into the coverage and the granularity of information. From this perspective, this study extends the understanding of physician's descriptive information in online consultation platform.

4.3 Practical Implications

This study also provides several practical implications. First, both the richness of self-descriptive information and expertise information has positive effects on patient's choice. Thus, appropriate doctor's self-descriptive information could possibly facilize patients, which indirectly affects the patient's choice.

Secondly, medical skill, social influence and the disease coverage are key factors the patients care about when choosing doctors in the online health community context. Thus, doctors are also made aware of how to display their own information in online consultation platform and what key information is needed to provide to patients. In one word, physicians can classify their information and provide as much self-descriptive information and expertise information to make up for the problems of information asymmetry, and to alleviate the tense doctor-patient relationship.

Thirdly, it provides some optimization directions for the designers of the online medical platform to improve the frequency and popularity of the community or website.

5   Conclusion

Rooted in signaling theory, this paper makes a comprehensive research and analysis on the influence of doctors' self-descriptive information on patients' decision-making in *Haoddf* Online. Moreover, we studied the impact of doctors' self-descriptive information, that is, the richness of doctors' personal descriptive information and expertise information, on patients' decision making. Except for the contributions the study has been discussed, this study also has some limitations. We chose *Haodf* online platform in this paper, however, due to the differences of platforms, the conclusions may not be applicable to other doctor-patient online medical platforms. In this paper, we took some random samples in *Haodf*, but we did not distinguish diseases and patient visits. In the future, more in-depth research can be done in these areas.

Acknowledgements. This study was supported by Humanities and Social Sciences Research Project of the Ministry of Education (22YJA630018), the Fundamental Research Funds for the Central Universities(2022JJ007) and Beijing Polytechnic(2023X019-SXZ).

References

1. Yang, H., Gao, H.: Personalized content recommendation in online health communities. Ind. Manag. Data Syst. **122**(2), 345–364 (2022). https://doi.org/10.1108/IMDS-04-2021-0268
2. Shah, A.M., Muhammad, W., Lee, K.: Investigating the effect of service feedback and physician popularity on physician demand in the virtual healthcare environment. Inf. Technol. People, ahead-of-print, ahead-of-print (2022). https://doi.org/10.1108/itp-07-2020-0448
3. Hampshire, K., Hamill, H., Mariwah, S., Mwanga, J., Amoako-Sakyi, D.: The application of signalling theory to health-related trust problems: the example of herbal clinics in Ghana and Tanzania. Soc. Sci. Med. **188**, 109–118 (2017). https://doi.org/10.1016/j.socscimed.2017.07.009
4. Yang, H., Du, H.S., Shang, W.: Understanding the influence of professional status and service feedback on patients' doctor choice in online healthcare markets. Internet Res. **31**(4), 1236–1261 (2020). https://doi.org/10.1108/intr-10-2019-0429
5. Gong, Y., Wang, H., Xia, Q., Zheng, L., Shi, Y.: Factors that determine a Patient's willingness to physician selection in online healthcare communities: a trust theory perspective. Technol. Soc. **64**, 101510 (2021). https://doi.org/10.1016/j.techsoc.2020.101510
6. Connelly, B.L., Certo, S.T., Ireland, R.D., Reutzel, C.R.: Signaling theory: a review and assessment. J. Manag. **37**(1), 39–67 (2011). https://doi.org/10.1177/0149206310388419
7. Zhu, F., Zhang, X.M.: Impact of online consumer reviews on sales: the moderating role of product and consumer characteristics. J. Mark. **74**(2), 133–148 (2010). https://doi.org/10.1509/jm.74.2.133
8. Li, H., Fang, Y., Wang, Y., Lim, K.H., Liang, L.: Are all signals equal? Investigating the differential effects of online signals on the sales performance of e-marketplace sellers. Inf. Technol. People **28**(3), 699–723 (2015). https://doi.org/10.1108/itp-11-2014-0265
9. Courtney, C., Dutta, S., Li, Y.: Resolving information asymmetry: signaling, endorsement, and crowdfunding success. Entrep. Theory Pract. **41**(2), 265–290 (2016). https://doi.org/10.1111/etap.12267
10. Zhou, J., Kishore, R., Amo, L., Ye, C.: Description and demonstration signals as complements and substitutes in an online market for mental health care. MIS Q. **46**, 2055–2084 (2022). https://doi.org/10.25300/MISQ/2022/16122

11. Li, J., Tang, J., Yen, D.C., Liu, X.: Disease risk and its moderating effect on the e-consultation market offline and online signals. Inf. Technol. People **32**(4), 1065–1084 (2019). https://doi.org/10.1108/itp-03-2018-0127

12. Chen, S., Guo, X., Wu, T., Ju, X.: Exploring the online doctor-patient interaction on patient satisfaction based on text mining and empirical analysis. Inf. Proc. Manag. **57**(5), 102253 (2020). https://doi.org/10.1016/j.ipm.2020.102253

13. DellaVigna, S., Gentzkow, M.: Persuasion: empirical evidence. Ann. Rev. Econ. **2**(1), 643–669 (2010). https://doi.org/10.1146/annurev.economics.102308.124309

14. Liu, Q.B., Liu, X., Guo, X.: The effects of participating in a physician-driven online health community in managing chronic disease: evidence from two natural experiments. MIS Q. **44**(1), 391–419 (2020). https://doi.org/10.25300/misq/2020/15102

15. Liang, H., Xue, Y., Zhang, Z.: Understanding online health information use: the case of people with physical disabilities. J. Assoc. Inf. Syst. **18**(6), 433–460 (2017). https://doi.org/10.17705/1jais.00461

16. Herzenstein, M., Sonenshein, S., Dholakia, U.M.: Tell me a good story and i may lend you my money: the role of narratives in peer-to-peer lending decisions. SSRN Electron. J. **48(Spec.)**, S138–S149 (2011). https://doi.org/10.2139/ssrn.1840668

17. Mousavi, R., Raghu, T.S., Frey, K.: Harnessing artificial intelligence to improve the quality of answers in online question-answering health forums. J. Manag. Inf. Syst. **37**(4), 1073–1098 (2020). https://doi.org/10.1080/07421222.2020.1831775

18. Li, Y., Yan, X., Song, X.: Provision of paid web-based medical consultation in china: cross-sectional analysis of data from a medical consultation website. J. Med. Internet Res. **21**(6), e12126 (2019). https://doi.org/10.2196/12126

19. Shah, A.M., Muhammad, W., Lee, K., Naqvi, R.A.: Examining different factors in web-based patients' decision-making process: systematic review on digital platforms for clinical decision support system. Int. J. Environ. Res. Public Health **18**(21), 11226 (2021). https://doi.org/10.3390/ijerph182111226

20. Fan, J., Geng, H., Liu, X., Wang, J.: The effects of online text comments on patients' choices: the mediating roles of comment sentiment and comment content. Front. Psychol. **13**, 886077 (2022). https://doi.org/10.3389/fpsyg.2022.886077

21. Li, Y., Ma, X., Song, J., Yang, Y., Ju, X.: Exploring the effects of online rating and the activeness of physicians on the number of patients in an online health community. Telemedicine e-Health **25**(11), 1090–1098 (2019). https://doi.org/10.1089/tmj.2018.0192

Impacts of Social Media Usage in Facilitating Social Commerce: The Roles of Social Support and Cultural Identity Change

Shangui Hu[1], Fengle Ji[2(✉)], and Dongyang Li[2]

[1] Ningbo University of Finance and Economics, Zhejiang, People's Republic of China
[2] Anhui University of Technology, Anhui, People's Republic of China
jfl13608928535@163.com

Abstract. The development of social media has led to an increasing number of customers engaged in cross-border social commerce environment wherein cultural differences exert impacts on their behaviors in different manners. However, how social media usage influences customers' cultural identity change and their engagement in cross-cultural social commerce remains under-investigated. Based on the S-O-R paradigm, this study explores the mediating role of cultural identity change in social media usage and engagement in social commerce and the moderating role of social support. A total of 2,058 samples from 135 countries were surveyed through an online data platform. The results of this study show that social media usage for information and social media usage for socializing both exert positive effects on international customers' cultural identity change and then boost their engagement in social commerce. In addition, social support positively moderates the relationship between different dimensions of social media usage and cultural identity change respectively.

Keywords: social commerce · cultural identity change · social support · social media usage · cross-cultural environment

1 Introduction

Enabled by the advancement of information technology and internet access, social media has become a ubiquitous tool assisting people's lives, not only affecting the way people communicate, relax, exchange, and interact but also changing their online shopping behaviors, such as social commerce (Liao et al. 2022). In contrast to traditional e-commerce, social commerce is a new type of online platform based on social media that allows customers to share news and comments on products. The new operation mode of business has a significant impact on the purchasing behaviors of other potential customers (Nakayama and Wan 2019). And due to the pattern of social commerce changed from seller-centered to buyer-centered, how to attract potential customers and increase customer stickiness through social media platforms is now an imperative issue for managers (Osatuyi et al. 2020). As such, exploring the factors that can affect customer engagement in social commerce has attracted a lot of scholarly attention, such as

G. Salvendy and J. Wei (Eds.): HCII 2023, LNCS 14052, pp. 276–285, 2023.
https://doi.org/10.1007/978-3-031-35921-7_19

social media usage (SMU) (Horng and Wu 2020; Tuncer 2021; Liao et al. 2022; Hu et al. 2022; Hu and Zhu 2022; Sohn and Kim 2020). Yet research findings on how social media use affects international customers' engagement in cross-cultural social commerce are inconsistent (Hu et al. 2022; Hu and Zhu 2022). In this regard, there is a great necessity to further clarify the pictures of how social media usage influences customers' social commerce, particularly in a complex cross-cultural environment (Fig. 1).

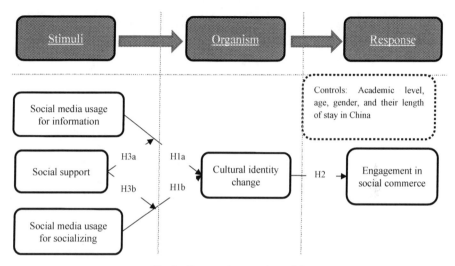

Fig. 1. Proposed research model

2 Conceptual Framework and Hypothesis Development

2.1 Social Media Usage and Cultural Identity Change

Social media usage covers two dimensions, information and socializing (Hu et al. 2020). Social media usage for information refers to international customers' usage of social media for access to cultural core values and codes of conduct about the social community, which meets the cognitive needs of international customers (Hu et al. 2017). According to social learning theory, the wealth of information resources available through social media contributes to the metacognitive and cognitive cultural intelligence of international customers (Hu and Zhu 2022). This increased cognitive ability allows international customers to change their old prejudices and stereotypes about the dominant cultural group, challenge their home country's cultural identity and possibly achieve identity with a foreign cultural group (Hu et al. 2020). Thus, we hypothesize that:

> H1a: social media usage for information increases customers' cultural identity change.

Social media usage for socializing purpose brings international customers closer to the dominant cultural groups, increasing their contact and fostering good relationships

(Hu et al. 2021). The well-established friendship helps international customers overcome the negative effects of cultural differences and adapt themselves to the mainstream cultural majority (Hu et al. 2020), which paves path for cultural identity change (Mao and Shen 2015). In addition, according to social identity theory (Mangum and Block 2018), intimate contact on social media platforms creates similarities, lowers cultural barriers and increases international customer's well-being, adaptation skills, and interests to follow the mainstream routine in culturally dominating group (Yampolsky et al. 2013; Hu et al. 2020; Waßmuth and Edinger-Schons 2018). Thus, we hypothesize that:

> H1b: social media usage for socializing increases customers' cultural identity change.

2.2 Cultural Identity Change and Engagement in Social Commerce

International customers who have managed cultural identity change demonstrate more satisfaction with the social commerce community concerning service quality, information quality, and loyalty when they interact with the social network community (Waßmuth and Edinger-Schons 2018; Angelini et al. 2015), and this emotional satisfaction may inspire international customers to enjoy the products and services of the foreign country and engage themselves in social commerce (Osatuyi et al. 2020). In addition, cultural identity can affect international customer's accessibility to relevant knowledge and the perceptions of the usefulness and reliability of access to information (Stanley et al. 2021). Therefore, cultural identity change enhances the international customer's ability to access and process information and deepen their understanding of products and services in cross-border social commerce, which eliminates the disadvantage of a lack of information for customer engagement in social commerce (Hwang et al. 2014). Thus, we hypothesize that:

> H2: cultural identity change increases customers' engagement in social commerce.

2.3 Moderating Role of Social Support

On the one hand, social support can ease the stress of international customers in a cross-cultural environment and make them feel cared for by members of the community. Emotional care facilitates international customers to maintain a long-term psychological attachment to the community when they use social media to socialize with the culturally dominating community (Lin et al. 2018; Ng 2013). Accordingly, customers will have the motivation to identify with the products and services in a cross-cultural context (Wang et al. 2020). On the other hand, international customers have access to a wealth of information about cross-border social commerce through social media (Hu et al. 2022). However, due to cultural diversity, customers can be faced with information asymmetries and misinformation (Wang and Herrando 2019). What's more, international customers may not fully comprehend the information they receive due to their inherent cognitive mindsets (Hu and Zhu 2022). Therefore, support from the social commerce community can help international customers identify the correctness of the information they receive through social media and help them understand it from a new perspective. Thus, we hypothesize that:

H3a: social support boosts the effects of informational social media usage on cultural identity change.

H3b: social support boosts the effects of socializing social media usage on cultural identity change.

3 Research Methodology

3.1 Sample and Procedure

In view of the impact of COVID-19, we collected data from international students in more than 40 Chinese universities in China with the help of school supervisors through online data collection platform, Wenjuanxing (www.wjx.cn). Two separate pre-tests were conducted to ensure the reliability and validity of the questionnaire prior to the formal data collection of the large sample. And finally, a total of 2058 valid questionnaires were collected from 135 overseas countries.

3.2 Measures

To measure the construct of social media usage, a six-item scale was used, which was adapted from Hughes et al. (2012). And we adopted a five-item scale from Busalim and Ghabban (2021) to measure customer engagement. We adopted a three-item scale from Sussman (2002) to measure cultural identity change. And a seven-item scale was adopted from Zimet et al. (1988) to measure social support.

According to prior research, the current study also listed students' age, gender, academic level, and length of stay in China to be controlled to avoid any potential confounding effects (Hu and Zhu 2022).

4 Analysis and Results

To test the reliability and validity, we examined factor loadings, Cronbach alphas, and composite reliability. The statistics demonstrated good results with the scores of Cronbach alphas and composite reliability higher than the required benchmarks of 0.7 (Naylor et al. 2012). To measure the convergent validity, we assessed all the items' loadings to ensure scores were above 0.7. And we assessed the composite reliabilities to ensure the scores were above 0.7. Finally, we worked out AVEs values to ensure they exceeded 0.5. This indicates that all variables demonstrate good reliability and validity (Table 1 and Fig. 2).

Consistent with H1a, SMU for information was positively related to cultural identity change ($r = 0.125$, $p < 0.01$). Further, as proposed in H1b, SMU for socializing also demonstrated a positive relationship with cultural identity change ($r = 0.262$, $p < 0.01$). Following the hypothesis development, we further examined the relationship between cultural identity change and engagement in social commerce. The result indicated that cultural identity change was positively related to engagement in social commerce ($r = 0.264$, $p < 0.01$). Thus H2 was supported well. Moreover, results indicated that social support positively moderates the relationships between two dimensions of social media usage and cultural identity change. To better depict the image of moderating effects of social support, we drew pictures of the simple slope (Figs. 3 and 4).

Table 1. Measurement of constructs

Constructs	Dimensions	Items	Loadings	CR	AVE	Cronbach alphas
SMU	Socializing	3	0.853–0.885	0.766	0.908	0.843
	Information	3	0.791–0.873	0.869	0.689	0.763
CIC		3	0.752–0.878	0.861	0.676	0.759
ESC		5	0.874–0.92	0.956	0.814	0.943
SS		7	0.853–0.919	0.967	0.808	0.960

Notes: SMU, social media usage; CIC, cultural identity change; ESC, engagement in social commerce; SS, social support

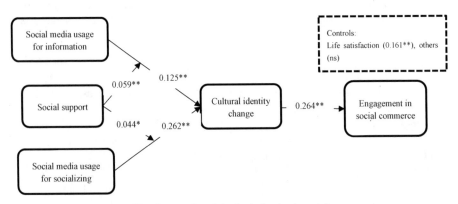

Fig. 2. Results of the hypothesized model

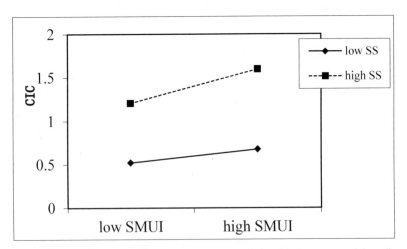

Fig. 3. Moderating effect of social support (SS) on the relationship between social media usage for information (SMUI) and cultural identity change (CIC)

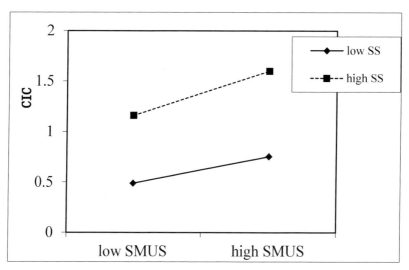

Fig. 4. Moderating effect of social support (SS) on the relationship between social media usage for socializing (SMUS) and cultural identity change (CIC)

5 Discussion

Based on the S-O-R model, this study explains the mechanism of the role of social media usage on international customers' engagement in cross-border social commerce from the perspective of cultural identity change and the moderating effect of social support on their relationships. And the current study makes significant theoretical contributions to existing research.

First, this study successfully applies the S-O-R model to the study of cross-border social commerce. Although previous research has shown that the S-O-R framework is widely used in social commerce research (Xue et al. 2020; Zhang et al. 2014), there has not been much attention paid to how this theoretical framework explains the behavior of international customers in cross-cultural social commerce. From an intercultural perspective, the study validates the psychological mechanism (cultural identity change) whereby external stimuli (social media usage) exerts impact on the behavioral response of international customers (engagement in social commerce). What's more, considering the cross-cultural pressures on international customers to engage in social commerce, this study argues that social support can have a significant impact on the psychological mechanisms (cultural identity change) that precede international customers' engagement in social commerce through social media platforms. Therefore, this study considers social support as another important stimulus for international customers when engaging in cross-cultural social commerce. The present study model remedies the inadequacy of existing studies that only examine social commerce in a single cultural context.

Second, this study found that cultural identity change among international customers is an important mechanism for enhancing social commerce engagement through social media platforms. How the use of social media based on different customer motivations promotes customer engagement in social commerce has not received much attention in existing research, especially in cross-cultural scenarios. And this study divides social media into two dimensions, information, and socializing, according to the different utilization purposes by international customers, each of which has a positive effect on cultural identity change from different perspectives, ultimately contributing to international customers' social commerce engagement. The study's findings are an important addition to the field of social commerce research.

Third, the data analysis confirms the positive moderating effect of social support between social media usage and international customers' cultural identity and ultimately influences customer engagement. Although previous research has demonstrated the positive role of social support in customer engagement in social commerce, the findings of this study were only validated in a single cultural context (Wang et al. 2020; Fan et al. 2019). Therefore, it is currently unknown how social support in a cross-cultural context explains international customer engagement in cross-cultural social commerce. In this regard, the findings of this study have enriched our understanding of the role of social support in different contexts.

In addition to the theoretical contributions, this study makes some practical contributions.

First, the findings of this study indicate the importance of differently motivated social media usage on international customers' cultural identity change and engagement in social commerce. Therefore, managers should focus on building social media platforms, especially based on customers' different motivations of usage. Influenced by both utilitarian and hedonic motivations, international customers use social media platforms to learn about the culture of products and services in cross-cultural social commerce to further determine their purchase intentions. So, managers should further optimize and improve social media platforms to meet the needs of customers with different usage motivations. To meet the need for utilitarian value, high-quality information about products and services should be made more accessible to customers via social media platforms. In addition, managers should offer high-quality after-sales service to reduce the impact of negative reviews on customers' willingness to buy for building a good reputation. And to meet the demand for hedonic value, managers should establish good communication channels on social media platforms for customers to interact and communicate with sellers or other potential customers, for example, the creation of fan interaction groups.

Second, this study concludes that cultural identity change is an important channel for international customers to engage in cross-cultural social commerce through social media platforms. This is because when international customers engage in cross-border social commerce, their home culture will limit their perceptions of the validity of information and influence their attitudes towards products and services (Nakayama and Wan 2019). Therefore, sellers need to focus on guiding and nurturing international customers to identify with the culture embedded in their products and services. On the one hand, sellers should provide more detailed and reliable information about their products and services through social media platforms, facilitating international customers to understand the content of the product and remove their original cultural perception bias to recognize the products and services in cross-cultural social commerce. On the other hand, sellers should increase their emotional interaction with international customers through social media platforms to build a trustworthy relationship to encourage customers to better comprehend the culture novelty reflected by their products or services and actively participate in cross-cultural social commerce.

Third, the results of the study confirm the positive moderating role of social support in facilitating international customers' cultural identity change through social media platforms. Therefore, managers should provide more social support to international customers through social media platforms to promote their cultural identity change and engage in cross-cultural social commerce. For example, sellers can use social media platforms to provide international customers with more detailed information about their products and to provide timely advice on any questions they may have. In addition, it is important to cater for the emotional aspects of international customers during the interaction process to address their cross-cultural social commerce stress. Further, companies can also match their online services to international customers according to their different regions.

6 Limitations

Although this study has made some contributions, some limitations need to be taken into account in subsequent studies. Firstly, as a multidimensional concept (Hollebeek et al. 2014), customer engagement is only studied as a holistic concept in this study. Secondly, this study only examines the factors influencing and mechanisms acting on international customers' engagement in social commerce in the Chinese context. Thirdly, the limitations of cross-sectional data should also receive the attention of subsequent studies.

References

Angelini, V., Casi, L., Corazzini, L.: Life satisfaction of immigrants: does cultural assimilation matter? J. Popul. Econ. **28**(3), 817–844 (2015)

Busalim, A.H., Ghabban, F.: Customer engagement behaviour on social commerce platforms: an empirical study. Technol. Soc. **64**, 101437 (2021)

Fan, J., Zhou, W., Yang, X., Li, B., Xiang, Y.: Impact of social support and presence on swift Guanxi and trust in social commerce. Ind. Manag. Data Syst. **119**(9), 2033–2054 (2019)

Hollebeek, L.D., Glynn, M.S., Brodie, R.J.: Consumer brand engagement in social media: conceptualization, scale development and validation. J. Interact. Mark. **28**(2), 149–165 (2014)

Horng, S.-M., Wu, C.-L.: How behaviors on social network sites and online social capital influence social commerce intentions. Inform. Manage. **57**(2), 103176 (2020)

Hu, S., Gu, J., Liu, H., Huang, Q.: The moderating role of social media usage in the relationship among multicultural experiences, cultural intelligence, and individual creativity. Inf. Technol. People **30**(2), 265–281 (2017)

Hu, S., Hu, L., Wang, G.: Moderating role of addiction to social media usage in managing cultural intelligence and cultural identity change. Inf. Technol. People **34**(2), 704–730 (2020)

Hu, S., Hu, L., Wu, J., Wang, G.: Social media usage and international expatriate's creativity: an empirical research in cross-cultural context. Hum. Syst. Manag. **40**(2), 197–209 (2021)

Hu, S., Ji, F., Wang, J.: Do we need to push harder when social commerce crosses borders: a cross-cultural empirical research. In: Salvendy, G., Wei, J. (eds.) Design, Operation and Evaluation of Mobile Communications: Third International Conference, MOBILE 2022, Held as Part of the 24th HCI International Conference, HCII 2022, Virtual Event, June 26 – July 1, 2022, Proceedings, pp. 256–263. Springer International Publishing, Cham (2022). https://doi.org/10.1007/978-3-031-05014-5_21

Hu, S., Zhu, Z.: Effects of social media usage on consumers' purchase intention in social commerce: a cross-cultural empirical analysis. Front. Psychol. **13**, 837752 (2022)

Hughes, D.J., Rowe, M., Batey, M., Lee, A.: A tale of two sites: Twitter vs. Facebook and the personality predictors of social media usage. Comput. Hum. Behav. **28**(2), 561–569 (2012). https://doi.org/10.1016/j.chb.2011.11.001

Hwang, I.J., Lee, B.G., Kim, K.Y.: Information asymmetry, social networking site word of mouth, and mobility effects on social commerce in Korea. Cyberpsychol. Behav. Soc. Netw. **17**(2), 117–124 (2014)

Liao, S.-H., Widowati, R., Cheng, C.-J.: Investigating Taiwan Instagram users' behaviors for social media and social commerce development. Entertainment Comput. **40**, 100461 (2022)

Lin, J., Li, L., Yan, Y., Turel, O.: Understanding Chinese consumer engagement in social commerce. Internet Res. **28**(1), 2–22 (2018)

Mangum, M., Block, R.: Social identity theory and public opinion towards immigration. Soc. Sci. **7**(3), 41 (2018)

Mao, J., Shen, Y.: Cultural identity change in expatriates: a social network perspective. Hum. Relat. **68**(10), 1533–1556 (2015)

Nakayama, M., Wan, Y.: The cultural impact on social commerce: a sentiment analysis on Yelp ethnic restaurant reviews. Inform. Manage. **56**(2), 271–279 (2019)

Naylor, R.W., Lamberton, C.P., West, P.M.: Beyond the "like" button: the impact of mere virtual presence on brand evaluations and purchase intentions in social media settings. J. Mark. **76**(6), 105–120 (2012)

Ng, C.S.-P.: Intention to purchase on social commerce websites across cultures: a cross-regional study. Inform. Manage. **50**(8), 609–620 (2013)

Osatuyi, B., Qin, H., Osatuyi, T., Turel, O.: When it comes to satisfaction … it depends: an empirical examination of social commerce users. Comput. Hum. Behav. **11**, 1106413 (2020)

Sohn, J.W., Kim, J.K.: Factors that influence purchase intentions in social commerce. Technol. Soc. **63**, 101365 (2020)

Stanley, M.L., Taylor, M.K., Marsh, E.J.: Cultural identity changes the accessibility of knowledge. J. Appl. Res. Mem. Cogn. **10**(1), 44–54 (2021)

Sussman, N.M.: Testing the cultural identity model of the cultural transition cycle: sojourners return home. Int. J. Intercult. Relat. **26**(4), 391–408 (2002)

Tuncer, İ: The relationship between IT affordance, flow experience, trust, and social commerce intention: an exploration using the SOR paradigm. Technol. Soc. **65**, 101567 (2021)

Wang, Y., Herrando, C.: Does privacy assurance on social commerce sites matter to millennials? Int. J. Inf. Manage. **44**, 164–177 (2019)

Wang, Y., Wang, J., Yao, T., Li, M., Wang, X.: How does social support promote consumers' engagement in the social commerce community? The mediating effect of consumer involvement. Inf. Process. Manage. **57**(5), 102272 (2020)

Waßmuth, N., Edinger-Schons, L.M.: Are people really strange when you're a stranger? A longitudinal study of the effect of intergroup contact on host-country identification. Int. J. Intercult. Relat. **67**, 58–70 (2018)

Xue, J., Liang, X., Xie, T., Wang, H.: See now, act now: How to interact with customers to enhance social commerce engagement? Inform. Manage. **57**(6), 103324 (2020)

Yampolsky, M.A., Amiot, C.E., de la Sablonnière, R.: Multicultural identity integration and well-being: a qualitative exploration of variations in narrative coherence and multicultural identification. Front. Psychol. **4**, 126 (2013)

Zhang, H., Lu, Y., Gupta, S., Zhao, L.: What motivates customers to participate in social commerce? The impact of technological environments and virtual customer experiences. Inform. Manage. **51**(8), 1017–1030 (2014)

Zimet, G.D., Dahlem, N.W., Zimet, S.G.: The multidimensional scale of perceived social support. J. Pers. Assess. **52**(6), 756–761 (1988)

Designing an Interactive Mobile Assessment Tool to Quantify Impact of the Environment on Wellbeing

Thomas Johnson[(✉)] and Eiman Kanjo

Department of Computer Science, School of Science and Technology,
Nottingham Trent University, Nottingham, UK
{thomas.johnson,eiman.kanjo}@ntu.ac.uk

Abstract. The ubiquity of mobile sensing and smartphone capabilities offer a significant opportunity to obtain real-world sensor data and momentary mental wellbeing fused at the point of exposure. In this paper, we present the design, implementation and evaluation and user experiences of Urban Wellbeing; a cross-platform mobile application, which aids in quantifying the relationship of the environment, behaviour and mental wellbeing. Urban wellbeing integrates: (i) real-time environmental sensor data in the form of Air Quality Index, (ii) momentary mental wellbeing assessment in the form of emojis, (iii) image and the type of environment and (iv) noise levels in decibels. We report early findings from trials conducted based on the design of Urban Wellbeing to promote engagement. Our preliminary results of Urban Wellbeing, tested with both iOS and Android smartphones demonstrate that it can be effective as a personal environmental and wellbeing sensing application and engaging for users.

Keywords: Urban Wellbeing · Environment · Mental Wellbeing · Air Quality · Ecological Momentary Assessment

1 Introduction

A significant impact of the growth in the world, particularly environmental factors (such as Particulate Matter 2.5, noise, and gases) within the environment are having a significant impact on our health [17,18], behaviour [10] and mental wellbeing [14]. As the population increases and our urban environments obtain more focus it is expected that 66% of the global population will live in urban areas by 2050 [11].

Recently, a World Health Organisation study found that 91% of the world's population is living in areas where air quality guidelines are not met which is resulting in over 4.2 million deaths each year [2]. In addition, many places across the UK where these guidelines are not being followed is resulting in more serious health conditions such as higher heart rate leading to heart disease and asthma [2], or even death [17].

© The Author(s), under exclusive license to Springer Nature Switzerland AG 2023
G. Salvendy and J. Wei (Eds.): HCII 2023, LNCS 14052, pp. 286–295, 2023.
https://doi.org/10.1007/978-3-031-35921-7_20

The use of sensor-based technologies and mobile sensing devices have the greatest opportunity of understanding the impact of exposures within a range of urban environments as well as quantifying the impact to individuals through assessment-based questionnaires [13,15]. Smartphone momentary wellbeing assessments using environmental factors is lacking with limited contribution of using objective sensor data. Specifically, previous research has only explored these using questionnaires with limited user interaction and data obtained from real-world sensors [3].

In this paper, we propose, discuss the design and explore the implementation of our environmental and wellbeing sensing system tool *Urban Wellbeing*, that is able to unobtrusively fuse wellbeing states and objective sensor data in the form of environmental factors such as air quality, noise and gain a perspective on the environment through image and location. Urban Wellbeing is an application that aims to bring us closer to understand the impact of urban environments on mental wellbeing as an interactive assessment tool

The rest of this work is organised as followed: Section 2 describes the background and related literature review. Session 3 discussed the system design, including the process participants complete to carry out an assessment. Section 4 shares the results from a set of users who have tested the design of Urban Wellbeing. Finally, Sect. 5 considers the conclusions drawn from this work and work to be considered in the future.

2   Background/Literature Review

As individuals, within each urban environment, we are exposed to a range of stressors, such as particulates, noise and gases which have been shown to result in a negative impact on our health [20], behaviour, physiology [16] and mental wellbeing [14]. The impact of our environment is largely dependent on the time, location and type we are in to experience the exposure. There has been considerable research attention to the impact of poor air quality within the environment particularly towards health related issues, however, there are still considerable opportunities to explore the impact on mental wellbeing. Recently a study found that mental wellbeing illnesses are steeply increasing and expected to cost the UK economy over £2 billion each year [21].

Across many studies, the combination of mobile technologies and sensors are becoming increasingly popular approaches to provide a greater insight into the impact of the environment direct at the point of exposure. This research opportunity highlights the potential of utilising technological resources whereby exposure to the environment can be accurately assessed and calculated [23].

Sensor fusion approaches have been shown to be effective when investigating the relationship between the environment, physiology, behaviour and wellbeing, including our own work. In particular, the DigitalExposome concepts can bring us closer to unravelling the impact of the environment on wellbeing, highlighting that particulate matter correlates with ElectroDermal Activity (EDA), Heart-Rate Variability (HRV) and results in a worsened wellbeing state when exposed to a high level. Additionally, using the concept of semantic trajectories using episodes has shown a worsened wellbeing can be caused by a polluted urban environment [12].

ExpoApp utilised a similar approach to study the short-term health impacts of high air pollution with the result demonstrating those who weren't able to access green spaces inhaled higher rates of air pollution [7]. Furthermore, 'Project HELIX' investigated the environmental impact on individuals living in urban environments demonstrating increased level of blood pressure, allergy and asthma illnesses for those who particularly living in urban environments [19].

An ecological momentary assessment (EMAs) involves capturing people's thoughts and behaviours at the moment of exposure repeatedly within an environment [1], [22]. The use of EMAs has been shown to be extremely popular within studies conducted to obtain a human perspective on wellbeing and the environment. A study in 2018 explored the use of EMAs as the context for collecting wellbeing, demonstrating that exposure to nature and daylight correlated with a better affective state [4].

Until recently, EMAs were carried out with as 'pen and paper' approach, which was effective in being able to assess wellbeing [24]. A significant growth and development of mobile technologies and their capabilities enables EMAs to be incorporated for a more portable assessment at the time of exposure. As such, a previous mobile application, *Urban Mind* [3] has used a smartphone mobile application approach to assess the environment through a series of questions based on an ecological momentary assessment. This approach demonstrates a good knowledge gained from EMAs into the natural features of the environment and the direct impact to wellbeing. In summary, the use of smartphones for momentary wellbeing assessment is lacking in terms of using objective sensor data which is linked to the exposure directly at the exact location.

3   System Design: Urban Wellbeing

To overcome the limitations of existing literature, we propose the design of *Urban Wellbeing* as a cross-platform (iOS and Android) interactive assessment tool that aids in supporting the work of unravelling the relationship between the environment and mental wellbeing. The mobile application encompasses a range of data collection types including: live sensor data from the Department of Environment, Food and Rural Affairs' Automatic Urban Rural Network (DEFRA AURN), image of current environment, momentary mental wellbeing (recorded using emojis), timestamp and location as identified at Fig. 1. The overall aim of *Urban Wellbeing* is to complete the assessment individually and as much as possible whilst going about your day or to carry this out in a different locations. This research has been approved by Nottingham Trent University Ethical Committee (application number 648). At the start of each assessment, participants must agree to carry out the study and are informed of their options, should they wish to withdraw from the study.

Fig. 1. The individual data types that are involved in the Urban Wellbeing assessment process. These involve: Air Quality data from live sensors, exact location, image of current environment, personal noise level, wellbeing labelled using emojis and timestamp of assessment event

3.1 Real-Time Wellbeing Assessment

To complete the assessment within *Urban Wellbeing*, users are required to record their wellbeing using five well-known emojis and text-equivalent meanings displayed on buttons as depicted at Fig. 2. The table also at Fig. 2 shows how wellbeing is calculated in terms of assigning an individual score to each emoji, from *1=negative/low* to *5=positive/high* . The 'Personal Index for Adults' self-assessment of measured satisfaction has been adopted to ask users how they are feeling with their life as a whole [6]. We have adapted this into the form of a five-point Likert SAM scale [5], to provide a proven method for self-reporting subjective wellbeing. There have been several studies that utilise this approach, including our own work [12,13] which has shown how momentary wellbeing can be effectively obtained, such as DigitalExposome [14], NeuroPlace [16].

Fig. 2. Urban Wellbeing assessment of wellbeing using emojis and table showing equivalent scoring compared to emojis

3.2   Environmental Image Capture

To gain an understanding into what the environment visually looks like when the assessment is taking place, participants are invited to capture an image using the in-build camera of the wider environment they are currently standing within. Depicted at Fig. 3 demonstrates this page in action, along with the image consent which participants must 'agree to understand' prior to being able to take the image. Whilst testing the Urban Wellbeing application, four images at Fig. 3 show examples of what was collected from several participants.

Fig. 3. Urban Wellbeing image capture along with 4 example images taken

3.3 Environment Air Quality and Noise

The final process for the assessment is to collect the environmental levels of air quality and noise which is relative to the participants' specific location. On clicking 'Capture' as depicted at Fig. 4, a loading bar will form around the noise icon which results in several processes of obtaining the participant's location, Air quality and noise level.

We gather air quality readings by using data collected by the DEFRA AURN stations [8] which are positioned across the United Kingdom. In particular, the data obtained includes: Real-time Air Quality Index, Air Quality Level and AURN station ID. The Air Quality Index is a process of combining all of the individual pollutants collected at each AURN station either taking the highest recorded value or averaging out the values across a period of time [9]. Secondly, noise is obtained from the assessment which is calculated by recording a series of noise clips in decibels which are collected over a period of 5 s. Finally, at this point all the data has been saved locally stored on the phone and with the timestamp (DD/MM/YYYY) added, the combined data is sent to a secure database ready for analysis. To protect users and in-line with ethics agreement, no data is stored in the database to identify a participant.

Hold the phone still and then press capture
to collect a sample of noise in the
environment. Once the assessment is
complete you will be moved to the next
page.

Capture

Fig. 4. Urban Wellbeing air quality and noise sampling

4   Results

A preliminary study has taken place to evaluate the design of the application
and performance as a tool to capture live environment sensor data and wellbeing, to aid in quantifying the relationship between the two variables. In total,
5 participants were recruited for testing of Urban Wellbeing and interviewed
following a full day of utilising the application in the wild. There was an equal
download of Urban Wellbeing made up of iOS and Android platform between
the participants.

When interviewed after using the Urban Wellbeing app for the day, it was
found that the majority (4) participants informed us that they enjoyed using
the mobile application to understand how the environment could play a part
in their wellbeing. Overall, these participants were able to use Urban Wellbeing
and complete the assessment process several times throughout their day. One
participant struggled with the concept and process through the application and
what they had to do. Some of the participants at times reported that the final
screen (Fig. 4) was a little slow at loading causing some issues with waiting
around for the assessment to be completed.

Another concern was that one participant hadn't clicked on the 'accept permissions' when prompted so therefore the application was not able to be used.
All participants agreed that there should be some sort of incentive to carry out

the experiment using the mobile application, with one stating perhaps a series of badges per environment or step counter activity.

Following discussions with all participants after their day, it was mentioned that a loading screen before the assessment starts should be presented which briefly explains the main ideas and understanding of the work to be carried out. As such, a landing page has been developed into the application with three separate pages detailing the app itself, the walk outline and how the results of this study will be used, as depicted at Fig. 5.

Fig. 5. Urban Wellbeing mobile application three landing screens to give a general overview of the application before starting the individual assessment

5   Conclusion and Future Work

The use of smartphones combining a ecological assessment tool and live sensor data has helped to develop a novel environmental assessment tool with fusing data at the source of exposure that demonstrates the potential to quantify the relationship between urban environmental factors and mental wellbeing. Individual assessments made up of (i) self-labelled wellbeing, (ii) environment image capture, (iii) air quality and noise collection shows the capabilities of understanding the changes within the environment at a more direct perspective, logging at the point-of-exposure. The preliminary trial involved five participants who tested the applications design whilst in a real-world environment and demonstrated the potential for the app to be used alongside daily life and to gain a closer understanding into how certain environmental factors can have a direct impact on their wellbeing.

In the future, a larger trial will be conducted with more participants to further demonstrate the impact not only of the Urban Wellbeing mobile application but the relationship between the environment and mental wellbeing, as well as to gather additional user feedback. There is further work that could be investigated such as an incentive to use the application to collect more reliable data. We envision future versions of the application could be used to notify users where they recently labelled their wellbeing as negative as a place to avoid and for urban planners to encourage the design of urban spaces.

References

1. Ecological momentary assessment - gov.uk. https://www.gov.uk/guidance/ecological-momentary-assessment
2. Air, C., Plan, S.: Clean air strategy plan (2011)
3. Bakolis, I., et al.: Urban mind: using smartphone technologies to investigate the impact of nature on mental well-being in real time. BioScience **68**, 134–145 (2018). https://doi.org/10.1093/biosci/bix149, https://academic.oup.com/bioscience/article/68/2/134/4791430
4. Beute, F., de Kort, Y.A.: The natural context of wellbeing: ecological momentary assessment of the influence of nature and daylight on affect and stress for individuals with depression levels varying from none to clinical. Health Place **49**, 7–18 (2018). https://doi.org/10.1016/J.HEALTHPLACE.2017.11.005
5. Bradley, M.M., Lang, P.J.: Measuring emotion: the self-assessment manikin and the semantic differential. J. Behav. Therapy Exp. Psychiatry **25**, 49–59 (1994). https://doi.org/10.1016/0005-7916(94)90063-9
6. Cummins, R.A., Ps, F.A.S.: Personal Wellbeing Index-Adult (PWI-A) (English) 5th Edition The International Wellbeing Group MANUAL 2013 Personal Wellbeing Index-Adult (2013)
7. Donaire-Gonzalez, D., et al.: Expoapp: an integrated system to assess multiple personal environmental exposures. Environ. Int. **126**, 494–503 (2019). https://doi.org/10.1016/j.envint.2019.02.054
8. Food, for Environment, R.A.D.: Automatic urban and rural network (aurn)- defra, uk (2018). https://uk-air.defra.gov.uk/networks/network-info?view=aurn
9. Geetha, A., Ramya, P.S., Sravani, C., Ramesh, M.: Real time air quality index from various locations. Int. J. Recent Technol. Eng. (IJRTE) **9**, 368–372 (2020). https://doi.org/10.35940/ijrte.b3493.079220
10. Haddad, H., de Nazelle, A.: The role of personal air pollution sensors and smartphone technology in changing travel behaviour. J. Transp. Health **11**, 230–243 (2018). https://doi.org/10.1016/j.jth.2018.08.001
11. Johnson, T., Kanjo, E.: Sensor fusion and the city: visualisation and aggregation of environmental & wellbeing data. IEEE (2021). https://ieeexplore.ieee.org/document/9562852
12. Johnson, T., Kanjo, E.: Episodes of change: emotion change in semantic trajectories of multimodal sensor data. IEEE (2023)
13. Johnson, T., Kanjo, E.: Urban wellbeing: a portable sensing approach to unravel the link between environment and mental wellbeing (2023). https://doi.org/10.1109/LSENS.2017.0000000, http://www.michaelshell.org/contact.html

14. Johnson, T., Kanjo, E., Woodward, K.: Digitalexposome: quantifying impact of urban environment on wellbeing using sensor fusion and deep learning, January 2021

15. Kanjo, E.: NoiseSPY: a real-time mobile phone platform for urban noise monitoring and mapping. Mob. Netw. Appl. **15**, 562–574 (2010). https://doi.org/10.1007/S11036-009-0217-Y

16. Kanjo, E., Younis, E.M., Sherkat, N.: Towards unravelling the relationship between on-body, environmental and emotion data using sensor information fusion approach. Inf. Fusion **40**, 18–31 (2018). https://doi.org/10.1016/j.inffus.2017.05.005

17. Laville, S.: Air pollution a cause in girl's death, coroner rules in landmark case—london—the guardian (2020)

18. Lee, B.J., Kim, B., Lee, K.: Air pollution exposure and cardiovascular disease. Toxicol. Res. **30**, 71–75 (2014). https://doi.org/10.5487/TR.2014.30.2.71

19. Maitre, L., et al.: Human early life exposome (helix) study: a European population-based exposome cohort, September 2018. https://doi.org/10.1136/bmjopen-2017-021311

20. Nieuwenhuijsen, M.J., Donaire-Gonzalez, D., Foraster, M., Martinez, D., Cisneros, A.: Using personal sensors to assess the exposome and acute health effects. Int. J. Environ. Res. Public Health **11**, 7805–7819 (2014). https://doi.org/10.3390/ijerph110807805

21. Perkbox: The 2018 UK workplace stress survey—perkbox (2018)

22. Shiffman, S., Stone, A.A., Hufford, M.R.: Ecological momentary assessment. Annu. Rev. Clin. Psychol. **4**, 1–32 (2008). https://doi.org/10.1146/ANNUREV.CLINPSY.3.022806.091415, https://pubmed.ncbi.nlm.nih.gov/18509902/

23. Asimina, S., et al.: Assessing and enhancing the utility of low-cost activity and location sensors for exposure studies. Environ. Monit. Assess. **190**(3), 1–12 (2018). https://doi.org/10.1007/s10661-018-6537-2

24. de Vries, L.P., Baselmans, B.M.L., Bartels, M.: Smartphone-based ecological momentary assessment of well-being: a systematic review and recommendations for future studies. J. Happiness Stud. **22**(5), 2361–2408 (2020). https://doi.org/10.1007/s10902-020-00324-7

Perception of Co-supervisors in Doctoral Education Towards Mobile Information Systems for Higher Education in Malaysia

Chee Ling Thong[1]([✉]) [iD], WeiLee Lim[2] [iD], and Shayla Islam[1]

[1] Institute of Computer Science and Digital Innovation, UCSI University, 56000 Kuala Lumpur, Malaysia
`chloethong@ucsiuniversity.edu.my`
[2] Graduate Business School, UCSI University, 56000 Kuala Lumpur, Malaysia

Abstract. In the post-Covid era, mobile information systems have greater potential for supporting the doctoral supervision process, including co-supervision pedagogy in doctoral education. However, little is known about its design and development. This study explores the potential of designing a mobile information system for doctoral co-supervision in higher education. It is anticipated that the contributions of this study (as consideration areas in the user requirements gathering phase) would help system designers when involved in designing mobile information systems. First, this study examines the main challenges doctoral co-supervisors face in Malaysian higher education institutions. A focus group interview examines ICT use and its integration with supervision pedagogies like meetings, reading draft, and giving supervisees feedback. A total of ten doctoral co-supervisors who have completed co-supervision with at least one doctoral candidate were interviewed at three Malaysian universities. According to the findings of our study, co-supervisors communicate using a variety of ICT, including email, mobile phones, Microsoft Teams, Skype, and social media platforms such as Facebook. Some of the supervisors use Microsoft SharePoint for collaborative writing. The majority of them saw the importance of integrating ICT with co-supervision pedagogy. The study also discovered the need for increased use of collaborative-based technology in promoting collaborative co-supervision pedagogy. These include virtual spaces for the scholarly community, such as an online discussion forum and a collaborative writing space for providing feedback on supervisees' report drafts. In future work, a mobile information system or digital collaborative tool that can accommodate a complex virtual space through cloud computing will be designed, and the proposed digital tool will empower rather than control or direct the process of learning.

Keywords: co-supervision · doctoral supervision · digital collaborative tool · mobile information system

G. Salvendy and J. Wei (Eds.): HCII 2023, LNCS 14052, pp. 296–306, 2023.
https://doi.org/10.1007/978-3-031-35921-7_21

1   Introduction

Mobile technologies have gained tremendous growth during the Covid-19 pandemic due to the high demand for the use of mobile technologies particularly when academicians (or co-supervisors) are located at different geo-graphic locations or while they are in motion such as traveling in a plane, traveling from one location to another, or work from home (relate to mobility). Mobile information system (MIS) becomes an important tool to be used by the co-supervisors to access to information resources particularly when they are on the move. In this study, MIS (or known as mobile web application) is defined as information system (IS) which gain services or access to information resources any-time and everywhere through IS hardware or mobile devices such as mobile phones, tablets, or laptops. These mobile devices are easily movable in space, and able to access to online information resources or services as long as wireless connection is provided [1]. Based on the findings of a study conducted in two universities in Australia, the need for an increased use of ICT as well as its integration with supervision pedagogy have been identified [2]. Their study concludes that the use of ICT increases high quality research output and supervision, particularly in enhancing supervision-student relationship by using Web 2.0 technologies. For example, supervision pedagogy began to change by supervisors in Australia [2], they developed more participatory relationships through notable collaboration and communication using new technologies. There is an increased use of social network such as Twitter and Facebook for disseminating their research findings or initiating their own academic communities. They discovered the needs for learning communities for supervisors which would enable supervisors to enter into dia-logues about supervision practices and to exchange ideas between new and experienced supervisors. Five years on, in post-Covid era the increasing emphasis in integrating ICT in co-supervision pedagogy in addressing doctoral supervision and related issues is becoming more intense. Hence, this study aims to investigate the main issues or challenges faced by doctoral co-supervisors and explore the current use of ICT and its integration with supervision pedagogies in institution of higher learning in Malaysia.

The research objectives are two-fold: 1) to find out what co-supervisors have to say about their experiences when 'working together' with co-supervisors, and on the basis of this data, investigate the issues or challenges faced by them in the start of a new working relationship with co-supervisors in the areas of co-supervision arrangements (roles and responsibilities) and supervision pedagogies (meetings and reading drafts and providing feedback); 2) to find out perception and experience of using ICT/digital tools and explore what system features are if supervisors had already begun integrating these technologies into their co-supervision process.

2   Literature Review

This section presents mobile information systems, mobile and web technologies, and issues and challenges of co-supervision in doctoral education.

2.1   Mobile Information Systems

Based on previous studies, the use of web technologies is more prevalent than mobile technologies in the area of doctoral supervision. Web 2.0 technology is the current version of the internet which all are familiar with. Whereas Web 3.0 is the latest web technology or process engine that uses blockchain advances. Metaverse is a new dimension which include social platforms, education, virtual training techniques that employ Web 3.0 technology. Web 3.0 more commonly used in financial sector. Many other sectors may begin to explore adopting Web 3.0 technologies, however at the point of this study, there are more relevant literatures on employing Web 2.0 technologies in higher education. Moar and Fraser [3] proposed creating a participatory supervision support platform (PSVSP) to support participatory doctoral research processes in virtual spaces using Web 2.0 technology. Virtual space enhances social interaction between the academic and doctoral students, student-supervisor relationship and overcome challenges such as low completion rates, low satisfaction with students' theses, and lack of support for supervisors or students [4]. It was reported that the supervisors' workload is already demanding, that requires robust framework of how to use web-based tools in reducing isolation in supervision and at the same time increase efficacies.

The Grattan Institute's Mapping Australian Higher Education [5] has discovered that research on doctoral supervision was underdeveloped. Ten years on, there is also a need to share the database across devices using cloud services. In the past ten years, some relevant literature found are: an online portal namely Form@doct as a resource rather than a network [6] and an online tutorial for doctoral candidate (Form@doct) in France; an international doctoral education network namely Doctoralnet® that was built to support students and their supervisors [7].

MIS or mobile web applications which hosted on an app and access from a web browser on a mobile device, are getting popularity. According to Information Technology Gartner glossary, mobile web applications (app) refers to "applications for mobile devices that require only a Web browser to be installed on the device" (URL: https://www.gartner.com/en/information-technology/glossary/mobile-web applications) [8]. DataReportal [9] reported the number of smartphone (or mobile devices) users reached 5.22 billion by the end of 2020, which represent 66% of world population.

Figure 1 shows digital growth in the past one decade reported DataReportal. Figure 2 shown the year-on-year change for total population (+1.0%), unique mobile phone users (+1.8%), internet users (+4.0%) and active social media users (+10.1%).

Figure 2 shows Internet users grew by 192 million over the past one year (Jan 2021–Jan 2022). The growth may continue in the post Covid era. The statistics shown the need arise in integrating digital tools into supervision particularly on approaches used to doctoral pedagogies. These statistics reported has become the motivation to study the perception of doctoral supervisors towards mobile information system or mobile web app.

Based on a literature study [11], some example of functionalities of the digital tools include notifications (dimension: communication and one-way interaction) such as email access and alert messages that allow reachability; communication (dimension: communication and two-way interaction) such as phone conversation and communication support (WA, MS Teams, Zoom); information access (dimension: data and one-way interaction) such as access reports/news/announcement/materials in learning management system (using search functionality); data processing (dimension: data and two-way interaction)

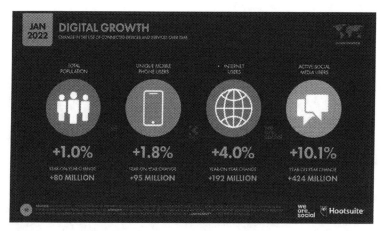

Fig. 1. Digital Growth [9] (Source: https://datareportal.com/reports/digital-2022-global-ove rview-report)

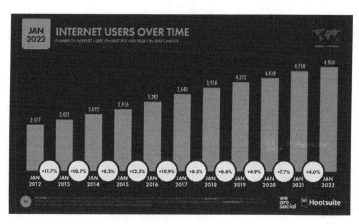

Fig. 2. Internet Use [10] (Source: https://datareportal.com/reports/digital-2022-global-overview-report)

such as access or sending logbook data in learning management system to co-supervisors using laptop/tablet/mobile devices, etc. In this study, functionalities of MIS are categorized into two dimensions: 1) study the main focus whether it is on communication or data processing; 2) study interaction between human/user (co-supervisors) and information system whether it is considered one-way or two-way (reciprocal) interactive.

Table 1 presents a summary of selected digital tools used to support doctoral co-supervision, what the tools are, its special features and limitations. Most of the relevant literature found capitalize on web-based tools which can accommodate complex interaction in virtual spaces through a web browser, e-portfolio or cloud computing [13].

It is discovered that most of the study explore web-based tools in collaborative environment, none of the IHL using mobile information systems or mobile web application to support doctoral co-supervision.

Table 1. Summary of Selected Digital Tools

Tool	What is it	Special features	Limitations
Doctoralnet (https://doctoralnet.com) [7]	Virtual space: Web-based international network. To unite doctoral students from nine countries	Online discussion and collaborative writing space	Hard to maintain a sustainable community and lack of strong digital pedagogy framework in terms of co-creation of knowledge
Virtual spaces [12]	A network for the exploration of resources and online discussion forum. To provide idea and prompt to encourage on-going reflection	Online resources and online discussion forum	Lack of mobile web application function (e.g. access online resources through web browser on mobile devices)
PSVSP [3]	Participatory Supervision Support Platform (PSVSP) is a web-based platform/application for improving doctoral supervision	Support different processes of supervision	Not identified
Facebook/Twitter (2023)	Create own communities and disseminate information	Web conference/sharing resources	Lack of specific functions to support supervision pedagogy
Microsoft SharePoint (2023)	Collaborative writing	Common virtual writing spaces for collaborative writing	Lack of discussion forum or virtual spaces for participatory supervision

2.2 Issues and Challenges in Doctoral Co-supervision

Based on literature study, co-supervision is likened a safety net for doctoral candidates as compared to single supervisory system [14]. The findings of earlier research shown that co-supervision in doctoral education is less explored [15] and this is reflected in handbooks on doctoral supervision [16]. Kalman and colleagues [15] reported the challenges of co-supervision appear in SIX (6) areas and they are challenges in communication, disagreement between supervisors, issues of commitment, issues of time and organization, issues of power responsibility, and challenges to practical realization of the research projects. Challenges in communication includes lack of communication with co-supervisors [17]; disagreement between co-supervisors which includes giving conflict advice or feedback to the candidates [17–19]; issues of commitment which includes inequitable recognition of the work of co-supervisors [17, 18, 20] and issues of power and responsibility which include unclear roles and responsibilities of supervisors [21].

This study focuses on investigating challenges in the areas of communication and issues of power and responsibilities (or roles and responsibilities) of co-supervisors. Referring to the framework or tool developed by Nave et al. [22], these two areas are grouped under co-supervision arrangements and pedagogies of supervision. This study also explores the use of ICT or digital tools and its integration with co-supervision arrangements such as define the roles and responsibilities of each supervisor and co-supervision pedagogies such as meetings and reading drafting and providing feedback to supervisees.

3   Methodology

The protocol employed in this study is qualitative in nature. Focus group interviews are used to elicit, analyze, and specify the requirements with stakeholders. Focus group interview is an unstructured, free flowing interview with a small group of people, and it is conducted in a flexible format [23]. The focus group consists of ten doctoral co-supervisors who have produced at least one doctorate graduate. The interview is conducted at three private universities in Kuala Lumpur, Malaysia. The interviewees are selected based on convenience sampling. Each interview takes up 30 min throughout a period of two months.

The interview questions are semi-structured with open-ended questions. These questions have been pre-tested among two experts to ensure clarity and sequence of the questions. The data collected are first transcribed and subsequently examined with thematic analysis for concise key considerations in designing the co-supervision MIS.

4   Results and Discussions

This section presents the descriptive results which are analyzed from the study.

4.1   Demographic

Basic demographics for the respondents are presented in Tables 2 and 3.

Table 2. Demographic of Co-supervisors (I)

Category	Response	n	%
Gender	Male	7	63.6
	Female	3	36.4

(*continued*)

Table 2. (*continued*)

Category	Response	n	%
Age	30–39	1	10
	40–49	7	70
	50–59	1	10
	>60	1	10
Years of experience	1–2 years	9	90
	>3 years	1	10

Most of the respondents are male (63.6%). Eight of them are aged more than 35 years old (90%) and two of them are between 30 to 35 years old (10%). All the co-supervisors have one to two years of experience in co-supervision, and only one senior co-supervisor have more than 3 years in co-supervision.

Table 3. Demographic of Co-supervisors (II)

Respondent	Area of research	Years in current institution	No. Student graduate
1	Statistics	3	5
2	Logistics Management	15	2
3	Applied Science	8	1
4	Mobile Network	3	1
5	Business and Management	10	1
6	Business	5	1
7	Business	2	1
8	Business	6	1
9	Business	10	3
10	Business	11	1

All of the co-supervisors classified themselves as having more than two years' experience of working (100%) and they have produced at least one successful complete doctoral candidate. Majority (70%) of co-supervisions from Faculty of Business. The next section discusses the interview results.

4.2 Interview Results

The results show none of the respondent uses any specific software or digital tool (or MIS) in supporting their work for co-supervision in their respective IHL. However, out of 10 respondents who participated in the study, 90% of them prefer to have MIS in assisting them in co-supervision. The desired features of the MIS are: it possesses an online repository (database) which store all the required information needed such as progress report (95.8%); it helps to generate meeting alert/notification on meetings (91.7%); and it is a mobile-based or web-based application (83.3%). Only 10% of the respondents do not prefer to have MIS with the reason of unable to predict how MIS could assist and to what extent it can help in supporting co-supervision. Overall results show that co-supervisors are looking forward to having such system in order to address the challenges faced by them during the co-supervision process particularly when they are supervising more than 5 students at the same time.

All respondents are using basic digital tools to facilitate co-supervision such as mobile phones and email for communication and exchange of information. Other applications used are Facebook, Twitter, Microsoft Teams (MT), Skype and editing software. Most of them using MT or Skype when unable to have face-to-face meeting due to country lock-down or Covid cases. All supervisors reported the use of Words documents to track changes in progress report or proposal or thesis draft and exchanging information or provide feedback of report or draft via email or during MT or Skype meeting. Some used social networking mediums such as Facebook to share written drafts. 'I use Facebook to communicate and read my students' work and give them feedback.......'[SUP7]. Only one co-supervisor reported his doctoral candidates are mostly at middle-age and not competent in using ICT. Therefore, he does not intend to use any specific software or system. It is found that a concern discovered about technology competencies among candidates. It is believed the gap can be narrowed down in future. Training is recommended to close the gap and increase technology experience [2].

According to the responses from all respondents, it is common for communication between co-supervisors at the beginning of the 'working together' for early discussion on the co-supervision arrangements. However, it is noted by a supervisor (principal supervisor) that she has more discussion with doctoral candidate than co-supervisor (second supervisor). She meets the co-supervisor after she has provided feedback to candidate on the thesis draft. Candidate is expected to improve the draft based on her feedback before meeting co-supervisor. 'He met me (principal supervisor) more than two times at the beginning of his PhD journey, as I take heavy responsibility than the co-supervisor'[SUP8], noting than principal supervisor involvement and much more participation in the co-supervision pedagogy and her power and responsibility are higher than co-supervisor.

5 Discussion and Implications

The findings of this study provided some insights that shed lights on current and future MIS or digital tools in Malaysia particularly in adapting to new normal in post-Covid era. In this section, the following insights are discussed:

1. Web-based tool using Web 2.0 technologies is still popular and it is reported by much research works in literature study. However, none of co-supervision using ICT (specific software or MIS) in doctoral supervision. The findings shown need arise increasingly in the post Covid era particularly supervision in collaborative manner. Quite a number of studies reported web-based tools are more popularly used in supervision pedagogy and it helps increase supervision quality research work and completion rate as well as reduce attrition rate. Some of the proposed features are virtual

spaces, online discussion forum and collaborative writing using Microsoft SharePoint or Dropbox or other web-based tools. It is also discovered that Web 3.0 technologies are not used by the supervisors at the time of this study. Although Web 3.0 is the latest web technology which is more advance than Web 2.0, Web 2.0 is still a mostly used technology in doctoral co-supervision. Moar and Fraser [3] reported Web 2.0 tools enabled greater dialogue and interaction between the supervisor and candidates rather than a passive viewing of content. It is perceived the importance of ICT and supervision pedagogy are combined into a research project in a more collaborative and collegial way. This may be considered as participatory supervision. On the other hand, Integration with supervision pedagogies such as meetings and reading drafts and providing feedback to candidates is not perform in collaboratively manner using digital technologies such as collaborative writing. It is also found that there is a lack of relevant literatures which published in year 2017–2022 particularly MIS or mobile web app. Most of the IHL use Skype, Microsoft Teams for meetings, phones or email or Facebook for communication or disseminate information. Some still prefer using conventional approach (face-to-face meetings with candidates).

2. It is discovered some key items are absent in early discussion in co-supervision. These items are:
   a. nature of the work involved. All respondents mentioned there is only verbal agreed understanding of what supervisors should be involved.
   b. formal institutional requests. This is mainly due to current heavy workload of supervisors, and it is perceived as an additional administrative burden to supervisors.
   c. division of work among supervisors. What supervisor should do to co-supervise effectively are not involved in the early discussion. All supervisors expect candidates learn how to manage their own research projects.
   d. distribution of effort across panel and committee. This is perceived as a great challenge when it comes to risk management and regulations for supervisory responsibilities.
   e. clarification of roles, responsibilities and expectations.

Principal supervisors work on 'trust' basis. Expectations on research output (such as number of publication) are not formalized with co-supervisors when they start 'working together'. However, most supervisors adhere to the regulations or code of practice set by their respective institutions such as timely completion or graduate on time. Code of practice outlines the responsibilities of both supervisors and candidates, ethical compliance, research practices, intellectual property and so forth. As to how to ensure efficiency (such as successful completion or frequency of meetings in one semester), are not included in early discussion. This could be addressed at institutional level.

The main issues are identified in this study. This data serves as input to user requirements gathering which serve as an important phase in the system development lifecycle approach. In the nutshell, the practical implication of this study is to assist system designer to discover the system architectural components.

6   Conclusion

As a conclusion, this research has successfully investigated the issues faced by doctoral co-supervisors and their perception towards using MIS in the co-supervision process including supervision pedagogy. Since participatory supervision is an important process in supervision pedagogy and doctoral co-supervisors have to work together in a collegiate and collaborative manner, this study concludes that these could be facilitated by MIS or mobile web app with functionalities such discussion forum and online shared repository containing progress reports and thesis drafts of doctoral candidates. Comments of supervisors are also captured as record and notification messages are sent to doctoral candidates when the report is provided comments by supervisors in a collaboratively manner. It is also found that web-based tools are more popular and mobile web app is preferred by most of the doctoral supervisors. In future work, a mobile web app is designed and developed based on the input provided by respondents.

Acknowledgement. This research work is supported by UCSI University, Malaysia.

References

1. Wang, S., Hsu, C., Taniar, D., Hung, P.: Mobile information systems [Guest Editorial]. China Commun. **12**(12), iii–iv (2015). https://doi.org/10.1109/CC.2015.7386074
2. Maor, D., Currie, J.K.: The use of technology in postgraduate supervision pedagogy in two Australian universities. Int. J. Educ. Technol. High. Educ. **14**(1), 1–15 (2017). https://doi.org/10.1186/s41239-017-0046-1
3. Moar, D., Fraser, B.: Designing a participatory supervision support platform for improving higher education degree supervision: A feasibility study. Office for Learning and Teaching, Higher Education Division, Department of Industry, Innovation, Climate Change, Science, Research and Tertiary Education (2015)
4. Phelps, R., Fisher, K., Ellis, A.: Organizational and technological skills: the overlooked dimension of research training. Australas. J. Educ. Technol. **22**(2), 145–165 (2006)
5. Norton, A.: Mapping Australian Higher Education. Grattan Institute, Melbourne (2012)
6. Malingre, L., Serres, A., Men, L.: Form@doct: designing innovative online tutorials for PhD students in France. IFLA J. **39**(1), 45–57 (2013)
7. Danby, S., Lee, A.: Researching doctoral pedagogy close up: design and action in two doctoral programme. Aust. Univ. Rev. **54**(1), 19–28 (2012)
8. Gartner: https://www.gartner.com/en/information-technology/glossary/mobile-web-applications (2022)
9. DataReportal. Digital 2021: Global overview report. https://datareportal.com/reports/digital-2021-global-overview-report (2021)
10. DataReportal Digital 2022:Internet use. https://datareportal.com/reports/digital-2022-global-overview-report (2022)
11. Gebauer, J., Shaw, M.J., Gribbins, M.L., Gebauer, J., Shaw, M.J., Gribbins, M.L.: Towards a specific theory of task-technology fit for mobile information systems. University of Illinois at Urbana-Champaign, College of Business Working Paper, 05–0119 (2005)
12. Stelma, J.: An ecological model of developing researcher competence: the case of software technology in doctoral research. Instr. Sci. **39**(3), 367–385 (2011)

13. Velte, T., Velte, A., Elsenpower, R.: Cloud Computing: A Practical Approach. McGraw-Hill, New York (2010)
14. Pole, C.: Joint supervision and the PhD: safety Net or Panacea? Assess. Eval. High. Educ. **23**(3), 259–271 (1998). https://doi.org/10.1080/0260293980230303
15. Kálmán, O., Horváth, L., Kardos, D., Kozma, B., Feyisa, M.B., Rónay, Z.: Review of benefits and challenges of co-supervision in doctoral education. Euro. J. Educ. **57**, 452 (2022)
16. Taylor, S., Kiley, M., Humphrey, R.: Handbook for Doctoral Supervisors (2nd edn.). Routledge (2018)
17. Olmos-Lopez, P., Sunderland, J.: Doctoral supervisors' and supervisees' responses to co-supervision. J. Furth. High. Educ. **41**(6), 727–740 (2017). https://doi.org/10.1080/0309877X.2016.1177166
18. Buttery, E.A., Richter, E.M., Filho, W.L.: An overview of the elements that influence efficiency in postgraduate supervisory practices arrangements. Int. J. Educ. Manage. **19**(1), 7–26 (2005). https://doi.org/10.1108/09513540510574920
19. Kobayashi, S., Grout, B.W., Rump, C.O.: Opportunities to learn scientific thinking in joint doctoral supervision. Innov. Educ. Teach. Int. **52**(1), 41–51 (2015). https://doi.org/10.1080/14703297.2014.981837
20. Grossman, E.S., Crowther, N.J.: Co-supervision in postgraduate training: Ensuring the right hand knows what the left hand is doing. S. Afr. J. Sci. **111**(11–12), 1–8 (2015)
21. Ukwoma, S.C., Ngulube, P.: Supervision practices in library and information science postgraduate research in Nigeria and South Africa. Afr. J. Libr. Arch. Inf. Sci. **30**(2), 127–142 (2020)
22. Wald, N., Kumar, V., Sanderson, L.J.: Enhancing co-supervision practice by setting expectations in a structured discussion using a research-informed tool. High. Educ. Res. Dev. **42**, 757–769 (2022). https://doi.org/10.1080/07294360.2022.2082390
23. Zikmund, W.G.: Business Research Methods, 7th edn. Thomson, USA (2003)

Research on the Influencing Factors and Mechanism of Sharing Accommodation Hosts' Resilience in the Post-epidemic Era

Junjing Wang[1] and Maomao Chi[2(✉)]

[1] Wuhan Technology and Business University, Wuhan 430065, China
[2] China University of Geosciences, Wuhan 430078, China
chimaomao@vip.163.com

Abstract. The rapid development of sharing economy (e.g., sharing accommodation) has become an essential driver of economic resilience. However, the COVID-19 outbreak hugely impacts sharing accommodation platforms and their hosts. How to actively cope with COVID-19 and develop resilience has become a complex problem in the industry. There is a lack of research on the formation mechanism of sharing accommodation hosts' resilience in the academic community. Based on the coping theory, this paper conducts a case study on the hosts of sharing accommodation platforms to explore the influencing factors and mechanisms of resilience. The results find the context-specific factors of threat appraisal, ability appraisal, problem-focused coping, emotion-focused coping, platform governance, and their relationship with resilience. This paper has important practical significance for guiding sharing accommodation platform enterprises and hosts to overcome difficulties.

Keywords: Sharing Accommodation Hosts · Resilience · Coping Theory · Platform Governance · Case Study

1 Introduction

As one of the most successful business models of the sharing economy, the sharing accommodation platform effectively links the idle accommodation space provided by the host with the tenant, improving the matching efficiency of both sides [1]. However, the COVID-19 epidemic has had a severe impact on the sharing accommodation industry. In China, the transaction scale in the sharing accommodation sector declines 29.8% in 2020[1]. Platform and hosts are facing unprecedented challenges.

In the face of external shocks, hosts urgently need the ability to bounce back and even forward their original operating status (namely, resilience). After the outbreak of COVID-19, hosts actively responded to the COVID-19 threats, and strengthened their capabilities in the coping process. Meanwhile, Airbnb announced over $250 million to support its host community [2]. Therefore, it is necessary to understand the influencing

---

[1] http://www.sic.gov.cn/News/568/11277.htm.

factors and mechanism of sharing accommodation hosts' resilience, so as to promote hosts and platforms to cope with external shocks and develop resilience.

Relevant studies mainly focus on the participation behavior of sharing accommodation hosts [3] and the management of the platform on the hosts [4] in the steady-state environment. Recently, scholars have begun to focus on the response of sharing accommodation hosts and platforms to the COVID-19 shock. For example, Xu, et al. [5] and Mont, et al. [6] qualitatively analyzed the hosts' coping strategies and platform management changes after the COVID-19 respectively. However, the current literature lacks resilience research on how hosts recover or even improve their operational performance under external shocks, and also ignores the impact of platform support.

Based on the above practical needs and theoretical limitations, this paper attempts to explore the influencing factors and mechanism of sharing accommodation hosts' resilience in the post-pandemic era. This paper adopts coping theory, which describes the cognitive and behavioral efforts made in the face of negative events [7], and introduces platform governance into coping theory.

This paper has two research contributions. On one hand, this paper deeps the academic community's understanding of the individual response to shocks and the formation of resilience in the platform environment, provides a theoretical framework for the study of hosts' resilience in a highly dynamic environment (VUCA), and enriches the research on the process mechanism of small and micro entrepreneurs facing shocks. On the other hand, this study provides suggestions for the crisis response of sharing accommodation hosts and platform enterprises, which is helpful to realize the high-quality and sustainable development of sharing accommodation industry and further develop the resilience of digital economy.

2   Theoretical Background

2.1   Research on Sharing Accommodation Hosts

Existing studies from the perspective of hosts mainly focus on the participation behavior of hosts and the management of hosts by platforms. First, the research on hosts participation behavior mainly focuses on the motivation of hosts participation [3, 8, 9], processes (such as hosts-tenants interaction [10]), and outcomes (such as how to be a super host [11, 12]).

Second, scholars also pay attention to the management of hosts by sharing accommodation platforms. For example, Leoni and Parker [4] explored Airbnb's governance and control of hosts through netnographic method. Through an inductive qualitative analysis, von Richthofen and von Wangenheim [13] revealed three strategies for host management. In the face of the COVID-19, sharing accommodation platforms needed to make significant changes to respond to the crisis [14].

Current research mainly focuses on the participation behavior of sharing accommodation hosts and the management of hosts by platforms in a steady state environment. Although some studies qualitatively analyze how platforms and hosts respond to the COVID-19, there is still a lack of research on the influencing factors and mechanism of hosts response and resilience in the post-pandemic era. In addition, the specific ways of governance of sharing accommodation platforms in the post-pandemic era and their impact on hosts' resilience have not been clarified.

2.2 Individual Resilience

Individual resilience is often defined as an individual's ability to quickly recover from shocks [15]. There are two streams in individual resilience research [16], the first stream regards individual resilience as a stable personality trait [17], while the second stream regards individual resilience as the result of dynamic processes [18].

The first stream mostly focus on the relationship between individual resilience and mental health [19], the relationship between individual resilience and individual or organizational performance [16, 20].

The second stream focus on the influence of internal factors (such as individual emotions, cognition, and behavior) and external factors (such as social support) on resilience. Most studies focus on how individuals form resilience in the coping process [21], and find that coping influence resilience. For example,. Zheng, et al. [22] found that travelers' travel fear in the context of COVID-19 affected travelers' resilience through four coping strategies.

Since the recovery or even improvement of the operation of the hosts after the outbreak of COVID-19 cannot be achieved without the active (adaptive) response of the hosts, this paper follows the research of the second stream. Hosts' resilience refers to the ability to bounce back or forward the original operation state in the face of the external shocks (such as COVID-19). It is concerned about how hosts form resilience through the coping process when facing the sudden impact of COVID-19.

2.3 Coping Theory

Coping theory was originally proposed by Lazarus [23], which mainly describes the cognitive and behavioral effort process of individuals in the face of negative events. According to Lazarus and Folkman [7] coping process model, the coping process mainly includes four main steps: negative event triggering, appraisal, coping strategy and outcome [24].

First, coping is often triggered by negative events [24]. Prolonged exposure to negative events may render adaptive capacity ineffective and individuals may reach a stage of exhaustion. Therefore, it is important to respond appropriately to negative events [25].

Second, individual's cognitive assessment of negative events plays a decisive role in the arousal and selection of coping strategies [26]. Cognitive appraisal mainly includes threat and capability appraisal [27].

Then, coping strategies are the core concept of coping theory, and are defined as behavioral efforts to manage threats [7]. Lazarus and Folkman [7] divided coping strategies into problem-focused and emotion-focused coping.

Finally, coping theory suggests that the ideal outcome is closure, meaning that there is no longer need to cope. However, the coping process does not always end with a definite end, and individuals may continue to be trapped in coping [28]. Based on the perspective of stress growth [29], an individual's effective coping effort will lead to an increase in resilience. In particular, many scholars treat resilience as an outcome of coping, suggesting that resilience is influenced by coping strategies [21, 30].

In summary, based on above four steps, this paper follows the dynamic viewpoint stream [18] to takes resilience as the outcome. This paper introduces the key variable of platform governance to consider the impact of platform support, and forms the framework to guide the research (see Fig. 1).

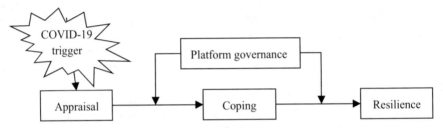

Fig. 1. Research framework of formation mechanism of sharing accommodation hosts' resilience in the post-epidemic era.

3   Methodology

3.1   Research Design

Based on the fact that the process of how sharing accommodation hosts form resilience under the epidemic is still unknown, this paper attempts to describe the coping and resilience formation process of hosts under the COVID-19 through case study, and reveal the influencing factors and mechanism hidden behind the phenomenon.

3.2   Data Collection

This paper recruited sharing accommodation hosts through purposive and snowball sampling techniques, and mainly contacted hosts through personal relationships, Weibo, and sharing accommodation platforms. Participants must: (1) operate a sharing accommodation business on a sharing accommodation platform (such as Airbnb, Tujia, etc.). (2) Joined the sharing accommodation platform before the COVID-19 (January 23, 2020) and has been operating since then.

The data mainly comes from semi-structured interviews online. Participants were informed of the purpose of the study before the interviews. All interviews were conducted in January 2022. Sampling continued until the 12th interview reached information saturation, which was followed by six additional interviews. 19 hosts volunteered to participate and completed the interviews, and each lasting between 30 and 70 min. Table 1 provides some sharing accommodation host demographics.

This paper also supplements diversified data sources to ensure mutual complementarity and cross-validation between data [31]. It includes: (1) online observation. Long-term observation of media accounts of sharing accommodation hosts. (2) Secondary data, such as corporate official website information, literature, industry reports, etc.

Table 1. Examples of sharing accommodation hosts' basic information.

Hosts' code	Sex	Age	Education	Job type	Participation Time	Number of properties
H1	Female	51	Junior college	Full-time	2018	1
H2a	Female	26	Undergraduate	Full-time	2018	20
H2b	Male	30	Unknown			
H3	Female	33	High school	Full-time	2020	7
H4	Female	33	Undergraduate	Full-time	2018	16
H5	Female	31	Undergraduate	Full-time	2017	2
H6	Male	26	Master	Full-time	2018	20
H7	Male	34	Undergraduate	Full-time	2019	100
H8	Female	24	Undergraduate	Full-time	2018	35
H9	Female	46	Undergraduate	Full-time	2016	14
H10	Female	30	Master	Part-time job	2018	3
H11	Male	32	Undergraduate	Part-time job	2018	7
H12	Male	27	Undergraduate	Full-time	2017	28

4   Date Analysis

Encoding is the first step of qualitative data analysis. In this paper, NVivo software is used to encode data in open, axial and selective encoding [30]. The coding process is done independently and discussed repeatedly by three members.

4.1   Open Coding

Open coding refers to the gradual labeling, conceptualization and categorization of the original data. This paper resulted in 60 concepts and 25 original categories (Table 2 showed the examples of open coding).

Table 2. Examples of open coding.

Label	Concept	Original category
Fewer orders, lower prices, staff costs......	Low revenue, high cost	Financial threat
Family disapproval, platform-host conflict......	Family disapproval, communication conflict	Social threat
Reduced hosts' service quality, reduced platform service efficiency......	Reduced service quality, difficult to maintain operations	Operational threat
Depression, nervousness......	Emotional stress	Psychological threat
Competitive accommodations, strong ability	Competitive products and services, capable	Self-efficacy
The expectation of the effect of the coping strategy, the calculation of the return rate......	Effect appraisal of coping strategies, risk appraisal of coping strategies	Response efficacy
Sales of local products, long-term rent, increase marketing......	Change the leasing model, change the price, increase the marketing, increase the service experience, and expand the new business form of accommodation	Increase income
Communicate with hosts to reduce rent, reduce staff salaries......	Reduce rental costs, reduce staff costs, reduce operating costs	Reduce cost
Understand the market, improve the emotional connection......	Understand customer needs, improve service experience, improve infrastructure, improve health environment	Improve service quality
Attract private domain stream through social media......	Establish private domain stream, switch to similar platform, build local accommodation platform, seek platform help	Change platform dependence
Understand the tenant refund, understand the platform requirements	Understand the tenant, understand the platform	Positive understanding

(continued)

Table 2. (*continued*)

Label	Concept	Original category
Compared to people infected or lost their lives……	Compare with other people, compare with other accommodations	Positive comparison
Believes that the epidemic can make him stand out, can accompany family	Believe the epidemic is a chance, believe the epidemic is a vacation	Cognitive reconstruction
Reading, traveling……	Reading, traveling, partying, running	Entertainment
Platform provides long-term rental function……	Long-term rental function, social media interface, direct selling function	Share resource
……	……	……

4.2 Axial Coding

Axial coding refers to the clustering analysis of the original categories obtained by open coding. Based on coping theory and existing literature, this paper finally forms 6 deputy categories and 4 main categories (Table 3).

Table 3. Axial coding.

Main category	Deputy category	Original category
Appraisal	Threat appraisal	Financial threat
		Social threat
		Operational threat
		Psychological threat
	Capability appraisal	Self-efficacy
		Response efficacy
Coping	Problem-focused coping	Increase income
		Reduce cost
		Improve service quality
		Change platform dependence
	Emotion-focused coping	Positive understanding
		Positive comparison
		Cognitive reconstruction
		Entertainment

(*continued*)

Table 3. (*continued*)

Main category	Deputy category	Original category
Platform governance	Platform governance	Incentive
		Formal control
		Informal control
Resilience	Hosts' resilience	Bounce back
		Bounce forward

4.3 Selective Coding

Selective coding refers to identifying the core category from the main category, and developing the theoretical framework in the form of a story line. This paper found that formation mechanism of hosts' resilience in the post-epidemic era could dominate all categories as the core category. The story line is: appraisal, coping, and platform governance can individually or jointly affect hosts' resilience. Specifically, in the face of the COVID-19, sharing accommodation hosts will make coping strategies based on the threats and capabilities appraisal to solve problems or alleviate negative emotions, so as to better rebound or improve the operation situation. And the platform governance will promote or inhibit the coping and resilience. Therefore, this paper constructs a resilience formation mechanism model (see Fig. 2), which is in line with the theoretical framework proposed in the previous section (Table 4).

Table 4. Examples of typical relationship.

Structure of typical relationship	The connotation of the relationship structure	Typical examples
Appraisal → Coping	Threat and capability appraisal of shocks influences coping strategies	H6: The monthly rent was a big cost, so we looked for long-term rent
Coping → Resilience	Emotion-focused and problem-focused coping strategies positively affect hosts' resilience	H1: Through the efforts in the pandemic, I feel that customer stickiness and offline services have been better done
Appraisal*Platform governance → Coping	Platform incentives, formal control, and informal control influence hosts to adopt coping strategies to deal with the evaluation	H8: We participated in the live broadcast of the platform, which bring about 10 orders

(*continued*)

Table 4. (*continued*)

Structure of typical relationship	The connotation of the relationship structure	Typical examples
Coping*Platform governance → Resilience	Platform incentives, formal control, and informal control affect hosts to form resilience from the implementation of coping strategies	H5: We will use good means of the platform to improve our image

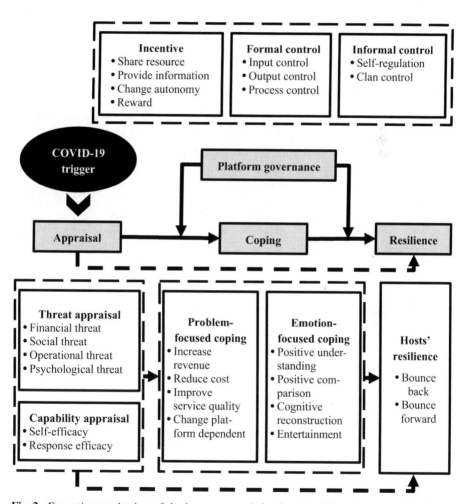

Fig. 2. Formation mechanism of sharing accommodation hosts' resilience in post-epidemic era.

4.4 Theoretical Saturation Test

Theoretical saturation is tested in two ways. First, after the 12th interview which has reached information saturation, this paper conducted six additional interviews. Second, this paper randomly collected 20 posts related to the epidemic from the network from March to June 2022. The codes obtained in this paper already approach saturation.

5 Findings

This paper focuses on the core category to makes a discussion of the influencing factors (including appraisal, coping and platform governance) and mechanism of resilience formation of hosts after COVID-19 outbreak.

5.1 Appraisal

Coping is often triggered by a negative event [24], and individuals evaluate the information they receive and decide what action they will take [26]. Previous studies believe that appraisal consists of threat appraisal and capability appraisal [26].

First, threat appraisal refers to the degree to which external shocks are considered dangerous [32]. The threat of COVID-19 perceived by hosts originates from financial, social, operational and psychological aspects. Financial threat is the primary source of threat, and 'complex guest situation (H10)' have caused difficulties in the operation. The hosts will also be subjected to social threats from 'family's incomprehension of the hosts' occupation(H5)', and psychological threats such as 'frustration (H5)'.

Second, capacity appraisal refers to the extent to which hosts believe their ability and effectiveness to deal with the threat when the external shocks occur, including self-efficacy and response efficacy. Self-efficacy refers to the degree to which hosts believe they have the ability to respond when the external shocks (such as COVID-19) occur [33], such as 'team is relatively competent (H6)'. Response efficacy refers to the degree of belief that response will avoid threats [33]. Hosts will evaluate the effectiveness of the following coping strategy by 'calculating the rate of return (H6)'.

5.2 Coping

The individual's cognitive assessment of negative events will evoke the their choice of coping strategies [26], which include problem-focused and emotion-focused coping.

Problem-focused coping refers to adaptive behavior that tries to change the objective reality by solving problems [34]. Hosts alleviate the difficulties by increasing revenue, reducing costs, improving service quality and changing platform dependence.

How to increase income is mostly concerned. Five strategies are summarized as follows: (1) Change the leasing model into long-term rental (H1). (2) Change the price, such as reduce prices to attract customers (H8). (3) Increase marketing promotion, such as 'sending some vouchers to tenants (H6)'. (4) Increase service experience, such as 'adding afternoon tea for local tourists (H9)'. (5) Expand new business forms, such as combining food (H1), play, real estate and shopping (H2).

Reducing costs can also alleviate threats. It mainly includes three types of costs: (1) Renting cost. (2) Employees' cost, such as '*replacing old employees with fewer professional and younger employees (H8)*'. (3) Marketing cost, such as establishing private domain stream (H2a).

Due to the COVID-19 requires higher hygiene, hosts improve service quality by: (1) Strengthening the understanding of customer needs (H2a). (2) Improving service experience, such as '*humanized communication (H2a)*'. (3) Improving infrastructure, such as upgrade accommodations with new sharing kitchen (H8). (4) Improving the health environment, such as '*each aunt is equipped with a camera (H7)*'.

The value creation of hosts cannot be separated from the participation of sharing accommodation platforms. After the COVID-19, hosts' dependence on sharing accommodation platforms has changed. (1) Focus on private domain stream, such as '*presenting life to others*' through social media. (2) Seek help from the platform, such as asking the customer service about '*order refund problem (H10)*'. (3) Switch to similar platforms. As mentioned in H4, '*X' order volume has decreased, so its' investment will be less*'. (4) Build a local accommodation platform. As H9 said, '*Now I am building my own platform, and I will not rely on others*'.

Emotion-focused coping refers to creating a positive perception of the environment, thereby mitigating negative emotions related to threats [34]. Hosts alleviate negative emotions by positive understanding, positive comparison, cognitive reconstruction and entertainment.

Under the COVID-19, both the platform and the tenants encountered difficulties, so the hosts first positive understanding others. Second, hosts make positive comparison with '*people who lost lives (H1)*'. Then, hosts (especially head hosts) regarded the epidemic as an chance or vacation (H2b). Finally, the hosts will adjust himself and the group mood through some activities, such as '*exercising (H5)*'.

5.3 Resilience

Based on the stress growth view, some studies have found that individual coping processes affect resilience. Hosts' resilience refers to the ability to bounce back or even forward the original operating state in the face of external shocks, which includes two dimensions: bounce back and bounce forward.

First, bounce back refers to the ability of hosts to return to their original operating conditions in the face of external shocks. Bounce back is mainly reflected in the recovery of hosts' operating performance and the adaptation to operational changes, such as '*survival (H2a)*'. Second, bounce forward refers to the ability to improve hosts' original operating status, including (1) better operating performance. As H2b said, 'The most intuitive feedback is to buy back'. (2) Better operating conditions. As H9 mentioned that '*I can fill in more content, and do not only be a room seller*'. (3) Stronger operational capability such as cognitive, strain, and communication ability.

5.4 Platform governance

This paper finds that platform support (platform governance) can affect individual coping and resilience. Platform governance refers to a set of main rules, constraints and incentives for sharing accommodation platforms to create and obtain value, including incentive, formal control and informal control.

Incentive refers to the degree to which a sharing accommodation platform promotes hosts' participation through mechanisms. (1) Resource sharing, such as '*long-term rental channel (H6)*' functions. (2) Provide information, such as '*improving the service department (H11)*'. (3) Change autonomy, such as '*Full refund without the consent of the hosts (H12)*' (4) Increase the reward, such as '*reducing commission and issue discount coupons (H4)*'.

Formal control refers to the extent to which the sharing accommodation platform expects the host to act in accordance with the platform objectives through rules and standards, including (1) input control, the platform continuously reviews the information of listings. (2) output control, the platform humanized calculated the performance of the hosts. (3) process control, the platform added epidemic prevention guidelines and standardized processes, such as '*the platform has an image upload entrance, and customers can see the daily elimination situation (H4)*'.

Informal control refers to the extent to which sharing accommodation platforms rely on norms and values shared with hosts to influence host behavior, including: (1) self-regulation, the platform will organize hosts' training and exchanging activities (H4). (2) clan control, hosts will rely on the belief shared with the platform to consciously and actively respond to the COVID-19 crisis (H10).

5.5 The Formation Mechanism of Hosts' Resilience

Based on the grounded theory, this paper analyzes the influencing factors and mechanism of hosts' resilience, and builds a mechanism model (see Fig. 2). The formation of hosts' resilience includes appraisal, coping and platform governance influencing factors. The logical relationship among these factors is as follows:

(1) Appraisal and coping are the main internal factors of hosts' resilience. The COVID-19 will trigger hosts' threat and capacity appraisal. Appraisal can directly affect resilience, but more by awakening hosts' coping strategies to form resilience. First, threat and capability appraisal enable the hosts to adapt and recover. For example, '*the team is capable of coping – adapt (H6)*'. Second, coping strategies play an important mediating role in appraisal and resilience. For example, '*financial threat – conversion to long-term rent – survival (H6)*'.

(2) Platform governance is the main external factor of hosts' resilience, which have a multiplicative effect with appraisal and coping. Most platform governance promotes hosts to better cope with threats and build resilience, such as '*financial threat * platform provides live broadcast – pre-sale using platform live broadcast (H8)*'. However, some platform governance hinder hosts coping and resilience, such as '*financial threat * platform reduces the autonomy of hosts to refund – the host cannot communicate with the tenant independently (H5)*'.

6 Discussion and Conclusion

6.1 Main Conclusion

Based on the coping theory, this paper analyzed the formation mechanism of sharing accommodation hosts' resilience in the post-epidemic era through grounded theory, and found the influencing factors and mechanism of sharing accommodation hosts' resilience. The main conclusions include: (1) Threat and capability appraisal triggered by COVID-19 shock will awaken the coping strategies and guide hosts to adapt to the shock. (2) hosts' problem-focused and emotion-focused coping strategies can promote hosts' resilience. (3) Hosts' resilience is the ability to recover or even exceed the original operating state, including bounce back and bounce forward. (4) The governance mechanisms of the sharing accommodation platform have a multiplicative effect with the hosts' appraisal and coping, which jointly affect the hosts' coping decision and resilience formation.

6.2 Theoretical Implications

The theoretical contributions of this paper are as follows: First, this paper supplements the concept of hosts' resilience under sudden crisis. Previous literatures regard individual resilience as a stable personality trait [19, 20], or the result of dynamic process, focusing on bounce back dimension [22]. This paper complements the dynamic process view [18], including bounce back and bounce forward dimension. This paper contributes to the measurement of sharing accommodation hosts' resilience in crisis situations.

Second, this paper enriches the research on the participation behavior (especially resilience) of sharing accommodation hosts under sudden crisis events. Previous studies mainly focused on hosts' participation behavior in steady environments [8–12]. This paper focuses on hosts' resilience under sudden crisis events, and finds the key elements and relationships of appraisal and coping. Therefore, this paper proposes a new theoretical basis for hosts participation research in VUCA environment.

Third, this paper deeply explores the governance of sharing accommodation platform and its impact on hosts' resilience under sudden crisis events. Previous literature mainly focused on software platforms and e-commerce platforms [35, 36], or governance of sharing accommodation platforms in steady environments [4, 13]. This paper focuses on the sharing accommodation platform governance under emergency crisis events, and finds platform governance has double-edged sword effect on host coping and resilience. Therefore, through the actual perception of hosts, this paper lays a foundation for future research on the impact of platform support on host participation behavior.

Fourth, this paper further extends coping theory by treating the results of coping as resilience. Based on the view of stress growth [29], this paper believes that individual adaptive efforts will lead to the improvement of individual adaptability. This paper further complements the influence of external support on individual coping, which lays a theoretical foundation for the study of individual coping with the impact of sudden crisis in the platform environment.

6.3 Management Implications

This paper has important management implications for sharing platform enterprises and their hosts on how to cope with the current highly dynamic environment (VUCA, such as COVID-19 impact), and sustainable development.

For sharing accommodation hosts. First, the threat appraisal and capacity appraisal are the influencing factors of hosts' resilience and coping. The host needs to maintain the agility of the environment (such as emergencies, platform changes and policy changes). Also, the host needs to master their capacity and the feasibility of possible coping strategies.

Second, the positive coping to shocks is the influencing factor of hosts' resilience, and coping plays an important mediating role in appraisal and resilience. When facing the shock, the host needs to reduce the negative emotions through positive understanding, positive comparison, cognitive reconstruction and entertainment. Also, hosts need to increase revenue, reduce costs, improve service quality and change platform dependence to solve the threat.

Finally, platform governance is also an important factor affecting hosts' resilience. Sharing accommodation hosts need to actively understand and respond to platform changes. For example, for incentives, hosts can actively apply functions such as long-term rent to increase revenue generation channels.

For sharing accommodation platforms. First, platforms should actively respond to shocks to promote the hosts' resilience under sudden crises. For example, for incentives, the platform can alleviate the difficulties of short-term rent through new functions.

Second, the governance mechanisms of sharing accommodation platforms need to be investigated in hosts, so that platform governance can more effectively promote the formation of hosts' resilience. For example, some hosts react that the platform does not have many long-term rent customers, so the effect is not very good.

6.4 Limitations and Opportunities

This paper still certain limitations. First, semi-structured interviews were used to make hosts recall after the COVID-19. Although there are some observations continuously, it is suggested that research should be carried out immediately when crisis events occur. Second, based on the COVID-19, this paper analyzes the coping and resilience of hosts' operation interruption. However, the epidemic is normalized, and future research can explore the dynamic relationship between these factors over time.

References

1. Jiang, Y., Balaji, M.S., Jha, S.: Together we tango: value facilitation and customer participation in Airbnb. Int. J. Hospitality Manage. **82**, 169–180 (2019)
2. Farmaki, A., Miguel, C., Drotarova, M.H., et al.: Impacts of Covid-19 on peer-to-peer accommodation platforms: host perceptions and responses. Int. J. Hospitality Manag. **91**, 102663 (2020)
3. Bremser, K., Wüst, K.: Money or love – Why do people share properties on Airbnb? J. Hospitality Tourism Manag. **48**, 23–31 (2021)

4. Leoni, G., Parker, L.D.: Governance and control of sharing economy platforms: hosting on Airbnb. Br. Account. Rev. **51**(6), 100814 (2019)
5. Xu, X., Huang, D., Chen, Q.: Stress and coping among micro-entrepreneurs of peer-to-peer accommodation. Int. J. Hospitality Manage. **97**, 103009 (2021)
6. Mont, O., Curtis, S.K., Voytenko, P.: Organisational response strategies to COVID-19 in the sharing economy. Sustainable Prod. Consumption **28**, 52–70 (2021)
7. Lazarus, R.S., Folkman, S.: Stress, Appraisal and Coping. Springer, New York (1984)
8. Dogru, T., Zhang, Y., Suess, C., et al.: What caused the rise of Airbnb? An examination of key macroeconomic factors. Tourism Manag. **81**, 104134 (2020)
9. Dolnicar, S., Talebi, H.: Does hosting on Airbnb offer hosts vacation-like benefits? Proposing a reconceptualization of peer-to-peer accommodation. J. Hospitality Tourism Manag. **43**, 111–119 (2020)
10. Cheng, M., Zhang, G.: When Western hosts meet Eastern guests: airbnb hosts' experience with Chinese outbound tourists. Ann. Tourism Res. **75**, 288–303 (2019)
11. Gunter, U.: What makes an Airbnb host a superhost? Empirical evidence from San Francisco and the Bay Area. Tourism Manag. **66**, 26–37 (2018)
12. Liang, S., Schuckert, M., Law, R., et al.: Be a "Superhost": the importance of badge systems for peer-to-peer rental accommodations. Tourism Manag. **60**, 454–465 (2017)
13. von Richthofen, G., von Wangenheim, F.: Managing service providers in the sharing economy: Insights from Airbnb's host management. J. Bus. Res. **134**, 765–777 (2021)
14. Gerwe, O.: The Covid-19 pandemic and the accommodation sharing sector: effects and prospects for recovery. Technol. Forecast. Soc. Change **167**, 120733 (2021)
15. Wieczorek-Kosmala, M.: A study of the tourism industry's cash-driven resilience capabilities for responding to the COVID-19 shock. Tourism Manag. **88**, 104396 (2022)
16. Aguiar-Quintana, T., Nguyen, T.H.H., Araujo-Cabrera, Y., et al.: Do job insecurity, anxiety and depression caused by the COVID-19 pandemic influence hotel employees' self-rated task performance? The moderating role of employee resilience. Int. J. Hospitality Manag. **94**, 102868 (2021)
17. Connor, K., Davidson, J.: Development of a new resilience scale: the Connor-Davidson resilience scale (CD-RISC). Depression Anxiety **18**, 76–82 (2003)
18. Egeland, B., Carlson, E., Sroufe, L.A.: Resilience as process. Dev. Psychopathol. **5**, 517–528 (1993)
19. Ran, L., Wang, W., Ai, M., et al.: Psychological resilience, depression, anxiety, and somatization symptoms in response to COVID-19: a study of the general population in China at the peak of its epidemic. Soc. Sci. Med. **262**, 113261 (2020)
20. Saad, S.K., Elshaer, I.A.: Justice and trust's role in employees' resilience and business' continuity: evidence from Egypt. Tourism Manag. Perspect. **35**, 100712 (2020)
21. Van der Hallen, R., Jongerling, J., Godor, B.P.: Coping and resilience in adults: a cross-sectional network analysis. Anxiety, Stress, & Coping **33**(5), 479–496 (2020)
22. Zheng, D., Luo, Q., Ritchie, B.W.: Afraid to travel after COVID-19? Self-protection, coping and resilience against pandemic 'travel fear.' Tourism Manag. **83**, 104261 (2021)
23. Lazarus, R.S.: Psychological Stress and the Coping Process. McGraw-Hill, New York (1966)
24. Salo, M., Makkonen, M., Hekkala, R.: The interplay of IT users coping strategies: uncovering momentary emotional load, routes, and sequences. MIS Q. **44**(3), 1143–1175 (2020)
25. Law, J., Pearce, P.L., Woods, B.A.: Stress and coping in tourist attraction employees. Tourism Manag. **16**(4), 277–284 (1995)
26. Crossler, R.E., Andoh-Baidoo, F.K., Menard, P.: Espoused cultural values as antecedents of individuals' threat and coping appraisal toward protective information technologies: Study of U.S. and Ghana. Inform. Manag. **56**(5), 754–766 (2019)
27. Floyd, D.L., Prentice-Dunn, S., Rogers, R.W.: A meta-analysis of research on protection motivation theory. J. Appl. Soc. Psychol. **30**(2), 407–429 (2000)

28. Lazarus, R.S.: From psychological stress to the emotions: a history of changing outlooks. Ann. Rev. Psychol. **44**, 1–21 (1993)
29. Lee, S.: Understanding the dynamics among acculturative stress, coping, and growth: a grounded theory of the Korean immigrant adolescent experience. Child. Youth Serv. Rev. **94**, 105–114 (2018)
30. Stratta, P., Capanna, C., Dell'Osso, L., et al.: Resilience and coping in trauma spectrum symptoms prediction: a structural equation modeling approach. Pers. Individ. Diff. **77**, 55–61 (2015)
31. Yin, R.K.: Case Study Research: Design and Methods. Sage Publications Inc, CA (2009)
32. Boss, S.R., Galletta, D.F., Lowry, P.B., et al.: What do systems users have to fear? Using fear appeals to engender threats and fear that motivate protective security behaviors. MIS Q. **39**(4), 837–864 (2015)
33. Lee, Y., Larsen, K.R.: Threat or coping appraisal: determinants of SMB executives' decision to adopt anti-malware software. Eur. J. Inform. Syst. **18**(2), 177–187 (2009)
34. Liang, H., Xue, Y.: Avoidance of information technology threats: a theoretical perspective. MIS Q. **33**(1), 71–90 (2009)
35. Song, P., Xue, L., Rai, A., et al.: The ecosystem of software platform: a study of asymmetric cross-side network effects and platform governance. MIS Q. **42**(1), 121–142 (2018)
36. Liang, C., Shi, Z., Raghu, T.S.: The spillover of spotlight: Platform recommendation in the mobile app market. Inform. Syst. J. **30**(4), 1296–1318 (2019)

The Relationship Between Enterprise Tax Credit and Business Credit Financing in the Mobile Commerce Environment

Qian Wang[✉], Peiyan Zhou, and Huiying Luo

Jilin University, 2699 Qianjin Street, Changchun City, Jilin, China
wq17860829005@163.com

Abstract. In recent years, mobile commerce has developed rapidly, bringing new opportunities and challenges to the business development of enterprises. Mobile commerce makes the production and operation of enterprises no longer restricted by time and space, helping enterprises to better adapt to the new market competition model. However, in practice, mobile commerce lacks the trust that exists in the physical transaction model between enterprises, resulting in its development being constrained by the credit problems that exist between enterprises. Tax credit, as an important part of enterprise credit, can reflect the actual credit status of enterprises. The State Administration of Taxation of China launched a tax credit rating activity for the whole country in 2014, using the form of grades to evaluate the tax credit of enterprises. In this paper, the relationship between corporate tax credit and business credit financing is studied with a sample of A-share listed companies in China from 2014–2021. The main findings of this paper are: there is a positive relationship between enterprises' tax credit and their commercial credit financing in the mobile commerce environment; compared with state-owned enterprises, commercial credit financing of non-state-owned enterprises is more significantly influenced by tax credit.

Keywords: Mobile commerce · Tax Credit · Commercial Credit Financing

1 Introduction

With the rapid development of the Internet and other technologies, the popularity of smartphones and the emergence of mobile commerce, people's shopping methods and shopping concepts are undergoing tremendous changes. According to the 50th Statistical Report on the Development Status of the Internet in China released by the China Internet Network Information Center, as of June 2022, the number of Internet users in China was 1.051 billion, with 19.19 million new Internet users compared to December 2021; the Internet penetration rate reached 74.4%, an increase of 1.4 percentage points compared to December 2021. According to the 2022 Communications Industry Statistical Bulletin issued by the Ministry of Industry and Information Technology of the People's Republic of China, the cumulative telecommunications business revenue in 2022 completed 1.58 trillion, an increase of 8% over the previous year. Total telecom

© The Author(s), under exclusive license to Springer Nature Switzerland AG 2023
G. Salvendy and J. Wei (Eds.): HCII 2023, LNCS 14052, pp. 323–334, 2023.
https://doi.org/10.1007/978-3-031-35921-7_23

business at the previous year's prices reached 1.75 trillion yuan, up 21.3% year-on-year. Emerging business revenues grew prominently, with data center, cloud computing, big data, Internet of Things and other emerging businesses developing rapidly. In 2022, total business revenues amounted to 307.2 billion yuan, up 32.4% over the previous year, and the proportion of telecommunications business revenues increased to 19.4% from 16.1% in the previous year, boosting telecommunications business revenues by 5.1 percentage points. Mobile Internet access traffic reached 261.8 billion GB, an increase of 18.1% over the previous year. The monthly average mobile Internet traffic per household (DOU) for the year reached 15.2 GB/household-per-month, up 13.8% from the previous year; the DOU for the month of December reached 16.18 GB/household, up 1.46 GB/household from the end of the previous year. The rapid development of mobile commerce brings more convenience and benefits to business transactions without time and space constraints, directly changing the business situation of commercial transactions and providing opportunities for enterprises to adapt to new market competition models and explore business opportunities.

Mobile commerce brings opportunities as well as challenges to the development of enterprises. Compared with physical transactions, this new business transaction model is virtual and unseen, and lacks the trust of the physical transaction model. In the mobile commerce environment, in order to achieve the transaction goals, both sides of the transaction often need to pay high credit costs. Enterprise credit problems can affect enterprise business credit financing due to high credit costs, which is not conducive to enterprises to gain financial advantages in the fierce competition. Therefore, credit problems are an important aspect that hinders the development of mobile commerce. In 2014, the State Administration of Taxation of China issued the Measures for Tax Credit Management (for Trial Implementation), which clarifies that taxation authorities will include all tax-paying enterprises in credit management. Tax authorities collect taxpayers' credit history information, internal tax information and external information on a monthly basis, set enterprises' tax credit into four grades of A, B, C and D according to the credit degree (M grade has been added since April 2018), and take the initiative to announce the annual list of A-grade taxpayers to the society. For taxpayers with A-grade tax credit evaluation, the tax authorities will adopt a series of incentive measures, such as providing green channels or special personnel to help with tax-related matters, implementing joint incentive measures with relevant departments, and other incentive measures in combination with the actual local situation. Thus, it promotes taxpayers' honesty and self-discipline and improves tax law compliance. China's tax credit rating system is gradually moving towards perfection. More enterprises take tax credit into consideration when making relevant decisions in order to improve the correctness of their decisions.

The main contributions of this paper: First, the current research on mobile commerce credit issues mainly focuses on the construction of credit system, and few articles focus on tax credit. This paper explores the relationship between tax credit and commercial credit financing in mobile commerce environment, which enriches the relevant research on mobile commerce credit issues. Second, this paper enriches the study of the economic consequences disclosed by tax credit ratings. The main reason why relatively little research has been conducted on corporate credit in the past is that the creditworthiness of firms is difficult to measure. In this paper, we collect the list of taxpayers with A-grade tax credit published by the State Administration of Taxation, take the A-grade tax credit rating as a reflection of corporate integrity, and use the data of listed companies from 2014–2021 as a sample to test whether paying taxes in good faith helps enterprises obtain business credit financing.

2 Theoretical Analysis and Research Assumptions

2.1 Tax Credit and Enterprise Credit

This paper considers tax credit as an important aspect of corporate credit. First of all, tax integrity refers to the integrity principle that enterprises follow in their taxation activities. Taxation activities of enterprises are closely related to their production and operation activities, and almost every business of enterprises will involve taxation issues. If an enterprise is dishonest in its business activities, such dishonesty will be reflected in the financial information of the enterprise, such as accounting entries, accounting statements, etc. The enterprise's tax information is in turn carried by the financial information formed by production and operation activities. Then the dishonesty of enterprises in business activities will affect the tax situation of enterprises, and thus the tax behavior of enterprises is also dishonest. If an enterprise is rated as A-grade taxpayer in tax credit rating, it can indirectly reflect that the enterprise also follows the principle of honesty in its daily operation activities. From the viewpoint of signaling theory, the taxation department releases the list of A-grade taxpayers with tax credit to the public, which actually transmits the signal that the A-grade taxpayers with tax credit are operating well, and thus helps to improve the business credit of enterprises themselves. Second, enterprises that are honest in their tax practices are likely to follow the principle of integrity in other behaviors as well. Companies with integrity have stricter requirements for their own behavior and ethical standards, are monitored by internal employees when making surplus management decisions, and are under constant scrutiny from the public, peers and other collaborators [1]. Companies often choose to be dishonest in their tax behavior to pursue immediate short-term benefits, but this can harm the long-term interests of the company. The information of A-grade taxpayer is like a business card endorsed by the government, showing the state's recognition of the enterprise's tax integrity, which is conducive to the overall improvement of the enterprise's reputation. From the development perspective of the previous period, integrity can help enterprises reduce the information mismatch with partners and help enterprises gain reputation. The behavior of a company that considers cost-benefit when deciding whether to be honest is inertial, so if a company is honest in its tax behavior, it is likely to follow the principle of honesty in other areas as well.

2.2 Tax Credit and Business Credit Financing

Business credit is a direct credit relationship between enterprises in the transaction of goods or services, formed by the purchase and sale activities with deferred payment or advance payment. The research on commercial credit is mainly based on alternative financing theory and buyer's market theory. The former believes that some enterprises with weak external financing ability have difficulty in obtaining sufficient funds, so they will obtain financial support from those enterprises with strong external financing ability through commercial credit [2]. The latter argues that commercial credit exists because suppliers sell more products faster by offering commercial credit to customers [3]. Companies generally do not have to pay for collateral, interest, etc. when obtaining funds through commercial credit financing. Partners often consider the risk of default of a company due to credit issues when making relevant decisions, so a company's creditworthiness may affect whether or not it can obtain commercial credit financing.

Under the mobile commerce environment, there is information asymmetry between enterprises and suppliers and customers, so enterprises need to pay high credit cost in order to realize transactions and achieve the purpose of transactions. An enterprise recognized as a taxpayer with tax credit grade A can effectively alleviate such information asymmetry, thus not only promoting the realization of transactions, but also facilitating enterprises to obtain commercial credit financing. Tax credit A grade indicates that enterprises follow the principle of honesty in their taxation activities, which is essentially an official authentication of the quality of financial reports of enterprises by tax authorities. By the information spillover effect of tax credit A grade, it can effectively alleviate the information asymmetry between enterprises and suppliers and customers, cultivate the trust relationship between enterprises, and then help enterprises to obtain commercial credit financing [4]. According to the theory of incomplete contract, since the contract between tax collection authorities and taxpayers is incomplete, there must be information asymmetry between them. Enterprises may take advantage of this information asymmetry to act opportunistically and thus achieve the purpose of tax avoidance. The tax credit rating has a series of incentive policies for honest taxpaying enterprises, which can complete the contract and motivate enterprises to reduce opportunistic behavior through the self-implementation mechanism of the contract. In order to achieve a higher tax credit rating, enterprises will reduce the opportunistic behavior of tax avoidance and refrain from tax evasion. The reduction of tax avoidance motivation is conducive to improving the quality of corporate financial reporting and information transparency [5]. When suppliers and customers decide whether to grant business credit to an enterprise, the financial information of that enterprise will serve as an important basis for decision making. Therefore, tax credit A-level recognition can alleviate the degree of information asymmetry between enterprises and suppliers and customers, thus helping enterprises to obtain business credit financing.

Paying taxes in good faith can improve a company's reputation and enable it to obtain a higher amount of business credit financing. Business credit financing is an important way for Chinese companies to obtain funds for their daily business activities. Companies need to consider various aspects when deciding whether to grant commercial credit to a partner. A wrong decision may lead to the inability to recover all the funds or even to the breakage of the enterprise's capital chain, thus endangering the survival of the enterprise. Tax authorities can collect taxpayers' tax credit information from tax management system, national unified credit information platform, official websites of relevant departments, news media or media when rating enterprises for tax credit.

Tax credit A grade reflects the recognition of tax credit status of enterprises by taxation authorities, which can help enterprises shape a good social image and improve their social reputation. According to reputation information theory, the formation of reputation as a signaling activity builds trust between the supply and demand sides of capital and improves the trust level between supply chain partners [6]. As a result, suppliers and customers believe that the business credit granted to taxpayers with A-grade tax credit can be recovered as expected.

In summary, enterprises paying taxes in good faith can reduce the information mismatch between enterprises in the mobile commerce environment and enhance their overall reputation, according to which, the following research hypothesis is proposed in this paper.

H: Enterprises that pay taxes in good faith are more likely to obtain business credit financing.

3 Data and Methodology

3.1 Data

The sample period of this paper is 2014–2021 because the State Administration of Taxation of China started to publish the list of taxpayers with A-grade tax credit from 2014. The tax credit data of enterprises are obtained from the website of the State Administration of Taxation through Python, and the rest of the data are obtained from the CSMAR database. If an enterprise's annual tax credit status is rated A by the tax authorities, the listed company is considered to be an honest tax-paying enterprise in that year. In this paper, the data were screened by (1) excluding the samples of ST and *ST class companies (2) excluding the samples of financial and insurance listed companies; (3) excluding the samples of companies with missing key variables. We obtained 1489 observations in 2014,1733 observations in 2015,1834 observations in 2016, 2159 observations in 2017, 2345 observations in 2018, 2518 observations in 2019, 2724 observations in 2020, and 3013 observations in 2021, for a total of 17815 observations. To avoid the influence of extreme values on study, all continuous variables involved in the regressions in this paper were subjected to the upper and lower 1% tail reduction. Table 1 provides a description of the variables and their definitions in this paper.

Table 1. Variables and variable definitions

Variable names	Variable definitions
HONEST	Enterprise's tax credit status is rated A by the tax authority, HONEST = 1, otherwise HONEST = 0
CREDIT	Commercial credit financing level,(Accounts Payable + Notes Payable + Receipts in Advance)/ Total Assets

(*continued*)

Table 1. (*continued*)

Variable names	Variable definitions
LEV	Total liabilities divided by total assets
BANK	Short-term loans at the end of the year t/total assets
CASH	Monetary capital at the end of the year t/total assets
SIZE	Natural logarithm of total assets
FIXEDASSET	Net fixed assets/total assets
ROA	Net profit/average total assets
SHRL	Shareholding ratio of the largest shareholder at the end of the year t
STATE	The property right of state-owned enterprises is 1, and that of non-state-owned enterprises is 0
OPINION	The standard unqualified opinion issued by the auditor in the current year, OPINION = 1, otherwise OPINION = 0
BIG4	The accounting statements of the current year are audited by the four major international accounting firms, BIG4 = 1, otherwise BIG4 = 0
DUAL	The chairman and general manager of the enterprise are the same person, DUAL = 1, otherwise DUAL = 0

3.2 Methodology

In this paper, we construct the following model to test the impact of companies paying taxes in good faith on business credit financing.

$$CREDIT = \beta0 + \beta1HONEST + \beta2LEV + \beta3BANK + \beta4CASH + \beta5SIZE + \beta6FIXEDASSSET$$
$$+ \beta7ROA + \beta8HRL + \beta9STATE + \beta10OPINION + \beta11BIG4 + \beta12DUAL + \sum YEAR + \sum INDUSTRY + \varepsilon$$

In this paper, control variables such as gearing ratio (LEV), nature of ownership (STATE) [7], fixed assets to total assets (FIXEDASSET) [8], audit quality (OPINION) [9] and year and industry dummy variables (YEAR, INDUSTRY) are set in the above model. The coefficient $\beta1$ of the variable HONEST in the model represents the impact of listed companies' integrity in paying taxes on business credit financing, and this paper expects $\beta1$ to be positive.

4   Empirical Tests and Results

4.1   Descriptive Statistics

Table 2 shows the results of the descriptive statistics of this paper. The mean value of CREDIT is 0.156, indicating that the proportion of accounts payable, notes payable and pre-receivables to total assets in the sample companies is 15.6% on average, and the overall amount of commercial credit financing is large; the mean value of HONEST is

0.617, indicating that 61.7% of the sample companies are selected as taxpayers with tax credit grade A; the mean value of STATE The mean value of STATE is 0.389, indicating that 38.9% of the sample companies are state-owned enterprises; the mean value of OPINION is 0.969, indicating that 96.9% of the sample companies received a standard audit opinion; the mean value of BIG4 is 0.068, indicating that 6.8% of the sample companies have hired an international Big 4 audit firm.

Table 2. Descriptive statistics

Variables	Mean	Std. Dev	Min	Max	p1	p99
CREDIT	0.156	0.114	0.005	0.509	0.005	0.509
HONEST	0.617	0.486	0	1	0	1
LEV	0.433	0.202	0.063	0.9	0.063	0.9
BANK	0.084	0.092	0	0.394	0	0.394
CASH	0.174	0.118	0.017	0.591	0.017	0.591
SIZE	9.746	0.588	8.666	11.507	8.666	11.507
FIXEDASSET	0.21	0.163	0.002	0.698	0.002	0.698
ROA	0.038	0.061	−0.244	0.196	−0.244	0.196
SHRL	34.759	14.913	8.78	75	8.78	75
STATE	0.389	0.487	0	1	0	1
OPINION	0.969	0.174	0	1	0	1
BIG4	0.068	0.252	0	1	0	1
DUAL	0.276	0.447	0	1	0	1

4.2 Multiple Regression Analysis

The regression results obtained in this paper, with HONEST as the core explanatory variable and CREDIT as the explained variable, are shown in Table 3. As can be seen from column (1) in Table 3, after controlling for the control variables and the time and industry dummy variables, the regression coefficient of honest tax payment (HONEST) on business credit (CREDIT) is 0.004 and is significant at the 1% level. This indicates that, under the same conditions, it is easier for companies rated A for tax credit to obtain business credit financing than for companies not rated A for tax credit by tax authorities. The hypothesis H proposed in this paper is verified, that is, it is easier for enterprises that pay taxes in good faith to obtain commercial credit financing.

Table 3. Linear regression

Credit	Coef	St.Err	t-value	p-value	[95% Conf	Interval]
HONEST	0.004***	0.001	3.06	0.002	0.001	0.007
LEV	0.433***	0.005	91.16	0	0.424	0.442
BANK	−0.386***	0.008	−45.58	0	−0.402	−0.369
CASH	0.041***	0.006	6.91	0	0.029	0.052
SIZE	−0.021***	0.001	−14.54	0	−0.024	−0.018
FIXEDASSET	−0.069***	0.005	−14.79	0	−0.078	−0.06
ROA	0.103***	0.012	8.71	0	0.08	0.126
SHRL	0.001***	0	11.70	0	0	0.001
STATE	0.007***	0.001	4.87	0	0.004	0.01
OPINION	0.026***	0.004	7.05	0	0.019	0.033
BIG4	−0.015***	0.003	−5.65	0	−0.02	−0.01
DUAL	−0.004***	0.001	−2.77	0.006	−0.007	−0.001
BANK	0.129***	0.014	8.97	0	0.101	0.157
YEAR	Yes					
INDUSTRY	Yes					
Observations	17815					
R-squared	0.488					

*** $p < 0.01$, ** $p < 0.05$, * $p < 0.1$

5   Robust Test

5.1   Changing the Metric of the Explained Variable

This paper changes the measure of the explained variable (CREDIT) and recalculates the level of commercial credit financing (CREDIT_1) of the firm for the year as the ratio of the sum of accounts payable and notes payable to total assets in the balance sheet. In this paper, we replace the original commercial credit financing (CREDIT) with the new commercial credit financing (CREDIT_1) for the regression test [10], and the results are shown in Table 4. As shown in column (1) of Table 4, the regression coefficient of tax honesty (HONEST) is 0.004, which is significantly greater than 0 at the 1% level, and the findings of the study remain unchanged.

Table 4. Robust test

VARIABLES	(1) CREDIT_1	(2) CREDIT_2
HONEST	0.004***(3.44)	0.007***(4.31)
LEV	0.344***(79.40)	0.458***(78.34)
BANK	−0.267***(−34.64)	−0.419***(−41.33)
CASH	0.018***(3.33)	0.041***(5.51)
SIZE	−0.02***(−15.14)	−0.021***(−11.81)
FIXEDASSET	−0.043***(−9.97)	−0.073***(−12.88)
ROA	0.062***(5.71)	0.115***(7.59)
SHRL	0***(10.52)	0.001***(11.33)
STATE	0.005***(3.94)	0.011***(5.81)
OPINION	0.021***(6.24)	0.029***(7.05)
BIG4	−0.005**(−2.01)	−0.015***(−4.55)
DUAL	−0.003**(−2.27)	−0.003*(−1.84)
BANK	0.107***(8.20)	0.120***(6.82)
YEAR	Yes	Yes
INDUSTRY	Yes	Yes
Observations	17815	12,078
R-squared	0.444	0.510

t-statistics in parentheses *** $p < 0.01$, ** $p < 0.05$, * $p < 0.1$

5.2 Delete the Sample for 2020 and Later Years

China saw the emergence of the COVID-19 at the end of 2019, which is likely to have a generalized impact on firms' operations in 2020 and 2021, and thus on their funding operations. The sample period of this paper covers the years 2020 and 2021, and to avoid the impact of the COVID-19 on firms' business credit financing, the paper removes all samples from 2020 and later years and re-executes the relevant regression process. As shown in column (2) of Table 4, the regression coefficient of tax honesty (HONEST) is 0.007, which is significantly greater than 0 at the 1% level. These results are still consistent with the baseline regression results and do not change the core findings of this paper.

6   Heterogeneity Analysis

State-owned enterprises, due to the nature of his property rights, have more resources available to them and are inherently more likely to gain the trust of other enterprises. Compared with state-owned enterprises, the business credit of non-state-owned enterprises does not have enough external guarantee. And the A grade of tax credit is the

Table 5. Heterogeneity analysis

VARIABLES	(1) CREDIT_3	(2) CREDIT_4
HONEST	0.005***(2.81)	0.003(1.20)
LEV	0.441***(75.08)	0.412***(52.18)
BANK	−0.419***(−38.98)	−0.344***(−25.49)
CASH	0.026***(3.78)	0.065***(6.00)
SIZE	−0.016***(−8.70)	−0.026***(−11.40)
FIXEDASSET	−0.044***(−6.75)	−0.093***(−13.42)
ROA	0.102***(7.66)	0.097***(4.14)
SHRL	0.000***(8.45)	0.001***(8.78)
OPINION	0.034***(8.01)	0.012*(1.76)
BIG4	−0.020***(−5.27)	−0.007**(−2.05)
DUAL	−0.000(−0.11)	−0.010***(−2.91)
Constant	0.091***(4.76)	0.184***(7.99)
YEAR	YES	YES
INDUSTRY	YES	YES
Observations	10,893	6,922
R-squared	0.465	0.534

t-statistics in parentheses. *** $p < 0.01$, ** $p < 0.05$, * $p < 0.1$

recognition of taxation integrity by taxation authorities, which is equivalent to providing a more authoritative credit endorsement for enterprises, which is exactly what non-state-owned enterprises lack. At the same time, state-owned enterprises have more economic resources and political support, so they have more excessive financing channels and financing means. In this paper, all listed companies in the sample are divided into two categories, state-owned and non-state-owned, according to the nature of property rights, and the impact of tax credit on corporate commercial credit financing is examined separately. In the grouped regression results in Table 5, CREDIT_3 in column (1) is the degree of commercial credit financing for non-state-owned enterprises and CREDIT_4 in column (2) is the degree of commercial credit financing for state-owned enterprises. As can be seen from Table 5, the regression result for non-state-owned enterprises is 0.005, which is significantly positive at the 1% level. That is, the impact of honest tax payment on business credit financing is more obvious among non-state enterprises.

7 Conclusion

This paper studies mobile business credit from the unique perspective of tax credit and analyzes the impact of tax credit on corporate business credit financing. This paper uses A-share listed companies from 2014–2021 as the research sample, and the tax credit rating of the State Administration of Taxation as a measure of corporate credit. The study finds that: enterprises that pay taxes in good faith are more likely to obtain business credit financing, and this result passes the robustness test of changing the measure of the explanatory variables and reducing the sample period; the heterogeneity analysis shows that the impact of tax credit on corporate business credit financing is more pronounced for non-state-owned enterprises.

Based on the above analysis, this paper puts forward the following suggestions. First, under the mobile commerce environment, good tax credit can help enterprises break the barriers arising from the credit problems of mobile commerce. Therefore, enterprises should pay attention to their own tax credit, have the advantages brought by good tax credit in the mobile commerce environment, and show stronger competitiveness in the competitive environment. Secondly, capital is the blood in the body of an enterprise, which is necessary for the production and operation activities of an enterprise. Without sufficient capital, the survival and development of an enterprise is not guaranteed. In order to make better use of this channel of commercial credit financing, enterprises should recognize the impact of tax credit rating on information asymmetry between enterprises and corporate reputation, regulate their behavior in production and operation activities, and realize the win-win situation of honest tax payment and improved business performance.

Acknowledgments. First of all, I would like to express my deep and sincere gratitude to my supervisor, Professor Peiyan Zhou, for his continuous valuable guidance throughout my research process, and it is a great honor for me to study under his guidance. In addition, I would like to thank all the teachers and students in the School of Business and Management of Jilin University for their valuable comments, which have helped me a lot to improve the quality of my thesis. I sincerely thank my dearest friends and members of my research group for their support. I am very grateful to my parents for their motivation, patience, love, and care throughout my education and life journey. Finally, I would like to thank all those who helped me directly or indirectly to complete my thesis. I sincerely wish you all the best in all your endeavors.

References

1. Guiso, L., Sapienza, P., Zingales, L.: The value of corporate culture. J. Financ. Econ. **117**(1), 60–76 (2015)
2. Bruno, B., Christian, G.: Trade credit and credit rationing. The Rev. Financ. Stud. **10**(4), 903–937 (1997)
3. Fabbri, D., Menichini, A.M.C.: Trade credit, collateral liquidation, and borrowing constraints. J. Financ. Econ. **96**(3), 413–432 (2010). https://doi.org/10.1016/j.jfineco.2010.02.010
4. Zhiwei, X., Shaoyu, L., Weihan, P.: Accounting information quality and firms' business credit financing-an empirical study based on an unexplained audit fee measure. Econ. Manage. Res. **38**(8), 124–135 (2017). (in Chinese)
5. Mihir, A., Desai, D.D.: Corporate tax avoidance and high-powered incentives. J. Financ. Econ. **79**(1), 145–179 (2005)
6. Xuejiao, S., Shuping, Z., Su, Y.: Can flexible tax collection alleviate corporate financing constraints-evidence from a natural experiment on tax credit rating disclosure. China Ind. Econ. **3**, 81–99 (2019). (in Chinese)

7. Huacheng, W., Huan, L., Shenghao, G.: Economic policy uncertainty, the nature of property rights and business credit. Econ. Theory Econ. Manag. **305**(05), 34–45 (2016). (in Chinese)
8. Yongjin, W., Dan, S.: Does geographic agglomeration promote inter-firm business credit? Manag. World **232**(01), 101–114+188 (2013). (in Chinese)
9. Yunshen, C., Yutao, W.: Audit quality, transaction costs, and business credit models. Audit Res. **158**(06), 77–85 (2010). (in Chinese)
10. Ma, L., Min, Z., Yi, Z.: Do supplier-customer relationships affect firms' business credit–an empirical test based on Chinese listed companies. Econ. Theory Econ. Manage. **302**(02), 98–112 (2016). (in Chinese)

Author Index

© The Editor(s) (if applicable) and The Author(s), under exclusive license
to Springer Nature Switzerland AG 2023
G. Salvendy and J. Wei (Eds.): HCII 2023, LNCS 14052, pp. 335–336, 2023.
https://doi.org/10.1007/978-3-031-35921-7

Printed in the United States
by Baker & Taylor Publisher Services